CORRECTIONS AND THE COMMUNITY

Louis P. Carney

Faculty of the Administration of Justice
Golden West College
Huntington Beach, California

Visiting Lecturer in Criminology
Chapman College
Orange, California

PRENTICE-HALL, INC., Englewood Cliffs, N.J. 07632

Library of Congress Cataloging in Publication Data

Carney, Louis P

Corrections and the community.

Includes bibliographical references and index.

1. Community-based corrections—United States.

I. Title.

HV9304.C35 364.6 76-19033

ISBN 0-13-178319-X

For Mary Josephine

Printed in the United States of America

10 9 8 7 6 5 4 3 2 1

Prentice-Hall International, Inc., *London*
Prentice-Hall of Australia Pty. Limited, *Sydney*
Prentice-Hall of Canada, Ltd., *Toronto*
Prentice-Hall of India Private Limited, *New Delhi*
Prentice-Hall of Japan, Inc., *Tokyo*
Prentice-Hall of Southeast Asia Pte. Ltd., *Singapore*
Whitehall Books Limited, *Wellington, New Zealand*

CONTENTS

PREFACE

This book anticipates the future and recaptures the past. Community-based corrections is not a new idea but, more properly, a renewed commitment. The accent on community-based corrections, however, has never been more insistent than it is today because traditional methods of correction, particularly of the institutional variety, have been singularly unsuccessful.

In 1967 the report of the President's Commission on Law Enforcement and Administration of Justice concluded that the American public must look to new methods and develop new perspectives, if the criminal justice system is to be a viable system. Six years later the National Advisory Commission on Criminal Justice Standards and Goals asserted that the most promising means of accomplishing that objective was community-based corrections. In the intervening years, that vision has been constantly reemphasized.

It is the position of the National Council on Crime and Delinquency that "imprisonment must be viewed as an alternative to community treatment."[1] The corrective endeavor should minimize, not maximize, penetration into the criminal justice system.

There is, as yet, no abundance of empirical data to demonstrate that community-based corrections is more successful than traditional methods,

---

[1] National Council on Crime and Delinquency, *Policies and Background Information* (Hackensack, N.J.: NCCD, 1972), p. 15.

but there is an abundance of evidence that prisons and juvenile correctional institutions have been infinitely less successful. The contemporary thrust of corrections—towards the community—is a reformative thrust, to the extent that it represents a repudiation of traditional methods. But it is also evidence of the humanistic philosophy that is infiltrating corrections. Above all, it is another way of seeking solutions to the fearful and distressing problems of crime and delinquency. Community-based corrections represents a rational redirection in corrections but, in the final analysis, it will be validated or invalidated on the basis of the hard data that it must itself produce.

This text proposes to offer a coherent view of community-based corrections in the perspectives of past influences, contemporary circumstances, and future hopes. A major thesis is that unless corrections changes its direction we shall have to abide a progressively ineffectual Criminal Injustice System. We cannot afford that desolate prospect. Community-based corrections is, at least, pregnant with promise.

Louis P. Carney

CORRECTIONS AND THE COMMUNITY

Door to Trenton prison cell. It was constructed in 1836. © *Corrections Magazine*. *Photo by Bill Powers.*

1

THE CRISIS IN CORRECTIONS

Those who cannot remember the past are condemned to repeat it.

George Santayana

Shortly before he died on October 22, 1975, Arnold Toynbee, an English historian of eminent distinction, said, "Our present society is truly repulsive." If that criticism is applicable to society in general, then we are surely entitled to great misgiving in appraising our criminal justice system. The sheer magnitude of crime, the volume of litigation that plagues our judicial machinery, and the dismal record of our prisons and juvenile institutions as instruments of correction are at least cause for grave concern, if not repulsion.

Dimensions of the Crisis

There is ample evidence to indicate that our prisons and juvenile institutions not only do not correct, but tragically contribute to the very antithesis of reformation. Indeed, as a noted contemporary authority has observed, "correction generally has not achieved more than a low estate." [1] We are obliged in conscience to seek alternatives.

THE IMPRISONED

The prison reflects an American penchant for warehousing its miscreants. One-half of the convicted felons sentenced to state institutions receive sentences in excess of five years, and one-quarter receive sentences of over ten years.[2] The penal system of the United States is by far the largest of its kind in the world. Throughout this nation there are more than 400 major penal institutions, approximately 800 juvenile detention and correctional facilities, and no less than 3,921 locally administered jails. In addition, there are state-operated jails in Connecticut, Delaware, and Rhode Island, and innumerable local lockups which detain persons for forty-eight hours or less. Of the 141,600 in the national jail population, according to a recent survey, more than 50 percent had not yet been convicted.[3] In 1975, a quarter of a million inmates were housed in the prisons of the U.S., a 10.5 percent increase over 1974.

Into this massive penal system nearly 3 million people are processed annually. On any given day, there are over 400,000 Americans incarcerated in some level of the penal system—about one in every 500 Americans. More than twice that number are under probation or parole supervision. Each day, 8,000 persons are sent to jails and penal institutions. In excess of one million children are handled annually by all of the juvenile courts in the United States.

Those that enter the system are predominantly the poor and the disadvantaged. More than half of the felons committed to the federal system, for instance, do not have a high school diploma, and more than two-thirds are unskilled workers. Yet studies confirm that the imprisoned do not suffer from subnormal intelligence. Rather, they have lacked opportunities to develop themselves vocationally and educationally.

CRIME AND DELINQUENCY

Crime and delinquency, the factors that thrust people into the correctional apparatus, are steadily and alarmingly increasing. The FBI reported that

---

[1] Sol Rubin, *Crime and Juvenile Delinquency* (Dobbs Ferry, N.Y.: Oceana Publications, 1970), p. 204.

[2] Sol Rubin, *The Law of Criminal Correction* (St. Paul, Minn.: West Publishing Company, 1973), p. 305.

[3] U.S. Department of Justice, Law Enforcement Assistance Administration, *Survey of Inmates of Local Jails 1972, Advance Report* (Washington, D.C.: U.S. Government Printing Office, 1974), p. 1.

Guards at McNeil Island Federal Penitentiary, c. 1900.

Crime Index Offenses increased 18 percent in 1974 over 1973.[4] A National Crime Panel survey of crime in the five largest cities in the United States revealed that approximately 3.2 million criminal acts of violence and common theft occurred in 1972. *The amount of crime reported by survey respondents was roughly twice that recorded by law enforcement agencies in the same cities for the same period.*[5]

In a recent survey undertaken by the Office of Criminal Justice Programs in the state of Michigan, it was discovered that 20 percent of all Michigan households had been victimized by crime. It was also ascertained that two-thirds of the people surveyed expressed fear of crime being committed against them.[6] This pervasive fear of crime had been earlier documented. The President's Commission on Law Enforcement and Administration of Justice reported that 43 percent of citizens sur-

---

[4] Federal Bureau of Investigation, *Crime in the United States, Uniform Crime Reports*, 1974. (Note: "Crime Index Offenses" include murder, forcible rape, robbery, aggravated assault, burglary, larceny-theft, and motor vehicle theft.)

[5] U.S. Department of Justice, LEAA, *Crime in the Nation's Five Largest Cities, Advance Report* (Washington, D.C.: U.S. Government Printing Office, April 1974). The first annual nationwide victimization survey (for 1973) was also conducted by LEAA. It revealed that serious crime occurred three times more frequently than it was reported (See *Criminal Justice Newsletter* 9-1-75).

[6] Michigan Office of Criminal Justice Programs, "The Michigan Public Speaks Out on Crime," Second Annual Survey, March 1974.

veyed stated that they did not go out after dark because of the fear of being victimized by crime.[7]

It is clear that the cold statistics of crime have deeper dimensions. Epidemic crime has the power to turn large numbers of citizens into something approaching what the noted Gestalt psychologist Fritz Perls calls "anxious automatons." But the statistics also demonstrate our persisting failure to contain crime and delinquency, and to "correct" those who commit criminal and delinquent acts.

And what of the cost of crime and the cost of correction? It is not a simple matter to develop accurate figures which reflect the cost of crime, but the adjective "staggering" will apply in any circumstance. Two authorities who have given the problem some painstaking attention concluded that "conventional" crime (robbery, burglary, serious larceny, and auto theft) costs an annual $600 million in direct property loss.[8] To this would have to be added the vast cost of processing offenders through the criminal justice system. For instance, the cost of administering the 373 courts of the California system alone was $210 million in 1971.[9] And this is but one component of one state's criminal justice system. A California county recently researched the manpower demands of judicial prosecution and discovered that 106 criminal justice personnel were involved in the judicial processing *of a single misdemeanant.*[10] If this inordinately expensive investment is an investment in failure, then the American public must truly reappraise its criminal justice methodology.

The cost of "treatment" is also astronomical. In 1973 it cost the taxpayers an average of $10,000 to keep a child in a detention facility; the average cost for an incarcerated adult was close to that figure. This is eight to ten times what it would cost for probation or parole supervision in the community. It is generally estimated that somewhat less than $2 billion is expended on corrections throughout the United States, but it is apparent that the cost of crime and criminal prosecution is inordinately higher than the amount expended to correct the offender. Further, the correctional effort takes place in a veritable hodgepodge of fragmented

---

7 President's Commission on Law Enforcement and Administration of Justice, *The Challenge of Crime in a Free Society* (Washington, D.C.: U.S. Government Printing Office, 1967). This commission will hereafter be referred to as the President's Crime Commission in the body of this text.

8 R. T. Galvin and R. Ashby, "The Cost of Crime," in Simon Dinitz and Walter C. Reckless, eds., *Critical Issues in the Study of Crime* (Boston: Little, Brown and Company, 1968), p. 24.

9 California Council on Criminal Justice, *1973 Comprehensive Plan for Criminal Justice* (Sacramento, 1973).

10 Louis P. Carney, *Introduction to Correctional Science* (New York: McGraw-Hill Book Company, 1974), pp. 92–93.

programming, conflict in philosophy, and jurisdictional complexity, so disjointed that the Keldgord Commission called it a "nonsystem."

THE PRESCRIPTION

The Keldgord Commission, following an exhaustive analysis of the California correctional system, stated in its recommendations:

> The single most important recommendation of this study is that the bulk of the correctional effort, its programs, and its resources be moved to the community level.[11]

This is an echo. Four years earlier, the President's Crime Commission had articulated the rationale for the new, community-based philosophy in corrections:

> The general underlying premise for the new direction in corrections is that crime and delinquency are symptoms of failures and disorganization of the community as well as individual offenders. In particular, these failures are seen as depriving offenders of contact with the social institutions that are basically responsible for assuring development of law-abiding conduct. . . .
>
> The task of corrections therefore includes building or rebuilding solid ties between offender and community, integrating or reintegrating the offender into community life—restoring family ties, obtaining employment and education, securing in the larger sense a place for the offender in the routine functioning of society. . . .[12]

The theme of the 1974 annual Congress of the American Correctional Association was "Corrections at the Crossroads." An avenue of promise leads to the community.

Violence and Protest

During recent years the pressures for social change have built up and sporadically exploded in our society, to such a degree that they cannot

[11] State of California, Board of Corrections, *Correctional System Study: The System* (Sacramento, July 1971), p. ix. This is popularly known as "The Keldgord Report" or "The Keldgord Commission" after its program director, Robert E. Keldgord.

[12] President's Crime Commission, *Task Force Report: Corrections* (Washington, D.C.: U.S. Government Printing Office, 1967), p. 7.

be ignored. A national commission established to assess the phenomenon of violence concluded that, next to the Reconstruction era, the 1960s were the most violent years in our history.[13] In the 1950s the thrust of the rebellion was against repressive governmental policies in the area of civil rights. The fact that there were more than two dozen major flareups in the prisons of the United States during that decade is quite significant.

Continuing through the sixties and into the seventies, riots have torn through the ancient instruments of correction. The revolt of the inmates in the Tombs (the New York City prison, since closed), the horrendous slaughter at Attica, and the bloody events in California's Soledad and San Quentin prisons were, perhaps, the most notable.[14] As the slave ultimately struck at his chains, the contemporary convict began to strike in earnest at the shackles in his obsolete tomb.

THE COURTS TAKE NOTE

As the above events were unfolding, the courts were becoming increasingly predisposed to sustain the prisoner's position. During the 1971–72 term of the United States Supreme Court, for instance, eight cases were heard that directly affected inmates, "and in each of them the offender's contention prevailed." [15] Prominent among complaints was that imprisonment under certain conditions constituted cruel and unusual punishment, in violation of the Eighth Amendment to the Constitution.

PROTEST IN THE PRISON

Elton B. McNeil has stated that the bulk of human aggression is caused by frustration.[16] Shostrom considers conflict as necessary, and says that

---

[13] Hugh Davis Graham and Ted Robert Gurr, "Violence in America, Historical and Comparative Perspectives," *Staff Report to the National Commission on the Causes and Prevention of Violence*, vol. 2 (Washington, D.C.: U.S. Government Printing Office, June 1969), p. 268.

[14] For a definitive work on prison disturbances, see the publication of the American Correctional Association: *Causes, Preventive Measures, and Methods of Controlling Riots and Disturbances in Correctional Institutions* (Woodridge Station, Washington, D.C., 1970); also Carney, *Introduction to Correctional Science*, Chapter 7.

[15] National Advisory Commission on Criminal Justice Standards and Goals, *Task Force Report: Corrections* (Washington, D.C.: U.S. Government Printing Office, 1973), p. 1. This commission will hereafter be referred to as the National Advisory Commission in the body of this text.

[16] Elton B. McNeil, ed., *The Nature of Human Conflict* (Englewood Cliffs, N.J.: Prentice-Hall, Inc., 1965), p. 28.

there can be creative conflict.[17] And Camus viewed revolt as an actual "principle of existence."[18] The prisoner may not be aware of these scholarly sentiments, but he is very frustrated; he revolts to create better conditions; and he battles to survive in the grim, obsolete prisons that are part of our "correctional" system. Meanwhile, the tempo of prison disturbances has continued with a steady cacophony and, as the National Advisory Commission correctly observed, these disturbances "confirm the feeling of thoughtful citizens that such institutions contribute little to the national effort to reduce crime."[19]

The Honorable A. Leon Higginbotham, vice-chairman of the National Commission on Violence, pleaded at the close of the deliberations of that body, for a moratorium on further studies of racism, poverty, crime, or the urban crisis. Instead, he urged *implementation* of the many meritorious recommendations already made by numerous commissions of the recent past.[20] If there is a time for implementation, it is now. Before the decade of the seventies has passed into history, it may be predicted that it will become the bloodiest and most violent in our prison history if the American people do not heed the insistent cry for correctional change; if they do not take steps to implement the clamorous recommendations of the President's Crime Commission, the Keldgord Commission, and the National Advisory Commission: *return the bulk of correctional endeavors to the community.*

The Failure of the System

The central fulcrum in the American correctional system, and its own creation, is the penitentiary. Contrary to popular supposition, the penitentiary is not an inheritance from our European forebears, but a domestic development. Its pristine architecture reflects our puritan heritage. Massive edifices of concrete and steel, the original penitentiaries were designed to facilitate solitary contemplation of one's misdeeds. It was felt that introspection in solitude was conducive to personal reform. It was also believed that if prisoners were allowed to associate, they would criminally contaminate one another, so some of the earlier penitentiaries in the

---

[17] Everett L. Shostrom, *Man, The Manipulator* (New York: Bantam Books, 1968), p. 127.

[18] Albert Camus, *The Rebel* (New York: Vintage Books, 1956), p. vii and throughout.

[19] National Advisory Commission, *Corrections*, p. 1.

[20] *To Establish Justice, To Insure Domestic Tranquility,* Final Report of the National Commission on the Causes and Prevention of Violence (Washington, D.C.: U.S. Government Printing Office, 1969), pp. 116–17.

United States entertained what is known as the silent and separate system.

Here is an echo from a penitentiary:

> There are no lines of communication with the administration whatsoever. We are not able to get help for problems, nor allowed to communicate with anyone on staff.
>
> I am up against some pressure because I have refused to play games with some of the so-called big-shots on the yard. Kicking one in the ———, knocking another down, and taking a knife away from a third, has not brought me any popularity. Refusing to yield to their sex games, refusing to pay-off, and refusing to become a part of the "convict" game, has made me an outlaw. I have been cornered twice, and managed to get out by pure luck and a few nasty tricks I had not forgotten how to play. . . . The only other solution would be to go into their Protective Unit. . . . Even if I were willing to, my counselor refuses to even talk to me let alone bring me before a classification committee. He told me, he is the one to decide what I need and when I need it, and he told me that he doesn't care what I may think about it.

Dungeon in the Old Stone Prison, Philadelphia, c. 1800. *Courtesy Pennsylvania Prison Association, Philadelphia.*

Sound like a missive from the yesterday of penology, from one of our earlier prisons? It was written in 1974 from a New England penitentiary.[21]

THE FAILURE OF THE PRISON

The preceding letter evidences the lack of progress in the prison as an instrument of correction, and it points up the wide chasm that so often exists between inmate and staff. There cannot be any meaningful rehabilitation under such adverse conditions. There are more than twenty-five prisons in the United States which are over one hundred years old. An additional thirty-six were built before 1900. The comment of the former director of the Federal Bureau of Prisons is as valid now as it was when he made it: "Most state prisons are outmoded, obsolete shells and cages to which other structures have been added as the philosophy and functions of the prison changed." [22]

Legitimate criticism of the prison has been increasing of late. A report by the New York City Board of Correction described prisons as "warehouses of human anguish and mirrors of social injustice." [23] Four convict-authors at the Indiana State Prison, who have served a collective fifty years in a dozen different American prisons, made this observation: "While all that talk about rehabilitation goes on and on, the whole system keeps right on doing what it has been doing for a century—demeaning, degrading, dehumanizing, and punishing," through the instrumentality of "a system of jails and prisons which are wretched pestholes, indecent crime-breeding swamps of iniquity into which are jammed the poor, the socially outcast, the ignorant, the emotionally disturbed and the mentally ill." [24] In 1976, a U.S. District judge characterized Alabama's prisons as "unfit for human habitation."

Certain factors which are inimical to treatment in the prison are measurable and observable. Others are not. It is evident that the prison is an abnormal environment. It is one-sexed, authoritarian, filled with the poor, the young, and the ethnic minorities. It is pervaded with perverted sexuality and satiated with despair. Numbers are substituted for names, individuals are stripped of their individuality, training and

---

[21] Personal letter from an inmate, July 13, 1974.

[22] From the introduction by James V. Bennett, U.S. Department of Justice, Bureau of Prisons, *Handbook of Correctional Institution Design and Construction* (1949).

[23] *Crisis in the Prisons: New York City Responds*, the 1971 Annual Report of the New York City Board of Correction, p. 3.

[24] H. Jack Griswold and others, *An Eye for an Eye* (New York: Holt, Rinehart and Winston, copyright © 1970 by H. J. Griswold, M. Misenheimer, A. Powers and E. Tromanhauser. Reprinted by permission of Holt, Rinehart and Winston, Publishers).

education are limited, and there is an oppressive convict code which makes life cheap and treatment unpalatable.

The psychic trauma, the institutionalization, the stigma, the anguish of separation from loved ones, the interrupted parenthood, and similar disabilities are not so easy to measure, but they are equally devastating to the human spirit. They are all countermilitants to correctional restoration.

VIOLENCE IN THE PRISON

On top of these disabilities, the prisons of this land are becoming centers of violence. In some jurisdictions county probation departments are subsidized (paid) by state government to screen out and supervise in the community the less serious convicted felons. This is having a disturbing side effect. It is causing some prisons to be imbalanced with the hard-core and the violence-prone offender. Overcrowding only exacerbates the

Early prison shop, probably in Leavenworth Federal Penitentiary, c. 1908. *Courtesy U.S. Bureau of Prisons.*

situation. In 1975, to forestall a "potentially explosive" condition, the state of Georgia took the unusual step of prematurely releasing hundreds of nonviolent offenders. In 1972 and again in 1973, Florida's director of corrections refused to accept new inmates because of dangerous overcrowding in the prison system.

Constitutional rights are also infringed. In 1975, a District Court judge in Massachusetts said that he would refuse to commit offenders to Concord Reformatory because of the inhumane living conditions in that institution. And in 1976, a U.S. District Court judge threatened to close all of the prisons in Alabama if flagrant violations of human rights weren't terminated.

Violence has become the hallmark for many prisons. For example, during a seven-month period from December 1, 1972, through July 1, 1973 there were 118 stabbings in the California prison system, seventeen of which were fatal.[25] During the first nine months of 1973 there were 344 escapes from California prisons.[26] In a 1973 murder trial, "Fat Carlos" testified that a "Mexican Mafia," with 200 members, exists in the California prison system, and it has a death code for betrayal. A convict-author in early 1972 wrote that there was "so much racial paranoia" in San Quentin that it wasn't necessary to incite violence. Any pretext would suffice "to start the killing." [27] The ironic thing is that these characteristics pertain to the California system, which is credited with being one of the best, if not *the* best system in the nation.

A MORATORIUM ON PRISONS

The Federal Bureau of Prisons, which has often taken a leadership role in progressive corrections, has surprisingly committed itself to a long-range plan of institution-building, in the face of consolidating opposition. It is equally surprising to note that authorities in California, faced with a 1974–75 budget slash, complained that the "biggest disappointment" was a loss of funds to build two new prisons.[28] Meanwhile, correctional bodies and professional organizations are speaking out for a moratorium on the construction of penal institutions.

The California Council on Criminal Justice, for instance, went on record on August 24, 1972, as unanimously opposing the federal plan to

---

[25] California Department of Corrections, *Correctional News Briefs* (Sacramento), July 24, 1974.

[26] *Los Angeles Times,* October 10, 1973.

[27] Edward Bunker, "War Behind Walls," *Harper's Magazine,* February 1972, p. 39.

[28] California Department of Corrections, *Correctional News Briefs,* July 3, 1974.

construct a new institution in California for youthful offenders.[29] The National Advisory Commission has recommended a ten-year moratorium on the construction of new prisons, and urges that the intervening period be one in which planning for noninstitutional facilities takes place.[30] In a succinct and compelling indictment, the Commission declared that the prison "is obsolete, cannot be reformed, should not be perpetuated through the false hope of forced 'treatment,' and should be repudiated as useless for any purpose other than locking away persons who are too dangerous to be allowed at large in free society. For the latter purpose we already have more prison space then we need." [31]

This study occupied two years and expended $1.75 million of Law Enforcement Assistance Administration funds. That is a costly investment of time and money, and it will be unpardonable if there is a lack of implementation and we are left with another collection of "meritorious" recommendations that will sit forlornly on library shelves. Yet, as an expert has pointed out, "the Bureau of Prisons, which could be phased out as an operating agency, has a mandate for a ten-year plan for new prisons, jails, and correction centers at a potential cost of over a billion dollars." [32]

The Recidivism Index

Recidivism is the technical term for repetitive criminal behavior. Correctionalists ordinarily employ the term in a more restricted sense, to indicate multiple *prison* commitments. In this frame of reference, a "three-time loser" would be an individual who has served three separate penitentiary sentences. The term is also used in a more generalized context, to describe the felonious re-arrest of previously convicted felons. For our purpose, it is a prospective criterion of the prison's failure as an instrument of correction.

THE CAREERS IN CRIME STUDY

Authorities in the field are not in universal agreement on the significance of recidivism as an evaluative tool, primarily because of conflicting data

---

[29] California Council on Criminal Justice, *Bulletin*, vol. 5, issue 8, September 15, 1972.

[30] National Advisory Commission, *Corrections*, p. 597.

[31] *Ibid*., p. 352.

[32] Milton G. Rector, President, National Council on Crime and Delinquency, from address delivered to the American Bar Association, cited in NCCD *News Fronts*, Autumn 1975, p. 5.

and an inability to establish decisive parameters. Two recent studies illustrate the dilemma.

In 1963 the FBI began to process criminal history data in order to document criminal recidivism. This project was called the Careers in Crime study. From 1963 to 1969, criminal history data on 240,000 offenders was processed for statistical use, and also to demonstrate the need for centralization of data collected in the light of criminal mobility and recidivism. At the beginning of 1970, the FBI began to convert offender records to computer form for the operational Computerized Criminal History File of the National Crime Information Center. The recidivism profile of the 207,748 offenders in the Computerized Criminal History File for the years 1970–1974 is shown in Fig. 1–1.[33] Of the total

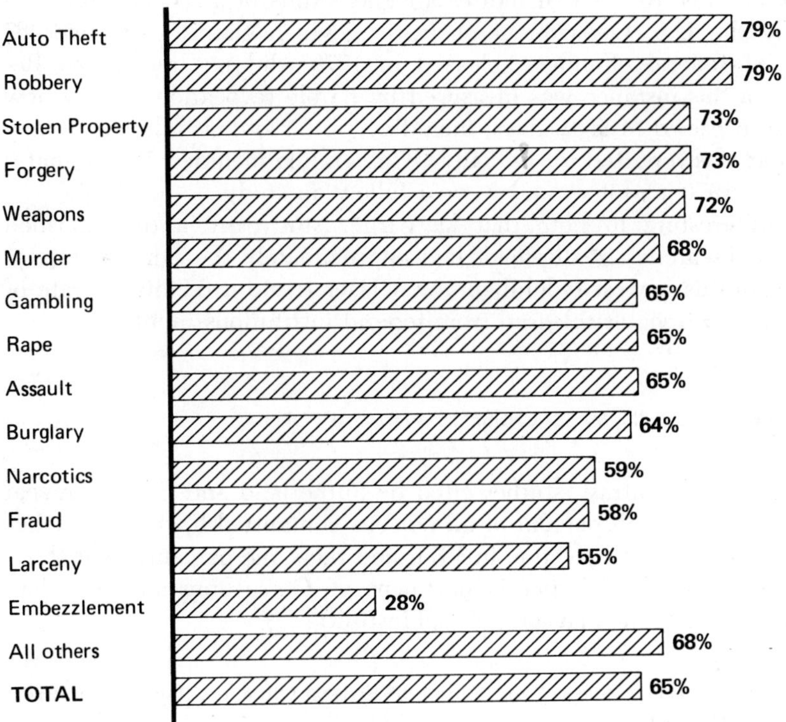

Fig. 1.1. Careers in Crime Study. *Source: Federal Bureau of Investigation, Uniform Crime Reports.*

---

33 Federal Bureau of Investigation, *Crime in the United States Uniform Crime Reports,* 1974, p. 49.

number in the profile, 135,470 or 65 percent, had been arrested two or more times. The average criminal career (span between first and last arrests) was five years and five months, and the average number of times each was arrested was four. The individuals in the study committed 835,000 documented offenses. In view of the fact that only about one-fifth of the serious crimes committed in 1972, for instance, were solved by arrest, this total must be considered a conservative figure.

It should be noted that the recidivism profile in Fig. 1–1 is of individuals who are older than would normally be the case. This results from the general practice of police agencies not to submit fingerprint cards on juveniles. As can be seen in the graph, the recidivism rate was substantial.

FEDERAL PRISON SURVEYS

In stark contrast to the FBI figures are the results of a recently released study by the U.S. Department of Justice, which claims that "over 67 percent of federal offenders released in 1970" did not recidivate. Recidivism in this instance was measured by parole revocation, or any new sentence in excess of sixty days, including probation, occasioned by any arrest that was reported to the FBI.[34] This sample included 1800 inmates released in 1970, and it was a two-year follow-up study.

It is interesting to note that an earlier study, by a distinguished American researcher in the field, had approximately the same results as obtained in this newest federal survey. Glaser found a recidivism rate of 35 percent for inmates released from federal institutions in 1956.[35]

RECIDIVISM IN MASSACHUSETTS AND CALIFORNIA

To continue the contrast, studies cited by Sutherland and Cressey reveal that approximately 85 percent of all persons committed to the Massachusetts Department of Correction in 1971, and the same percentage of those committed to the California Department of Corrections in 1969, had previously served time in a correctional institution.[36]

---

[34] Bureau of Prisons, "Success and Failure of Federal Offenders Released in 1970," *Advance Report*, Washington, D.C., April 11, 1974.

[35] Daniel Glaser, *The Effectiveness of a Prison and Parole System* (New York: Bobbs-Merrill Co., 1964), p. 20.

[36] Edwin H. Sutherland and Donald R. Cressey, *Criminology*, 9th ed. (New York: J.B. Lippincott Company, 1974), p. 608.

CONFLICTING CRITERIA AND CONCLUSIONS

One of the obvious difficulties with recidivism data is that the criteria employed often differ in terms of what constitutes recidivism. Correctional philosophy often fluctuates with changes in administration, and this philosophy, whether progressive or repressive, may have profound influence on a given body of correctional statistics. Furthermore, some of the studies cited pertain to recidivism among prisoners, among ex-prisoners, and among re-arrestees who may not be re-imprisoned. It is appropriate, at this stage, to echo the National Advisory Commission's cautious observation, that recidivism "should be the primary but not the only evaluative criterion." [37]

One conclusion, nevertheless, is inescapable. An extraordinarily large number of offenders in correctional institutions and on parole have been in prior difficulties with the law and are recidivists. The studies document, at the very least, sustained criminality in this group. An important point to keep in mind, however, is that the majority of offenders do not become reinvolved in serious felonious activity. It is the highly selective, *imprisoned* offender who has most frequently been in prior criminal difficulities.

We must be concerned with recidivism because it is an index of the success or lack of success of *programs*. More important, it is also an index of the success or lack of success of *systems*, and it is the entire criminal justice system that is under scrutiny. It is conclusive that the prison is not effective in aborting continued criminal careers for the large number of recidivists in its midst.

The National Advisory Commission, in its opening comments, made a statement that provides a fitting ending for this section:

> The failure of major institutions to reduce crime is incontestable. Recidivism rates are notoriously high. Institutions do succeed in punishing, but they do not deter. They protect the community, but that protection is only temporary. They relieve the community of responsibility by removing the offender, but they make successful reintegration into the community unlikely. They change the committed offender, but the change is more likely to be negative than positive.[38]

---

[37] For a good examination of the recidivism issue, see the National Advisory Commission, *Task Force Report: Criminal Justice System*, 1973, Standard 6.7. The Commission feels that recidivism can only tell us about *program effectiveness: Corrections*, p. 514.

[38] National Advisory Commission, *Corrections*, 1973, p. 1.

And that is but one more documented argument for a shift in the correctional emphasis—to the community.

Social, Cultural, and Causal Factors

If one were to look critically and objectively at the primary characteristics of the imprisoned in this nation, one might well be tempted to paraphrase Emma Lazarus: "Send me your poor, your tired masses, the wretched refuse of your affluent land, your young, and I will warehouse them."

THE POOR IN THE SYSTEM

Our prisons are so filled with the young, downtrodden poor that the President's Crime Commission cited this as a fact of compelling interest early in its overview of the American criminal justice system: "It is with the young people and the slum dwellers who have been embittered by the painful social and economic pressures that the criminal justice system preponderantly deals."[39] It is quite surprising, therefore, to discover that the Crime Commission's Task Force Report on Corrections scarcely touches upon this vital dimension of crime and justice in the United States.

Poverty itself is a form of imprisonment. The have-nots experience not only the normal frustrations that are the lot of all men but, in addition, the agonies that derive from the status of poverty itself. In a society that places great importance on professional or vocational standing, the unemployed poor become the butt of a vicious circle of rejection and discrimination. They are not only vulnerable to the pangs of want, but also more susceptible to exploitation. Some recent experiments conducted by the City University of New York are illustrative. In one instance, researchers "lost" money in conspicuous places. After making sure that pedestrians "found" the money, the researchers returned and told the "finders" that the money belonged to them. The researchers were dressed differently, some wearing workman's clothing and others modish business suits with ties. Nearly 80 percent of the finders returned the money to the well-dressed researchers, but only 38 percent did to the less well dressed, clearly indicating a bias based on status inferred from dress.

The family is the basic social unit, and the one that fundamentally provides the meaningful experiences and security for its members. But a family's emotional stamina is sapped by poverty, and the family in-

[39] President's Crime Commission, *The Challenge of Crime in a Free Society*, p. 6.

stitution is eroded by welfare. Many of the poor are on welfare. A significant 1974 congressional study of welfare programs in 100 counties revealed that welfare tends to split up families, because it is so designed that welfare income increases as the family disintegrates, but it decreases as the family integrates. It is common knowledge that gross numbers of delinquents are the products of broken homes. Minorities are also more frequently represented among the poorer segments of our society, and are thus the victims of double discrimination, poverty, and criminal justice bias.

THE SYSTEM'S VICTIM: THE MINORITY

The mere fact that a large number, or even a disproportionate number of a minority group is convicted, does not *de facto* prove discrimination. But sufficient evidence does now exist to demonstrate that blacks, for example, have been discriminated against in the administration of justice. In the noteworthy *Furman* decision, which held that capital punishment constituted cruel and unusual punishment, two United States Supreme Court Justices made statements, in their respective opinions, indicating their belief that such discrimination was, indeed, a fact.[40]

When the death penalty was abrogated on June 29, 1972, there were 631 persons awaiting execution on death rows across the United States. Of that total, 55.6 percent were black.[41] Blacks constitute approximately 11 percent of the population of the United States. Marvin Wolfgang, a distinguished authority in the field of criminology, made a very careful study, with an associate, of the racial aspects of sentencing in those states in which rape is a capital offense. The study led to the conclusion that "sentences of death have been imposed on blacks in a way that exceeds any statistical notion of chance or fortuity."[42]

In 1970 a total of 2,520 males and 85 females were committed to the New York State Department of Correctional Services from New York City. Of that total, 85 percent were nonwhite.[43] Is justice, fortuity, or a discriminatory system responsible for that racial imbalance?

---

[40] Justices William O. Douglas and Thurgood Marshall, *Furman v. Georgia*, 408 U.S. 238.

[41] CALM, Inc., *Newsletter*, 6, no. 1, October 1972. (CALM stands for Citizens Against Legalized Murder.)

[42] Marvin E. Wolfgang and Marc Riedel, "Race, Judicial Discretion, and the Death Penalty," *The Annals of the American Academy of Political and Social Science*, vol. 407 (May 1973), 119–33. An excellent source book for the student interested in the issue of capital punishment is Hugo Adam Bedeau, ed., *The Death Penalty in America* (Garden City, N.Y.: Anchor Books, 1967).

[43] State of New York, Department of Correctional Services, *Characteristics of New Commitments 1970*, VI, no. 1, 1.

The vast majority of prison inmates also suffer from reading deficiencies. Illiteracy correlates with poverty and the lack of opportunity, which are oppressors of the minority. As the National Advisory Commission pointed out, "A productive exercise of legal rights and responsibilities is based on a competency in English and an understanding of American culture."[44] The denial of adequate literacy, which is a defect in our educational system, is in effect a denial of the exercise of full legal rights, including the right to stay out of the criminal justice system.

SEGREGATION IN THE PRISON

The bitter gall of discrimination has also followed the disadvantaged into the prison itself. Black inmates in San Quentin refer to that institution as the "inner city," implying that it is just a relocated ghetto. It was not until 1968, in fact, that the United States Supreme Court invalidated segregation in correctional institutions.[45] One of San Quentin's more famous inmates wrote about what happens to the segregated minority:

> His have-nothing status, the absence of the all-important controls, predisposes him to impracticality, he can never relax, he is or becomes the desperate man. And desperate men do desperate things, take desperate positions; when revolution comes he is the first to join it. If it doesn't come he makes it.[46]

And so we have the latest pathological development spawned in the American correctional system, the phenomenon of the "political prisoner," a term that could not heretofore be found in any conventional dictionary.[47]

Let George Bernard Shaw conclude this section: "The conclusion is that imprisonment cannot be fully understood by those who do not understand freedom."[48] Those who do will see the wisdom of redirecting the correctional effort.

---

[44] National Advisory Commission, *Community Crime Prevention*, 1973, p. 151.

[45] *Lee v. Washington*, 390 U.S. 333.

[46] George Jackson, *Soledad Brother* (New York: Bantam Books, 1970), p. 245.

[47] For an excellent contemporary analysis of this phenomenon, see Stuart A. Brody, "The Political Prisoner Syndrome," *Crime and Delinquency*, 20, no. 2 (April 1974), 97–106.

[48] George Bernard Shaw, *The Crime of Imprisonment* (New York: Philosophical Library, 1946), p. 125.

The Search for Justice

The objective of the whole criminal justice procedure is to secure justice. In an address delivered to the Wilshire Bar Association on July 23, 1974, Justice Macklin Fleming of the California Appellate Court described that procedure as a "chronic scandal." He was particularly incensed by the interminable delays in processing cases, reminding his listeners of the legal axiom that "Justice delayed is justice denied."

WHAT IS JUSTICE?

What is justice? Well, it obviously means many things to many people. Theologians and philosophers have long pondered the meaning of justice, as have legal scholars. In its most primitive sense it signifies equality; it involves giving every man his due. Among the learned philosophers who wrote at length on this virtue, Aristotle and Aquinas spring to mind. Both viewed justice as having several forms.

According to Thomas Aquinas, justice has three basic dimensions, each dimension concerning the relationships among men. The first is the relationship of members in a community among themselves, which is covered by *commutative justice.* The second governs the relationship of the community (state) as a whole to its individual members, and its known as *distributive justice.* The third concerns the relationship of the individual to the whole community (state), and is regulated by *legal justice.*[49] All three dimensions are implicitly operative in the criminal justice system, at least in the abstract. It is interesting to note that Aquinas considered justice "the most excellent of all the moral virtues" because it was "most akin to reason,"[50] which, of course, is what supposedly elevates man above less developed forms of life.

The search for justice in the judicial-correctional system is essentially a search for distributive justice, as well as a search for a balance between distributive and legal justice.

JUSTICE, GUILT, AND RESPONSIBILITY

There is another critical issue at stake in the whole process of adjudication of guilt and imposition of sentence, and that is the question of the

---

[49] Hans Meyer, *The Philosophy of St. Thomas Aquinas* (St. Louis: B. Herder Book Co., 1946), p. 395.

[50] *Summa theol.*, II, q. 66, a. 4.

degree of responsibility of the individual offender. The social sciences are tending more and more toward a deterministic view of man, that is, one in which criminal man is essentially viewed as having *involuntarily* entered into a life of crime or a criminal act. He is not considered culpable because of the uncontrolled forces of environment and heredity, but he is held accountable to society for his disruptive behavior. This was the position of the nineteenth-century criminologist, Enrico Ferri, and it is being resurrected today.[51]

Not everyone can be comfortable with a theory that denies man self-determination. The opposing view to determinism is that man is fundamentally in control of his destiny and is the master, not the slave, of his environment. He may have this capacity for self-determination impaired by infancy, insanity, immaturity, or chemical interference, but he is essentially self-determinative. The *voluntarist* or *indeterminist* agrees with the *determinist* that "the concept of responsibility . . . is at the core of the criminal process." [52] But he has a different interpretation of responsibility.

Men, however, do not have to unravel and solve this philosophic problem in order to be just men and to have a just system. In striving to make the criminal justice system a viable one, we will actually be engaged in resolving the philosophic problem. The blindfolded lady of justice is not really interested in partisanship. She is very much interested in Justice.

JUSTICE IN A PRACTICAL CONTEXT

From a practical viewpoint, the criminal justice machinery is a ponderous complexity that begs to be reformed and streamlined. A 1970 survey revealed that a grand total of 46,159 public criminal justice agencies exist on the state and local level. There are, interestingly, almost as many courts as there are enforcement agencies, 13,235 compared to 14,806. About one-fifth of the agencies deal with prosecution and defense but, significantly, prosecutors' offices outnumber defenders' offices by a 23-1 ratio. Correctional agencies constitute 16 percent of the total, basically consisting of 4,435 agencies for adults, 724 for juveniles. There are 2,445 probation offices included in the correctional 16 percent.[53]

---

[51] Nicholas N. Kittrie, "Will the XYY Syndrome Abolish Guilt?" Institute for Studies in Justice and Social Behavior (Washington, D.C.: The American University Law School, 1971).

[52] *Ibid.*, p. 28.

[53] U.S. Department of Justice, LEAA, National Institute of Law Enforcement and Criminal Justice, "Criminal Justice Agencies in the United States 1970," (Washington, D.C.: U.S. Government Printing Office).

From such a complexity it is no wonder that justice is so often an absent commodity. In 1953 the prestigious *Annals* repeatedly stressed the urgency of reforming the criminal justice system.[54] It is an infinitely more urgent necessity today.

JUSTICE AND REFORM

The search for justice will require a thrust for reform in all three of the major components of the criminal justice system, the police, the courts, and corrections. The police will have to understand that they have an important role in diverting juveniles *from* the system. Something will also have to be done to reduce the large number of immortal criminal records that are maintained by police agencies. Niederhoffer calls this "criminal justice by dossier."[55] Eternally maintaining records of this nature causes ex-offenders to be perpetually labeled. Records and labels are conspiratorial elements that offset reformation and forestall justice.

Burdened courts that mete out inequitable sentences uniquely defeat justice. Despite the evidence that severe sentencing is not conducive to reformation, sentences appear to be growing longer. A case in point is the recent New York law that makes a life sentence mandatory for conviction of sale of hard drugs.

The disparity in sentencing that plagues our courts is a grievous affront to our sense of justice. Numerous cases can be cited. In a recent instance in New York, a member of the New York Stock Exchange and his firm were convicted of manipulating stock trades worth $20 million, through secret Swiss accounts. The defense attorney, a former federal judge, likened his client's offense to a traffic infraction! The defendant was fined $50,000. In another case before the same judge, an unemployed, black shipping clerk, the father of two children, who had a prior felony conviction for robbery, was charged with stealing a $100 television set. He was sentenced to a year in jail.[56] The reader should understand that we are using *disparity* to imply manifest injustice in sentencing practices. There is no implication that sentences cannot be different in similar circumstances in the interests of justice.

---

[54] *Annals of the American Academy of Political and Social Science,* vol. 287, May 1953.

[55] Arthur Niederhoffer, "Criminal Justice by Dossier: Law Enforcement, Labeling, and Liberty," in *Current Perspectives on Criminal Behavior,* Abraham S. Blumberg, ed. (N. Y.: Alfred A. Knopf, Inc., 1974), pp. 46–47.

[56] National Coordinating Committee for Justice Under the Law, *NCCJL REPORTS,* 11, no. 4 (November–December 1973).

Justice in the correctional component will require both rational methods of correcting and adequate protection for the public. As Conrad has stated, rehabilitation continues to be a meritorious objective, but its achievement "in a correctional structure" is no longer considered a practical possibility by informed authorities.[57] The protection of the public is paramount, so the dangerous offender must be institutionalized. The problem of determining who is dangerous, however, is a very perplexing problem. No formula currently exists that would enable such a diagnosis. The definition of dangerousness is generally applied to individuals whose crimes involve grievous physical injury or death to the victim, or who are chronic, serious offenders. It is easier to say that the majority of offenders should be subjected to community-based methods of correction.

THE GOALS OF JUSTICE

The criminal justice system cannot operate in a vacuum, divorced from the large body of law-abiding citizens it ostensibly protects. With crime rampant and senselessly violent, a pervasive fear is abroad in the land. People have expressed fear of going out at night, fear for their personal safety, and fear of being the victim of property and assaultive offenses. This was documented in surveys undertaken by the President's Crime Commission, and reaffirmed in a more recent survey conducted in the state of Michigan.[58] The whole point of national reform of the criminal justice system is, ultimately, to enhance the security of the community. But that security will not be enhanced by dealing vengefully with the products of the criminal justice system, nor by the denial of simple justice.

In 1974 the American Bar Association drafted proposed legislation to create a National Institute of Justice. That proposal acknowledged the critical need for an agency to appraise "the effectiveness and quality of justice and the administration of law, including but not limited to civil and criminal justice . . . ."[59]

Conscionable men cannot let injustice in the criminal *justice* system endure.

---

[57] John P. Conrad, "Corrections and Simple Justice," *The Aldine Crime and Justice Annual 1973* (Chicago: Aldine Publishing Company, 1974), p. 516.

[58] Michigan Commission on Criminal Justice, *The Michigan Public Speaks Out on Crime,* Second Annual Survey, January 1974.

[59] American Bar Association, Commission on a National Institute of Justice, Draft Proposal: *A Bill for an Act Creating a National Institute of Justice,* January 1974, p. 1.

Two-tiered prison cell. *Courtesy South Carolina Department of Corrections.*
Photo by Ken Sturgeon.

Review Questions

1. What is meant by the statement: "The prison reflects an American penchant for warehousing its miscreants"? What statistical data can you suggest to support this contention?
2. Give some statistical data that will demonstrate the astronomical cost of crime and the cost of corrections.
3. How would you explain the increasing number of disturbances in America's prisons?
4. Give five reasons for the failure of the prison to attain its correctional objective.
5. Name the different ways in which the term *recidivism* is used, including the manner in which it is used in your textbook.
6. Who was responsible for the Careers in Crime Study, and what were the conclusions of that study?
7. Evaluate recidivism in terms of the various studies of recidivism cited in this chapter.
8. Describe the American prisoner in terms of sociocultural factors.
9. What were the three types of justice according to Thomas Aquinas?
10. Does man have free will? Write out the rationale for your answer and then develop a system of penalties for criminal behavior on the basis of your philosophy.

2

THE HISTORICAL PRELUDE

Hatred never ceases with hatred;
hatred only ceases with love.

Guatama Buddha

In his efforts to civilize himself, man has known occasional failures. One failure has persisted with more than the usual pathos: the fruitless effort to discover an effective yet compassionate way in which to deal with the criminals spawned by society. One of the earliest methods of coping with anti-social behavior, practiced by preliterate societies, was banishment. The offender was literally expelled from the security and nurture of his community, and abandoned to alien and hostile tribes. This was a merciless approach, as banishment was tantamount to capital punishment, so certain was its outcome. But this was not an isolated case of mercilessness.

The Heritage of Punishment

For some inexplicable reason, men have most often resorted to severe punishment as the method of counterattacking the criminal in society's midst. We say inexplicable because history has amply demonstrated that severe, brutal punishment has not had the intended effect: to diminish crime.

Despite the high amount of crime which characterizes contemporary Western civilization, lawlessness is not exclusively a modern phenomenon. The thirteenth-century reign of King Edward I (1272-1307), for instance, was considered a lawless era. Edward himself was considered a strong king and was a prolific lawmaker, and historians have called him "The English Justinian." But during his reign the Statute of Westminster lamented the fact that "felonies increase from day to day." [1] The king, following a still popular practice, appointed numerous special commissions, over 200 in nineteen years, "to seek out, arrest, and sometimes try ill-doers. . . ." [2]

Although punishment became progressively severe in the intervening centuries, the volume of crime obviously did not abate. There were in excess of 200 capital offenses in England during the early part of the nineteenth century, with hanging being the penalty for many minor felonies, including pickpocketing. Yet pickpockets used to attend the public hangings of their confederates to ply their trade.

There is evidence that severe punishment is a concomitant of civilization. The cultural anthropologist, Ellsworth Faris, maintained that primitive societies that have had no contact with modern societies do not resort to punishment as we know it.[3]

Civilized man has run the gamut in devising physical and lethal punishments to inflict on the traducer of the social mores. Offenders have been thrown to wild animals, impaled on stakes, boiled in oil, staked out in the sun with eyelids propped open, beheaded, stoned, guillotined, electrocuted, gassed, drowned, crushed, placed in a sack with poisonous snakes, incinerated, disemboweled, mutilated, dismembered, flogged, and even crucified. Nor were these methods of punishment exclusively employed by "primitive" societies.

When Thomas Harrison was sentenced in 1660 for his participation in the killing of the Stuart king, Charles I, the presiding judge made this pronouncement:

---

[1] Ralph B. Pugh, "Some Reflections of a Medieval Criminologist," *The Raleigh Lecture on History, Proceedings of the British Academy* (London: Oxford University Press, 1973), LIX, 3.

[2] *Ibid.*

[3] Ellsworth Faris, *The Nature of Human Nature* (New York: McGraw-Hill Book Company, 1937), pp. 86–93. For other viewpoints see, for example, the acclaimed authority on primitive law, E. A. Hoebel, *The Law of Primitive Man* (Cambridge, Mass.: Harvard University Press, 1954); and Harry Elmer Barnes and Negley K. Teeters, *New Horizons in Criminology* (Englewood Cliffs, N.J.: Prentice-Hall, Inc., 1963), particularly pp. 285–90.

> The judgment of the court is, and the court doth award, that you be led back to the place from whence you came, and from thence to be drawn upon a hurdle to the place of execution; and there you shall be hanged by the neck; and being alive shall be cut down and your privy members to be cut off, your entrails to be taken out of your body, and you, living, the same to be burnt before your eyes, and your head to be cut off, your body divided into four quarters, and your head and quarters to be disposed of at the pleasure of the King's Majesty, and may the lord have mercy upon your soul.

The passage of time did not appreciably soothe the savage heart. Two centuries after Thomas Harrison was summarily disposed of, a trial concluded in a Federal District Court for the Territory of New Mexico. Roy Bean was the presiding judge, and an adobe stable was utilized as a temporary courtroom. In passing sentence, Judge Bean demonstrated a flair for lyrical poetry—and a commitment to the deathless philosophy of severe punishment.

> Jose Manuel Miguel Xavier Gonzales, in a few short weeks it will be spring. The snows of winter will flee away, the ice will vanish and the air will become soft and balmy. In short, Jose Manuel Miguel Xavier Gonzales, the annual miracle of the year's awakening will come to pass, but you won't be here.
>
> The rivulet will run its purring course to the sea, the timid desert flowers will put forth their tender shoots, the glorious valleys of this imperial domain will blossom as the rose, still you won't be here to see.
>
> From every treetop some wild woods songster will carol his mating song, the butterfly will sport in the sunshine, the busy bee will hum happily as it pursues his accustomed vocation, the gentle breeze will tease the tassels of the wild grass, and all nature, Jose Manuel Miguel Xavier Gonzales, will be glad, but you. You won't be here to enjoy it because I command the sheriff or some other officers of this county to lead you out to some remote spot, swing you by the neck from a nodding bough of some sturdy oak, and let you hang until you are dead.
>
> And then, Jose Manuel Miguel Xavier Gonzales, I further command that such officer or officers retire quickly from your dangling corpse, that the vultures may descend from the heavens upon your filthy body, until nothing shall remain but the bare, bleached bones of a cold-blooded, copper-colored, blood-thirsty, throat-cutting, chili-eating, sheep-herding, murdering son-of-a-bitch.

As Justin Atholl observed, having made a refined study of the civilized art of hanging, it would seem that if hanging is to be done away with, it will have to be by general clemency rather than outright abolition, which "would be in keeping with our reluctance to break with old traditions . . . ."[4]

CAPITAL PUNISHMENT

Capital punishment is the most ancient of punishments, and one of the most persisting. It has been the subject of inflamed dialogue and much intellectual combat. It has taken many forms, several of which have already been mentioned. In the Western world, hanging, electrocution, gassing, and shooting have been the more enduring forms. Because of its prominence in our heritage of punishment, it merits more than passing attention.

Hanging was introduced into England by the invading Germanic tribes in 449 A.D.,[5] and it must have fitted in well with the English temperament, for Duff, in his definitive work on this method of capital punishment, dedicated it to:

THE HANGMEN OF ENGLAND

and to similar

CONSTITUTIONAL BULWARKS

everywhere

It is related that toward the end of the seventeenth century a beleaguered ship laboring in heavy seas in the vicinity of Cape Horn was relieved to detect the desolate land now known as Patagonia. As the ship drew near, the lookout reported seeing a gallows that had been erected on the forbidding land, and the passengers "were much comforted by finding a gibbet standing, a proof that Christian people had been there before."[6]

It is perhaps noteworthy that the apex of capital punishment occurred during the wretchedly cruel late eighteenth and early nineteenth centuries in England, and equally noteworthy that capital punishment was

---

[4] Justin Atholl, *Shadow of the Gallows* (London: John Long, Ltd., 1954), p. 218.

[5] Charles Duff, *A New Handbook on Hanging* (Chicago: Henry Regnery Company, 1954), p. 11. It is of historical interest that this book was publicly burned by the Nazis as "a dangerous political tract."

[6] Atholl, *Shadow of the Gallows*, p. 11.

abolished *de jure* [7] in that land in 1969, a matter of 1,520 years after the introduction of hanging.

The United States was necessarily a latecomer to official execution, the first victim to be dispatched by "manufactured lightning" (electrocution) being William Kemmler, who was executed on August 6, 1890 in Auburn prison. In fact, there has been a progressive decline in the use of capital punishment in this country. In a forty-year period, from 1930 to 1970, a total of 3,959 prisoners were executed under civil authority in the United States; [8] there were no executions in the last three consecutive years of that period. The culmination of this trend took place on June 29, 1972, when, in a very close 5–4 decision, the United States Supreme Court ruled that capital punishment was cruel and unusual punishment.[9] The California State Supreme Court had made an earlier, more decisive 6–1 ruling to the same effect,[10] asserting that the death penalty "was incompatible with the dignity of man and the judicial process," as well as being a specific violation of the Eighth Amendment, which bars cruel and unusual punishment. San Quentin's death row was closed down on September 13, 1972. It was not particularly noticed, but that was the first anniversay of the crushing of the Attica revolt.

The dispute on this matter will undoubtedly be endless. In California, more than a million signatures were obtained to place an initiative on the California ballot to restore capital punishment. It was restored, effective January 1, 1974. Less than six months after the abolition of capital punishment, a Gallup Poll indicated that public support for the death penalty was the highest it had been in twenty years. And less than three months after the California State Supreme Court's historic action, a three-time killer sent a startling letter to the attorney-general of California in which he warned that a bloodbath would take place in San Quentin during the following two years, because convicts construe the abolishment of the death penalty as license for them to kill—correctional officers.[11]

In 1971, even before the United States Supreme Court decision, the then governor of Pennsylvania declared that there would be no executions during his tenure, and his attorney-general condemned capital punishment as violative of the Eighth Amendment.

---

[7] *De jure* abolition is abolition by specific statute, as opposed to *de facto* abolition, which means abolition through nonapplication of the penalty, even where enabling statutes are "on the books."

[8] "Capital Punishment 1930–1970," *National Prisoner Statistics,* no. 46 (August 1971).

[9] *Furman v. Georgia,* 408 U.S. 238.

[10] *People v. Anderson,* 6 Cal. 3d 628; 100 Cal. Rptr. 157 (2-18-72).

[11] Martinez (California) *News-Gazette,* March 11, 1972.

Before either of these events the National Council on Crime and Delinquency, in a 1968 *amicus curiae* (friend of the court) brief, attacked capital punishment on another front, the imaginative allegation that it constituted a violation of due process because execution renders due process inoperable. Errors that might occur in the proceedings, and be subject to appeal, are placed beyond juridical review by the death of the would-be appellant.

As far back as 1963 the governor of California had thrown the California legislature into a furor when he asked that body to enact a moratorium on capital punishment. One of his prime contentions was that capital punishment "weakens the very society it is meant to protect, because it shames the public conscience and denies the entire rehabilitative concept of modern penology." [12] In the decade of the sixties, 207 death sentences were imposed in California courts.[13]

And as recently as 1972 the director of the California Department of Corrections, a department believed by many to be the finest in the country, came out in favor of capital punishment.[14]

This is our heritage.

Coercive Corrections

Corrections is, of course, coercive. The subtle issue is whether coercive corrections and rehabilitation can be successfully wedded. We'll deal with that in more detail later. For the moment it is enough to affirm that correctional sanctions are imposed by the state with all of its coercive might. The individual who does not submit to conditions imposed by the court, or who repudiates a sentence by fleeing from it, will assuredly face the prospect of additional (coercive) penalties imposed by the state. Increasing penalties demonstrate the faith of the criminal justice system in coercive punishment. The ultimate *noncapital* sanction is life imprisonment, and that is perpetual coercion. To secure compliance by coercion is to secure compliance by force. The National Advisory Commission put this in appropriate perspective: "The typical response to coercion is alienation, which may take the form of active hostility to all social controls or later a passive withdrawal into alcoholism, drug addiction, or dependency." [15]

---

[12] Statement of Governor Edmund G. Brown on Capital Punishment, transmitted to the California Legislature on January 31, 1963.

[13] Los Angeles Police Department *Legal Bulletin*, January 29, 1970, citing article in the October–November 1969 issue of the Los Angeles County District Attorney's *Legal Information Bulletin*.

[14] Santa Rosa (California) *Press Democrat*, January 25, 1972.

[15] National Advisory Commission on Criminal Justice Standards and Goals, *Task Force Report: Corrections* (Washington, D.C.: U.S. Government Printing Office, 1973), p. 223.

If men are merely compliant, they are not asserting their individual destinies; in a word, they are being forced to conform rather than being attracted by appealing norms. Alienation is the natural end product of this type of a system. Conrad, who defines alienation as "the resistance to the exercise of power generated in its subjects," considers the theory of compliance to be a bleak prospect for corrections.[16] The element of coercion in corrections may well be, as Conrad said, ineradicable, but it is practically a contemporary axiom that reformation should be secured through *persuasion* rather than *compulsion.* The former implies an internalization of socially desirable norms; the latter produces alienation and further anti-social behavior.

THE PRISON

The prison, of course, represents the culmination of coercive corrections. Many are surprised to discover that the penitentiary is an American contribution to penology, although the word "penitentiary" was coined by the English prison reformer, John Howard. It derives from the Latin word, *paenitentia,* meaning penitence. The concept of the penitentiary evolved through two prison systems that developed within a decade of one another, the Auburn system in New York (1819) and the Pennsylvania system, whose Eastern State Penitentiary opened in 1829.[17] Influenced by the religious convictions of the Quakers, who believed that reformation and redemption could be achieved through solitary contemplation, absolute silence and absolute segregation was required of inmates in the Pennsylvania system. In the Auburn system, which was the one generally adopted in American penology, congregation was permitted but absolute silence was required.

It was mentioned earlier that banishment was a primitive form of punishment. It is an ironic paradox that our modern penitentiaries, for the most part, are erected in rural areas, far distant from the urban centers from which most offenders come, continuing the ancient tradition of banishment. The original intent of imprisonment, as Glaser has noted, was to assure "that certain types of offenders would be usefully

---

[16] John Conrad, "Reintegration: Practice in Search of a Theory," in Criminal Justice Monograph, *Reintegration of the Offender into the Community,* U.S. Department of Justice (Washington, D.C.: U.S. Government Printing Office, June 1973), pp. 14, 15.

[17] In terms of historical accuracy, the Walnut Street Jail, erected in Philadelphia, began the penitentiary system in the United States when legislation was passed establishing the principle of solitary confinement, productive work, strict discipline, and segregation of the more dangerous offenders. This occurred in 1790.

Sing Sing convicts in lock-step and traditional striped prison garb, c. 1900. *Courtesy of the New York State Department of Correctional Services.*

employed."[18] Thus, the so-called work ethic was an additional influence on the development of the penitentiary.

THE PRISON PARADOX

The prison constitutes an exercise in the paradoxical. It endeavors to punish and to treat simultaneously. It must punish the offender to protect the community, and it must restore the offender to a different (noncriminal) lifestyle to further protect the community. The prison milieu is an abnormal environment in which the inmate is supposed to be prepared for adaptation to a normal environment, the free world. Yet it is an indisputable fact that "the conditions of imprisonment and the requirements for successful adjustment there differ radically from

---

[18] Daniel Glaser, *The Effectiveness of a Prison and Parole System* (New York: The Bobbs-Merrill Company, Inc., 1964), p. 224.

San Quentin cell block. © *Corrections Magazine.* *Photo by Bill Powers.*

those prevailing in the free community." [19] Adjustment to a prison community merely indicates adjustment to a prison community. There is no basis for inferring that rehabilitation results from expedient adaptation. The Presidential Task Force on Corrections showed cognizance of this phenomenon when it stated, "Recidivistic offenders who are committed to a life of crime often learn to adjust to imprisonment well and strive to make the most favorable impression in order to obtain the earliest opportunity to be free to engage in crime again." [20]

There are numerous problems that are peculiarly characteristic of the prison environment. Homosexuality, wheeling and dealing, education in crime techniques, depersonalization, loneliness, and the pangs of separation from family are just a few of the problems that immerse the prisoner. The prison is a major economic operation, as well as an intended correctional device. The administrators have to maintain an efficient and a *controlled* operation.

PRISON RIOTS

Prison riots and disturbances not only are of major concern to the administration, but are a prospective source of demoralization among staff. They necessitate diverting professional staff to custodial functions and can literally cripple the operation of the institution for a period of time. The Federal Bureau of Prisons has stated that "the potentials for disorder within an institution are in inverse ratio to the effectiveness of institutional management and control." [21] It concedes, however, that this analysis means nothing without an understanding of the precipitating factors in disorders, such as overcrowding, inequitable sentencing, political manipulation, and poor parole policies.

Although prison riots are not a new phenomenon in the American prison system, the decade of the sixties was punctuated with an inordinate number, which have continued with appalling drama into the seventies. Louis Nelson, the recently retired warden of San Quentin, who is known as "Big Red" to the convict population, predicted that prisons will become unmanageable in the next decade. Nelson was particularly critical of lawyers and judges, citing an instance in which a judge ordered him to make two books available to a convicted burglar.

---

19 President's Commission on Law Enforcement and Administration of Justice, *Task Force Report: Corrections* (Washington, D.C.: U.S. Government Printing Office, 1967), p. 56.

20 *Ibid.*

21 U.S. Bureau of Prisons, *Prisoner Management and Control* (Washington, D.C.: U.S. Government Printing Office, 1969), p. 1.

The aftermath at Attica. Note dead bodies in foreground.

One of the books described how to make a bomb and the other how to pick locks.[22]

Of course, there are many factors responsible for prison disturbances.[23] There is a renewed thrust to preserve and extend civil rights. There is an increasing recognition that men and women who have been incarcerated have not lost all of their civil rights and they should not be merely controlled automatons. The increasing use of subsidy and diversionary tactics has tended to leave the prisons imbalanced with the more violence-prone

[22] *Los Angeles Times*, July 5, 1974.

[23] A good source book is the following: American Correctional Association, *Causes, Preventive Measures, and Methods of Controlling Riots and Disturbances in Correctional Institutions* (Woodridge Station, Washington, D.C.: American Correctional Association, 1970). See also this author's assessment, *Introduction to Correctional Science* (New York: McGraw-Hill Book Co., 1974).

type of inmate. Internal problems, such as depersonalization, sexual deviance, and staff sadism, have contributed to disturbances. The prison revolutionary has also appeared on the scene, and the ugly issue of racism has made its presence felt. The apogee was the bloody massacre at Attica and the saga of the Soledad Brothers. While all of these elements are descriptive of the prison institutionally, they also evidence the fact that the prison is, by nature, ill-equipped for the reformative function.

THE PRISON EXPERIENCE

In recent years there has been a deluge of documentary-type books and articles which focus on the devastating, desolating experience of imprisonment. One that is dreadfully pertinent gives an account of the deplorable conditions in the New York City House of Detention for women. After a four months' study, the author concluded that it "may be one of the most infamous women's prisons in the country. . . ." [24] The book deals with conditions in the mid-1960s, not the mid-1860s, as one might easily suppose from just reading it. It tells of rats and cockroaches infesting the cells, of rampant homosexuality, of brutally insensitive vaginal examinations of young teenagers on brief commitments for civil rights demonstrations, of denial of fundamental constitutional rights, of inadequate medical services, of dark, confining, dungeon-like cells. It also tells of staff apathy and sadism, of unavoidable sexual molestations by lesbians, and the pitiful agony of addicts in withdrawal, and the lonely tears of the ingenuous.

The stench of perversion permeates our correctional institutions. A recent analysis of the studies made on homosexuality in prisons has led to the conclusion that somewhere between 30 and 45 percent of the inmates engage in this type of behavior.[25] And the naive and the innocent are frequently victimized.

Irwin discusses another debilitating factor in the prison experience, in this instance referring to the California system. The imprecise method of determining the actual sentence a man must serve in California (because of the indeterminate sentence) creates a "profound sense of injustice against the conventional society . . . and is related to increased loss of commitment to the conventional society," and, as he observes, "has not greatly furthered the correctional goal." [26] Nor have the prisons.

---

[24] Sara Harris, *Hellhole* (New York: E.P. Dutton & Co., Inc., 1967), p. 9.

[25] U.S. Department of Justice, National Institute of Law Enforcement and Criminal Justice, "Homosexuality in Prisons" (Washington, D.C.: U.S. Government Printing Office, February 1972), pp. 12, 13.

[26] John Irwin, *The Felon* (Englewood Cliffs, N.J.: Prentice-Hall, Inc., 1970), p. 50.

The Shift in Correctional Philosophy

The change in attitude toward the criminal offender cannot be pinpointed as having commenced at any specific time, quite obviously. Both the dramatic and the imperceptible have conspired over a long period of time in the evolution of the philosophy of reconstruction. The ancient, vengeful philosophy of *lex talionis* can still be consistently documented in many areas of the world and, indeed, in many systems within our own United States. The chasm probably reflects the "cultural lag" between the insights developed by academicians and professionals in the field, and technical ignorance on the part of the broader spectrum of society that is not so knowledgeably blessed. Besides, it is much easier to discuss a criminal dispassionately in an ivory tower than it is in your burglarized home. In any event, many forces and factors, some ancient, some embryonic, have contributed to the development of the contemporary correctional philosophy.

SOME FACTORS INFLUENCING THE CHANGE

No era or time has cornered the market on cruelty—nor the market on compassion. These are traits that do not belong to time but to man. Compassion is a distinctly human attribute. It contains the essence of love, the seeds of human dignity, and the lofty sentiment of altruistic concern. Hence, it can be expected that it would struggle to surface in man at least as often as his baser impulses. One factor, therefore, that is responsible for the changing philosophy is man's fundamental capacity for contemplating his misguided brother with compassionate concern.

It was the private sector and the religious communities that first demonstrated positive concern for the imprisoned, in the historical context. The selfless devotion of St. Vincent de Paul to the galley ship convicts, the pioneering effort of Pope Clement XI in developing the first institution for wayward children, the monumental efforts of the Quakers to bring about the birth of constructive concern in our early prisons, and the creation of the Philadelphia Society for Alleviating the Miseries of Public Prisons, are scattered examples.

Early reformative efforts in our prisons dealt mainly with attempts to involve prisoners in work, to institute prison visitation, and to introduce education behind bars.[27] If a general impetus to reform could be identified,

[27] There was, for instance, a school operating in the old Walnut Street Jail. *Cf.* Rex A. Skidmore, "An American Prison School in the Eighteenth Century," *Journal of Criminal Law, Criminology and Police Science*, 46, no. 2 (July–August 1955), 211–13.

it might be the almost simultaneous developments of probation and parole. John Augustus, a Boston shoemaker, interceded with a magistrate's court in 1841 to have some misdemeanants released to his supervision and custody. His solicitude and humane concern were responsible for an incredible success rate with those entrusted to his care. The preceding year, in the brutal penal colonies of Australia, a new governor of Norfolk Island, Captain Alexander Maconochie, instituted a gradual release system, culminating in a "ticket of leave," the forerunner of parole. Subsequent refinements were introduced by Sir Walter Crofton, who had become director of the Irish prison system in 1854. The "Irish System" was, in turn, introduced into Elmira Reformatory in New York, and ultimately into the penal philosophy of the United States.

From a practical standpoint, the most influential factor in the changing philosophy in corrections was the development of the scientific approach. The detached and objective stance of the physical scientist in his search for empirical truths influenced the social scientist in his quest for behavioral truths. The beginnings of scientific inquiry in the field of criminology took place in the latter part of the eighteenth century, particularly in Italy and England. Although his views are generally discredited today, the Italian psychiatrist-anthropologist Cesare Lombroso attempted to apply systematic study to criminal behavior. The Classical School of Criminology sought to mitigate the brutality of punishment, and the later, so-called Italian School of positivists contributed typological concepts and a more truly scientific viewpoint.

It has to be reiterated, however, that the shift in correctional philosophy is still in labor and does not yet have the legions of adherents that it merits. Regretfully, one must acknowledge that the words of a perceptive observer made at the first prison congress in 1870 are applicable over a hundred years later. He said that "the champions of different schools are [in large measure still] ranged in the field of abstractions. . . ." [28] Reconstruction is not only philosophically palatable, it is also practically beneficial. It is time to move from abstraction to compassionate practicality.

THE FAILURE OF THE SYSTEM

The evidences of failure in our present system of corrections have been amply documented. The failure is in the area of justice as well as in the area of reformation; it is in our philosophy and in our institutional in-

[28] Signor Martino Beltrani Scalia, "Historical Sketch of National and International Penitentiary Conferences in Europe and America," *New York Prison Association, Twenty-sixth Annual Report,* cited in Joseph Eaton, *Stone Walls Not a Prison Make* (Springfield, Ill.: Charles C Thomas, 1962), p. 197.

struments of correction; it is documented in our recidivism data, and in the enormous cost of the criminal justice system in terms of the return on our investment; it can also be documented in the barbarisms that continue to exist, and the apathy that is the handmaiden of brutality.

Here are some facts. The National Advisory Commission has called for a moratorium on the building of prisons, yet the Federal Bureau of Prisons has a $700 million program for constructing sixty-five new institutions, twenty-nine of which are intended for completion by 1982.[29] Comparable planning, if not on such a vast scale, is going on in a number of states. In Florida a few years ago, following the historic Gideon decision,[30] over a thousand prisoners were released from custody because they had not been provided with legal counsel during their trials. A follow-up study was made in which this group was compared with a similar number of individuals who had fully completed prison terms, often of longer duration. The "Gideon" releasees showed a recidivism

Leavenworth Penitentiary under construction, using prisoners as the construction force, c. 1900. *Courtesy U.S. Bureau of Prisons.*

---

29 National Coordinating Committee for Justice Under the Law, *NCCJL Reports,* 11, no. 4 (November–December 1973).

30 *Gideon v. Wainwright,* 372 U.S. 335 (1963).

rate that was half that of the control group. The implications concerning the effects of prison "treatment" are obvious.

A recent study of prison releasees revealed that there was no significant difference in subsequent recidivism rates between those prisoners who received treatment while imprisoned and those who did not.[31]

THE CONTEMPORARY PHILOSOPHY

Reform and research have been co-sponsors of the more enlightened approach to criminal misbehavior. The National Advisory Commission sees this trend as essentially beginning after World War I in this country, precipitated by the prodigious research of the husband and wife team of Sheldon and Eleanor Glueck[32] at Harvard University. It was the Gluecks who "initiated the empirical test of programs by examining the experience of those exposed to them over considerable periods."[33]

According to the *Manual of Correctional Standards* of the American Correctional Association, the modern philosophy of rehabilitation receives practical application in the three "continuous phases of the correctional process: probation, institutional training and treatment, and parole."[34] It is our position that treatment rarely occurs in the prison setting, and that the accent of contemporary philosophy should be as was stated in the Preface. The prison must be considered an alternative to the community rather than the reverse. The American Correctional Association has said it well: "It is contrary to progressive correctional philosophy and is becoming increasingly repugnant to the social conscience of our people to imprison an offender for a long period, without regard for his personal characteristics, merely because his custodial segregation affords society protection for the time being."[35]

Punishment Versus Treatment

The argument for the abolition of most prisons, for community-based corrections, for alternative correctional programming, and for diversion from the criminal justice system is not an argument *per se* for the aboli-

[31] Gene Kassebaum, David A. Ward, and Daniel M. Wilner, *Prison Treatment and Parole Survival* (New York: John Wiley, 1971).

[32] Eleanor Glueck passed away in 1972.

[33] National Advisory Commission, *Corrections,* p. 497.

[34] *Manual of Correctional Standards* (American Correctional Association, College Park, Md.: 1971), p. 6.

[35] *Ibid.,* p. 7.

tion of punishment. It is, rather, an argument for rational penal sanctions. It would obviously be an exercise in futility to define a crime in the penal code, to list its essential ingredients, and to fail to attach some sort of sanction (penalty) to the crime. The issue is really one of appropriately defining punishment. We are beyond the point where we can tolerate the vengeful or the dehumanizing as an acceptable penal sanction.

THE DEFINITION OF PUNISHMENT

The most popular current notion of punishment is that it provides *protection* for society and *reformation* of the offender. An earlier writer concluded a modest exploration by reiterating the popular view, "that punishment is justice; that justice implies the giving what is due. . . ."[36] One is readily tempted to respond, "But *what* is due?" It should be apparent, even to the beginning student, that the question of free will is vitally and inextricably intertwined with the question of punishment.

Punishment can be defined in many different ways and from the point of view of many different disciplines. Philosophers and theologians find it their proper province; political philosophers dwell on the issue (i.e., should an *additional* punishment be inflicted on ex-President Nixon after the "punishment" of resignation?); behavioral scientists, particularly criminologists, are vitally concerned with the question of punishment.

Punishment has been considered necessary to *restore moral equilibrium*. The utilitarian school of political philosophy, which included Jeremy Bentham, defended punishment on the grounds of *social utility*. That is, unless the state imposed it, there would be no effective check upon undesirable behavior. *Expiation* is an ancient rationale; that is, the offender is made to suffer as atonement. *Retribution*, the old code of an eye for an eye, is an enduring defense of punishment. It has been securely felt that *deterrence* is the primary reason for punishment, that it will teach a redirective lesson both to the offender and to potential offenders.

The theologian and the philosopher, from their eternal and universal frames of reference, can develop definitions of punishment. But the behavioral scientist, in the realm of changing corrections, has to be content with weighing the issue in the light of attained objectives. He will make a good beginning if he heeds the wise distinction made by the esteemed

---

[36] F.H. Bradley, "The Vulgar Notion of Responsibility," in Gertrude Ezorsky, ed., *Philosophical Perspectives on Punishment* (Albany: State University of New York Press, 1972), p. 110. For the student interested in a more wide-ranging examination of the philosophical asepcts of punishment, this is an excellent source as is J. Gerber and P. McAnany, eds., *Contemporary Punishment, Views, Explanations and Justifications* (South Bend: University of Notre Dame Press, 1972).

Karl Menninger. The distinction is between *punishment* and *penalty*, between "pain inflicted over the years for the sake of inflicting pain," and "a predetermined price levied automatically." [37]

ORIGIN AND OBJECTIVES OF PUNISHMENT

Punishment is coeval with man. An eighteenth-century writer, retrospectively probing our dim beginnings, suggested that the right to punish commenced with the first crime, which in turn gave rise to the first criminal law. These first laws were really the expression of a need "for social intercourse, not of agreements between free men." [38] Others have seen punishment as evolving from revengeful intratribal and intertribal encounters, and still others delving into the murky past consider that crime and punishment are somehow associated with, and derive from, torts, or personal injuries. Be that as it may, the contemporary correctionalist is more interested in the objectives of punishment, and whether or not those objectives are secured.

The fundamental objective of punishment is control. Punishment is intended, whether successful or not, to control and diminish behavior that society considers unacceptable. It has been traditionally held that punishment includes the following elements: expiation, retribution, deterrence, and reformation. These are what Clemmer calls the "ordinary objectives." [39] All of these are subsumed under control, but which controls are the most effective is by no means settled. We do know that severe punishment has not succeeded, and that it is falling into disuse. As John Conrad said, "Punishment alone is so ineffective that it cannot survive for long without compassion . . . compassion requires intelligence and discrimination, as well as generosity." [40] But our criminal justice system has been solidly based on the concept of deterrence in the past. Is it effective?

DETERRENCE

Deterrence has ordinarily been conjoined with severe or excessive criminal penalties or sanctions. But one factor is often overlooked, as LaPiere

[37] Karl Menninger, *The Crime of Punishment* (New York: The Viking Press, Inc., 1968), p. 202.

[38] Comte d'Hautefort, *Observations* 1767, quoted in George G. Killinger and Paul F. Cromwell, Jr., *Penology: The Evolution of Corrections in America* (St. Paul: West Publishing Co., 1973), p. 1.

[39] Donald Clemmer, *The Prison Community* (New York: Holt, Rinehart and Winston, 1966), p. 181.

[40] John Conrad, *Crime and Its Correction* (Berkeley: University of California Press, 1965), p. 302.

The cemetery at Sing Sing Prison, c. 1905. *Courtesy of the New York State Department of Correctional Services.*

astutely observed: ". . . physical sanctions . . . depend on the individual's reaction to pain and injury. They can be effective only to the extent that he fears being physically hurt."[41] This prompts the speculation: Is the objective of punishment to bring endurance from the strong and submission from the weak? In actual fact, ". . . physical punishment, or the threat of physical punishment, only restrains behavior. It does not make the individual accept or inwardly approve of the norm. . . ."[42] That might be, however, a completely separate issue. If the objective of deterrence is to prevent the recurrence of undesirable behavior, and it actually does, it is obviously not essential for the governing norm to be accepted.

The evidence with respect to deterrence is rather conflicting. According to a State Assembly study in California, for example, extended prison sentences, have been shown to be ineffective. This study revealed that although California ranks fifth in the nation in the

---

[41] Richard T. LaPiere, *A Theory of Social Control* (New York: McGraw-Hill Book Company, 1954), p. 221.

[42] *Ibid.*

length of its prison sentences, it has a much higher crime rate than states with shorter penalties. More significantly, it was shown that most offenders discover what the penalties for their crimes are *after* they have performed the criminal acts.[43] There is far from universal agreement among scholars on the effects of deterrence but, as Professor Zimring has suggested, those studies that profess to show a negative correlation between longer prison sentences and deterrence should at least stimulate experimentation with shorter sentences.[44]

In contrast, Andenaes speaks of the efficacy of deterrence in his native Norway with respect to drunk driving offenses. In Norway, jail sentences are peremptorily imposed for "unfit driving" involving an amount of alcohol in the blood (0.05 percent) far below that necessary to make a person even mildly intoxicated and considerably below the limit in the United States (0.10 percent in California, for example). Yet "for most people the risk seems too great."[45] He also points out that a large number of the population who were actively involved in resistance to the German invaders during the occupation refrained from active involvement after the Germans introduced capital punishment for this activity.[46]

Many other studies could be cited, but it will suffice to conclude by stating that there is a renewed interest among social scientists to assess more accurately the deterrent effect of punishment. As one writer expressed it, "It is naive to suppose that punishment exists in a vacuum. . . ."[47] Punishment very probably has a decided deterrent effect, but the punishment inflicted must be constructive and the penalty rational. A penalty may be effective, yet undesirable. It is well to remember that the very loss of liberty is punishment, and the very fact of having a public agency, however benevolent, intruding into one's private existence, even in a community-based setting, can be construed as a form of punishment.

TREATMENT

One of the most eloquent men in history, Edmund Burke, once declared that men of intemperate minds cannot be free. Their passions forge their

---

[43] California State Assembly, Progress Report of the Assembly Committee on Criminal Procedure, *Deterrent Effects of Criminal Sanctions* (Sacramento, May 1968).

[44] Franklin E. Zimring, *Perspectives on Deterrence,* National Institute of Mental Health, Center for Studies of Crime and Delinquency, January 1971, pp. 106–7.

[45] Johannes Andenaes, "The General Preventive Effects of Punishment," in Leon Radzinowicz and Marvin E. Wolfgang, eds., *Crime and Justice Volume II: The Criminal in the Arms of the Law* (New York: Basic Books, 1971), p. 90.

[46] *Ibid.,* pp. 89–90.

[47] William J. Chambliss, "The Deterrent Influence of Punishment," *Crime and Delinquency,* 12, no. 1 (January 1966), p. 75.

fetters. In view of the vast complexity and uncertainty that surrounds the concept of treatment, it is tempting to suggest that treatment is merely any and all efforts that seek to break the fetters of the intemperate. Unfortunately, it is just not that simple, for we would probably get into a deep discussion on just what constitutes intemperateness. Treatment implies restoration, which is a presumption that a less than whole state exists in the "client." Let us try to narrow the definition.

TREATMENT DEFINED

It is most common to tackle the definition of treatment in a medical context, for doctors have been the traditional healers, at least since Hippocrates formalized the commitment of the physician to patient wellbeing. It was only natural that the so-called "medical model" would creep into the practice of correctional "treatment." That was a misfortune. A patient is not ordinarily responsible for his illness. To attribute involuntary "sickness" to a criminal is to relieve him of responsibility for his actions. Further, criminal behavior is often a survival mechanism, a description that cannot be given to an illness. Some correctional authorities feel that the medical model has retarded rather than facilitated progress in corrections.[48]

The eminent psychiatrist Karl Menninger devotes several pages to an exploration of the meaning of treatment, emerging with an interesting if equivocal definition. He hastens to deny that crime is a disease or an illness, but he wishes it would be considered an illness so that it could be treated. This enigmatic view is explained through his definition of two words. *Diseases* are "undesired states of being" susceptible to established physical and pharmaceutical methodology. *Illness,* on the other hand, signifies "a state of impaired functioning."[49] If a man steals bread to preserve his life, is he in a state of impaired functioning? An able critic protests Menninger's view that the secret of success lies in replacing the punitive attitude with the therapeutic attitude. Dr. Thomas S. Szasz caustically observes, "From this perspective, a lobotomy performed with a therapeutic attitude is more humane than a money fine imposed with a punitive attitude."[50]

Many efforts at defining treatment are merely definitions of "a treatment approach." Fox, for instance, speaks of preparing the inmate "by

---

[48] See for example Richard J. Clendenen, "What's the Matter with Corrections?" *Federal Probation,* 35, no. 3 (September 1971), 8–12.

[49] Menninger, *Crime of Punishment,* p. 254.

[50] Thomas S. Szasz, "Crime, Punishment, and Psychiatry," in Abraham S. Blumberg, ed., *Current Perspectives on Criminal Behavior* (New York: Alfred A. Knopf, 1974), p. 281.

therapy or conditioning so that his responses to stress will be socially acceptable responses."[51] But *conditioning* can be a nasty word, and behavior modification, with its operant *conditioning,* has been under vigorous attack recently. The Law Enforcement Assistance Administration has put an embargo on grants for behavior modification programs involving brain surgery, aversion therapy, or drug treatment.[52] A veritable furor has developed over the practice of conditioning inmates through psychosurgery. It has been alleged that lobotomies were secretly attempted at a California prison in 1968 but were terminated "when the news leaked out."[53] It has also been revealed that a paper entitled "Man Against Man" was read to a conference of prison administrators in 1962,

The Federal Correctional Institution at Butner, North Carolina. During the planning stages, this institution was to be designated "The Behavioral Research Center," but adverse public reaction to behavior modification caused this designation to be officially withdrawn. It opened in May 1976. *Courtesy U.S. Bureau of Prisons.*

---

[51] Vernon Fox, *Introduction to Corrections* (Englewood Cliffs, N.J.: Prentice-Hall, Inc., 1972), p. 37.

[52] *Los Angeles Times,* February 15, 1974.

[53] *NCCJL Reports,* 11, no. 3 (September–October 1973). See also "The Case Against Psychosurgery," *Psychology Today,* 7, no. 12 (May 1974).

in which it was explained how the North Korean brainwashing technique could be applied to American convicts.[54] Unsupervised medical experiments have also been conducted in Alabama's Draper prison.

The issue of a definition is a cogent one, for the question of normal versus abnormal is by no means resolved. The psychological categorization of mental illnesses has been seriously challenged and embarrassingly tested. Stanford University conducted a recent experiment in which eight experimenters, feigning mental illnesses, were admitted to psychiatric wards. Subsequent to entering, they resumed normal behavior, but were still "treated" as if they were ill.[55] The director of that experiment, writing in *Science,* a thoroughly respected journal, has bluntly stated that "the view has grown that psychological categorization of mental illness is useless at best and downright harmful, misleading, and pejorative at worst."[56]

Gibbons seems to have most lucidly captured the essence of the modern correctional treatment approach when he says, "the treatment point of view is hardly more than a broad orientation to offenders which stresses that something positive should be done to miscreants, but in which details are not spelled out."[57] There is a positive dearth of concrete evidence affirming the effectiveness of any particular treatment tactic. It stands to reason that if one existed it would be in universal use. Thus we can simply define treatment in the field of corrections as the mobilizing of all available human knowledge, and the implementation of all scientifically validated reformative strategies, tailored to the individual need, not repugnant to reason and compassion, which are designed to enable the individual to fulfill his potential for human growth and development, at relative peace with himself and his community.

RESEARCH

There are many questions to be answered in the field of correctional research. Despite the indecision in defining treatment, "rehabilitation is going to be a key word in corrections."[58] In other words, the objective

---

[54] *Ibid.*

[55] D.L. Rosenhan, "On Being Sane in Insane Places," *Science,* Vol. 179 (January 19, 1973), 250–57.

[56] *Ibid.,* p. 250.

[57] Don C. Gibbons, *Society, Crime, and Criminal Careers* (Englewood Cliffs, N.J.: Prentice-Hall, Inc., 1968), p. 493.

[58] This statement was part of the opening remarks of E.B. Witten, vice-president of the Joint Commission on Correctional Manpower and Training, to a research seminar conducted in Washington, D.C., July 6–7, 1967; *Research in Correctional Rehabilitation* (Washington, D.C.: Joint Commission on Correctional Manpower and Training, December 1967).

of corrections remains clear, but the methodology remains elusive. There is a possibility that has not occurred to too many people heretofore, and that is that we might be overly preoccupied with correcting in the criminal justice system. There is a growing feeling that when "criminal law invades the sphere of private morality and social welfare, it often proves ineffective and criminogenic." [59] Suppose, for example, that certain offenses were removed from the penal code and the behavior previously penalized suddenly became wholly permissible. Vagrancy and gambling are good examples. Now what becomes of the validity—or even the necessity—of all of the torrent of previous "research" findings, diagnoses, and treatment prescriptions? It would appear that before we can truly define the treatment thrust, it is imperative that we overhaul the criminal justice system—until it is actually operating in its proper sphere of competence, protecting *society*. The criminal justice system has been literally overburdened with inappropriate action, and this in turn forestalls legitimate progress in corrections. There is much for research to tackle in this area.

RESEARCH DATA

Another area of concern relates to what researchers call the "data base." That is, how extensive, how valid, and how meaningful is the research information available? Many conclusions have been drawn from meager data, and this does not advance the cause nor the status of correctional research. In the very recent past, the director of the research center of the National Council on Crime and Delinquency at Davis, California, used the word "deplorable" to describe the "breadth or scope of information that is available." He drew particular attention to the fact that the President's Crime Commission, a governmental agency, had to contract with a private agency to ascertain the number of individuals incarcerated in the United States.[60]

THE FUTURE OF RESEARCH IN CORRECTIONS

We are faced with two compelling conclusions at this point in our review: The prison is a generally ineffective instrument of correction, and we critically need additional empirical data if we are to progress in the

---

[59] National Advisory Commission, *Corrections,* p. 11.

[60] Don M. Gottfredson, "Current Information Bases for Evaluating Correctional Programs," *Research in Correctional Rehabilitation* (Washington, D.C.: Joint Commission on Correctional Manpower and Training, December 1967), p. 28.

nebulous pursuit of "treatment." Experimentation is the handmaiden of research. It follows that imaginative and bold experimentation is going to be necessary to advance our understanding of criminal man and to discover restorative treatment techniques.

In 1870 the American Prison Association held its first and most memorable meeting in Cincinnati. At that time it drew up its famous Declaration of Principles. These principles have never been completely implemented. They were incredibly foresighted, considering the time. The fifth principle is pertinent here: "The prisoner's destiny should be placed measurably in his own hands; he must be put into circumstances where he will be able, through his own exertions, to continually better his own condition . . ."

It would seem that the normalizing community would be the appropriate "circumstances." The opportunity to become directly involved in his own "treatment," and to make direct restitution to his victims, would more likely better his condition, as well as the community's. This would be preferable to the interminable warehousing in a criminogenic milieu that goes on in our system today.

In Sweden approximately 80 percent of its convicted offenders are given suspended sentences or placed on probation. But they must also forfeit up to one-third of their pay, proportioned in terms of the seriousness of their offenses. There are life sentences in Sweden for very serious offenses, but even lifers are given three-week vacations in the community during incarceration. Prisons in Sweden are furnished in comfortable and homelike motif, and the inmates are permitted frequent short furloughs for home visits. A modified Swedish system would appear to be an improvement on the major warehousing system that we have in the United States.

There are some very promising developments in this country, however, which we shall discuss in subsequent chapters.

RESPONSIBILITY

An issue that is conveniently avoided, but hauntingly ubiquitous, is the question of free will and personal responsibility in the matter of criminal behavior. We have already stated that there are many mitigants to the exercise of free choice, but gainsaying these, are men sufficiently free in their deliberations as to render them responsible for the consequences of, and hence, the penalties for, their actions? It is not appropriate to undertake a deep philosophic excursion to resolve this quandry, but both treatment and penal sanctions imply responsibility. We are not dealing with automatons. The word "deliberation" derives from the Latin root meaning "to ponder," or literally to ponder on a scale (*Libra*), as in a scale of alternative choices. In the controversy over free will, philosophers point to the capacity for reflection in the human. Man does not always reflect before he acts, but when he does he opts for a course of action which he might not have undertaken had he not submitted the issue to reflection. The philosopher Titus asked: "Why should a man stop and deliberate if the choice is not influenced by the deliberation?" [61]

Fortunately, the exercise of compassion does not depend on a prior knowledge of whether or not man is responsible for his actions, but the complete man in the criminal justice system, particularly in the correcting component, should ponder this issue well. Is dignity separable from freedom? Did John F. Kennedy mock us when he urged us to heed the command of Isaiah, to "undo the heavy burdens and to let the oppressed go free"? [62] The Don Quixote of contemporary psychiatry, Dr. Thomas S. Szasz, with his customary penetrating clarity, provided a foundation from which to contemplate the issue of freedom and responsibility: "Progressive freedom, independence, and responsibility lead to being human; progressive enslavement, dependence, and irresponsibility, to being a thing." [63]

Review Questions

1. Do you favor or oppose capital punishment? Why? Set up a class debate on the issue.
2. What is meant by the term "coercive corrections"? Explain fully.
3. What were the more significant developments, and which were the more important institutions, in the history of the penitentiary in the United States?
4. What reasons could you give to explain the prison's inability to contribute to rehabilitation?
5. When did the "shift in correctional philosophy" take place, and what factors were responsible for this shift?
6. What was the Gideon decision and what was the significance of this decision in terms of imprisonment?

---

[61] Harold H. Titus, *Living Issues in Philosophy* (New York: American Book Company, 1946), p. 168.

[62] Inaugural Address of President John Fitzgerald Kennedy, January 20, 1961.

[63] Szasz, *Crime, Punishment, and Psychiatry,* p. 283.

7. How would you define punishment? What interesting distinction did Karl Menninger make?
8. What is the origin and what are the objectives of punishment?
9. How would you define treatment? How does Gibbons view correctional treatment?
10. What role does research have in the future of corrections? Why?

3

DIVERSION STRATEGIES AND LEGAL DIMENSIONS

Why should I hurt thee?
This world surely is wide enough
to hold both thee and me.

Laurence Sterne

Diversion is not synonymous with community-based corrections, but it is part of the generic community correctional effort. The distinction lies in the fact that diversionary tactics are aimed at keeping people *out of* the criminal justice system, and particularly out of its institutional component, whereas community-based corrections refers to the total spectrum of correctional programming that takes place in the community, sometimes as a sequel to institutionalization.

Diversion: Definition, Critique, and Rationale

There are compelling practical reasons for diversion. The criminal justice system is grievously overburdened. A United Nations Report released on August 9, 1974, revealed that there were 200 persons imprisoned in the United States for every 100,000 of the population.[1] This

[1] *Los Angeles Times,* August 10, 1974.

is ten times the rate of the Netherlands. In 1973 the U.S. Congress "failed to enact a single new law in the field of criminal justice." [2] In that same year, over 420,000 persons were arrested in the United States on marijuana charges.[3] This was just under 70 percent of all drug arrests for that year and represented a 43 percent increase over the previous year. Some marijuana offenses are classic examples of nonconforming behavior susceptible to criminal justice diversion.

Diversion is also to be distinguished from *prevention*. The latter refers to efforts aimed at precluding the development of infractions of the law, whereas diversion is introduced *after* legally prohibited behavior has taken place. The National Advisory Commission defines diversion as "formally acknowledged and organized efforts to utilize alternatives to initial or continued processing into the justice system." [4] This definition introduces the specific element of *formal acknowledgment*. The reason for this is to give diversion formal recognition as a legitimate part of the correctional machinery. In terms of processing, "diversion implies halting or suspending formal criminal proceedings against a person who has violated a statute, in favor of processing through a noncriminal disposition or means." [5]

THE ORIGIN OF DIVERSION

Informal diversion has occurred since the birth of the criminal justice system, but with only unofficial recognition. The wide exercise of discretion by police officers, particularly in the diversionary handling of juveniles, is a case in point. Informal diversion, in fact, occurs at every stage of the criminal justice processing. The district attorney diverts when he declines to prosecute prosecutable offenses. The court diverts when it avoids imposing a more severe disposition, opting for a lesser or suspended sentence. Probation is, of course, diversion epitomized.

In trying to analyze the origins of diversion, Carter concludes that three factors are basically involved: the insufficiency of the criminal justice system, the desire of the citizen to become actively involved in the system's workings, and recognition of the fact that crime is actually

---

[2] National Coordinating Committee for Justice under the Law, *NCCJL Reports*, 11, no. 4 (November–December 1973).

[3] Federal Bureau of Investigation, *Crime in the United States, Uniform Crime Reports, 1973* (Washington, D.C.: U.S. Government Printing Office, 1973).

[4] National Advisory Commission on Criminal Justice Standards and Goals, *Task Force Report: Corrections* (Washington, D.C.: U.S. Government Printing Office, 1973), p. 73.

[5] *Ibid.*

spawned in the community. These are the influences which have paved the way for diversion.[6] But there have also been less obvious influences that are just as much a part of the historical move toward this method of corrections.

In some major urban areas "detached workers" (detached from social agencies) infiltrate juvenile and youth gangs, attempting to work from within to divert the members from criminality. This concept was pioneered in the 1930s under the influence of some of the outstanding sociology faculty at the University of Chicago, men such as Ernest W. Burgess, H. D. McKay, and Clifford R. Shaw. It was fittingly called the Chicago Area Project. In more recent times, the New York City Youth Board has employed this technique rather extensively.

Another influence has been the recognition that criminal behavior should be treated at its source. Kansas wheat is not harvested in Oregon, nor is a Brazilian meningitis outbreak treated in Ireland. Where crime originates, ideally, treatment ought to originate. And that introduces the concept of individualizing treatment, which is something that has a greater likelihood of occurring in the community milieu, with its normalizing backdrop.

The legal system itself is a critical element, for it can obstruct or facilitate the use of community resources as alternative modes of dealing with offenders. The Advisory Council of Judges showed an awareness of this fact by stipulating, in its Model Sentencing Act, that, "For a correctional system to be effective, the sentencing judge should have the power to choose without restriction among the forms of sentence, according to the condition of the defendant and the requirement of public protection." [7]

There are many other factors which might be cited as contributing to the development of the concept of diversion, but it is not necessary to enumerate them exhaustively. Some of the more important include the fact that the stigma of incarceration might be avoided; professional and economic opportunities would not be denied to the convicted person; less serious offenses might be more appropriately handled by some other type of agency; and recidivism would be reduced by lessened opportunity for criminal contagion which is inevitably present in the penal institution.

It should be categorically understood that diversion should be entertained only for those offenders whose behavior can be effectively dealt

---

[6] Robert M. Carter, "The Diversion of Offenders," *Federal Probation*, XXXVI, no. 4, 31–36.

[7] Advisory Council of Judges of the National Council on Crime and Delinquency, *Model Sentencing Act* (1971).

with in the community. For the major felons, particularly those inflicting a severe degree of injury or death, or for individuals whose psychotic or otherwise unmanageable behavior requires the security of custody, institutionalization is, of course, indicated.

CRITICISMS OF DIVERSION

Some critics feel that diversion by the court has one fatal flaw: it gives a dangerous degree of discretion to the judiciary. With no established guidelines, it is maintained, the large number of judges would contribute to considerable conflict in method and introduce an inconsistency into the system of justice. This in turn would bring disregard for the law and would complicate the police officer's role. The response to this valid criticism is well stated by Eleanor Harlow, who conducted a perceptive review in this area for the National Conference on Crime and Delinquency: "The proponents of diversion . . . are advocating that pre-judicial disposition be made a conscious and clearly defined policy; that the process of diversion be given some procedural regularity; and that the decisions be made on the basis of explicit and predetermined criteria."[8] Precisely. Pre-judicial diversion should not remain a random and inconsistent event, but become a clear, conscious policy and procedure.

It is also feared by some that discretionary power is unseen power and, therefore, it could be subverted by individuals in the system to serve purely personal objectives. This is also a valid criticism. It is rebutted in the same fashion as above, that is, abuse of discretionary power will be neutralized if procedural regularity is instituted.

Another criticism concerns the possibility of screening out serious offenders instead of the lesser offenders for whom diversion is more appropriate. The facts are that the majority of offenders processed into the system are misdemeanant, or lesser offenders. In a relatively recent survey of twelve states, conducted by the American Bar Foundation, it was found that an amazing 93.5 percent of all persons charged, exclusive of traffic offenses, were charged with misdemeanors.[9] As to the possibility of serious offenders being unworthily diverted, there are so many filters and controls in the system that alarm is hardly justified.

---

[8] Eleanor Harlow, Review: "Diversion from the Criminal Justice System," *Crime and Delinquency Literature,* 2, no. 2 (April 1970).

[9] Lee Silverstein, *Defense of the Poor* (Chicago: American Bar Foundation, 1965), pp. 123–24.

EVALUATING DIVERSION

We obviously do not yet have an integrated, highly systematized, regulated and unified program of diversion. The great financial burden on the correctional system is for institutional care, not for community alternatives. The vast majority of those who commit crime are never brought to justice, for they are never apprehended. The protracted processing through the criminal justice system, the brutalities and deprivations of the obsolete, unreformable prisons, and the consequent stigma inherited through both are ill-designed to enhance the rehabilitative objective. But they are persuasive reasons for alternative action.

Favorable evidence is not completely lacking. In Washington, D.C., a diversion strategy known as Project Crossroads was evaluated in 1971. This project provided counseling and job assistance for young, first offenders. There was a fifteen-month follow-up period in which the recidivism rate was measured. A 31.4 percent rate was found for those who participated in the community counseling and service program, compared to a 45.7 percent rate for a control group not involved in the project's services. The evidence affirmed the fact that recidivism was directly related to a reduction in participation in the program. There have been other successful pilot programs, and we shall be discussing many of them in subsequent chapters.

THE ARGUMENT FOR DIVERSION

The favorable reasons for diversion far outweigh the negative criticisms. The principal ones may be summarized as follows:

1. *Diversion contributes to decriminalization.* It is a settled fact that the system tends to criminalize in direct proportion to the amount of time that the individual spends in the system. The National Advisory Commission urges, as a "basic principle," that all efforts be directed toward reducing the involvement of the offender "in the institutional aspects of corrections."[10] In addition, some mentally incompetent persons, because of the absence of diversionary flexibility, are subjected to criminal processing, which is often contrary to the protective intent of the respective legislatures.[11] *Diversion will neutralize criminalization.*

2. *Diversion will prevent social stigma.* Behavioral scientists have long

---

[10] National Advisory Commission, *Corrections,* p. 232.

[11] The National Advisory Commission considers this "a major benefit" to be obtained from diversion. Cf. National Advisory Commission on Criminal Justice Standards and Goals, *Courts* (Washington, D.C.: U.S. Government Printing Office, 1973), p. 28.

emphasized the fact that a criminal record is a serious impediment to rehabilitation. It is a stigma maintained by an unforgiving society. The Advisory Council of Judges, by substituting "person" for "prisoner" in the Model Sentencing Act,[12] obliquely recognized this problem. Diversion will neutralize problems (and consequent stigma) which haunt those who have been processed into the system, such as bonding, securing employment, emigrating, and being able to enter a specialized profession. Persisting obstructions in these areas can well redirect an individual into criminal behavior. Records should be maintained on dangerous offenders, but to perpetually stigmatize the run-of-the-mill offender "threatens to destroy the correctional process," as a Canadian study phrased it.[13] *Diversion will contribute to the rehabilitative process by neutralizing social stigma.*

3. *Diversion will prevent collapse of the criminal justice system.* The National Advisory Commission flatly stated that "The significance of diversion is evidenced primarily by the role it plays in keeping the criminal justice system in operation."[14] The average citizen, including, perhaps, the reader of this textbook, has a sublime faith in the system. That it might be on the brink of collapse is inconceivable. It is probably generally known that the system moves slowly and is overworked. But consider some hard data that are not generally known. In 1974 a total of 10,192,000 serious felonies (murder, aggravated assault, forcible rape, robbery, burglary, grand larceny, and auto theft) were reported to the police. There were a resultant 2,164,100 arrests, and of that number, 81 percent or 1,752,921 were prosecuted. Twenty-nine percent of that 81 percent had their cases dismissed or were acquitted.[15] In view of the fact that crime is underreported two to four times (the percentage is more likely higher),[16] it can be seen that a microscopic number of criminal offenders are actually prosecuted. What would happen if the criminal justice efficiency rate were to increase, even a modest percentage, and diversionary tactics eliminated? It is self-evident that the criminal justice

---

[12] Advisory Council of Judges, *Model Sentencing Act*, p. 29.

[13] *The Report of the Canadian Committee on Corrections*, "Towards Unity: Criminal Justice and Corrections" (Ottawa: The Queen's Printer, 1969), p. 407.

[14] National Advisory Commission, *Corrections*, p. 74.

[15] Federal Bureau of Investigation, *Crime in the United States, Uniform Crime Reports 1974* (Washington, D.C.: U.S. Government Printing Office, 1974), pp. 10, 179, 46.

[16] The President's Crime Commission, through the National Opinion Research Center of the University of Chicago, undertook the first survey ever conducted to ascertain the volume of underreported crime: President's Commission on Law Enforcement and Administration of Justice, *Task Force Report: Crime and Its Impact—An Assessment* (Washington, D.C.: U.S. Government Printing Office, 1967), pp. 17–18.

system would be inundated, and the cost of its maintenance would become abortive. *Diversion enables the system to keep operative.*

4. *Diversion offers an alternative to the counterproductive practice of incarceration.* Factors already cited, including recidivism data, affirm the fact that institutionalization is ordinarily counterproductive to the rehabilitative process. It is also more costly. The per capita cost of institutional treatment is substantially higher than that of community treatment. In a Des Moines, Iowa, diversion program, selected convicted felons are permitted to stay in the community in halfway houses. One selected case will illustrate the factor of comparative cost. Barbara ——— was convicted of manslaughter for killing her drunken, gun-wielding husband. A three-year sentence served in prison would have cost the taxpayers $24,000. Three years in the community cost $2,000. While in the community, Barbara paid $1,000 in taxes. The actual saving to the community, therefore was $23,000. *Diversion substitutes a normal environment for an abnormal one, and at a substantially reduced cost.*

5. *Diversion enables community resources to be more widely employed in the correctional endeavor.* It also permits more members of the community to become vitally involved in an essentially local problem, the prevention of crime and the correction of criminal behavior. The community has an impact on behavior—and on criminal behavior. There are also an incredible number of community resources, in urban areas particularly. What has been sadly lacking is not resources but well-lighted avenues to the resources. The local community has enough at stake to illuminate the way and to imaginatively create new resources for the human challenge of mending disordered lives. *Diversion can permit the correctional system to offer a brokerage service in community resources.*

Establishing Norms for Diversion

For diversion to prove its worth, it must be discreetly employed. That brings up the important question of selection and screening. It is obvious that incarceration is the only avenue for some offenders. And whether or not the prison is an effective treatment instrument, the security of the community will take precedence in situations involving seriously dangerous or violent offenders. But what criteria should be applied in screening those eligible for diversion?

SCREENING FOR DIVERSION

The National Advisory Commission lists four positive and four negative categories, here paraphrased: [17]

[17] National Advisory Commission, *Courts.*

Diversion Indicated

1. Relative youth of the offender
2. Victim willingness to forego conviction
3. Mental or emotional impairment for which treatment is available in the community
4. Crime being significantly related to a factor, such as employment or family problems, that can be remedied in the community

Diversion Contraindicated

1. History of physical violence toward others
2. Involvement with syndicate crime
3. Anti-social life style ingrained and especially resistant to change
4. A special need to prosecute to discourage others from similar type of offense

The Commission makes a necessary qualification: "The criteria for invoking diversion must vary according to the nature of the program and the type of criminal activity."[18] You cannot divert to nonexistent programming. On the other hand, the fact that some areas are richer in resources reaffirms the imperative need to overhaul the criminal justice system and to make appropriate resources universally available.

GUIDELINES

At the present, no standard criterion for diversion exists. It is important, therefore, that agencies operating diversion programs clearly spell out the selection and operational criteria. The diversion program should also be administered by the criminal justice component directly concerned, such as the police, the prosecutor, the courts. Diversion should not be contemplated where criminal behavior has not occurred, because it is an *alternative* mode of handling *those who have violated criminal statutes.*

At the present time, we have limited knowledge about the real effectiveness of diversion. But while empirical data does not exist in abundance, there have been promising results in existing programs. We have already seen that the Washington, D.C., Project Crossroads has had a substantial degree of success. Even more favorable results have resulted from the VERA Institute's Manhattan Court Employment Project. This is a diversionary project in which individuals are screened into a program

---

[18] *Ibid.*, p. 32.

consisting of individual, group, and vocational counseling. Paraprofessionals are utilized in the program. The emphasis is on substituting socially acceptable values, and career development. Over a twelve-month period offenders who had successfully completed the program were compared with a control group selected from the general court population. It was found that the re-arrest rate for participants in the Court Employment Project was 1.9 percent compared to 29.6 percent for the control group. That is a very substantial index of success.

THE PURPOSE FOR SENTENCING

Many individuals think of sentencing only in a punishment context, mainly because of the punishment philosophy that permeates our judicial system. But sentencing actually has multiple objectives. These aren't always mutually agreed upon, but do include the following: punishment, segregation, reformation, deterrence, imposing society's formal condemnation for the behavior of the criminal, and rewarding those who conform by punishing those who do not. According to the Model Penal Code of the American Law Institute, the purposes of sentencing are the following:

1. To prevent the commission of offenses
2. To promote the correction and rehabilitation of offenders
3. To safeguard offenders against excessive, disproportionate, or arbitrary punishment
4. To give fair warning of the nature of the sentences that may be imposed on conviction of an offense
5. To differentiate among offenders with a view to a just individualization in their treatment
6. To define, coordinate, and harmonize the powers, duties, and functions of the courts and of administrative officers and agencies responsible for dealing with offenders
7. To advance the use of generally accepted scientific methods and knowledge in the sentencing and treatment of offenders
8. To integrate responsibility for the administration of the correctional system in a state department of correction [19]

---

[19] American Bar Association Project on Minimum Standards for Criminal Justice, *Standards Relating to Sentencing Alternatives and Procedures* (New York: Institute of Judicial Administration, 1968), Appendix B, "Model Penal Code Sentencing Provisions," p. 306. Used with permission of the American Bar Association. The ABA Standards are printed in 18 volumes. Price is $3.25 for a single volume; bulk order prices are $2.50 ea. for 10–24 of the same title, and $2.00 ea. for 25 or more of the same title. They may be ordered from ABA Circulation Dept., 1155 E. 60th Street, Chicago, IL 60637.

Reviewing the wider purposes of sentencing, it is clear that the Model Penal Code encourages alternative and discretionary sentencing.

SENTENCING DISCRETION

While there are certain offenses for which there is no judicial alternative, such as mandatory imprisonment for first-degree murder, the vast majority of offenses may be handled in multiple ways at the discretion of the court. The American Bar Association takes the position that "The sentencing court should be provided in all cases with a wide range of alternatives."[20] It further urges the sentencing judges to meet and confer in sentencing institutes where collective wisdom may be exchanged and where new developments and techniques may be disseminated. Wide discretionary power on the part of the judiciary is desirable, for it will enable us to reaffirm the human truth so aptly expressed by Shakespeare in *The Merchant of Venice:*

> The quality of mercy is not strained;
> It droppeth, as the gentle rain from heaven
> Upon the place beneath: it is twice blessed;
> It blesseth him that gives, and him that takes.

It will also make justice more probable.

THE DANGEROUS OFFENDER

The guidelines and criteria for diversion outlined in the preceding sections clearly suggest that diversion connot be reasonably extended to all offenders. In some instances the statutes are rightfully preclusive, as where there is aggravated bodily harm or actual premeditated murder. Some offenders are poor candidates because of behavioral patterns that are symptomatic of violence potential. In other instances, public policy will not tolerate alternative action. In the final analysis, diversion is a calculated risk, but it can be a *reasonably* calculated risk. The protection of the community must be uppermost in the minds of those administering the criminal justice system. Consequently, individuals of such manifest menace as Charles Manson and Fred Gomez Carrasco quite plainly could not possibly be subjected to diversionary community programming. For an entirely different, but equally valid, reason, organized criminals, or

[20] *Ibid.*, p. 48.

gangsters, are unfit candidates for diversion. The President's Crime Commission, in fact, specifically recommended extensive prison sentences for the organized crime entrepreneurs.[21]

What constitutes "dangerousness" in an offender is not always easy to pinpoint or define. In contemporary corrections, "dangerousness" is equated with violence *potential.* But we can predict, or discover, violence potential only on the basis of *past* behavior. In another sense, violence potential is a diagnosis applicable to the whole human race, for violence is truly a capacity of the human species. The issue of "dangerousness" actually reduces itself to a question of demonstrated *past* capacity for violence or serious menace to the community. A persistently assaultive individual would quality as having the capacity for *future* violence, and a syndicate gangster would pose a serious menace.

Screening some offenders into an institutional setting should not prevent continuing research to discover alternate methods of treating even the so-called dangerous offenders. A great deal of interesting work is being accomplished in this regard at the famous Herstedvester Detention Center in Denmark. At Herstedvester it is recognized that there is a group of chronic offenders whose "demands on their abilities exceeds the possibilities they have for satisfying these demands."[22] In other words, some recidivistic offenders lack the capacity to maintain themselves in orthodox but stressful social roles. In Denmark it is felt that it is preferable to provide these individuals with some sustaining income rather than permit them to be subjected to the stresses that will provoke recidivism. So they are provided with a "disability pension." While this may seem like a very radical innovation, it is a very sensible idea because the cost of the modest pension is more than offset by the reduction in criminal behavior. The evidence to date is proving this approach to be successful. Those involved in the program were the chronic, high hazard offender, or those whom the superintendent, Dr. Sturup, forthrightly calls, "the relatively unintelligent, spineless, chronic criminals."[23] A five-year follow-up study of ninety-one of these "pensioned" offenders showed a recidivism rate among the property offenders (65 percent of total) of "only 20 percent." There was an "even better" result with the sex offenders and the aggressive offenders.[24] Considering the traditional approach toward this type

---

[21] President's Commission, *Organized Crime,* p. 19.

[22] Georg K. Sturup, M.D., "The Abnormal Dangerous Offender," paper presented at the Law, Psychiatry and Corrections Program sponsored by the American Bar Association's Commission on Correctional Facilities and Services and the World Correctional Service Center, held at the Royal Society of Medicine Meeting, London, England, July 19–20, 1971.

[23] *Ibid.*

[24] *Ibid.*

of offender, the above results are all the more remarkable. They also call into question the National Advisory Commission's third exclusionary category of behavior contraindicating diversion, "an ingrained anti-social life especially resistant to change."

PROTECTING THE PUBLIC

Although the criminal justice system has multiple objectives, its fundamental objective is to protect the community. Diversionary efforts must cautiously weigh the risk of victimization of the community. If there is disproportionate victimization, it will not only bring diversion into disrepute, but also contribute to a lack of faith in the justice system, and obstructive hostility on the part of the public. The public has to be a partner in these endeavors, for it is the public that is being serviced and it is the public that is bearing the burden of the system.

It is also imperative that fundamental research be undertaken before programs of diversion are impetuously launched. Professor Franklin E. Zimring of the University of Chicago Law School detects a tendency to oversell diversion and community-based programs without sufficient proof that they actually work,[25] and he points out that some negative research findings have actually been repressed.[26] But the present system has failed and community-based corrections has not yet been adequately tested.

Some sicentifically designed research projects are on the drawing boards, however, and data which will permit a more definitive evaluation will assuredly be available in the near future. The National Institute of Law Enforcement, for instance, has commissioned David Fogel, executive director of the Illinois Law Enforcement Commission and former director of the Minnesota Department of Corrections, to develop a detailed operational proposal for a new prison system.

The significant thing, in terms of diversion, is that Fogel's theoretical construct contraindicates imprisonment for property offenders. He divides offenders into basic groups: (1) the hard-core felons who would receive flat sentences, (2) those offenders who would need to be placed in small "custody centers," but who could be taught "lawful behavior," and (3) property offenders who would not be imprisoned but who would be diverted to community supervision.[27]

---

[25] Cited in *Criminal Justice Newsletter*, 5, no. 10 (May 20, 1974), 2. See also Zimring's penetrating evaluation, *Perspectives on Deterrence*, National Institute of Mental Health, Center for Studies of Crime and Delinquency (Washington, D.C.: U.S. Government Printing Office, January 1971).

[26] *Criminal Justice Newsletter*, 5, no. 10 (May 20, 1974), 2.

[27] *Criminal Justice Newsletter*, 5, no. 12 (June 17, 1974), 3.

Another interesting project is in embryo in Washington, D.C. The National Coordinating Committee for Justice Under Law has an ambitious program planned in which it "will obtain custody for criminal offenders before they are sent to prison, and provide these offenders with a sociological and vocational rehabilitation program."[28] Those in the program will live in apartments, which will be designed to become a housing cooperative if necessary, and they will be paid a salary commensurate with the median income in the United States, pro-rated in terms of family circumstance and size. Participation in the program will be voluntary and will entail a two-year training stint. The twin goals are to provide the participant with a healthier outlook on life and a marketable job skill. A control group will be set up and there will be follow-up evaluations to determine the influence on recidivism. Every effort will be made to associate the offenders in compatible groupings, in terms of economic, social, and intellectual dispositions. This project will be discussed in further detail in Chapter 5.

In the final analysis, the lack of success of traditional methods, and the increasing burden on the criminal justice system, argue forcefully for alternative methods.[29] They argue with equal force for scrupulous care in planning and research, for the public cannot conscientiously be expected to abide a decline in its protection.

Police Collaboration in Diversion

The door to the criminal justice system is almost invariably opened by the police officer, so the importance of the police agency cannot be overemphasized, particularly as a degree of diversion has always been within the broad discretionary powers of the police function. It is estimated, for example, that over half of the juveniles picked up by the police are handled informally and released, a classic example of diversion. The police component in the criminal justice system must realize its potential for diversion and must come to understand that certain cooperative ventures with the community, in diverting offenders, are just as much a valid police function as is the arrest of serious offenders. The police officer is a protector, not a prosecutor.

---

[28] *NCCJL Reports,* 11, no. 2 (July–August 1973).

[29] For a good review of the failure of correctional treatment, see Eugene Doleschal and Nora Klapmuts, "We Need Criminals," *Intellectual Digest,* IV, no. 9 (May 1974), 15–17.

THE HISTORICAL PRECEDENT

If a precedent is needed for the cooperative citizen-police role, we need only look to the historical development of the police. The American police system is basically inherited from the English system, although it has altered considerably with the passage of time. The Anglo-Saxon mind was distrustful of a centralized police force, which was the fashion on the Continent proper, where the prime function of the police was to support a monarchy or a czardom. The English police system developed as a decentralized system. Ironically, decentralization has been criticized in contemporary times, because there is a need in this country for a national penal code that will standardize penalties and sentencing options.

The first *organized* police force in England was created by legislation engineered by Sir Robert Peel in 1829.[30] In earlier times, the responsibility for protecting the community fell upon the citizens themselves in what was known as the "mutual pledge" system. Each and every individual was responsible for maintaining the peace, and was, in fact, a peace officer. This is the historical precedent for blending the police and the community in a mutual effort to maintain the peace.

THE CONTEMPORARY ROLE OF THE POLICE

It is common knowledge that the modern policeman has had to endure increasing hostility on the part of an unsympathetic public, in addition to the normal hazards of his profession. The reasons for this are complex, but the rebellious sixties and the increasing thrust for civil rights have contributed to the polarization of police and citizen. Basically an agency of authority, the police force has developed as a paramilitary organization in a society increasingly opposed to governmental authority. The hostile reaction to the Vietnam war, the rebellion of minorities, and the sexual revolution are some of the social changes that have confronted an essentially conservative agency, whose function and philosophy have not changed as rapidly as some social values. Because the foot patrolman has largely given way to advanced technology, and because the computer age has overtaken the police profession, the citizen is being forced into

[30] The first *official* police force was created by Edward I of England in 1285 with the promulgation of the Edict of Winchester; it provided for local groups of 100 each to undertake the responsibility of maintaining the peace in their respective districts.

a more impersonal relationship with the police officer. The police themselves are not unaware of this, and programs such as "Officer Bill," ride-alongs, and the team approach to community policing, as is practiced in Los Angeles, Hartford, Winston-Salem, and other cities, are counterbalancing efforts.

Certain professions tend to develop a *weltanschauung* or world outlook based on the functional operation of the profession or vocation. A barber, for example, is bound to scrutinize the head of a person; a social worker is more likely to see poverty, human misery, and injustice; the elements of danger and authority, so closely interwoven in his job, assuredly colors the policeman's view of his universe. This phenomenon has complex side effects, but in the police profession it notably gives rise to a clannish esprit de corps, a we-against-them attitude, and a prevailing tendency to seek "tough" enforcement of the law.[31] It follows that a particular problem in police cooperation in diversion is that police tend to look upon a diminution in the severity of sentence as "unreasonable leniency." Plea bargaining, in which the defense attorney and the district attorney bargain the sentencing disposition, is often viewed by the police as "brought about by a prosecutor's permissiveness or his inefficiency in not being able to try all cases brought to him by the police."[32]

POLICE-COMMUNITY COOPERATION

Because of the factors touched upon above, the police agency has not been predisposed to become actively involved with the community in the type of advisory committee or association that would enable it to become more closely tuned in to the community's needs. It is believed that the first police advisory committee came into existence in 1955,[33] in St. Louis. Its stated objective was to promote cooperation with the community and its social agencies. In the 1960s there was more growth in this area, with advisory committees being developed in such cities as New York, San Francisco, and Cincinnati. Unfortunately, the citizens in the committees tended to be those who saw eye to eye with the police, and a healthy give and take was neutralized.[34]

---

[31] For a study that specifically deals with the policeman's role, see Jerome H. Skolnick, "The Policeman's 'Working Personality,'" in Norman Johnston, Leonard Savitz, Marvin E. Wolfgang, eds., *The Sociology of Punishment and Correction* (New York: John Wiley and Sons, Inc., 1970), pp. 3–16.

[32] National Advisory Commission, *Courts*, p. 6.

[33] President's Commission on Law Enforcement and Administration of Justice, *Task Force Report: The Police* (Washington, D.C.: U.S. Government Printing Office, 1967), p. 156.

[34] *Ibid.*, p. 157.

Among the many recommendations of the President's Crime Commission, none was more heralded than the Youth Service Bureau, for it was designed to provide a wide range of services which would permit the police and the courts to divert youthful offenders away from the criminal justice system. Yet, five years after the Crime Commission's recommendation, a survey discovered that only 150 such bureaus were in operation in the United States.[35] This is unfortunate, because the Youth Service Bureau provides an ideal vehicle for police-community cooperation in diversion.

SOME POSITIVE PROGRAMS

The picture isn't a completely dismal one because some positive programs involving police collaboration in diversion have been developed. There is a Family Crisis Intervention Project in New York City, for which police officers are specifically trained to intervene in domestic conflicts on a teamwork basis. If the officer-team is unable to resolve the situation, provision is made for referral to another social agency. This pilot program has been demonstrably successful (not one homicide in 926 families in conflict that were dealt with), and has been emulated in Chicago, Denver, and Oakland. Similar programs are underway in Peoria, Jacksonville, New Orleans, Syracuse, and Columbus, Georgia.

In Santa Clara County, California, the 601 Diversion Project[36] is designed to divert 77 percent of the children who would normally be referred to the probation department. "Reward" funds are channeled into twelve law enforcement agencies who are participating in diverting the children into community-based programs. This is a well-planned program with concrete objectives spelled out, and one that should provide meaningful data to aid in the critical analysis of diversion.

California seems to be pioneering in this area, for similar programs are in operation in Los Angeles County involving the sheriff's office and the County Probation Department—in Pleasant Hill, where a Youth Service Bureau is staffed by three policemen and two community aides; and in Richmond, where an LEAA-funded pilot project, aided by the California Youth Authority, is testing the capacity of the police department to give direct services to predelinquents, including counseling and crisis intervention, without having to expend the traditional amount of time in re-referrals.

---

[35] Sherwood Norman, *The Youth Service Bureau* (Paramus, N.J.: National Council on Crime and Delinquency, 1972).

[36] The number 601 is taken from the governing Welfare and Institutions Code which covers the essentially "status offenses" of juveniles. See Chapter 8 for further discussion of "status offenses."

A real breakthrough occurred on March 1, 1970, when a social service unit was actually established and a police-social work team made operational in the Wheaton, Illinois, police department. The project was funded by the city of Wheaton and the Illinois Law Enforcement Commission.[37]

There are natural limitations on police involvement in diversion. The limitation of role perception, preclusion by actual statute in some instances, the lack of appropriate training of police officers, a limited fund of knowledge in the behavioral sciences, and manpower restrictions are a few. But it would be a sad mistake to underemphasize the profound influence of the police service in diversion. It may have been delimited in the past; it is not too Quixotic to hope that it may be unlimited in the future.

Pretrial Intervention

The cherished values of any society are embedded in the laws of that society, and those laws receive their ultimate interpretation in the courts, through which justice is purportedly dispensed. In reality, the courts of the United States are in grave difficulty. There is a serious backlog of cases, and there is little hope for immediate alleviation. Crime is on the upsurge, and the population of the United States is expected to increase 50 percent by the year 2000. We are fast reaching the point where half of our population will be under twenty-five years of age, a fact of pointed significance when we consider that 75 percent of all crime is committed by young people. This will further tax the courts.

The institutionalized court system has been resistant to change. Attacks on this institution are increasing. Some of the more radical lawyers are ignoring traditional decorum and openly attacking the court. The public is also more than usually hostile. As the nature of crime becomes more serious, the threat to the public is graver, and the delays in court processing continue unresolved. The 1971 National Conference on the Judiciary, which was held in Williamsburg, Virginia, expressed its concern about the need for court reform in a statement issued by the learned gathering, which included the President of the United States and the Chief Justice of the United States Supreme Court.

PRETRIAL DELAY

The uncommon procrastination in processing cases is disturbing not only to defendants, but also to witnesses, jurors, and others whose lives

[37] Harvey Treger, "Breakthrough in Preventive Corrections: A Police-Social Work Team Model," *Federal Probation*, XXXVI, no. 4 (December 1972), 53–58.

are unpredictably interruped by trial participation. Again and again we hear the echo of the judicial truism that justice delayed is justice denied. It is evident that court reform is an imperative need. Pretrial diversion could be a prospective part of that needed reform.

The state of New Jersey had recent cause for optimism when it first observed that its backlog of trial cases had begun to decline. The trend was detected during the fall of 1973. Although there was a heartening decrease of over 4,000 cases over a one-year period, the fact remains that in early 1973 there was still a backlog of almost 112,000 cases.[38] Multiply that circumstance by the remaining states and the federal judiciary and the dimensions of the problem become painfully clear.

DISPARITY IN SENTENCING

Rigidity in sentencing is not a judicial ideal, for the concept of justice implies variability in punishment, and the court should rightfully have wide-ranging discretion. What is deplorable is the contrast in severity of sentences for similar offenses, not merely in widely scattered states, but sometimes by different judges in the very same court system. A twenty-month study of the sentencing practices of judges in the Detroit Recorder's Court provides a graphic example. One judge imposed prison sentences in over 75 percent of the cases he handled, while a colleague did so in only about 35 percent of his cases. One judge, who consistently imposed sentences twice as lengthy as those of the most lenient of his associates, also imposed some of the most liberal sentences in other cases. The inference is obvious—subjective bias was allowed to color the sentencing.[39]

A concern that indirectly relates to disparity in sentencing is the inadequacy of defense services. It is generally conceded that competent counsel can favorably influence the court's disposition in many cases. But a current survey of 73 percent of the counties in the United States revealed that "the majority of a random sample of [court-] assigned attorneys had little training or experience in handling criminal cases. . . ."[40] The

---

[38] *Criminal Justice Newsletter,* 5, no. 11 (June 3, 1974), 3. For an analytical review of the causes of delay in felony cases, see Law Enforcement Assistance Administration, National Institute of Law Enforcement and Criminal Justice, "Analysis of Pretrial Delay in Felony Cases: A Summary Report" by Lewis Katz (Washington, D.C.: U.S. Government Printing Office, May 1972).

[39] Cited in President's Commission on Law Enforcement and Administration of Justice, *Task Force Report: The Courts* (Washington, D.C.: U.S. Government Printing Office, 1967), p. 23.

[40] *Criminal Justice Newsletter,* 5, no. 9 (May 6, 1974), 1.

seriousness of this finding is compounded by the fact that 65 percent of all felony defendants are unable to afford private attorneys.

THE BASIC ISSUES IN PRETRIAL INTERVENTION

Although a good and impressive case can be made for pretrial intervention in theory, there are complexities in the practical arena. It is too easy to overlook the fact that this type of intervention constitutes a unique bypassing of the justice system. Intervention, of course, presupposes that the defendant is diverted to some sort of rehabilitative alternative in the community, but that does not resolve the point that has been raised in the minds of the legal purists. An even more important issue than that of bypassing the system, is that of safeguarding due process. It has to be remembered that the individual who is the recipient of pretrial diversion, the person originally charged or arrested, has not had his guilt legally established at the time that pretrial intervention and diversion take place. The danger of presumption of guilt, therefore, is very real. While the defendant's consent should be obtained before he is involved in pretrial diversion, disguised coercion may induce his consent.

Questions have also arisen concerning the right to bail guaranteed under the Constitution, as well as protection against self-incrimination. The remaining due process safeguards also raise sticky issues. What about the right to a speedy trial, particularly where diversion involves an extended period of participation in a rehabilitative operation in the community? What about the protective rules of evidence? The nagging fact is that the concept of pretrial intervention, and subsequent diversion, contains the threat of substituting a sociological system of programming for a judicial system of law and constitutional safeguard. It will not be easy to resolve this dilemma.[41]

PILOT PROGRAMS

Although the pretrial intervention concept is still in embryo, the Commission on Correctional Facilities and Services of the American Bar

---

[41] An excellent review of these and other facets of this dilemma is contained in the following article: Nancy E. Goldberg, "Pretrial Diversion: Bilk or Bargain?" reprinted from NLADA by World Correctional Service Center, Chicago, undated. For another incisive critique, see Robert W. Balch, "Deferred Prosecution: The Juvenilization of the Criminal Justice System," *Federal Probation*, XXXVIII, no. 2 (June 1974), 46–50. For additional informative material, see the U.S. Department of Labor, "Pre-Trial Intervention," *Final Report*, July 31, 1974; the American Bar Association Report, *Pretrial Intervention Strategies: An Evaluation of Policy-Related Research and Policymaker Perception*, November 1974; and the U.S. Department of Justice Report by Joan Mullen, *The Dilemma of Diversion*, 1975.

Association has a National Pretrial Intervention Service Center in Washington, D.C., and it is currently setting up pilot programs in approximately a dozen cities, with funding from the U.S. Department of Labor. It is expected that increasing enlightenment will emerge from that body's ongoing explorations of the legal and practical issues involved in pretrial intervention.[42] There is no standard format for screening, diverting, or programming, because pretrial intervention is a new concept, dating from the mid-1960s. Several contemporary efforts appear to be based on the Washington, D.C., model of Project Crossroads, which was mentioned earlier.

Others take a more frontal approach. The State of Georgia, for example, eliminated chronic drunkenness from its criminal code by reforming the statutes in 1974. An Alcoholism Advisory Council was formed, and the drunk offender now comes under public health rather than criminal provisions of Georgia law. In the same year, the police chief of Darwin, Australia, a town noted as a "drinker's paradise," arbitrarily issued a directive prohibiting his policemen from arresting drunks. There is a suspicion, however, that this unusual form of diversion resulted from expediency rather than idealism.

A more important consideration than how the diverted individual is programmed, is *who* exercises the discretionary judgment? The police are vitally involved. The prosecutor cannot be ignored. The court must acquiesce. Probation has a strategic function. Social agencies must inevitably be part of the model. Nor can the public defender be excluded. It is likely that the prototype for the future may be incubating in places as far apart as Connecticut, Hawaii, and Oregon.

Connecticut. In 1971, in New Haven, Connecticut, an organization was formed and designated the New Haven Pretrial Diversion Program. Located in the Sixth Circuit Court district, it represented Connecticut's first effort to provide a mechanism for joining representatives of the criminal justice system, and other interested parties, for the purpose of examining the pretrial process and developing pilot programs for diversion. It is quite eclectic in membership, drawing from the principal components of the criminal justice system, as well as the Bar Association and the Yale Law School. Like Project Crossroads, after which it was modeled, it focuses on counseling and vocational assistance to the diverted.

Hawaii. The National Clearinghouse for Criminal Justice Planning

[42] For a scholarly assessment of the legal ramifications from the lawyer's point of view, consult: American Bar Association Commission on Correctional Facilities and Services, National Pretrial Intervention Service Center, "Legal Issues and Characteristics of Pretrial Intervention Programs," Washington, D.C., April 1974.

and Architecture, funded by a Law Enforcement Assistance Administration grant, is developing an intake service center to handle pretrial diversion in Hawaii. Considerable foresight is evidenced in the fact that the center will operate as a part of the court system. Selected arrestees will be diagnostically examined at the center and screened for their eligibility and suitability. With the court's protective mantle, the technical, legal questions of custody, jurisdiction, preventive detention, disposition without trial, and diversion itself are in greater likelihood of being definitively clarified.

Oregon. In December 1972 the Honorable Richard L. Unis, presiding judge of the Multnomah County (Oregon) District Court, dissatisfied with the traditional sentencing options open to him with respect to misdemeanants, established the Alternative Community Service Program. The key to the program is the individual arrestee's agreement to perform a certain amount of work for a nonprofit agency, in lieu of a traditional court disposition (See Fig. 3–1.) The "donated" work is scheduled by the Alternative Community Service Program so as not to conflict with the arrestee's own regular work schedule. This program is particularly interesting because it was initiated by a judge, channels the selectees into productive community service, and is showing a high success rate. See Fig. 3–2 for the selection procedure.

Initially there were fifteen participating nonprofit agencies; the number has since grown to more than 300. In the first eighteen months of its existence, 32,123 man-hours of community services were contributed by 1,179 individuals who had been charged with misdemeanors. More than 80 percent successfully completed their volunteer service. Several were absorbed into the regular work force of the respective nonprofit agency. The collateral benefits are extremely important:

> More jail space is now available for the serious offenders, the probation officer's caseload has been substantially reduced, and the community involvement in the program has made the citizenry more aware of the Court's function and responsibility in the criminal justice system.[43]

The court is not only the fulcrum in the criminal justice system, and the guardian of our lawful freedoms, it is also the venue in which the legal questions about pretrial intervention and diversion will ultimately be

---

[43] Undated cover letter by Wesley D. Carter, District Court Administrator, District Court of the State of Oregon for Multnomah County, Portland, Oregon.

District Court Of Oregon For Multnomah County
1021 S. W. 4th Avenue Room 154
Portland, Oregon 97204
248-5191

District Court Of Oregon For Multnomah County
ALTERNATIVE COMMUNITY SERVICE PROGRAM AGREEMENT

After being advised by the court of the Alternative Community Service Program, I voluntarily agree to perform____________hours of unpaid community service for a non-profit agency. I agree to abide by the following conditions of the program:

1. A schedule will be arranged for me that is agreeable with me and with the agency. This schedule will enable me to complete the work program prior to the assigned "due date" (_______________). This schedule can only be altered with permission of the District Court Program Coordinator or the non-profit agency supervisor. Failure to comply with this schedule, i.e., no show or tardiness, will result in termination of the assignment.

2. Should my contribution of services be unsatisfactory or be performed with an uncooperative attitude, as assessed by the agency representative or the District Court Program Coordinator, the assignment will be terminated.

3. I understand that should I experience any difficulties or problems in performing the volunteer services to the assigned non-profit agency, I am to contact the District Court Program Coordinator for resolution of the problem.

4. Additional Conditions:

I have read, or had read to me, the conditions under which I will be assigned an agency through the District Court Alternative Community Service Program and the conditions under which this assignment will be continued. I fully understand that my failure to comply with the above conditions will result in the termination of this assignment and the referral of this case back to the sentencing judge for appropriate disposition.

Signature of the Assignee____________________________________

Witness and Title__________________________Date_______________

Fig. 3.1. The Multnomah County (Oregon) Alternative Community Service Program Agreement.

decided. It appears that the trend is toward a more liberal interpretation of the rights of the citizens, even those citizens who have become entangled in the criminal justice system.

DISTRICT COURT OF THE STATE OF OREGON
for MULTNOMAH COUNTY

1021 SOUTHWEST FOURTH AVENUE
PORTLAND, OREGON 97204

WESLEY D. CARTER
COURT ADMINISTRATOR

The following is a detailed description of the procedure used during intake and placement for volunteer work through the Alternative Community Service Program:

1. Referral slip is received from the court indicating the number of hours to be performed, which do not usually exceed 80, and the due date by which the work must be completed. The volunteer accompanies this referral and is interviewed for the volunteer work.

2. A review is made of the volunteer's prior criminal record. A determination is made of the manner in which this record may relate to the agency where the volunteer is referred.

3. In order to more effectively match a volunteer with the agency of their choice, a brief appraisal is made of the volunteer's abilities, health, interests, transporation, hobbies, attitude and work schedule.

4. Unless the court has indicated otherwise, the volunteer is asked if he/she has any preference in mind where they will perform the volunteer work. If so, is it feasible, is it non-profit, does it meet the standards required of the program? If there are no suggestions, a review of the participating agencies is made to find the most appropriate agency. Factors considered are those listed in Number three, in addition to their place of residence and their employment address.

5. When the appropriate agency is selected, the "contact person" for that agency is called and asked if they have work for a volunteer with specified hours to give and with the required skills.

6. The volunteer is given a written copy of the agency's name, address, phone number, time schedule and contact person. The volunteer is advised that if anything should arise that would prevent him/her from keeping the scheduled appointments with the agency, the volunteer should call the participating agencies supervisor to make other arrangements. Under no circumstances may the time be rescheduled past the due date established by the court, unless approved by the District Court Program Coordinator. It is made clear to the volunteer that it is his/her responsibility to follow through with and to complete the assignment as agreed upon.

7. The participating agency's reply card, a copy of which is enclosed, is filled out in duplicate by the District Court Coordinator. One copy is forwarded immediately to the agency and one copy is kept with the volunteer's file. The volunteer signs the Alternative Community Service Program Agreement, a copy of which is enclosed, in duplicate. One copy is given to volunteer and one copy is kept with the file.

For further information regarding the Alternative Community Service Program, please call or write Judge Richard L. Unis, Mr. Wesley D. Carter, District Court Administrator or Mrs. Katherine Zimmerman, program coordinator, Multnomah County District Court, 1021 S. W. 4th Avenue, Portland, Oregon 97204. Phone: 503/248-5191 or 248-3957.

Fig. 3–2. Selection procedure in the Multnomah County Alternative Community Service Program.

Review Questions

1. How would you define "diversion" and how would you describe its origin?
2. What are the major criticisms of diversion?
3. What are the major arguments in favor of diversion?
4. According to the National Advisory Commission on Criminal Justice Standards and Goals, when is diversion indicated?
5. According to the National Advisory Commission, when is diversion contraindicated?
6. According to the Model Penal Code, there are eight fundamental purposes for sentencing. What are they?
7. What interesting correctional innovation was introduced at the Herstedvester Detention Center in Denmark and with what results?
8. Why does the police component in the criminal justice system have an important role in diversion?
9. What is meant by pretrial intervention? What basic issues are involved in this concept?
10. Describe Oregon's Alternative Community Service Program.

4

THE ROLE OF THE COMMUNITY

The criminal justice system should become the agency of last resort for social problems. The institution should be the last resort for correctional problems.

National Advisory Commission on
Criminal Justice Standards and Goals, *Corrections*

Just before the last game of a particularly dismal season in which his Chicago Bears had won but one game, George Halas is reputed to have instructed his quarterback, "If we win the toss, let's try and recover the fumble."

In the arena of competitive sports, it is evident that even fumbling can be a cause for hilarity. But when there are fumbles in the correctional system, there is no room for mirth, for the result is irreparably damaged humans, a lessening of the stature of justice, and a diminished faith in the correctional endeavor.

The Legacy of Failure

In the preceding chapters we took a critical look at both recidivism and rehabilitation as they related to traditional methods of "correction." It should be evident that we can no longer avoid the well-documented fact that our institutional instruments of "correction" have abysmally failed to achieve their stated objectives. In the words of the National Advisory Commission, "The prison, the reformatory, and the jail have achieved only a shocking record of failure." [1]

Confirming the blunt indictment of the National Advisory Commission, the American Assembly of Columbia University, surveying the status of prisoners in the United States concluded: "Most correctional institutions are and can be no more than mere warehouses that degrade and brutalize their human baggage." [2] Throughout the final reports of these two influential bodies, it is reiterated that the only promise for the future of corrections lies in community-based correctional programming.

The community must be educated in the new philosophy, and the major elements of the criminal justice system must become supportive of this new thrust. The findings of modern correctional theorists must be translated into action by the community. This chapter concerns itself with the community's role in that transition.

THE RATIONALE FOR REDIRECTION

In the preface to their criminology textbook, Haskell and Yablonsky state that "Crime is now recognized by most people as a moral corruption that is apt to and does infect all strata of society." [3] We might well ask ourselves, in this context, if crime is pervasive moral corruption, how effectively will it be dealt with if only a microscopic minority of the corrupt are selectively institutionalized? Are the selectively punished liable to respond with reconstructive remorse, or with a retaliatory sense of injustice?

Redirection of the correctional effort does not mean that all prisons will have to be immediately and summarily shut down. There will always be a need for the secure incarceration of certain offenders whom society considers too dangerous to be at liberty. Nonetheless, as the National Advisory Commission has declared, "It is essential to abate use of institutions." [4] The redirection of correctional efforts must not be made out of maudlin

---

[1] National Advisory Commission on Criminal Justice Standards and Goals, *Task Force Report: Corrections* (Washington, D.C.: U.S. Government Printing Office, 1973), p. 597.

[2] Lloyd E. Ohlin, ed., *Prisoners in America* (Englewood Cliffs, N.J.: Prentice-Hall, Inc., 1973), p. iv.

[3] Martin R. Haskell and Lewis Yablonsky, *Criminology: Crime and Criminality* (Chicago: Rand McNally College Publishing Company, 1974), p. v.

[4] National Advisory Commission, *Corrections,* p. 1.

sentimentality, nor "out of sympathy for the criminal or disregard of the threat of crime to society. It must be made precisely because that threat is too serious to be countered by ineffective methods." [5]

COMMUNITY ORIENTATION

The community will have to adopt the philosophy and the concept of community-centered corrections for it to be effective. It is incumbent upon the theoreticians of contemporary corrections to demonstrate the feasibility, promise, and economy of the new corrections, balanced against past failures. Not only is crime pervasive in our society, *the fear of crime* is pervasive. One writer actually considers this anticipatory fear to be itself an acute social problem which may be more difficult to solve than crime itself.[6] It is commonly understood that fear derives largely from apprehension about the unknown. This fear might be substantially abated if the community were to be collectively and directly involved in the task of neutralizing criminal behavior.

CITIZEN INVOLVEMENT

In this chapter, reference to the "citizen's" role is a reference to the general community. We will deal with the more specialized concept of the citizen volunteer in Chapter 13. According to the Keldgord Report, "Citizen involvement in corrections is at least as old as the field of corrections itself." [7] It was citizen concern that was responsible for the shift from corporal punishment to incarceration, which took place in the eighteenth and nineteenth centuries. The contemporary move toward community-based corrections similarly reflects a citizen response to the failure of imprisonment.

After a comprehensive survey of the California correctional system, the Keldgord Commission simply but succinctly stated, "It is the view of this study that the most effective service which can be rendered to an offender, consequently resulting in the best protection of society, and probably also offering society the greatest economy, is community-based service provided by the local level of government." [8]

There is another cogent reason for citizen participation in corrections.

---

[5] *Ibid.*

[6] James Brooks, "The Fear of Crime in the United States," *Crime and Delinquency,* 20, no. 3 (July 1974), 241–44.

[7] California Board of Corrections, *California Correctional System Study, Task Force Report: Institutions* (Sacramento, July 1971), p. 96.

[8] *Ibid.*

As society is collectively responsible for the conditions that breed injustice and crime, it bears an equal responsibility for collective remedial action. Two writers in the field have recently made the novel suggestion that the imprisoned felon is actually engaged in "vicarious expiation." He is atoning not for his own sins but for society's failure to provide a milieu that would have enabled individuals to find constructive alternatives to criminal behavior.[9] Whether or not this particular view can be accepted, no one can deny the collective responsibility of the community to abate injustice and to neutralize criminogenic factors in society.

It is unlikely that the transition to community-based corrections will be an orderly process. It is improbable that it will ever be a total process, but it should become an extensive operation. For this to happen, apathy will have to be overcome and concrete evidence will have to be accumulated to convince the skeptic. There are many correctional activities currently based in the community which can be prototypes for further development and expansion. In addition, some reprogramming of existing facilities can be pursued as fundamental preliminaries in the transition.

LEGISLATING CHANGE

Before community-centered correctional programming can become a more extensive reality, enabling legislation will have to be passed. As traditional methods of correction are displaced, funding, support, and legislation will be needed to sustain the transition. So far this has been happening in a piecemeal fashion, but a major piece of unifying legislation known as the Allied Services Act was introduced to Congress in 1974. The intent of this act was to assist the states in establishing comprehensive human services programs. This could have provided a needed stimulus for community correctional activities. As of early 1976, however, the Allied Services Act was still pending in the House Committee on the Post Office and the Civil Service, with a dismal prognosis for successful passage. Nevertheless, it is a harbinger of a changing attitude on the part of the federal government, and it is likely that a similar act will have more success in the future.

AFFIRMATIVE ACTION

The phrase "affirmative action" is ordinarily thought of in connection with fair employment practices, but we suggest that it has a wider application

---

[9] John F. Else and Keith D. Stephenson, "Vicarious Expiation: A Theory of Prison and Social Reform," *Crime and Delinquency*, 20, no. 4 (October 1974), 359–72.

in the criminal justice system. The long history of discrimination against ethnic minorities and women has obviously not been restricted to employment opportunities. Our repeated references to the fact that the prison system is disproportionately populated with the ethnic minority and the socio-economically disadvantaged supports this thesis.

Presidential decrees and fair employment laws in the 1950s and early 1960s did little to modify employment discrimination. In 1964 Congress passed legislation which also provided for federal legal enforcement, and the influential Civil Rights Act came into being. Substantially amended in 1972, this act specifically prohibits discrimination on the basis of sex, national origin, color, religion, or race. While the narrower focus of this act is on employment, its wider application is that we can no longer tolerate discrimination in any form. If the criminal justice system exists to deal almost exclusively with the economically disadvantaged and the downtroden, then it is a discriminatory system.

As the community is brought closer to its responsibility in the area of correction, it must follow that it has to take full cognizance of the discriminatory factors that breed crime. It must also recognize that it is imperative to involve all segments of the community in the restorative effort of corrections, and this means not only sensitively understanding cultural differences, but also opening opportunities for minorities to contribute to the solutions *on a professional level.* Part of the essence of the concept of community-based corrections is that the decisions must be collectively influenced by all segments of society. In the words of the late U.S. Supreme Court Justice John Marshall Harlan, uttered in 1896, "Our Constitution is color-blind. But until society translates that ideal into everyday practice, the decision-maker who is color-blind is blind to injustice."

One of the glaring disparities in the correctional systems of the United States is the disparity between the racial makeup of the inmate population in the nation's penal institutions and the corresponding number of minorities employed in the correctional systems. In 1972 the Association of State Correctional Administrators issued a policy statement committing that organization to eradicating the shortage of minorities in corrections.[10] In the arena of community corrections, the disparity continues. To truly facilitate the regeneration of the client in the community-centered correctional program, an appropriate effort must be made to recruit minorities and to utilize their insights and special talents. The failure to do so would be to perpetuate one form of blindness to injustice.

---

[10] For appropriate citations, and for an expanded discussion of this problem, including legal issues, see Daniel L. Skoler and Ralph Lowenstein, "Minorities in Correction," *Crime and Delinquency,* 20, no. 4 (October 1974), 339–46.

Immediate Contemporary Challenges

The transition to a fluid, community-centered correctional system will naturally be a long, sometimes painful, metamorphosis. Many of the theoretically desirable changes will not occur in our lifetime. There are many changes, however, that are possible of realization in the impending future. A few of those selective stepping-stones merit discusion.

REMOVING THE STIGMA OF CONVICTION

In the present system of criminal justice, a conviction is practically ineradicable. An ex-inmate is always labeled an "ex-con" or something equally derogatory. His criminal past is permanently embedded in police and court records and dogs him throughout his life. The ex-felon status bars an individual from better jobs, and brings other civil disabilities. The situation is analogous to that of the black man buried in the innermost recesses of the ghetto, who is expected to accept his lot and adjust to his circumstances when he knows that a better world exists. The ex-felon, particularly the one who is genuinely remorseful and motivated toward personal regeneration, is constantly reminded of the fact that he is not quite a whole citizen, yet he is expected to endure this limitation.

Pardons may be obtained in some circumstances, and the records of minors and certain misdemeanants may be expunged, but the procedure is often laboriously complicated. In California, for example, a man convicted of first-degree burglary and sentenced to the penitentiary, with no prior criminal history, would have to wait at least seven years and two months *after he is released from prison* before he could become eligible to be pardoned. And pardon is not automatic. Society must develop procedures whereby the onerous stigma of "ex-con" may be more speedily removed. It is vengeful to continue punishment endlessly, especially when the correctional objective is social reintegration.

DEVELOPING COUNTY CORRECTIONAL SYSTEMS

Several authorities have suggested that certain criminal justice functions could be readily and efficiently amalgamated on the county level. There is some thinking that all pre-sentence activities should be under uniform administration. For example, local detention and probation could be unified. There is often a county jail sentence accompanying probation, which would suggest some sort of professional unification of the local agencies of detention and probation. Furthermore, the county jail could be converted from its present low station in the criminal justice system, to become the nuclear community detention center.

PHASING OUT THE CITY JAIL

The first survey of jails in this country, surprisingly, did not take place until 1971, when a LEAA census determined that 4,037 existed. That number had shrunk to 3,921 by mid-1972.[11] The indications are that the local lockup (the city jail) is giving way to the larger, county-operated facility, under the jurisdiction of the sheriff. This is graphically demonstrated in California. In 1960 city jails in that state held 22 percent of all incarcerated adults. By 1969 that percentage had shrunk to only 9 percent.[12] Although it does not have the most jails (Texas does), California has the highest number of jailed inmates (25,348), almost double the number of the second leading state, New York (15,190).[13]

The fact that the city jail is unable to provide treatment or rehabilitation programming might be reason enough to have its functions absorbed into the county facility. The basic justification for its phase-out, however, is the fact that it represents a costly duplication of effort. The cost/benefit factor in the county jail was assessed by the Keldgord Commission in 1971, because data for the fifty-six local jails in California was not available. It cost the community $6.50 per day to keep an individual incarcerated in an average county jail in California. Using the hypothetical case of a young, male, first offender who has been sentenced for second-degree burglary, and using the traditional sentence of six months in the county jail as a condition of probation, the benefits to the community were assessed. With good time and credits, the young man would normally serve an actual 130 days, which would cost the community $835. For this investment, the following was charted:

---

[11] U.S. Department of Justice, Law Enforcement Assistance Administration, *Survey of Inmates of Local Jails 1972: Advance Report* (Washington, D.C.: U.S. Government Printing Office, 1974), p. 1.

[12] California Correctional System Study, *Institutions,* p. 99.

[13] *Survey of Inmates of Local Jails 1972,* p. 5.

Table 4-1. Cost/Benefit of County Jail Incarceration

Dispositional Response to Burglary	*Level of Benefit*
Isolation from community	High level of certainty
Vengeance	Subjective—dependent upon the victim's evaluation
Deterrence (prevention of future criminality by offender)	Undetermined—highly questionable
Deterrence (prevention of others from committing similar acts)	Undetermined—may have some effect
Correction	Undetermined

Source: California Board of Corrections, *California Correctional System Study, Task Force Report: Institutions,* Sacramento, July 1971.

In an interesting sidelight, when thirty jail administrators were surveyed to determine what they considered *should be* the primary function of their respective jails, the overwhelming first choice (16) was "To rehabilitate." "To punish" was a distant second (6). When the question was phrased in terms of what *is* the purpose of the jail, "To punish" garnered twelve votes to lead; "To rehabilitate" and "To house prisoners" tied for second, each with five votes.[14] In this respect, the jail adimnistrators are uncommonly enlightened.

DEVELOPING YOUTH CORRECTIONAL CENTERS

We will devote particular attention to the unique problems of the young offender in Chapter 8. At this time it is necessary only to emphasize the fact that whatever redirection is accomplished in corrections, it must preeminently involve redirection of juveniles *away from* the institutional machinery of corrections. In the survey of the California system, cited above, it was ascertained that 44 percent of the county jail inmates were between the ages of eighteen and twenty-five.[15] This is an appalling statistic, for the jail is the launching pad of criminalization.

The concept of a youth correctional center is, unfortunately, still mainly a concept rather than a reality. The youth correctional center is not to be confused with the Youth Services Bureau, which we shall describe shortly. The former is a correctional facility, designed for the high delinquency area. It involves intense interaction with the community, the use of paraprofessionals, and shared decision-making, with contributions from the

---

[14] California Correctional System Study, *Institutions,* p. 22.

[15] *Ibid.,* p. 100.

client as well as the staff. Ideally, the case supervisor would continue his interest in and his association with his ward after the latter has left the correctional facility. The President's Crime Commission envisioned youth correctional centers as "small-unit correctional institutions for flexible, community-oriented treatment." [16]

The Youth Services Bureau is also largely a concept, although the President's Crime Commission urgently recommended this type of facility as far back as 1967. The Youth Services Bureaus are envisioned as agencies that "would act as central coordinators of all community services for young people and would also provide services lacking in the community or neighborhood, especially ones designed for less seriously delinquent juveniles." [17] The Crime Commission recommended that police agencies avail themselves of the diagnostic facilities of the proposed Youth Services Bureaus, *with diversion in mind.* Localized facilities to meet the needs of youthful offenders and predelinquents are infinitely more important *before they go into the system,* than anything that is developed after the labeling and stigmatizing that result from incarceration.

Community Development and Integrated Human Services

The integration of human services is a concept that has been receiving significant attention recently. Since 1973 the Council of State Governments, supported by the U.S. Department of Health, Education, and Welfare, has had as one of its goals "to serve as a catalyst by bringing ideas and people together to consider practical solutions to the problems of state government." [18] It was quite natural that the problems in corrections would come within their purview. In an evaluative study, three possibilities were considered for organization of the correctional endeavor. Corrections could exist as a separate department; it could be merged with the police function in a department of criminal justice; or it could be placed in a large human resources agency (HRA). Despite some organiza-

---

[16] President's Commission on Law Enforcement and Administration of Justice, *The Challenge of Crime in a Free Society* (Washington, D.C.: U.S. Government Printing Office, 1967), p. 173. For a capable analysis of the youth correctional center concept, consult George Saleeby, "Youth Correctional Centers: A New Approach to Treating Youthful Offenders," *Federal Probation,* XXXIV, no. 1 (March 1970), 49–53.

[17] President's Commission, *The Challenge of Crime in a Free Society,* p. 83. See also the President's Commission, *Task Force Report: Juvenile Delinquency and Youth Crime,* 1967.

[18] *Human Resource Agencies: Adult Corrections in State Organizational Structure* (Iron Works Pike, Lexington, Kentucky: The Council of State Governments, October 1975), p. v.

tional difficulties, the study clearly pointed to the last-named option as the desirable one.[19] Having resources for human services integrated has obvious advantages. It can also contribute to wider community involvement in planning for change.

In an editorial in the "mini-journal" of the National Center for Youth Development, the point is made that we do not have any clear-cut, demonstrably effective approaches to delinquency prevention, because we have neglected to consider the dynamics in the everyday living and working existences of individuals. One of the conclusions made in that editorial could become the theme of community-based corrections in general:

> We are suggesting consideration be given to an approach we call *community development.* This involves broad participation in the planning of change. A sense of community becomes real when people work together towards a common goal. There is not much of a sense of community in the nation today, we hear people saying. But we believe it can be fostered through a positive approach to problem solving that involves people working together to *develop a community.*[20]

The common goal in the present instance is a more intelligent, effective correctional system. To effect that type of change requires broad community participation. The exciting thing about any concerted effort of this nature is that an extremely important by-product is a greater degree of community cohesiveness. The community is the reservoir of resources in the drama of human development and redevelopment. In this section we will review some of the ways in which that reservoir is being tapped in the furtherance of community-based corrections.

THE VERA INSTITUTE AND "SUPPORTED WORK"

The VERA Institute of Justice (VERA) is a nonprofit business corporation chartered by the state of New York. Its fundamental commitment is to criminal justice reform, and its basic goals are (1) to reduce the social cost of crime, and (2) to secure bona fide re-entry of ex-addicts and ex-felons

---

[19] *Ibid.*

[20] National Center for Youth Development of the National Council on Crime and Delinquency, *Soundings,* 1, no. 6 (November–December 1974), 2. Used with permission.

into society, primarily through the vehicle of "supported work." "Supported work," as conceived by VERA, "provides for the placement of marginally employable individuals such as ex-addicts and ex-offenders in low-stress, on-the-job training in socially useful public or quasi-public jobs."[21]

This viewpoint recognizes the almost insuperable challenge faced by the disadvantaged in securing decent employment when their underprivileged status is compounded by a felony conviction. It realistically expects that when new job skills and experiences are learned, confidence in handling attendant job responsibility will follow, and criminal life styles will have diminishing attraction. "Supported work" is also intended as a method for reducing the vicious welfare trap. VERA's motto in this enterprise could well be "a paycheck instead of a welfare check." The participants receive a paycheck instead of a demeaning welfare voucher. This paycheck combines earnings, regular welfare entitlements, and a diversity of government grants and allocations. When he is ready, the individual is moved totally into the private employment sector.

Ex-addicts in the VERA program have actually been placed as custodians in New York City police stations and in other governmental agencies in the city. In operation since 1972, the "supported work" program has shown such a degree of promise that the Ford Foundation has commissioned a study of the project to determine how it can be expanded in scope and replicated in other areas. It constitutes a classic example of the community functioning in a role consistent with the thrust of redirected corrections.

OPPORTUNITIES INDUSTRIALIZATION CENTER

Another successful organization that is attacking embryonic crime through vocational assistance to the disadvantaged is OIC, which began in a Philadelphia jailhouse in 1964 and now has centers in over 100 cities in three continents (North America, South America, and Africa). OIC is a multiracial, community-based program, in partnership with the business community and the minority communities (including poor whites). It is devoted to training and placing the unemployed, the underemployed, the uneducated, the undereducated, and the unskilled in the job market. In the United States, in the first eight years of its existence it trained 116,000 persons for useful jobs, placed 71 percent of them, saved approximately $100 million in welfare payments, and added $500 million to the nation's economy.

---

[21] Graham S. Finney, "Supported Work: Present Operations, Future Prospects," Ford Foundation *Information Paper,* February 1974, p. iii.

THE NACORF PROJECT

"The fragmentation, duplication and inefficiency characterizing most human services delivery constitute substantial evidence of the current system's inadequacy to fulfill its primary objective."[22] Propelled by this premise, the National Association of Counties Research Foundation (NACORF) designed a project "to clarify and document the status of human services delivery in six counties, and to assess the potential impact of the proposed Allied Services Act. . . ."[23]

Selecting a "heterogeneous mix" of six counties, five-member teams were dispatched to undertake on-site evaluation of the counties: governmental structure, demographic characteristics, level of human services, status of services integration, and attitude toward the Allied Services Act. Technical services were also provided to the participating counties.[24] Some of the major findings of this research project were:

1. County agencies should be the principal sponsors of allied services.
2. Local self-determination in government is an indispensable requirement for creative response to human services needs.
3. Human services problems are mutual problems, so services among dispensing agencies must be cooperative.
4. Federal grants for planning and implementation should be authorized, preferably for minimal five-year periods.
5. A forum for the ongoing and regular exchange of views should be built into any plan.
6. "In the final analysis, the considerable effort needed to change the fragmented delivery of human services requires a willingness on the part of individuals—from outreach workers to policy-makers—to work for institutional change."[25]

The integration of human services is not specifically conceptualized as a criminal justice vehicle, but the application is evident in the Declaration of Purpose of the Allied Services Act of 1974:

---

[22] The National Association of Counties Research Foundation, "Human Services Integration at the Community Level: A Six-County Report," *Executive Summary*, Washington, D.C., January 1974, p. 1.

[23] *Ibid.*, p. 5. As we noted earlier, the Allied Services Act was still pending in a House Committee, with a bleak prognosis for successful passage.

[24] Blue Earth County, Minnesota; Contra Costa County, California; Orange County, New York; Maricopa County, Arizona; Shelby County, Tennessee; and Marion County, Indiana.

[25] NACORF, *Executive Summary*, pp. 15–19.

> The Congress finds that there is a great need in the Nation today to better relate our human services programs in order to improve their effectiveness in restoring dependent individuals to a status of personal independence, dignity, and economic self-sufficiency.[26]

The 1974 Act proposed a "demonstration effort," which would be budgeted annually at $20 million and be evaluated after five years. It would be an essential beginning by the federal government to design a program which, in the words of HEW Secretary, Casper W. Weinberger, "will help streamline an uncoordinated bureaucratic jungle that the Federal government unwittingly created in its zeal to provide a vast array of social services to citizens in need." [27]

Alternative Dispositions for the Intoxicated Offender

Community-based programs which provide alternative methods of treatment for the self-victim offender are a related part of the redirection of corrections. Of particular value are those that deal with the public inebriate because of the large number of drunken offenders that clog the criminal justice system.

THE ST. LOUIS DETOXIFICATION PROGRAM

The St. Louis police department, under a grant from the Office of Law Enforcement Assistance (now known as the Law Enforcement Assistance Administration), had the distinction of establishing the first detoxification program in the United States, in 1966. Under this program, the police officer takes the public drunk to a hospital rather than to the police station for booking. "The three major goals of the program were to provide medical assistance, to facilitate rehabilitation of the patients, and to reduce public expenditures." [28] The individual was expected to undergo a seven-day program at the hospital, but could exercise the option of being processed through the courts. Few exercised this option. Evidence indi-

---

[26] Sec. 2(a), (1).

[27] U.S. Department of Health, Education, and Welfare, "The Allied Services Act of 1974, *Fact Sheet,* January 1974, p. 3.

[28] Helen Erskine, "Alcohol and the Criminal Justice System: Challenge and Response," U.S. Department of Justice, LEAA, National Institute of Law Enforcement and Criminal Justice, January 1972, p. 12. See also the *LEAA Project Report,* submitted to the LEAA by the St. Louis Metropolitan Police Department, undated. This report contains the Project Summary, Final Project Report, and Final Evaluation Report (Grant #284 [S.093]).

cates that a degree of police hostility remains a factor to be dealt with,[29] but the project must be considered a milestone. It is currently funded by the State of Missouri at the St. Louis State Hospital.

THE DISTRICT OF COLUMBIA ALCOHOL REHABILITATION PROGRAM

A comparable program was developed in the District of Columbia about a year and a half after a court ruling that "chronic alcoholism is a defense to a charge of public intoxication, and therefore not a crime. . . ."[30] A significant difference from the St. Louis project is that in the District of Columbia project nursing care rather than rehabilitation and counseling is emphasized. It also limits itself to a maximum of three days of care, and accepts self-referral cases. Some reinforcement for the program came with passage of the District of Columbia Alcoholic Rehabilitation Act of 1968. An assessment of this program turned up the same unfortunate hostility on the part of the police as was encountered in the St. Louis project. It is believed that this results from the police officers' feeling that dealing with a detoxification pickup is a low-priority police matter.[31]

THE VERA INSTITUTE SKID ROW SERVICE

The VERA Institute also operates a service for Bowery skid row drunks, but it accents service to the inhabitant of skid row, rather than specifically to drunks. It also uses civilian "rescue squads" and utilizes a medical clinic as a detoxification center.[32]

All three of these programs, though differing in operating procedures and in the degree to which police assistance is utilized, are valuable penetrations into the rigidity of a system that heretofore considered drunks fodder for the criminal justice system. It is a concept central to "the new corrections" that the "common" drunk should not be a *criminal* justice product.

Local Community Service Programs

Legislation such as the Allied Services Act aims at integrating human services. The inference should not be drawn that this is pioneer legislation,

---

[29] *Ibid.*, p. 13.
[30] *Easter v. District of Columbia*, 361 F.2d 50 (1966).
[31] Erskine, "Alcohol," p. 15.
[32] Erskine, "Alcohol," p. 18.

for many integrated local programs of great significance are already operative. We will briefly review a selected few here.

DAYTON, OHIO, CITIZEN COOPERATION PROGRAM

In 1972 the Dayton police department inaugurated the nation's first deliberate effort to unite the citizens and the police department in formulating the operational policies of the police agency. In view of the traditional enmity that exists between the American citizen and the police officer, and the jealousy with which the police have traditionally guarded their prerogatives, this was a remarkable undertaking. It was wisely felt that if the police are to secure maximum support from the community, they must be responsive to input from the community. The Dayton Citizen Cooperation Program operates in this fashion:

1. Experienced officers go out into the field to determine how certain laws are enforced, the project starting with the assumption that "we don't know."
2. From the data elicited, a narrative is developed which, with questions, is sent to a list of 200 cross-sectional community leaders for their opinion "on what they would expect from a policy on the subject."
3. A cross-section of those with the "best responses" is selected to sit down with the police representatives to thrash out a policy. This is the task force, and four graduate students assist the task force.
4. Tentative drafts are drawn up and widely circulated throughout the police department, where officers from the rank of lieutenant on up review the proposal and make recommendations. The police director has the final word and it is he who signs the policy and issues the general order.[33]

The Fraternal Order of Police bitterly opposed this project when it was first proposed, but now supports it. The participants are confident that the program will be a success. Its real significance is that it represents a cooperative congealing of local community sentiment and reemphasizes that the police have a proper function in local community corrections. As President Lyndon B. Johnson declared in a message to the Congress, "Police operations—if they are to be effective and responsible—must . . . remain basically local. It is the fundamental premise of our constitutional structure and of our heritage of liberty."[34]

---

[33] For additional details on this program, consult *Criminal Justice Newsletter*, 5, no. 7 (April 8, 1974), 1–2.

[34] President Lyndon B. Johnson, "Crime: The Challenge and the Response," *Message to the Congress on Crime*, February 7, 1968.

THE COLUMBUS CITIZEN DISPUTE SETTLEMENT PROGRAM

Another exemplary program "offers a constructive answer to a troubling problem: how to provide better service to the public without further burdening an already overloaded system." [35] This is the Columbus (Ohio) Citizen Dispute Settlement Program, created in the fall of 1971 and funded by the Law Enforcement Assistance Administration.

The primary thrust of this program is in the area of minor criminal offenses and family disputes. These offenses and disputes are cooperatively handled by the local prosecutor's office and hearing officers especially trained in mediation.

It is interesting to note that "The emphasis is on a lasting solution to an interpersonal problem rather than a judgment of right and wrong." [36] Before any warrant is issued, the disputants are invited to an administrative hearing, which is held in the evening or on a weekend for the convenience of the parties involved. It is felt that a nonjudicial confrontation between the parties involved will most often eliminate the need for intervention by the court, which often exacerbates the feelings of the litigants.

In addition to easing the tensions between the individuals, another objective is to reduce the workload of law enforcement and other elements of the criminal justice system. This is possible because complaints are administratively rather than criminally processed. A major intent is to eliminate the stigma of an arrest record. The Columbus Citizen Dispute Settlement Program is a conciliatory rather than a penal process.

Referrals are screened by a student clerk, and law students are employed as hearing officers. If the offense seems to be too serious or inappropriate for referral to the Night Prosecutor's Office, alternative referral may be made to another agency, such as the police or a social agency. Hearings are scheduled approximately one week from the time of referral and are conducted informally and without the trappings and procedural rules of evidence common to a court of law. Filing a criminal complaint is considered a final alternative. It has been resorted to on only rare occasions.

As an added resource for long-enduring family disputes, a Family Counseling Division was added to the project in January 1974. Clients may avail themselves of this service after initial screening. Local seminary students, who have extensive counseling experience, conduct sessions

---

[35] U.S. Department of Justice, LEAA, "Citizen Dispute Settlement," *Fact Sheet,* undated, p. 3.

[36] *Ibid.*, p. 5.

twice weekly in the Prosecutor's Office. There are no rigid criteria for determining who may be diverted to the program, but there are two fundamental guidelines, represented in the following questions:

1. Is the respondent potentially dangerous and should he or she therefore be dealt with under more secure conditions?
2. Could discussion and confrontation resolve the matter?[37]

In a one-year period, from September 1972, a total of 3,626 complaints were referred to the night prosecutor and hearings were duly scheduled. Slightly over one-third of the complainants failed to appear. Only 100 cases required rehearing because of noncompliance, and only 84 criminal complaints were filed. In a two-month period, 461 bad check cases were heard. Restitution was made in 290 cases; promises to pay were recorded in another 156 cases; and only 15 had to be referred for court action.

It has been estimated that the cost averaged $20 for each case diverted. There was obviously also a vast savings from nonuse of major court facilities, as well as in social and economic areas. It can justifiably be concluded that the Columbus Citizen Dispute Settlement program is a model project and holds the promise of substantial benefit. It should be widely emulated.

POLK COUNTY'S EXEMPLARY PROJECT

Under the sponsorship of LEAA's National Institute of Law Enforcement and Criminal Justice, a program was instituted to single out and designate as Exemplary Projects, noteworthy innovations in the criminal justice system. A significant reduction in crime, or singular achievement in improving the quality of justice, were among the more important criteria employed in selecting programs for this distinction. The first project to be so designated was the correctional system introduced in Polk County, Iowa, in 1971.

Primarily because of overcrowding, the State of Iowa condemned the Polk County Jail in 1970 and ordered it closed by April 15, 1971. The Polk County Board of Supervisors, instead of building a new and costly county jail, decided instead to create a comprehensive, community-based correctional system for the county. With financial support from the Des Moines Model Cities, and funding from LEAA, a County Department of Court Services was established on March 1, 1971. Through this agency, four major components were coordinated and integrated to offer alter-

[37] *Ibid.*, p. 10.

natives to the traditional penal institution. The four major components provided units for:

1. Pretrial release screening
2. Pretrial community supervision
3. A county-administered probation function
4. A community-centered corrections facility

The sub-units are centrally administered and have resulted in notable improvements in the Polk County criminal justice system. The essential manner in which each functions is as follows:

Pretrial Service. Two separate but complementary units are involved in the pretrial screening. Pretrial Release (OR—release on own recognizance) was actually established in 1964, but it is now administered by the new Department of Court Services. Its main objective is to effect a reform in the traditional bail bond system. Candidates are screened on the basis of an "objective community stability point scale," which is patterned on the pioneer VERA-Manhattan Bail Reform Project.[38] The defendant must earn a minimum of five points, calculated on the basis of stability factors in residence, employment, family circumstances, and prior criminal history. If eligibility is earned, the court is notified. If the individual is released by the court, the only service provided to him is that he will be notified when his court appearance is scheduled.

During the first nine years of the operation of this program, over 7,000 defendants were released on recognizance. Only 1.8 percent of the first 1,022 defendants released OR failed to appear in court. Reflecting the court's confidence in the program, OR recommendations were accepted by the court in 97 percent of the cases.

Supervised Pretrial Release. The second pretrial service unit is the Supervised Pretrial Release Program, referred to in the program as Community Corrections. This program handles those who do not qualify for recognizance release and who indicate need for supervision in the community. Practical services are provided, including individual and family counseling, vocational assistance, referral for specialized counseling and diagnostic evaluation, and educational upgrading. Most of these services are provided by community agencies through referral. During the first three years of this program, it was estimated that supervision services in

---

[38] U.S. Department of Justice, LEAA, National Institute of Law Enforcement and Criminal Justice, *A Handbook on Community Corrections in Des Moines* (Washington, D.C.: U.S. Government Printing Office, 1973), pp. vii–viii.

the community cost approximately $670 per client. A follow-up evaluation by the National Council on Crime and Delinquency indicated a 20 percent recidivism rate. This compares favorably with the rate of 37 percent that obtained under traditional bail bond releases in Polk County.[39] Perhaps the most important finding of this program is that an individual's ability to post a cash bond for release is not a valid criterion for release.

Probation and Pre-Sentence Investigation. Probation had existed as a county function since the 1960s, but it was transferred to the Department of Court Services in the reorganized project. Since the transfer, probation has been increasingly utilized by the courts. There was almost a threefold increase in the number of persons placed on probation in 1971. In 1973 there was a 20 percent revocation rate, which is considerably below the national norm.

Residential Service. In June 1971 the Ft. Des Moines Facility was established, rounding out the community-centered program of corrections. This is a residential facility, described as "nonsecure"[40] and designated for male offenders. Somewhere in the neighborhood of 75 percent of the individuals eventually confined to this facility have drug problems, yet there has been no unusual increase in problems despite the fact that there are no traditional security devices at the residential facility.

Community services are used almost exclusively in servicing the residents of the Ft. Des Moines Facility. In contrast to the ordinary penal facility, the only "in-patient" service offered is one-to-one counseling and therapy. The deliberate emphasis is on the community-based nature of the facility and, therefore, the community's resources are viewed as essential for the inmate's reintegration.

Over 90 percent of those committed to the residential center were convicted of felonies. The rated capacity of the facility is fifty-two. Up to 90 percent of all the inmates are either engaged in vocational or educational improvement programs, or are employed. Almost all of those who are employed work in private businesses in the community. The re-arrest rate for releasees from Ft. Des Moines is 35.7 percent, which contrasts with the 50 to 70 percent national rate for releasees from penal institutions. In the fall of 1972 a similar facility was added for female offenders, although it has functioned more as a halfway house than the residential facility for the males. It also doubles as a shelter-care facility for Supervised Pretrial Release clients and female probationers. The rated capacity

---

[39] *Ibid.*, p. viii.
[40] *Ibid.*, p. x.

is only six, but it is in keeping with the emphasis on individualized care in community-oriented programming.

Great credit is due to the visionary citizens of Polk County, Iowa, for this pioneering community-based correctional effort. Evaluation of the program showed that it saved state and county correctional systems approximately $454,000 in 1973. It is, indeed, a model project and it, too, should be widely emulated.

The Major Benefits to the Community

In a National Advisory Commission Progress Report, it is stated that "The thrust towards community-based corrections supports the most significant philosophical trend corrections has experienced in years." [41] By this time, the reader should be convinced of the merit of diverting major portion of the correctional process to the community. It should only be necessary, in concluding this chapter, to recapitulate the major benefits to be derived. The community must be mobilized and given this vital role in corrections for the following compelling reasons:

ECONOMIC

By diverting corrections into the community, the community's resources can be most advantageously used, and the horrendous cost of institutionalization can be avoided. The national average for institutionalizing an adult offender in the traditional prison is close to $11,000 annually. The Polk County project demonstrated that supervision could be accomplished in the community for as little as $670.

MANPOWER

There is a chronic shortage of manpower in the criminal justice system. A National Correction Survey, for instance, reported that probation officers with cases in excess of seventy-one probationers were responsible for more than 50 percent of all juvenile cases and approximately 90 percent of all adult cases.[42] Thirty-five cases was the suggested norm. This is

---

[41] U.S. Department of Justice, LEAA, National Institute of Law Enforcement and Criminal Justice, *Progress Report of the National Advisory Commission on Criminal Justice Standards and Goals* (Washington, D.C.: U.S. Government Printing Office, May 1972), p. 32.

[42] President's Commission, *Corrections*, pp. 98–99.

but one facet of community corrections, but it graphically portrays the opportunity for auxiliary support by the community's manpower reserve.

TREATMENT

Treatment holds more promise when the others who are significant in a client's life, such as family members, are more accessible. When the correctional effort is community based, family members and significant others can be directly woven into the rehabilitation plans, drawn upon for nurture and support, and contacted for invaluable insights.

NORMALIZATION

A major criticism of the prison system is that it constitutes an artificial environment. This is well documented. It challenges credulity to realize that the correctional system expects prison inmates to emerge from the artificial and pathological environment of the prison as normal. The community is the normal habitat of the individual even when he is in conflict with the law. Aside from cases involving grave pathology, it is reasonable to expect that normalization is more likely to occur in a normal milieu. Moreover, that is where the precipitants for the criminal behavior were spawned, and where they can be most constructively attacked.

FAMILY COHESION

The family is the nuclear social agency. Though it is being threatened by divisive forces and "broken" by divorce, psychopathology, and crime, the healthy family is still the fountainhead of an individual's emotional stability. Dispatching lawbreakers to distant institutions severs the nurturing ties of the family. Community-based treatment offsets that negative factor.

RECIDIVISM

Defining recidivism is not as simple as one might think, and much controversy surrounds this problem, principally in terms of the criteria used to determine recidivism. Irrespective of the controversy, adequate evidence exists to affirm a high rate of recidivism among the inmates of our penal institutions. The Progress Report of the National Advisory Commission says, "the majority of those who are sent to penal institutions will return." It also says, "In contrast, the return rate of those assigned to community-based programs appears to be significantly lower." [43] This is a heartening index rather than clearcut evidence that all community based correctional programs result in a reduction in recidivism.

Although it has been alleged that the success rate of community-based programs is due to the selection process, it has not been established that this factor is solely responsible for the reduction in recidivism. It appears evident that there are independent, therapeutic variables at work in the community that do not exist or are negated in the prison environment.

The foregoing six areas illustrate the major benefits to be derived from community-based corrections. We should also recognize as an important influence the growing realization on the part of the community that it has a responsibility to be actively involved in its own affairs. Moreover, there is a distinct trend toward increased participation by the citizenry in governmental functions. Beyond the desire to participate, there is also a developing recognition that the community can have a therapeutic impact on its delinquent citizens, if its resources and will are constructively mobilized.

In an official policy statement, the National Council on Crime and Delinquency succinctly developed the perspective on community-based corrections, and it provides a fitting culmination for this chapter:

> To allocate funds for institutions before making the greatest use of community correction will increase rather than decrease institutional populations; it will absorb manpower and money that would be better used for community correction. Instead of wasting massive sums on a system that has not worked in the past and is not likely to work in the future, we should first allocate funds for expanded community treatment.[44]

Review Questions

1. Why does the National Advisory Commission state that, "It is essential to abate use of institutions"?
2. Two writers in the field have suggested that imprisoned inmates are, in effect, undergoing "vicarious expiation." What do the authors mean to convey by this term?

---

[43] *Progress Report of the National Advisory Commission*, p. 33.

[44] National Council on Crime and Delinquency, Policy Statement, *Crime and Delinquency*, 8, no. 4 (October 1972), 332. Used with permission.

3. In what manner has the concept of affirmative action been applied, in this chapter, to the imprisoned? To the professionals in the criminal justice system?
4. The transition to a community-based correctional system will require many changes and take a long time to accomplish. Some changes, however, could be realized in the impending future. Name and discuss the four "challenges" discussed in this chapter that could result in such changes.
5. When thirty jail administrators were interviewed to determine what *should* be the primary function of the jail, what was the overwhelming first choice? What was the second choice? Did the responses differ when the question sought to discover what *is* the purpose of the jail? In what fashion?
6. How did the President's Crime Commission envision the Youth Services Bureau?
7. Discuss the VERA program of "supported work."
8. Describe one of the alternative programs for inebriates that were discussed in this chapter, the St. Louis Detoxification Program, the District of Columbia Alcohol Rehabilitation Program, or the VERA Skid Row Service.
9. What are the principal elements of the Columbus Citizen Dispute Settlement Program? How would you evaluate the success of this program?
10. The National Institute of Law Enforcement and Criminal Justice of LEAA instituted an Exemplary Project program. What was the first project so designated, the history of its development, and the principal aspects of this program?

5

PRE-INSTITUTIONAL CORRECTIONAL SUBSTITUTES

I hope and believe that by far the greater number of the officers serving in our prisons are naturally honorable and kindly men, but so were the slave-owners before the Civil War.

Thomas Mott Osborne, *Within Prison Walls*

In 1974 an inmate at the California Men's Colony, a state penitentiary, sued in court to get *less* strawberry shortcake, complaining that the rich foods served on the prison menu had caused him to become overweight. It was an exceptional situation. Few prisons are so opulent.

In reality, prisons are dehumanizing, depersonalizing facilities intrinsically lacking the capacity to rehabilitate. In the year of the strawberry shortcake in California, Florida was closing the doors to its state prisons for the third time in three years. Director of Corrections, Louie Wainwright, took this action because of severe overcrowding. With a rated capacity of 9,000 prisoners, the Florida prisons were bulging with 11,000. The Lake Butler Prison Reception Center presented a graphic example of the plight of corrections in Florida. Built to accommodate 726 prisoners, it held almost twice that number (1,163) when the director took his unusual action.

The prison is punitive. It isolates and it conceals. It warehouses and it banishes, but it rarely reforms. There is ample evidence that the prison accomplishes the very opposite of that for which it was designed. The National Advisory Commission has unequivocally stated that "the failure of major institutions to reduce crime is incontestable," and it calls for an abatement in the use of prisons.[1]

It will probably always be necessary to have some secure correctional facilities of the institutional variety. Pathological criminals, for example, and those who are uncontrollably violent or dangerous, will need custodial constraint. But the emerging trend and the dictate of reason point toward diversion *from* the system for the great majority of our criminal and delinquent offenders. It bears repeating that there is no sure method for determining who is "safe" and who is "dangerous." It is believed that "80 percent to 90 percent of inmates" are not dangerous.[2] In Chapter 3 we examined the rationale for diversion and explored some pilot programs. In this chapter we will expand our awareness of pre-institutional, diversionary concepts and tactics in the criminal justice system.

Assumptions About Crime

A great number of citizens make simplistic assumptions about crime. Some of the more popular assumptions are: The criminal is always completely culpable. The cause-and-effect relationship between the willful criminal and the criminal act is always direct and unmediated. Imprisonment should be automatically imposed, and it is inevitably curative. Severity of punishment is positively correlated with reformation. Criminal behavior is the natural end result of a dispassionate, intellectual decision, which is not influenced by social factors or social institutions.

This book does not take the deterministic position that all criminal behavior is foreordained. It does take the position that crime and criminal behavior cannot be fully understood without taking into account sociocultural factors; that it is insufficient to explain crime and criminal behavior on the basis of a psychogenic theory that ignores the impact of culture; that in addition to predisposing, uniquely individual factors, crime is also shaped by the influence of social roles, negative cultural programming, and our social institutions.

Our civilization will crumble in the dust of exculpation if the *victim's* sense of justice is destroyed. The criminal must be appropriately dealt with if justice is to have any meaning. Our premise is simply that

---

[1] National Advisory Commission on Criminal Justice Standards and Goals, *Task Force Report: Corrections* (Washington, D.C.: U.S. Government Printing Office, 1973), p. 1.

[2] *Criminal Justice Newsletter,* 6, no. 10, Nov. 10, 1975, quoting Milton J. Rector, president of the National Council on Crime and Delinquency, p. 2.

a community-based approach is a more rational approach to human reconstruction. Most criminals are neither guiltless nor blameless, but society must share the guilt and the blame. The majority of our offenders are redeemable. If they are not redeemed, the result will be additional criminal depredations, and a more burdensome cost for the criminal justice system.

SOME COST CONSIDERATIONS

The cost of administering the criminal justice system is staggering. During fiscal 1970–71, for example, the total criminal justice expenditures in the United States amounted to $10,513,358,000. More than 20 percent, or $2,291,073,000, represented direct expenditures on corrections.[3]

In that same fiscal year (for the month of October 1971) salaries for criminal justice personnel in state and federal agencies came to $929,-473,000 for the total system, and $184,819,000 for corrections personnel.[4] In view of the fact that 68 percent of all corrections personnel work in institutions,[5] the enormous cost of warehousing offenders can be readily deduced. Without minimizing the primary importance of the human quotient, it must be recognized that there is also a monumental economic factor to be considered in opting for community-based corrections. The financial benefits to be derived from certain types of community programming, however, such as restitution, contain the promise of extensive savings.

OUR CULTURAL VALUES AND OUR CRIME

In a materialistic culture such as ours, which places a high value on tangible possessions, socio-economic status, and purchasing power, the have-nots are subjected to greater disintegrative pressures than are the haves. We live in a society that preaches the democratic ideal, but the rich and the poor are polarized, and the vanishing middle class is battered and burdened. The "dog-eat-dog" philosophy is one result of a highly

---

[3] U.S. Law Enforcement Assistance Administration and U.S. Bureau of the Census, *Expenditures and Employment Data for the Criminal Justice System: 1970–71* (Washington, D.C.: U.S. Government Printing Office, 1973), p. 11.

[4] *Ibid.*

[5] Joann B. Morton, Kirkwood M. Callahan, and Nicholas A. Beadles, eds., *Readings in Public Employee/Management Relations for Correctional Administrations* (Athens, Ga.: Corrections Division, Institute of Government, University of Georgia, November 1973), p. 4.

competitive culture, and the "system" becomes the enemy. In a social system that enables millionaires to escape paying income taxes while it victimizes the less fortunate with a perplexing, bewildering maze of incomprehensible tax forms, should we wonder at a beat-the-system ethic? Crime is one end result of the institutionalized conflicts which are bred in this type of culture.

Add some further cultural precipitants, such as searing racial injustices, the furrows of poverty ploughed across our land, the recurrent specter of fratricidal war, rampant hedonism, the immunity enjoyed by syndicate and white-collar crime, a beleaguered criminal justice system, the inflation-recession cycle, and the matrix of crime and criminal behavior begins to unfold. In this context, a simplistic approach to the problem of crime is almost obscene.

Before any significant inroads can be made into the crime problem, major alterations will have to be made in our social philosophy and in some of our social institutions. There will have to be, ultimately, "a willingness on the part of every citizen to give of himself, his time, his energy, and his imagination." [6]

A DIFFERENT SET OF ASSUMPTIONS

The assumptions concerning crime that we described as being held by a large number of citizens, are really misconceptions. There are assumptions that are not misconceptions and are more in the nature of compelling truths. The crime prevention task force of the National Advisory Commission based its report on three such fundamental assumptions.

1. Citizen apathy and indifference contribute to the spread of crime.
2. Private and public agencies outside the criminal justice system influence rises and declines in crime rates.
3. Community crime prevention efforts have demonstrable benefits for existing institutions and agencies which are organized for the achievement of primary goals other than crime prevention.[7]

From these basic working premises, we can elicit the following propositions:

1. Citizen outrage without citizen involvement only serves to kindle frustration, which germinates further crime.

---

[6] National Advisory Commission, *Task Force Report: Community Crime Prevention* (Washington, D.C.: U.S. Government Printing Office, 1973), p. 2.

[7] *Ibid.*, p. 1.

2. When there is an efficient and responsive delivery of remedial services, alienation is decreased, the public confidence is restored, and there is an automatic, inhibitory influence on the crime rate.

3. When public and private agencies sponsor reconstructive programs, they simultaneously serve their own economic needs.

CRIME PREVENTION

It must be repeatedly stressed that without a conscious, organized effort to prevent crime, our puny efforts in dealing with symptoms will be utterly ineffectual. Palmer has observed that we "are not a preventive society. We tend to take action after a problem has attained large-scale proportions." [8] It will be difficult to undo this predisposition, but it is absolutely imperative if crime is to be influentially dealt with. Poverty must be attacked, recreational needs must be fulfilled, our blighted ghettoes and barrios must be renovated, social services must be available to those in need, and, above all, the indignation of the citizen must be translated into concerned action. That is why the community-based correctional effort is so critically important: it contains the vehicle for turning citizen indignation into concerned citizen involvement. Something else is also needed: concern for the plight of the victim.

Victim Compensation

One of the gravest deficiencies in our system of justice is the deplorable neglect of the victim. Justice requires a fine balancing of the scales. Brutalization of offenders will not advance the cause of justice, but neither will neglect of the victim. The "square john" who respects the law, and who strives to conform to society's normative dictates, has his incentive diminished when the only concern expressed appears to be for the criminal.

VICTIM NEGLECT

Let us consider a hypothetical case. You are assaulted by an individual whom you discover prowling in your garage, and you suffer moderate injuries which require medical attention, at today's exorbitant prices. Because the would-be felon did not have the opportunity to misap-

[8] Stuart Palmer, *The Prevention of Crime* (New York: Behavioral Publications, 1973), p. 9.

propriate any of your property, and because your injuries were of the "moderate" variety, the charge is reduced to trespassing, a misdemeanor, and the defendant is subjected only to a fine. What portion of the fine is given to you, the innocent victim, to assuage your feelings and to mitigate your medical expenses? Nothing, of course.

Change the scenario and make the offense a felony assault, from which you receive serious injuries. The defendant is convicted and sent to prison. There his medical, educational, vocational, and maintenance needs are fully serviced, at no cost to him. His teeth are fixed, his health is mended, his educational level is improved, he is provided with work skills, and he receives "all the trimmings" on such solemn occasions as Christmas. Supposing you, the victim, are poor—and it is the poor who are the primary victims of crime—and you have no medical insurance, a large family, and a limited income. You cannot even provide "all the trimmings" for your family at the proper holidays.

If you are the victim of a felony assault under such circumstances, you can be potentially destroyed financially, or be reduced to the demeaning existence that is the lot of the welfare recipient. Nor will sophisticated, scholarly theories about rehabilitation assuage your personal agony. The average victim of crime has a more pragmatic view of justice: Who provides *free* therapy to the child victim of a sexual molestation to forestall permanent psychosexual damage? Who redresses the rape victim? What social agency compensates the modest homeowner who has his household furnishings purloined during an absence from home? How palpable is society's concern for the maimed victims of her predators? What is happening to the sense of justice in these victims?

The answer is too painfully clear. The professionals in the criminal justice system can document an unending litany of recriminative complaints made by victims in our society. What, for example, was I to tell the woman, paralyzed for life from the neck down, whom I had the occasion to interview? She had taken a gunman's bullet that was intended for another, and had to spend the rest of her life immobilized. She employed every verbal device she could command to prolong my visit, for her tragedy had earned her nothing more than almost total neglect, and she hungered for a human contact. Her assailant had already been released from prison and was in the "free world." It was she who had been imprisoned.

If the criminal justice system continues to neglect the victims in its midst, then it will forfeit the right to include "justice" in its title. Society has a solemn obligation to bring succor to its victims. Thomas Jefferson said that governments are instituted among men to secure the rights of citizens. If government fails to secure those rights, isn't it reasonable to hold the government liable for its failure to do so?

In recent years, concern for the victim's plight has generated both compensatory legislation and a degree of controversy. The controversy, according to one commentator, is centered in the criticism that victim compensation statutes intrude into the province of private insurance and stifle "sturdy individualism." [9] This is an insubstantial criticism, however. The obligation of the state to its citizens is well settled historically, and no matter how desirable it would be to have a nation completely populated with sturdy folks, we know that it can never be. There are more compelling considerations than sturdiness. A sustained belief in justice is one.

PIONEER EFFORTS IN VICTIM COMPENSATION

Some promising developments have taken place in the recent past with respect to victim compensation and victim restitution. Beginning with New Zealand's Criminal Injuries Compensation Act of 1963, government has increasingly come to recognize its responsibility for the forgotten members of society, its victims of crime. Shortly after New Zealand set the modern example, Great Britain announced a plan for compensating victims of crime and violence. Presented to both Houses of Parliament on June 24, 1964, the nonstatutory "Scheme," as the English refer to it, became operational on August 1, 1964. California passed enabling legislation in 1965, New York in 1966, Massachusetts in 1968. In 1972 New Jersey joined the ranks of states with compensation statutes, which now also include Nevada, Hawaii, and Maryland.

On September 18, 1972, legislation to provide victim compensation up to $50,000 cleared the United States Senate 74–0. The proposed Victims of Crime Act of 1972 stipulated that the purpose of the Act was "to commit the United States to meet its moral obligation to assist the innocent victim of violent crime. . . ." [10] Unfortunately, the Congress was not so conscious of its "moral obligation," for the Act didn't get out of committee.

VICTIM COMPENSATION IN GREAT BRITAIN

Because it was one of the pioneer programs, and has so widely influenced compensation efforts in other jurisdictions, it will benefit us to explore the

[9] J. Ll. J. Edwards, "Compensation to Victims of Crimes of Personal Violence," *Federal Probation*, XXX, no. 2 (June 1966), 3. This article provides an excellent summation of victim compensation, and is recommended reading.

[10] H.R. 12458, 92d Congress, 2d Session.

British system in a little more detail. One of the more admirable qualities of the British approach is its flexibility. New Zealand, for instance, stipulates by statute those offenses which give rise to eligibility for compensation claims. The British system is not a statutory system, but a "Compensation Scheme," administered by a nine-member Criminal Injuries Compensation Board. Other major systems limit compensation to victims of violent crimes. The British Scheme, in contrast, spells out eligibility in the following manner:

> The Board will entertain applications for *ex gratia* payment of compensation in any case where the applicant or, in the case of an application by a spouse or dependant . . ., the deceased, sustained . . . personal injury directly attributable to a crime of violence (including arson and poisoning) or to an arrest or attempted arrest of an offender or suspected offender or to the prevention or attempted prevention of an offence or to the giving of help to any constable who is engaged in arresting or attempting to arrest an offender or suspected offender or preventing or attempting to prevent an offence.[11]

Under the British Scheme, awards have been granted for injuries resulting from threats of violence. In one such instance, a 14-year-old who was running away from several youths who had tried to extort money from him was struck by a bus and injured. A full award was given. Awards have also been granted where injuries have resulted from recklessness or accidental causes, including a case in which two older bullies dropped a twelve-year-old boy and broke his wrist. In direct violence cases, a fifteen-year-old rape victim was granted $3,000 upon presentation of evidence of resulting psychiatric problems, and a coal miner whose eyesight was permanently damaged in a street assault was granted $35,250.

Gallantry, unfortunately, is not covered. A man on a train noticed a young woman running frantically across the railroad tracks, in clear danger from the "live rail." He leaped from the train and led her to safety, but suffered an injury to his neck for his chivalry. It transpired that the young woman had been the victim of an "indecent assault," and it was from her accoster that she had been fleeing. The Criminal Injuries Compensation Board ruled that the gallant gentleman was not eligible for an award because he suffered his injury attempting to save a girl rather than attempting to arrest a suspected offender.

There is an admirable flexibility built into the British system, in that

---

[11] Cmnd. 4812. Criminal Injuries Compensation Board, *Seventh Report,* Accounts for the Year Ended 31st March, 1971 (London: H.M.S.O., November 1971), p. 23.

the amount of compensation is discretionary with the Criminal Injuries Compensation Board. Approximately $45 million was paid out in claims during the first decade of the English program, and more than $9 million in 1974 alone. In the United States, compensation is limited by statute. On July 1, 1974, California increased the amounts available to victims of violent crimes to a maximum of $23,000. Prior to 1974 the maximum in California had been $5,000, which led one authority to comment caustically that "the State of California has acted in a manner incompatible with its reputation in the field of corrections. . . ."[12]

LIMITATIONS IN COMPENSATION

There are two problems inherent in compensation programs. The first is cost. Expenditures in this country have not been unusual so far, but that is because there is vast ignorance in the public sector concerning the existence of these compensatory statutes. There are over 90,000 violent crimes committed in California each year, for example, yet only 2,000 claims were filed in a five-year period. This compares with 12,215 claims filed under the British system *during a one-year period,* fiscal 1973–74. It can be predicted that any victim compensation program will become a great financial burden unless a sound method of financing such a program is developed.

The second problem relating to compensation programs, simply stated, is this: *Gratuitous compensation paid by the state is not a satisfactory substitute for punitive restitution paid by the offender.* The only reasonable offset for the inordinate expense of gratuitous compensation is to require the criminal to make restitution as part of the corrective discipline meted out for his offense. The word "punitive" has an onerous connotation for a great many correctional theorists, because they attach vengeful attributes to the word. But satisfaction to society and to the victim is an integral part of the philosophy of punishment.

Restitution

Professor Schafer very effectively copes with the problem of gratuitous compensation when he points out that "a kind of spiritual satisfaction is implicit in any system of punishment," and if this were generally recognized, "a new concept of punishment might arise, strengthening the

[12] Edwards, "Compensation," p. 7. (In 1972 California disbursed $523,000 to indemnify but 267 victims.)

restitutive character of punishment on the one hand and, on the other, infusing compensation with a punitive quality." [13] Punitive, in this context, denotes the obligatory nature of restitution.

PIONEERING EFFORTS IN RESTITUTION

Contrary to popular belief, crime *does* pay, and often handsomely. When it pays at the expense of the conforming, law-abiding, innocent victim, then justice is being subverted. When the criminal is obliged to compensate society and his victim, there will be an increased faith in justice and a strengthening of the moral bonds between men. In 1971 Pennsylvania's penal code was amended to compel criminals to make restitution to their victims. A law passed in England in 1972 obliges criminals to make full restitution. When they are unable to do so, they are required to work on community projects, thereby making restitution to society.

While still a novel idea, restitution by the offender to the victim directly, or to the commonweal of society, has begun to take root. Restitution is an option in the Alternative Community Service Program in Multnomah County, Oregon, as we learned in Chapter 3. A middle-aged woman, suffering her first arrest for shoplifting a blouse, as an example, was sentenced to work as a receptionist in an adoption agency for thirty hours on Saturdays. In its first two years, approximately 2,500 offenders were sentenced to a variety of community services, such as helping the blind, working with children in recreational and athletic programs, preparing foodstuffs for the needy, and doing maintenance and construction work in public institutions.

In Salem, Massachusetts, District Judge Samuel E. Zoll has introduced a comparable practice with juvenile offenders, requiring the offenders to polish fire engines, plant seedlings in the town parks, clean up vandalized schools, and do similar restitutive chores. A physician in Phoenix, Arizona, facing a five-to-life sentence for illegal sale of liquid amphetamine, was sentenced to serve seven years as a practicing physician in Tombstone, Arizona, a town that had no doctor. In this type of sentence, not only is justice tempered with mercy, it is also tempered with redemptive wisdom.

The Georgia Department of Corrections Offender Rehabilitation, subsidized by an LEAA grant, instituted the Georgia Restitution Program in late 1974. The interesting thing about this program is that it services both

---

[13] Stephen Schafer, "The Proper Role of a Victim-Compensation System," *Crime and Delinquency*, 21, no. 1 (January 1975), 45. The student who is interested in further information in this area may also profitably consult Schafer's definitive work, *Compensation and Restitution to Victims of Crime* (Montclair, N.J.: Patterson Smith Reprint Series, Publication No. 120, 1970).

probationers and parolees. In its first eighteen months of operation, 315 participants, released to live-in community centers, were engaged in programs of monetary or public service restitution. Citizen volunteers assisted the staff at the centers.

THE MINNESOTA RESTITUTION PROGRAM

Fourteen states currently have provision for some form of restitution. One of the more noteworthy restitution programs is in Minnesota. The Minnesota Department of Corrections has been truly innovative in its approach to corrections. In 1974 institutional services accounted for 69 percent of the Department's budget, the balance going to community programs. The Department, in a policy statement, committed itself to reversing those percentages.[14] The Minnesota Restitution Center in Minneapolis is a residential, community-based correctional facility which epitomizes the thrust in Minnesota corrections.

Operated by the Department of Corrections, and funded by a grant from the Governor's Commission on Crime Prevention and Control, the Restitution Center works to negotiate contracts of restitution between offenders and victims, and operates a program to divert individuals from the prison environment. Ongoing research and evaluation are built into the program. The distinction which we made earlier between compensation and restitution is categorically recognized in this program. In the words of two faculty members at the University of Minnesota, who reviewed the program, "the concept of restitution clearly denotes that the individual offender rather than the state, repays the victim." [15]

THE OPERATIONAL PROGRAM

There are two distinct phases in the Minnesota restitution program. Restitution contracts are negotiated in the prison to which the offender has been committed, and they must be approved by the parole board. This is the first phase. The second phase is that of actual restitution, which takes place after the selected offender has been transferred to the Restitution Center. Developing the contracts before implementing restitution has obvious advantages. For one thing, voluntary participation can be assured. The nature and extent of restitution can also be decided. It

[14] Minnesota Department of Corrections, *Mission Statement 1974.*

[15] Joe Hudson and Burt Galaway, "Undoing the Wrong," *Social Work*, May 1974, p. 314. Professor Galaway was formerly director of the Restitution Center.

is normally cash payment from earnings, but can be in the nature of services, although these cannot be direct personal services to the victim. The willingness of the victim to participate is essential. This is ascertained prior to the offender's enlistment in the program.

The restitution program is restricted to property offenders, and exacting criteria have been established for screening into the program. The candidate must not have possessed a weapon during his commitment offense, for instance, and there must be no detainers (warrants) lodged against him. He must also come from one of the seven metropolitan counties making up the Minneapolis-St. Paul geographic area. This last criterion is especially significant. It underscores the intent of the program to personally involve the offender in making restitution, which would be a remote likelihood if he were to live some distance from the victim.

While the parolee is involved in the restitution program, he is expected to live at the Restitution Center and be subject to the supervision of the Center's staff. When employed, he must also contribute to his maintenance at the Center. Individual and group counseling is provided, as well as job placement assistance. This last element is obviously crucial, for direct restitution cannot be made if there is no income. The parolees in the program are advanced through four stages of increased responsibility and liberty, the final phase featuring full-time residence in the community.

There is one serious problem facing the Minnesota restitution program. The Community Corrections Act of 1974 subsidizes counties to retain offenders in the community and, in fact, penalizes them financially if they don't. This has resulted in a great reduction in committed property offenders—the pool from which the restitution program draws. It could jeopardize the program. So far, offenders have paid more than $14,000 in restitution in the Minnesota program.

BENEFITS FROM RESTITUTION

The following are the principal benefits derived from this type of community-based correctional program, here paraphrased from the observations of Hudson and Galaway: [16]

1. In terms of remedying damages and restoring a sense of justice, it is much more logical to involve both the doer and the victim in the process than it is to merely isolate the doer and ignore the victim, which has been our tradition.

---

[16] *Ibid.*, p. 317.

2. With restitution requirements clearly stated in contract form, the offender always knows where he stands not only with respect to fulfillment of the contract, but also with regard to his own success.

3. Restitution requires the offender to be actively involved, and not merely a passive recipient of the "system's" correctional "treatment."

4. Through restitution, the offender is provided with a very concrete method of reparation for his wrongs. This has the secondary advantage of providing a constructive method of dealing with his guilt, thereby enhancing his sense of self-esteem.

5. Victims, who harbor a reservoir of bitterness, tend to have more positive feelings toward those who restitute than those who are imprisoned.

The financial savings that accrue are quite important, of course, but the greatest benefit is the restoration of the dignity of both the offender and the victim, in the context of strict justice and in the spirit of reconciliation.

Alternative Sentencing

In his lonely desolation as an imprisoned felon, the celebrated man of letters, Oscar Wilde, proclaimed that crime would cease when punishment ceased, or when it was treated as a form of dementia if it did occur. While we can no longer afford the misguided luxury of presuming that all criminals are demented, we are obliged to conclude that unmitigated punishment as a philosophy of correction is untenable. It has been well stated that the "correctional system serves most effectively for the protection of society against crime when its major emphasis is on custody and rehabilitation, rather than custody and punishment." [17] "Rehabilitation" is perhaps the most overworked word in the correctional vocabulary. For our purpose it can simply mean the restoration of an offender into a constructive role in society.

There is no greater punishment for a free creature than the deprivation of liberty. There can be no more effective method of communicating society's displeasure with criminal behavior than by the assumption of control over the offender. It is not necessary, nor is it humane, to add physical or psychological punishment, for that embitters rather than reforms. The emphasis must be on the reconstruction of the individual in the context of justice.

---

[17] National Advisory Commission, *Task Force Report: Criminal Justice System* (Washington, D.C.: U.S. Government Printing Office, 1973), p. 255.

DIVERSION REVISITED

It is reported that President Lincoln, when told about General Grant's heavy drinking, replied that he would provide the same beverage for some other generals, if only he knew what it was. The elixir of correctional reconstruction has not yet been manufactured, so it cannot be distributed to the generals warring against crime. But, surely, some wisdom must have accumulated from the wars that have already been fought. This, at least, we should have learned: The prisons have not rehabilitated to any substantial degree. The community is a much more normalizing milieu than the prison in which to attempt the restorative effort.

But how is this to be accomplished in the community? Through what type of program? The failure of some community programs and the promise of others chart the course of the future. Some important groundwork has already been done.

In Chapter 3 we explored some of the theoretical problems in pretrial intervention, and learned something of programs underway in Connecticut, Hawaii, and Oregon. Closely akin to pretrial intervention, but less legally complicated, is alternate sentencing. This is simply a method of sentencing that utilizes a substitute for imprisonment. It is based, theoretically, on the rehabilitation principles mentioned in the preceding section. In England, Community Service as a sentencing alternative was made a part of the Criminal Justice Act of 1972. This permits the judge, in many types of offenses, to waive imprisonment for anyone over seventeen and to substitute a penalty of from 40 to 240 hours of voluntary, unpaid work in the community. The sentence must be completed within a year on the offender's own time.

A most promising and, indeed, unique alternative sentencing program is taking place in Michigan. It is unique in that it is specifically aimed at the recidivist. When speakng of diversion, one ordinarily thinks of the first-term offender, the one with the most corrective potential; but the Michigan program, in effect, maintains that if a principle is valid, it deserves application irrespective of the offender's status.

THE MICHIGAN COMMUNITY TREATMENT PROJECT FOR REPEAT OFFENDERS

It is a deeply entrenched judicial tradition to impose a more severe sentence upon a repeat offender than upon a first offender. This was classically demonstrated in the sentences handed down in the Circuit Court of

Oakland County, Michigan, in 1971. During that year, 530 offenders were sentenced. There was a positive correlation between a history of recidivism and commitment to an institution, as the following data illustrate:[18]

	Percent Committed
First offenders	25
One prior conviction	44
Two or more prior convictions	74

Though it is a normal response to treat the recidivist with greater severity, the Michigan project raises the question of whether this is a logical response. The judges of the Circuit Court had been concerned about developing alternatives to prison sentences. Fortuitously, the National Council on Crime and Delinquency (NCCD) was looking for a project site for a similar experiment at the same time. There followed a broad, collaborative undertaking by the courts, the probation department, the NCCD, the prosecuting attorney, the State Department of Corrections, the county commissioners, the Office of Criminal Justice Programs, and the Sachem Foundation to design a community-based program for repeat offenders. The Community Treatment Project for Repeat Offenders was the end result.

The majority of offenders enrolled in this program are property offenders. Although some of the individuals have been guilty of assaultive offenses, they are generally not violent or dangerous. Most are young males in their twenties, who could characteristically be described as immature persons from deprived family circumstances, either impoverished or broken homes.

The heart of the program is the involvement of a broad base of community resources and services in partnership with a wide spectrum of professionals with specialized expertise, with the objective of providing intensified human services as determined by the individual needs of the clients. General supervision is provided by probation officers, with no more than thirty-five cases permitted in each caseload. Intensive individual and group counseling is employed. Small task groups are formed to probe and identify the factors precipitating the individual's delinquent behavior.

Referrals are made to a variety of private and public agencies, and many professionals contribute time and services. Bankers, doctors, architects, lawyers, teachers, real estate brokers, seminarians, and many others offer special assistance and counsel. There is a heavy accent on volunteer services. Some fees can be paid for the clients, clinical services are provided

[18] The National Council on Crime and Delinquency, *Instead of Prison,* undated Report on the Community Treatment Project for Repeat Offenders, p. 5.

for drug and related problems, psychological testing is available, and technical and academic training is offered. Family counseling as well as employment training and placement assistance are also included. In short, the community is literally mobilized in toto in the reformative effort. This is a project that truly epitomizes the concept of community-based corrections. What have the results been?

RESULTS OF THE PROJECT

It costs the Michigan Department of Corrections more than five times as much to imprison an individual as it does to maintain him in the Project for Repeat Offenders. The annual cost of imprisonment was $3,967 in 1973; in contrast, it cost $725 to service an individual for one year in the project. In mid-1973 there were 164 offenders in the project. Of that number, eighty were from a group that normally would have been sent to prison. In other words, there was a savings of $360,000.[19] This was an operational savings. To this would have to be added the savings derived from keeping families off the welfare rolls, as well as various tax and sales revenues resulting from the activities of the clients in the community.

So much for economics. What of the more meaningful factor of recidivism? A randomly selected group of persons sentenced to prison was compared with a randomly selected group from the probation pool. The extremely low rate of recidivism for the hard-core offenders was a "hallmark accomplishment." By mid-1973, preliminary results showed "that only 2.5 percent of repeat offenders, who would normally be sent to prison but instead were assigned to the project, had to be terminated for new offenses or technical violations. This recidivism rate is far below the national rate of more than 60 percent and even lower than the rate for regular probationed offenders in the county." [20] Not one of the offenders who failed in the project was convicted of a crime involving danger to the public.

The success of the Community Treatment Project for Repeat Offenders has encouraged criminal justice officials in Michigan to expand this concept and to develop additional, similar projects. As the NCCD appropriately commented, "This project is a viable, proven alternative to imprisonment. It needs to be replicated. It behooves government and community leaders to examine it carefully." [21]

---

[19] *Ibid.*, p. 14.
[20] *Ibid.*, p. 1.
[21] *Ibid.*, p. 16.

The PORT Program

Another community-based program that has had a dramatic impact on correctional thinking is the so-called PORT Program. PORT is an acronym for Probationed Offenders Rehabilitation and Training. Established in Rochester, Minnesota, in October 1969, PORT is essentially a "live-in, community-based, community-directed, community-sponsored treatment program for both adults and juveniles." [22] The heavy emphasis on "community" in this definition is not unintentional. On the contrary, it reflects a strong commitment to local control of corrections. *Corrections Magazine* considers the PORT Program a model for future community corrections.[23]

THE ORIGIN AND OBJECTIVES OF THE PORT PROGRAM

PORT was conceived when two District Court judges, Donald T. Franke and O. Russell Olson, became dissatisfied with the lack of sentencing alternatives avaliable to the court. The medical director of the local state hospital, Dr. Francis Tyce, cooperated by permitting an experimental program in community corrections to be housed on the hospital grounds. The success of the preliminary efforts led to a two-year organizational attempt at enlisting the community's support, which was surprisingly successful. The cooperation of police agencies was especially notable. The PORT Program was then initiated.

PORT is a private, nonprofit corporation with four basic objectives.[24]

1. To control criminal and delinquent behavior without resorting to institutional or probationary programs
2. To reduce commitments to state institutions from the geographical area served by PORT
3. To provide a new and less expensive method for rehabilitating society's offenders
4. To see if the PORT method of control works and might be replicated in other areas of Minnesota

---

[22] *PORT 1971*, undated report by the Hon. O. Russell Olson, President, PORT of Olmsted County, p. 2.

[23] *Corrections Magazine*, 1, no. 3 (January–February 1975), 26.

[24] Nevin Doran Hunter, Robert M. Pockrass, and Luanne Hostermann, *Probationed Offenders and Rehabilitation Training: An Evaluation of Community Based Corrections* (Mankato, Minn.: Urban Studies Institute, Mankato State College, undated, c. 1974), p. 3.

In 1975, under the provisions of the Community Corrections Act, the state contributed $84,000 to the PORT Program. Additional funding comes from the counties involved (Olmsted, Dodge, and Fillmore), as well as from "tuition" costs levied on the participants. There are private contributors also. In fact, almost half of the first year's budget was contributed by the community.[25] A grant has also been received from the Law Enforcement Assistance Administration (LEAA). Program objectives include critical analysis of the program, so that it does not succumb to self-fulfilling prophecy.

THE OPERATIONAL PROGRAM

The PORT community correction center is on the grounds of the Rochester State Hospital. Referrals come from the district, juvenile, and municipal courts. For every adult diverted from a prison commitment to this program the county must pay the state $16 per day, which is what it would cost to maintain the individual in prison. The cost of juveniles is $35 per day. In the first ten months of 1974, only five individuals were committed to state prison from the participating counties, and no juveniles were committed to traditional state institutions.

As in the restitution program which we have already examined, the participant must sign a contract before being admitted to the PORT Program.[26] Restitution may be part of that contract. Adults in the program must pay $18 per day toward their upkeep, and the welfare department contributes some of the cost of the juveniles' maintenance. A board of directors runs the program, and membership on the board is almost equally divided between members of the criminal justice system and citizens elected by the community at a regular meeting conducted for that purpose.

The core of the treatment program in the correction center is "a combination of group treatment and behavior modification. . . . Confrontation, frankness, honesty, trust, care, reality testing, and decision-making are the ingredients of the group process." [27] The individual arriving at the institution is launched from the bottom level of a five-stage classification system. These stages proceed from minimal through maximal freedom.

---

[25] Francis A. Tyce, "PORT: Community Rehabilitation for Legal Offenders," *Hospital and Community Psychiatry*, March 1971, p. 23.

[26] "The contract provides the basis for an individual's involvement in the program, describing the major areas of concern during the program, criteria for leaving the program, and tentative post-discharge plans": *Corrections Center Operating Policy Manual*, III—1.

[27] Olson Report, *PORT 1971*, p. 4.

The main PORT facility. © *Corrections Magazine.* *Photo by Bill Powers.*

Maximal freedom is defined as "freedom commensurate with that of an individual of the same age in the community." [28] Progress through the stages is made by earning points, and through group decisions. This is reminiscent of the system introduced into the penal colonies of Australia in 1840 by Alexander Maconochie, but is, naturally, infinitely more sophisticated.

The community and its resources are heavily utilized. Students from junior colleges are employed as counselors, and paraprofessionals are used. The public schools are involved, as are the traditional agencies such as Mental Health and the Department of Vocational Rehabilitation. The services provided by community agencies are not duplicated in the center. In this way, the community and its resources are the sustaining force of the program, and therefore the community actually runs the program. A sixty-five-member advisory committee brings legal, financial, employment, and preventive expertise to the project; no vital area is left uncovered.

EVALUATING THE PORT PROGRAM

It is rather difficult to evaluate any correctional program, for a number of reasons. For one thing, there are so many variables involved that any one of them could have a positive or negative influence that might escape analysis. Furthermore, correctional goals for the individual offender are

---

[28] *Ibid.*

not precisely delineated. What, for example, should be construed as success for a socio-economically disadvantaged, thoroughly criminalized, highly suggestible individual of dull normal intelligence? Researchers in human behavior are far from consensus when it comes to the matter of changing human behavior. The success or failure of the PORT Program, if those terms really have applicability, can perhaps be best placed in the context of an observation made by the director of the project, Jay Lindgren: "I think the greatest cure for crime is growing up. If you can grow up in a place that allows you, when you are ready, to make some decent decisions about how you want to live your life, I think if anything is going to have an effect on rehabilitation, it's that." [29]

In terms of hard statistical data, a follow-up study of 165 participants in the program indicated a 35 percent recidivism rate; that is, 58 out of 165 program participants were either convicted of new offenses or committed to institutions for probation violations. When the recidivism rate was refined on the basis of adults and juveniles, it was determined that greater success had been obtained with the adult offenders. There was

A rap folk-singing session in the PORT Program with residents of the program and volunteer counselors. *Courtesy of Rochester, Minnesota,* Post-Bulletin.

[29] Quoted in *Corrections Magazine,* I, no. 3 (January–February 1975), 28.

only a 23 percent failure rate with the adults, but a 45 percent failure rate with juveniles.

Several evaluative reports on the PORT Program have come to a shared conclusion, which is encapsulated in the following abstract: [30]

> PORT's first four years continue to indicate the promise of community-based corrections. . . . The program has served virtually all of the offenders referred by the local courts . . . and has been a viable alternative to institution commitment. Outcome data available indicate that the program controls the participating offenders more economically and humanely than the institutional alternative. Moreover, this [*sic*] data also seem to indicate that PORT is more efficient and effective than incarceration.[30]

The best accolade that can be given to the PORT Program is the number of projects that have been modeled after it. Several have been developed in other sections of Minnesota, but it has also been the prototype for projects in other states, such as the Reality House program in Columbia, Missouri. PORT currently plans to develop training institutes, so that the principles behind this type of community-based correctional effort may be imparted to other professionals in the field.

The NCCJL Alternative-to-Prison Program

One of the most ambitious alternative-to-prison programs is being developed by the National Coordinating Committee For Justice under the Law (NCCJL), a nonprofit organization based in Washington, D.C.

ORIGIN AND OBJECTIVES OF THE NCCJL PROGRAM

The NCCJL came into being in the spring of 1972, basically dedicated to investigating prisoner grievances and prison strikes. Investigations undertaken by the NCCJL "revealed central causes of prison unrest that called for more than bandaid therapy or the rhetoric of outrage." [31] A program was devised that at first glance seems incredibly idealistic, but at a second look, utterly rational.

---

[30] *Program Report,* PORT Fourth Annual Meeting, Kahler Hotel, Heritage Hall, October 25, 1973, p. 8.

[31] National Coordinating Committee for Justice under the Law, *NCCJL Reports,* 4, no. 2 (February 1975), 1.

Convinced by its studies that the vast majority of the imprisoned come from minority and socio-economically deprived groups, that Attica and other disturbances have only produced rhetoric in favor of prison reform, and that bureaucratic "solutions" to the crime problem are designed to breed failure, the NCCJL decided to create a radical alternative to imprisonment. A model was developed that would "respond to the background needs most common to those people having the best chance of being incarcerated in this country—the hard-core unemployables." [32] A broad-base support was solicited in the community, beginning with Superior Court judges in the District of Columbia, probation officials, and funding sources. A most comprehensive program was blueprinted.

THE OPERATIONAL PROGRAM

"Basically, the alternative-to-prison program is a three-year investment in individuals who come from an environment that is short on education and training, but long on opportunity for getting involved with crime. NCCJL will obtain custody for criminal offenders before they are sent to prison and provide these offenders with a program that has two principal thrusts: technical training and resocialization." [33]

Determined to substitute action for rhetoric, the NCCJL intends to provide housing not only for the program participants, but also for their families. In addition, each participant will be provided a just living wage that is calculated on the national median income. The wage scale, which will apply to all NCCJL program participants, is based on the following formula: [34]

Dependents	*Hourly Rate*	*Weekly Salary*	*Annual Income*
1	$4.00	$160.00	$8,320.00
2	4.50	180.00	9,360.00
3	5.00	200.00	10,400.00
4	5.50	220.00	11,440.00
5	6.00	240.00	12,480.00
6	6.50	260.00	13,520.00
7	7.00	280.00	14,560.00
8	7.50	300.00	15,600.00
9	8.00	320.00	16,640.00
10	8.50	340.00	17,680.00

---

[32] *Ibid.*

[33] NCCJL, *Alternative to Prison Program,* undated program and policy statement, p. 3. Used with permission.

[34] *Ibid.*, p. 4.

Each "trainee" will be required to deposit one-fourth of his gross salary in the program's cooperative savings program. If the three-year program is completed, the full amount is refunded; otherwise it is applied to rent and maintenance. In condemning the "tremendous build-up in hardware mentality in relation to the crime problem," NCCJL "is proposing an extremely sensible alternative to the present legal justice system that will erase two major factors contributing to the failure of the present system: the lack of individual economic independence and the lack of personal confidence." [35]

Participants in the alternative-to-prison will live in a normal community setting with trained counselors. Technical on-the-job and classroom training will be given in mechanics, the building trades, and clerical services during the first year in the program. Specialized training will be given according to aptitude and preference during the second year, and the third year features "on-the-line" experience. In addition to training in employable skills, "the program will make a concentrated effort to re-socialize the participants through community development and adjustment to a new environment, rather than by applying *Clockwork Orange* behavior modification experiments that tend to destroy individuals." [36] Those involved in the program, and their dependents, will live rent free in a NCCJL housing facility during the training program.

ATTACKING MAJOR MISCONCEPTIONS

There is no questioning the fact that our prisons are filled with the poor and the disadvantaged. The NCCJL program attempts to go right to the root of the problem: economic insufficiency created by limited vocational skills. It is a program that plans to react vigorously against four major misconceptions about the American penal system that contribute to the ineffectiveness of that system:

1. That the United States can have a high unemployment rate, large unskilled work force, inadequate housing and simultaneously reduce the crime rate
2. That the American legal justice system is equitable
3. That the "law and order" monies spent during the past decade have been successful in preventing crime
4. That the present legal justice system works [37]

---

[35] *Ibid.*, p. 2.
[36] *Ibid.*, p. 3.
[37] *Ibid.*, p. 1.

Although the NCCJL is but one of a number of proliferating alternative, community-based correctional programs, it is the first of its kind. No other program has so decisively attacked the underlying *social causes* of crime, nor taken such a radical stance to counter the frequently described, but infrequently modified, inequities in our criminal justice system and in our social institutions. This pioneering effort contains the nucleus of the justice that must permeate the efforts of tomorrow's shapers of criminal justice.

Synopsis

After reviewing some of the more noteworthy efforts to substitute community corrections for prison "treatment," we can conclude that sporadic progress is being made. As the search for innovative community corrections goes on, it is accompanied by the recognition that there must be a comparable growth in training for this new thrust in corrections, as well as some effort to coordinate activities. Pretrial diversion, for example, will soon have several hundred different projects operating in the United States. Coordinating leadership could be given in this area by the American Bar Association which, through its Commission on Correctional Facilities and Services, has established a National Pretrial Intervention Service Center in Washington, D.C.

New ideas and new terms are infiltrating the literature. It is now popular to define any concentrated, pre-institutional effort to abort imprisonment, other than probation, as "intensive intervention."[38] But old terms, such as "crime prevention," must be ever in the forefront. Too many steel doors are being closed after the fact. Yet there are impressive developments in this area also. Denver has begun a High Impact Anti-Crime Program. By an intensive victimization survey, it seeks to compile data that will permit the actual prevention of crime.[39] San Francisco has a "Boozer Cruiser" which picks up drunks for treatment instead of criminal prosecution. Cleveland has a preventative Crime Impact Program that is earning high praise. A crime-specific Master Plan has been developed by that city, which has a concrete goal of reducing "impact crimes" (robbery, burglary, and "street assaults") by 20 percent in five years.[40] The offender,

---

[38] This concept is given capable and exhaustive translation in Eleanor Harlow, "Intensive Intervention: An Alternative to Institutionalization," *Crime and Deliquency Literature,* 2, no. 1 (February 1970).

[39] Denver Anti-Crime Council, *Analysis of 1972 Denver Victimization Survey,* December 1, 1974.

[40] National Advisory Commission, *Criminal Justice System,* p. 248.

the victim, and the crime setting will be intensively scrutinized, and a concentrated effort will be made to eliminate the causes of crime.

The weight of crime is very great. The prisons are literally groaning with their share of the burden. They are unsuccessful in reducing crime, and they are seriously overcrowded. Florida has thrice refused to take prisoners into its prison system because of overcrowded conditions. The Oklahoma State Penitentiary has more than three times its rated capacity of prisoners. In Georgia, prisoners are doubled up in 8′ by 5′ cells, because of overcrowding. This volatile condition is not limited to these few states, but is characteristic of the nation at large.

There is a collective strength available to lighten that burden in many diverse ways. It has only to be mobilized. It resides in the community.

Review Questions

1. Name five of the common assumptions made about crime and the criminal and explain why those assumptions are not valid.
2. Can you suggest some sounder assumptions? What are they?
3. The text states that one of the gravest deficiencies in the criminal justice system in the neglect of the victim. Victim compensation statutes and programs have developed to offset this deficiency. Describe the basic characteristics of the British Scheme for victim compensation.
4. One type of response to the neglect of the victim is restitution. Minnesota has a unique restitution program. Describe its basic method of operation.
5. What are the five major benefits to be derived from a restitution program?
6. What is meant by "alternative sentencing"? What is unique about the Michigan Community Treatment Project For Repeat Offenders?
7. Describe the model PORT Program, its origin, and its objectives.
8. One of the more dramatic and ambitious programs is the NCCJL Alternative to Prison Program. Why is this program "dramatic and ambitious"? Describe the NCCJL program in terms of its origin and objectives. How would you evaluate this type of program?
9. It is stated in the beginning of this chapter that this text does not take a deterministic position, but takes the position that crime will not be fully understood without taking into account sociocultural factors. Exactly what is meant by this statement? Elaborate.
10. Professor Schafer has stated that "a kind of spiritual satisfaction is implicit in any system of punishment." What is the full implication of this statement?

6

POST-INSTITUTIONAL COMMUNITY-BASED PROGRAMS

All my major works have been written in prison. . . .
I would recommend prison not only to aspiring writers
but to aspiring politicians, too.

Jawaharlal Nehru

At a Democratic Convention in Sacramento in January 1975, newly elected Governor Jerry Brown engaged in an impromptu give-and-take session with those present, during which he made the observation that prisons "don't punish, so what the hell do they do?" That rhetorical question could be partially answered by looking at some of the events in the California prisons.

In 1971 there were 545 felonies committed *within* the California prisons of such gravity as to be prosecuted in the courts, with convictions being obtained in 90 percent of those cases. In 1972 the total number of serious crimes committed in prison had risen to 676, also with a 90 percent conviction rate. In 1973 the imprisoned had committed 983 felonies. Criminal complaints, however, were filed in only 41.6 percent of these cases, and the conviction rate dropped to 80 percent. In 1974 there were eighty-seven stabbings and twelve inmate fatalities *in San Quentin alone*. Putting the governor's perplexed question in the perspective of the recent history of the nation's largest prison system, the very least that can be said is that prisons are breeding accelerated institutional violence, and prosecutory apathy.

Men and women, however, will undoubtedly be going to prison for a long time to come. Spiraling crime and violence in our society will guarantee it. In our vision of the future, we may anticipate that only the hard-core, dangerous offenders will be committed to prison. Before we reach that Utopia, our energies should be directed toward releasing the *nondangerous* offender as rapidly as possible, consistent with wisdom.

Work Release

Temporary or conditional release from prison has long been permitted for a number of reasons, such as for educational purposes or for home visitation, but the greatest development in this area has been in work-related programs. The terms "work release" and "work furlough" are often used interchangeably, but there is a distinction to be made. *Work release,* strictly speaking, refers to the practice of permitting imprisoned individuals to work in the community at regular employment, usually during the daytime hours, and to return to the institution after the day's work has been completed. *Work furlough,* on the other hand, involves a "temporary pass" that enables the prisoner to go into the community to seek post-release employment. In a broader sense, both permit the individual to develop expanding ties to the community prior to formal release from prison. Over 350,000 inmates go out on furloughs annually in the U.S., but these are not all work furloughs.

The work release concept was pioneered in Wisconsin in 1913, through legislation introduced by state Senator Henry A. Huber. Despite its early origin, work release had a delayed infancy, and did not experience any substantial development until after World War II. The Federal Bureau of Prisons did not introduce work release into its system until the Prisoner Rehabilitation Act was passed in 1965. Our focus will be deliberately on work release on the state and federal level. This should not obscure the fact that a vast number of highly successful work relase programs operate out of the nation's county jails. This is of profound significance because there are so few rehabilitation programs in jails. For instance, in the San Rafael (Calif.) County work release program, in operation since 1959, work releasees can dine at home and enjoy conjugal visiting.

Although we will be examining work release and work furlough simultaneously, purely as a convenience, the reader should be careful to keep the distinction between the two clearly in mind. It might also be kept in mind that any community-based program is only as good as the people, planning, selection, and administration of that program. There have been some embarrassing failures.

"BENIGN NEGLECT" IN CALIFORNIA

In California a Temporary Community Release program was designed, not merely to accommodate the search for a job, but for broader pre-release planning. It was felt that other important functions could be accomplished as well, such as securing a driver's license, meeting the parole agent, and reestablishing family relationships.

In 1972 a monthly average of 305 prisoners were released on TCR's from the state's twelve prisons. In 1973 that average had declined to 127 per month, representing a 58.4 percent reduction over the previous year. There was an additional decline in 1974, when the monthly average dropped to 93 (26 percent). It was acknowledged that the program was dying as a result of "benign neglect." [1]

Despite the consequent decline in popularity of the Temporary Community Release program, California had only a 2 percent escape rate among those released on TCR's over a five-year period (1969–74).[2] Sometimes programs fail because of defects in management and selection. The California program appears to have withered from apathy. The ultra-liberal correctionalist blinds himself to real dangers, while the ultra-conservative blinds himself to the promise of human redemption. But what can be said of the apathetic? What is needed is a concerned but moderated approach that will balance risk and hope. Progressive correctional developments must be permitted to unfold without being nipped in the bud by either liberal or conservative myopia—or moderate apathy.

THE WASHINGTON, D.C., DEBACLE

The most extensive use of the furlough has taken place in Washington, D.C. In fiscal 1974, almost 900 inmates made 38,500 trips into the community.[3] Unfortunately, several tragic events brought the entire furlough program under fire. On June 11, 1971, two furloughed prisoners shot a man during a burglary of his home, and the victim subsequently died. On September 25, 1974, FBI agents arrested another furloughee. They discovered a sawed-off shotgun in a box that he was carrying. What made this particular incident all the more distressing was the fact that the

---

[1] William P. Sidell, "Temporary Community Release Program" (mimeographed), May 13, 1974.

[2] Sidell, "Temporary Community Releases," February 20, 1975.

[3] Michael S. Serrill, "Furloughs in D.C.: A Tense Issue," *Corrections Magazine*, 1, no. 4 (March–April 1975), 53.

arrested man was the "entertainment coordinator" for the prison complex, and he had been permitted to visit the community to coordinate visits by outside groups to the prisons of Washington, D.C.

A crescendo of criticism subsequently reduced the Washington, D.C., program to a trickle of what it used to be. Condemnations came from jurists, federal grand juries, and the office of the U.S. Attorney. Allegations of corruption were mixed with charges that violent prisoners, many with years remaining before they would be eligible for parole, were being released on furloughs. The U.S. Attorney's report claimed that "seven out of ten of the men who escaped from Lorton during fiscal 1974 fled while on furlough." [4] The embattled District of Columbia Corrections Director, Delbert Jackson, defended his program—the most liberal in the United States—and maintained that prisoners released on furlough had all attained medium security and were properly eligible.

A SOUND CONCEPT

These failures are reminiscent of the catastrophic failure of the Don Lugo work furlough program in California, which was permanently shut down in 1972 following unbelievable mismanagement. It was reported that a safe containing $7,000 had been misappropriated from the prison facility by inmates and never recovered. In addition, widespread criminal behavior had been attributed to the residents of the facility, and serious crimes, including murder and arson, had been perpetrated by releasees.

Work furlough is fundamentally a sound correctional *concept*. It permits gradual reentry into the free community and gives the furloughee the opportunity to develop a solid program prior to release. It is also economically sound. California's first furloughed prisoner was paroled after a little over four months on the work furlough program. During the period of his furlough, he earned $2,460 working for a San Francisco automobile dealer. He paid $476 in taxes and had $234 withheld from his salary for Social Security. His expenses in the community, including meals, totaled $675, and he also paid the amount of $270 to defray the cost of his maintenance while a prisoner at San Quentin. He was also able to pay $76 in union dues and put $550 into a savings account.[5] When defects occur, they are usually defects in selection and management, not in concept.

---

[4] *Ibid.*, p. 54. Lorton refers to the correctional complex at Lorton, Virginia, which is the institution from which the individuals were furloughed. Although in Virginia, it is operated by the District of Columbia.

[5] California Department of Corrections, *Correctional News Briefs*, 9, no. 5 (March 21, 1969).

The maximum security unit at Lorton. © *Corrections Magazine.* *Photo by Bill Powers.*

THE NEW YORK RELEASE PROGRAM

In startling contrast to the problem-plagued District of Columbia program and the apathy-infected California program, New York's venture into work release appears to have been more efficiently and successfully operated. A relative latecomer despite having one of the largest correctional systems in the United States, New York instituted its first work release program at the Auburn facility in January 1970. From that point through July 1974, a total of 2,121 inmates participated. The New York program explodes some misconceptions about work release. In particular, it seriously questions the traditional exclusion of those individuals who have had convictions for assaultive offenses.[6] A random sample follow-up study of 161 New York cases revealed that no arrests had occurred for new offenses during work release; yet almost 55 percent of the individuals on

[6] This was found to be the most frequent basis for exclusion in a survey conducted of work release: Lawrence S. Root, "State Work Release Programs: An Analysis of Operational Policies," *Federal Probation,* XXXVII, no. 4 (December 1973), 52–58.

work release had originally been committed for violent or assaultive crimes, robbery alone accounting for 42.2 percent of the total.[7]

CRITIQUE OF THE NEW YORK PROGRAM

New York's program is operating in ten correctional facilities, but the data for the study are drawn from three institutions, the Auburn Correctional Facility, the Elmira Correctional Facility, and the Rochester Community Correction Center. The study covers the period from January 1, 1970, through July 31, 1974. It focuses on a very representative cross-sectional group, because Auburn is a maximum security prison, Elmira is for younger offenders, and Rochester is a community-based correctional center.

With respect to overall performance, it was determined that 75.2 percent of the sample performed satisfactorily while on work release during the period of the study. Of the 24.8 percent removed from the program, the greatest number were for violation of work release conditions, such as alcohol indulgence (prohibited in the program) and late returns. Only six cases actually absconded.

Obvious benefits are accruing. Although the participants were predominantly unskilled or semi-skilled workers, "the mean hourly wage paid to work release participants in nearly all types of employment situations . . . was $2.00 or more per hour." [8] It actually ranged to over $8.00 per hour. New York law permits the earnings from work release to be used to support dependents, to make institutional commissary purchases, or to pay fines. Nevertheless, the average amount received by a work release inmate upon his relase was $558. Of the 118 men who were released during the study period, 42 percent continued in their work release job or in similar employment. The preliminary indications are that the New York program is operating on a successful formula.

THE ESSENCE OF WORK RELEASE

The public will always overreact to correctional failures, sometimes with justification. If the work release program is not to receive negative criticism, the public must be convinced of its rehabilitative utility. That will most assuredly come from results, and results will be positive if the pro-

---

[7] State of New York, Department of Correctional Services, *Work Release Program January 1970–July 1974* (October 1974), 18.

[8] *Ibid.*

Work release coordinator in Dallas counsels federal releasee.
Courtesy U.S. Bureau of Prisons. Photo by Leo M. Dehnel.

grams are legally instituted and conscientiously managed, and if the participants are scrupulously screened into the program. Both the public and the correctional sector must recognize work release for what it actually is. The Federal Bureau of Prisons defines it well:

> Community Work is not a substitute for probation or parole. It is not part of an internal system of punishment and reward. Nor is it an obligatory means of offsetting the cost of public welfare payments to dependent families. It is intended to be a selective resource for the correctional treatment of certain offenders.[9]

[9] Federal Bureau of Prisons, *Community Work: An Alternative to Imprisonment* (Washington, D.C.: Correctional Research Associates, 1973), p. 3.

EDUCATIONAL RELEASE

Not quite on the scale of work release, but meriting equal attention, is the practice of educational or study release. The focus here is not on employment but on preparation for professional or vocational careers. Inmates on educational release are permitted to travel to the community to attend classes. South Carolina, for instance, has an extensive program of both academic and vocational release, in which inmates are permitted to attend college or vocational classes in the community. Prisoners from Trenton, Rahway, and Leesburg State Prisons in New Jersey have been attending Mercer Community College since 1971, when a Prison Education Network Program was instituted. The first twenty-eight furloughed inmate-students in this program received Associate of Arts degrees in 1973.

The Federal Bureau of Prisons refers to its program as "study-release," and, like South Carolina, permits inmates to attend both academic and vocational classes in the community. In 1972, for example, twenty-eight female inmates at the Women's Division of the Terminal Island, California, prison were enrolled in eleven different college and trade schools, studying such courses as fashion design, computer programming, and journalism. The ages of the students ranged from 18 to 57.[10]

The largest educational release program is probably the one in operation at New York's Ossining State Correctional Facility. In 1974 there were sixty inmates from this prison attending Hostos Community College in the Bronx, New York. While enrolled in the college program, the furloughed prisoners are permitted to participate fully in the college program, both academic and extracurricular. Inmates are selectively screened for this study release program. To be eligible, an inmate must be within one year of a parole release, and not be a high-risk type of individual.

Educational release is a particularly productive type of community corrections, for it enables an individual to enhance his employability, develop his intellectual faculties, and graduate to a free existence in community living all at the same time.

Prerelease Programs

Prison is a scarring experience. Release to the "free world," therefore, should be graduated for the majority of inmates. One of the emerging

---

[10] *Federal Bureau of Prisons Annual Report, 1973,* p. 11.

trends in preparing inmates for eventual return to the community has been the development of community prerelease centers. Although *pre*-release preparation does not always imply *post*-institutional programming, the focus in both is on corrections in the community; thus both warrant consideration at this time.

In its broadest definition, a community prerelease center is a *community-based,* transitional step in the reintegration of the offender into mainstream society. It is organized to impart skills and provide resources that will minimize the trauma of reentry. The program emphasis in a particular center, however, can vary within a fairly flexible range. The emphasis can be on employment, treatment, education, or general resocialization. In its narrowest definition, a prerelease program is an *institutional* program tailored to prepare an inmate for community living. Although the prerelease center may be an adjunct to a work release program, we are dealing with it separately because it has wider ramifications than mere employment facilitation.

THE CALIFORNIA EXPERIENCE

It is a common state of affairs in corrections to encounter unbridled enthusiasm for every new program introduced on the part of those instituting the program. An ever-present danger is the pitfall of self-fulfilling prophecy. This occurs when subjective bias operates to influence favorable results.

Hard data, which would permit critical evaluation of the prerelease center, are rather limited. A classic example is the prerelease program established in one of California's smaller prisons in 1965. Described by a departmental spokesman as "the most ambitious prerelease program in California," [11] it was nonetheless severely criticized by research analysts in the same department, who observed that "the program sought to meet the needs of inmates in general and thus met the needs of none in particular." [12]

One hundred inmates who had received parole dates, or who had conditional RUAPP releases established (Release Upon Approval of Parole Program), were selected for the program; early releases reduced this number to eighty-three. The inmates were involved in five orientation courses, each lasting five weeks, conducted over a period of eighteen

---

[11] Ben Lohse, "Pre-Release Operations: Institutions," California Department of Corrections, May 1967 (mimeographed).

[12] Norman Holt and Rudy Renteria, "Prerelease Program Evaluation: Some Implications of Negative Findings," *Federal Probation,* XXXIII, no. 2 (June 1969), 44.

months. For three months before the program went into operation, a correctional counselor made a sustained and extensive effort to enlist the community's support and resources, in both the private and public sectors. This effort was considered a primary objective in the planning of the program.

An inherent deficiency appears to be the fact that a great deal of orientation activity of the lecture variety took place, but not enough concrete assistance was given in the form of post-release program development. For example, courses were given on How to Get a Job, Educational Opportunities, Wardrobe Tips, Motor Vehicle Operation, Tips on Buying a Car, and How to Fail on Parole. But this general orientation did not meet specific needs. As Holt and Renteria noted in their critique, "Third termers found out about the conditions of parole, single men heard about Aid to Needy Children, and a halfway house was described to men with well-formulated residential plans." [13]

The program was evaluated by means of questionnaires, interviews, and feedback from an inmate participant observer whose status was not revealed to staff. Parole agents took part in the program as instructors, and a survey of inmate attitudes toward the parole agents was also conducted after the instruction. In this survey, it was determined that 57 percent of the respondents showed no change in attitude, 14 percent had an improved positive attitude, but 29 percent had become more negative in their attitude toward the parole agents.[14] The implications of this finding are obvious.

AN ANALYSIS OF FAILURE

The most fundamental criticism of the program was that the inmate participants were unmotivated "volunteers." Many of the inmates were beset by personal concerns and were not positively inspired by the broad, general approach. In addition, the lectures were of inconsistent quality. It might be said that the program failed because, like most program failures, it was poorly planned, unenthusiastically supported, erratic in operation, and "overly committed and bogged down with traditional prerelease programs." [15]

Many useful conclusions can be drawn from this program's failure. The prisoner who is about to be released on parole tends to think in concrete terms. Assurances of community concern, advice on esoteric subjects, and

[13] *Ibid.*
[14] *Ibid.*, p. 42.
[15] *Ibid.*, p. 45.

technical information will be wasted unless they are integrated with positive release programming. The most successful prerelease program will be the one that actually phases the inmate into a quality caliber job in the community. When a man has to depend on others for his subsistence, his feeling of self-worth depreciates, and he finds himself in a fertile climate for criminal relapse.

Adequate preplanning of the prerelease program is also essential, and there must be a system of ongoing feedback to permit appropriate modifications in the program. Screening into the program must also be meticulous and purposeful. No program should be launched without enthusiastic support for the program and its objectives by staff and participants. It should also be obvious that a progressive thrust cannot be established on traditional foundations. Progressive thrusts are, after all, diversions from tradition, in this particular case a tradition of failure.

THE SOUTH CAROLINA PRERELEASE PROGRAM

South Carolina opened its first prerelease center in 1964, and it currently has seven such centers in communities. Behind the program in South Carolina is a basic philosophy that recognizes that "the finest institutional treatment programs cannot always adequately prepare inmates for sudden transitional strife incurred as a result of their return to the free community. As such, many individuals released from confinement are destined to reenter the cyclical pattern of failure which likely predisposes them to further periods of incarceration." [16]

To counteract the negative elements in the transition, legislation was passed in South Carolina empowering the creation of centers "without the place of their confinement" in which inmates could be placed; while there, they could be trained for employment and eventually permitted to work gainfully in the community while still serving their sentences. Their wages are paid directly to the Department of Corrections by their employers. After maintenance is deducted, the balance of the inmate's wages, at the discretion of the Board of Corrections, is disbursed to the inmate, allotted to his dependents, or deposited in his account.

Residents of the centers are thus enabled to make social adjustments, through training and indoctrination, to the changing customs and fashions of the wider society. The empowering statute places only limited restrictions upon the type of programs that may be established. The most important are that center residents may not displace other employed workers

---

[16] South Carolina Department of Corrections, *1970–71 Annual Report, Community Pre-Release Programs,* p. 3.

in the community, and that they must be paid the standard scale for the work that they perform.

Functionally, the South Carolina Department of Corrections' Community Pre-Release Program is a combination of three distinct programs: the Work Release Program; a Ninety-Day Accelerated Pre-Release Program; and Project Transition. The last-named is "a newly organized effort to apply most modern management techniques to the problem of reducing recidivism." Whereas the national recidivism rate runs in excess of 50 percent, the South Carolina Project Transition claims to have obtained "a remarkable rate of 14 percent overall and 9 percent for those offenders processed through community-based work release centers."[17] The community is intimately involved in these correctional endeavors, and Project Transition operates with Job Coach Volunteers in the respective communities. When an inmate is finally released, it is with the assurance that he will be going to "quality employment" with people in the community who are vitally interested in his welfare and progress because they have been personally involved in the preparation of his return to the community.

Evidence, which is accumulating, suggests that prerelease programs reduce recidivism, particularly among those offenders with limited criminal histories.[18]

The Halfway House

The halfway house can be considered the incubus of the community correctional center, although no unbroken line can be drawn from the prototype to the therapeutically oriented community correctional center. This is because it is difficult to pinpoint the origin of the halfway house. Many diverse developments contributed to its birth, but it is generally considered that concern for the abused child was a principal factor.

HISTORICAL FORERUNNERS

In the eighteenth and early nineteenth centuries, 90 percent of all the criminals hanged were under twenty-one years of age, and a large number of these were children under ten. This was a period of time which led

[17] South Carolina Department of Corrections, *Project Transition Job Coach Manual*, undated, p. i.

[18] See especially the careful study: Daniel P. LeClair, "An Analysis of Recidivism Among Residents Released From Boston State and Shirley Pre-Release Centers During 1972–73," Massachusetts Dept. of Corrections, August 1975. Mass. opened its prerelease centers in 1972 for inmates within eighteen months of a parole date.

Charles Dickens to call his native land "one of the most bloody-minded countries on the earth."[19] In time, concern for the neglected and delinquent child led to the development of different types of shelter care. Shelter care facilities for vagrant children can be traced at least to the late eighteenth century in England. If any one word typifies the growth of the halfway house or shelter care movement, it is *concern*—concern for the neglected, institutionalized, and brutalized child, leading inevitably to concern for the adult ex-offender.

Religious groups have long been associated with efforts to help the man or woman coming out of prison. The St. Vincent de Paul Society, the Salvation Army, the Volunteers of America, and the Quakers have all been vitally involved in this compassionate endeavor. The involvement of the government came later. In general, it can be said that the halfway house emerged in the latter half of the nineteenth century. Credit is usually given to movements within Europe, but as early as 1845 the Quakers opened a halfway house in New York City, which is still in operation and still known as the Isaac T. Hopper Home. The creation of the halfway house was not without opposition and hostility. Keller and Alper relate that when a halfway house opened in New York in the late 1890s, the American Prison Association charged that expansion of these edifices would create "a permanent class of undesirable citizens."[20]

Spurred by pioneering efforts in Massachusetts, New York, New Jersey, and Pennsylvania, the halfway house movement grew steadily. Concern for the female ex-offender was manifested as early as 1864, when the Temporary Asylum for Discharged Female Prisoners was opened in a Boston suburb. According to the latest directory of the International Halfway House Association, there are over 1700 halfway houses in the United States. A brief look at some of the better-known ones will be useful.

NORMAN HOUSE

Norman House in London has been called "the prototype of the halfway house movement,"[21] a claim which may be disputed but which is not unmerited. It was established in 1954 as "a small family home" for twelve recidivists by a sensitive and dedicated former "prison visitor," Merfyn

---

[19] Charles Dickens, *American Notes* (London: Thomas Nelson and Sons, 1904), p. 59; cited in Oliver J. Keller, Jr., and Benedict S. Alper, *Halfway Houses: Community-Centered Correction and Treatment* (Lexington, Mass.: D.C. Heath and Company, 1970), p. 3.

[20] Keller and Alper, *Halfway Houses,* p. 7.

[21] Merfyn Turner, "The Lessons of Norman House," *Annals of the American Academy of Political and Social Science,* vol. 381 (January 1969), 39.

One of London's Three Norman Houses.

Turner. Turner worked at Pentonville, a maximum security English prison, most famous, perhaps, for being England's first penitentiary. Turner held the belief that the courts did not have to send such a large number of its defendants to prison. Further, he was very unimpressed with prison diagnoses, and became very aware of what little was done for the recidivist. He conceded that he could do nothing for the psychotic or the psychopath, but he could do much for the "inadequate" offender. Turner defines "inadequate" offenders as "People who do not appear to be markedly ill, mentally or morally, but who yet fail to find a secure place in an accepted pattern of social life and, having little capacity for making satisfactory personal relationships, express themselves through crime, alcoholism, personal eccentricities, or vagrancy."

Turner also experienced considerable hostility from "the prophets of doom." As he phrased it, "If the sun had been changed into darkness and the moon into blood, the pessimists would not have been dismayed." [22] The halfway house was set up in a Victorian house in a private park in London, and the residents, including Turner and his wife, lived "as any family lives." That is, the communal living fundamentally took place on the ground floor. The upstairs bedrooms were shared, but were for sleeping. "They were not a means of escape from the family life." [23]

---

[22] *Ibid.*, p. 41.

[23] *Ibid.*, p. 43. "Family style" has also been specifically designated as a cornerstone of Crofton House, a halfway house in San Diego, California, established a decade after Norman House: Bernard C. Kirby, "Crofton House: An Experiment With a County Halfway House," *Federal Probation*, XXXIII, no. 1 (March 1969), 54.

Pi House, St. Paul, Minnesota. Residential facility for female offenders. *Courtesy Minnesota Department of Corrections.*

The program operated in a group setting, but the strongest ties were developed between the individual residents and the staff members. The core of the program was a sustained effort to fulfill the lost needs of the residents, to counter their inadequacies, and to deliver to them genuine affection and concern. The Norman House is now an integrated component of the national Aftercare Service, and a second halfway house has been established.

DISMAS HOUSE

Perhaps the best-known halfway house in the United States is Dismas House in St. Louis. Of particular importance is the fact that Dismas House represented the resurgence of the halfway house as a correctional device in the United States. Founded in 1959 by the "Hoodlum Priest," as Father Charles Dismas Clark was known, Dismas House is a non-

Dismas House.

denominational, racially integrated facility that has been approved by the Federal Bureau of Prisons as a prerelease community center for federal prisoners. Dismas House was "the result of the enthusiasm and tireless efforts of a priest who personally involved himself in asuming responsibility for men released from prison." [24] With the able assistance of his long-time friend, Morris A. Shenker, a prominent Jewish attorney in St. Louis, an old public schoolhouse was purchased and became the nucleus of the halfway house.

Like other pioneers, Father Clark was the object of much abuse. Dubbed "The Hoodlum Priest" because of his association with criminals, he was once described by a district attorney as a "pernicious influence." [25] But from the founding of Dismas House through January 1, 1975, that "pernicious influence" enabled 4,363 ex-inmates to become residential participants in a program of compassionate concern, and an additional 7,055 nonresidents to be helped.[26] Father Clark died in 1963.

---

[24] Keller and Alper, *Halfway Houses,* p. 112.

[25] Fred Warshofsky, "Father Clark's Underworld Parish," *Coronet,* February 1961.

[26] Father Dismas Clark Foundation, "Dismas House," *1974 Annual Report.*

His successor, Father Fred L. Zimmerman, the present director of Dismas House, was the recipient of the St. Louis Humanities Award in 1974. He was selected as a "gruff saint honored for helping men," as St. Louis publicly acknowledged the important contribution of the halfway house for the ex-offender.

THE DISMAS HOUSE PROGRAM

The Dismas House program, originally offering residence and job assistance only, has developed into the complete community correctional center. Efforts are made by professional staff to meet the total needs of the residents—social, vocational, and emotional. Through a cross-sectional board of directors, the community is intimately involved in the effort.

Most of the residents are state parolees (26 percent) and federal prereleases (63 percent). The balance are probationers, direct referrals, and a limited number of pretrial referrals by the courts. The Missoui State Department of Vocational Rehabilitation assists in educational placement, and an in-house Alcoholics Anonymous group contributes to the rehabilitative program. In addition to residence [27] and basic necessities, each resident is provided with needed counseling, aid in obtaining employment, and complete medical care.

Primarily to nurture his sense of self-respect and responsible self-determination, each employed resident is expected to contribute to his subsistence.

The average length of stay at the halfway house was 8.1 weeks in 1974, and the average daily occupancy was forty. A total of 274 job placements were made during the year, but this statistic does not give the comprehensive picture of vocational assistance. A number of the men placed had had a series of jobs before they obtained the type of work most suitable for them; including these would swell the total of 274. Each resident has an assigned counselor and is obliged to participate in counseling, job placement, budgeting, and special treatment activities. Bringing drugs or alcohol into Dismas House is grounds for automatic expulsion.

We have made repeated statements about the disadvantaged backgrounds of the vast majority of our imprisoned offenders. The factors of discrimination and disadvantage are highlighted in the clientele serviced by Dismas House, as portrayed in Table 6–1. This also illustrates the important function being performed by the halfway house.

---

[27] Private and semi-private rooms are provided for the residents.

Table 6–1. Social Background Study of Dismas House Residents

Race	*1973*	*1974*
Black	53%	56%
White	47%	44%
Average Age	32	32
Teen	2%	2%
20–29	45%	50%
30–39	27%	26%
40–49	18%	16%
50–59	6%	4%
60+	2%	2%
Familial Background		
Adopted	8%	5%
Parents never married	4%	3%
Natural family disrupted by death of a parent	23%	35%
Natural family disrupted by divorce or separation	30%	27%
Natural family remained intact	35%	30%
Marital Status		
Single	35%	42%
Married	32%	27%
Divorced	20%	20%
Separated	13%	9%
Widowed	—	2%
Formal Education		
0–8 grades	30%	16%
9–11 grades	34%	31%
High school graduate	35%	25%
* G.E.D.	—	27%
College graduate	1%	1%
Previous Employment		
Unskilled laborer	74%	65%
Skilled laborer	15%	27%
Clerical work	4%	4%
Sales	6%	3%
Managerial	1%	1%

Prior Felonies with Conviction	*1973*	*1974*
None	36%	38%
One	28%	27%
Two	21%	20%
Three	6%	5%
Four	4%	5%
Five	3%	3%
Six or more	2%	2%
Nature of Most Recent Offense		
Murder or manslaughter	3%	4%
Felonious assault	7%	2%
Fraud, bad checks	16%	10%
Narcotics	6%	6%
Burglary	18%	14%
Robbery	13%	20%
Stealing, other than auto	14%	16%
Unlawful use or theft of auto	13%	10%
Sex offense	—	3%
Illegal use of weapons	—	7%
Other	10%	8%
Participated in Institutional Programs		
Employable skills learned in prison	42%	52%
Participated in prison educational programs	48%	52%
Nature of Most Recent Release from Prison		
Parole	32%	26%
Prerelease, state & federal	65%	63%
Direct commitment to Dismas House (court, parole, probation, pretrial)	3%	11%

* High school equivalency.

Source: Reprinted from *Dismas House Annual Report, 1974.*

The halfway house is basically a transitional program, whose objective is to provide residential and program services for only that period of time sufficient to facilitate the reintegration of the ex-offender into the community. This is also the basic purpose of Dismas House, although the length of stay is governed to a great degree by the requirements of participating agencies. With parolees, that is determined through case conferences conducted by the parole officer and the director of the program. Both state and federal prereleasees come for a period of time predetermined by the sending institutions, and they leave at the end of that period. The length of stay of the other residents is determined by individual adjustment to the program.

VIEWING THE HALFWAY HOUSE CRITICALLY

As halfway houses spring up across the country, there obviously exists a pervasive conviction that this is a promising correctional tool. It must be pointed out, however, that there has been very limited research done on the effectiveness of the halfway house from a purely scientific viewpoint. Research must take cognizance of the broader impact of the community effort on the total criminal justice system. One recent evaluative survey insists that federal guidance is a necessary prerequisite to establishing a halfway house, basically because of the role of federal funding.[28]

It is not sufficient merely to compare the costs of community-based corrections with traditional prison costs. It may be that community recovery costs more than penal incarceration, but the value of redemption from a criminal way of life can scarcely be put on a simple dollar and cents basis. The real question is: How much are we prepared to invest financially in costly programs which are fruitful in terms of correction? Obviously the investment will increase as the philosophy of corrections shifts to community-based corrections. The obligation that devolves upon community-based corrections is to prove its worth to the honest skeptic.

THE OHIO COMMUNITY TREATMENT SURVEY

There has been one major effort to critically evaluate the halfway house. A Law Enforcement Assistance Administration grant through the State of Ohio Department of Development has enabled the Ohio State University Program for the Study of Crime and Delinquency to implement

[28] Report to the Congress by the Comptroller General of the United States, *Federal Guidance Needed If Halfway Houses Are To Be A Viable Alternative To Prison,* May 28, 1975.

a study of the eight halfway house systems in Ohio. Besides broad evaluation, objectives of the study were "to develop a direction for future services, establish standards, and improve services and programs."[29]

This was a most comprehensive undertaking, and resulted in a two-volume report. It is not possible to review that report in any detail here, but some comments are in order: "The basic results of this study favorably report the effectiveness of halfway houses in the correctional process."[30] It was asserted that halfway house residents make a significantly better adjustment, in terms of both rehabilitation and socialization, than do ex-offenders released directly to parole. This conclusion takes on added significance in the light of the claim, included in the survey, that it is the "more difficult clientele" that is deployed to the halfway house.

The survey reiterated the basic premise of this text, that correctional agencies alone are powerless to correct crime, because the roots of crime are buried in social causes. To make community-based corrections truly effective, the entire community must become concerned and supportive.

The Community Correctional Center

The student has, perhaps, noticed that there is a lack of precision in many of the terms and concepts of "the new penology." Such terms as "work release" and "work furlough" are used interchangeably at times, and yet are given separate identities. The same can be said of "community correctional center" and "halfway house." They are interpenetrating concepts, but also embody distinctive differences, which we will discuss shortly.

Work release programs sometimes operate in community correctional centers. Oklahoma's "exemplary system" of Community Treatment Centers, for example, serve prerelease *and* work release functions. The generic term "community-based corrections," in fact, has received so many different interpretations that it has been accused of having "lost all descriptive usefulness except as a code-word with connotations of 'advanced correctional thinking' and implied value judgments against the "locking up" and isolation of offenders."[31]

---

29 Richard P. Seiter, Harry E. Allen, and John J. Baumeister, *Initial Statement Regarding the Study of Ohio Halfway Houses,* Ohio State University, Program for the Study of Crime and Delinquency, 1973, p. 5.

30 Seiter, Allen, and Baumeister, *Evaluation of Adult Halfway Houses in Ohio, Vol. II,* Ohio State University, Program for the Study of Crime and Delinquency, December 1974, p. 85.

31 Benjamin Frank, ed., *Contemporary Corrections* (Reston, Va.: Reston Publishing Company, 1973), p. 207, citing Public Health Service Publication No. 2130, *Community Based Correctional Programs.*

Metropolitan Correctional Center, New York City.
Courtesy U.S. Bureau of Prisons.

The California Department of Corrections uses community correctional centers to "house and provide treatment to a type of offender who is without resources in the community, is less motivated, and has a lower expectancy base for parole success than the general inmate population." [32] The emphasis here is on the poorer risks.

The San Mateo (California) County Probation Department operates a therapeutic community correctional center program, known as Ellsworth House, for serious offenders, but limited to jail releasees. It encourages the residents not to see themselves as either criminals or mental patients, but as "people who have problems which have led them to anti-social behavior and thus brought them into conflict with the criminal justice system." [33] The program operates on the therapeutic community principle, utilizes behavior modification, and gives the residents substantial re-

[32] California Department of Corrections, Parole and Community Services Division, Report to the Legislative Analyst, *Community Correctional Centers 1972,* Abstracted from Cover Letter.

[33] H. Richard Lamb and Victor Goertzel, "A Community Alternative to County Jail: The Hopes and the Realities," *Federal Probation,* XXXIX, no. 1 (March 1975), 34.

sponsibility for decision-making. Ellsworth House approaches the pure concept of the community correctional center, because it is a twenty-four-hour total program, intimately intermeshed with the community and its resources, and with therapists and professionals in the criminal justice system. It is, ironically, located in a converted mortuary.

Until such time as the lexicon of corrections can be rendered more definitive and can become more universally agreed upon, precise definition will continue to be a problem. To assist the student's broader understanding, we have opted to make distinctions where appropriate, but it must be recognized that the boundaries will often be blurred. In this context, we have employed the term community correctional center generally to describe a community-based correctional facility that is more therapeutically oriented, and which consists of a broad range of rehabilitative services, frequently including work and study release. (The Federal Bureau of Prisons uses the term "residential center" as a synonym for community correctional center.)

We have used the term halfway house, on the other hand, in the traditional fashion, to depict a community-based facility operating as a transitional device for easing the pangs of reentry and primarily providing residential and employment assistance. Group counseling and other supportive services are occasionally a part of the halfway house program, and a given halfway house, such as Dismas House, can actually be called a community correctional center.

THE FEDERAL COMMUNITY TREATMENT CENTERS

The reintegration program of the Federal Bureau of Prisons is basically centered in its community treatment centers (also referred to as residential centers). They are dedicated to providing a variety of prerelease services to selected inmates who are within three to four months of the conclusion of their institutional sentences. There are fifteen of these centers in nine metropolitan areas. During fiscal year 1973 almost 1,800 offenders received employment assistance, counseling for personal problems, aid in restablishing community ties, and help in furthering their education through these centers. Another function of the community treatment center is to provide pre-sentence study and diagnosis for the federal courts and the United States Board of Parole. Of the almost 1,800 that were processed, approximately 300 were cases of this nature.[34]

When an offender is released to an area where the federal system does not have a community treatment center, contracts are negotiated

[34] Federal Bureau of Prisons, *Annual Report, 1973*, p. 15.

The award-winning Metropolitan Correctional Center in Chicago.
Courtesy U.S. Bureau of Prisons.

with public and private agencies to provide this service. At the present time the Bureau of Prisons has contracts with over 100 different public and private agencies in 40 different states. Residential and prerelease services were provided to 1,700 federal offenders in this fashion in 1972. In 1974 this contract system with other agencies was computerized, permitting the Federal Bureau to match the offender's needs with particular community resources. A population accounting system has also been implemented that will permit follow-up evaluation from the prerelease phase through the post-release phase.

THE CANADIAN EXPERIENCE WITH THE RESIDENTIAL CENTER

In 1972 the Solicitor General of Canada commissioned a Task Force on Community-Based Residential Centres. The purpose of the Task Force was to examine what is known as "the C.R.C. movement" in Canada, and to make appropriate recommendations concerning this form of community correctional endeavor.

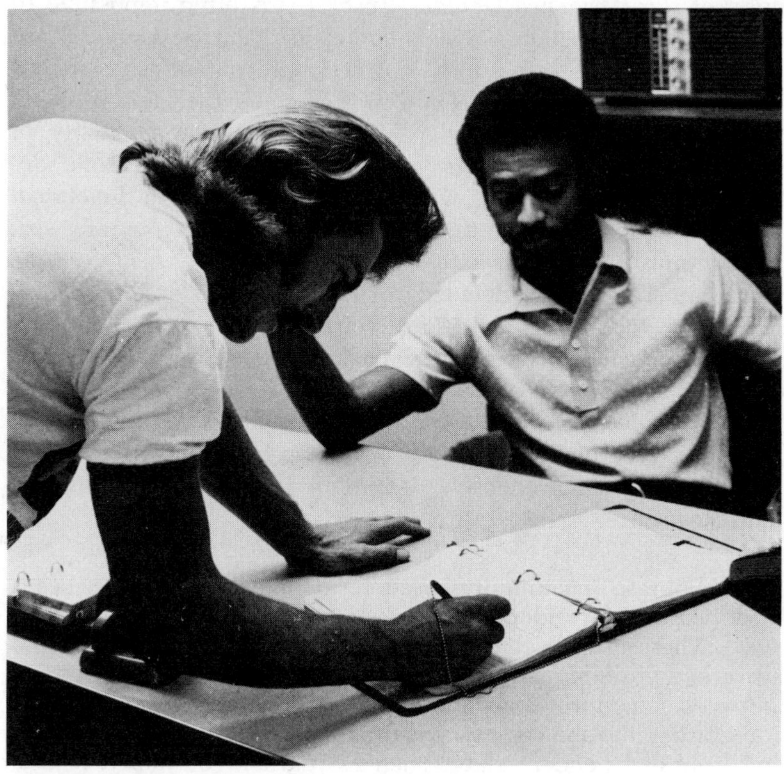

Inmate checking out of Community Correctional Center.
Courtesy U.S. Bureau of Prisons. Photo by Leo M. Dehnel.

In Canada the development of the Community-Based Residential Centres has been largely a function of the private sector. The Canadian Centres, which are considered "innovative programming," serve three basic purposes: (1) to divert from the criminal justice system and from incarceration, (2) to reduce the length of the sentence, and (3) to provide temporary relief from incarceration.[35]

The Task Force immediately encountered the problem which we raised at the beginning of this section: the perplexing overlap between the multi-purpose residential center and the halfway house. As the Task Force stated, Canada provides "a bewildering picture of residences offering everything from overnight accommodations to relatively permanent 'counter cultures' where residents make a long-term commitment to the programme and the ideology which underlies it."[36]

Definition of the Residence Center. Just as it is often impossible to draw rigid lines of distinction between prerelease centers, work release centers, halfway houses, community correctional centers, and similar community correctional programs, so do we encounter the same problem when we attempt to define "offender." This term has applicability to prisoners, ex-prisoners, probationers, parolees, adults, and juvenile delinquents. Keeping this in mind, we must be content with *functional* distinctions, and we must realize that any definition of a community correctional center must be a *generic* one.

The Canadian Task Force decided to adopt the broadest of definitions. Ex-offender was taken to be "any person convicted of a criminal offence, who either currently or in the past, has been on probation or in prison."[37] It appears that this definition inexcusably excludes the parolee, but it can be inferred that parolees are included in that portion of the definition which pertains to those who have been "in prison."

A rather long, but comprehensive definition was adopted to describe the residential centre:

> The phrase "community-based residential centre" describes a wide variety of residential services for many kinds of persons in need. These include the physically handicapped, the elderly and disturbed or delinquent children, as well as offenders. They stand between some form of complete institutionalization and complete integration into the community, providing a service to those moving from a dependent status such as "patient" or "inmate," to a less dependent one such as "dischargee" or "parolee." Equally, they may be provided as alternatives to a more comprehensive level of institutionalization as in probation camps or hostels or group homes, i.e., for persons moving from an independent status

---

[35] Department of the Solicitor General, *Report of the Task Force on Community-Based Residential Centres* (Ottawa: Information Canada, 1973), p. x.

[36] *Ibid.*

[37] *Ibid.*

> to a dependent one. They tend, by and large, to be funded by sources other than the residents. They differ from institutions in that they tend to be smaller, more informal and to provide easier access to the community. They differ from boarding houses and hostels in that those responsible for their administration perceive of themselves as offering something in addition to room and/or board. This extra programme may range all the way from assistance in obtaining employment to intensive group counseling or a complete alternate life-style.[38]

Although this is a rather long definition, it is a quite useful one, for the accent is functional. The community correctional center, by whatever name, services those in need who are *in medias res,* between some form of institutional existence and a free existence in the community. The range of services is from simple sustenance for basic needs to milieu therapy which attempts to change the very life style of the resident. The center tends to be smaller than institutions, more informal in operational policy, proximate to the community, and funded by sources other than the residents—in other words, by a public or private entity. If the student will grasp these ingredients, he will have discovered the élan vital of the community correctional center.

BASIC FINDINGS OF THE CANADIAN TASK FORCE

The Task Force uncovered the fact that there are 156 C.R.C.'s in Canada for adult ex-offenders, with a gross capacity of approximately 5,700 beds. On one randomly selected night in 1972 approximately 3,000 of those beds were occupied. A great variety of program services are offered, but the quality of the facilities, and the distribution, are uneven. Furthermore, there are no commonly accepted standards by which to evaluate the programs. This finding reaffirms the need to develop standard guides for the development and operation of the community correctional center.

Nineteen of the residential centers are exclusively for women, with a total maximum bed capacity of 220, and 26 centers are coeducational. An interesting trend was noted. Those centers whose primary orientation is toward the ex-offender are showing an increasing predisposition to also accepting nonoffenders. Funding for the centers consists of "a jungle of types, sources, responsibilities, criteria, and standards." [39] The Task Force deplored the fact that while most inmates indicate a need for this

[38] *Ibid.*

[39] *Ibid.*, p. 9.

transitional type of service, the centers are not operating at maximal capacity, nor, indeed, is their existence broadly known by the imprisoned.

CONCLUSIONS OF THE TASK FORCE

The conclusions of this major survey can be universally applied to the community correctional center wherever it is planned. It should, first of all, be understood that community-based corrections is more than a rational thrust in corrections. It is also the culmination of some philosophic and criminologic insights about crime, criminal behavior, and rehabilitation. Above all, the move to the community is an indictment of the prison as a corrective instrument. The Task Force pointed out the incongruity of expecting the mass prison to promote individual self-sufficiency. Massification obviously does not breed individualism:

> Prisons are "total" institutions, characterized by the concentration of power in the hands of the keeper, and the almost complete absence of formal power among the kept. Whatever value this may have in maintaining control, *it is a model of human influence essentially identical to that employed by the offender when he commits his offense!* [40]

Rehabilitation in the prison setting is a Utopian dream, because instead of encouraging responsible self-determination, the prison culture nurtures "enforced dependency on the non-negotiable authority of others." Traditional corrections has attempted to impose its solutions for change on the offender, but in so doing, the imposers "miss a crucial determinant of human behavior: one can impose solutions if one's object is to punish or to contain behavior, but one cannot if one's object is to change it." [41]

This is, in effect, an argument for a type of community-based correctional programming, envisioned in the community correctional center, in which the resident is an active, self-directing participant in his own correcting. By self-directing, we mean that he is actively involved in the crucial decision-making about his own destiny. Correction cannot be superimposed; it must be adopted.

The Canadian Task Force was of the opinion that the community correctional center is a development in corrections which is only now beginning to realize its potential, and the members of the Task Force strongly endorsed this development. Their numerous recommendations and con-

---

[40] *Ibid.*, p. 30.

[41] *Ibid.*

clusions can be reduced to a few generic principles which must be adopted to ensure the orderly development of this contemporary thrust:

1. Concise objectives must be articulated for the community correctional center.
2. A method must be devised for ongoing evaluation.
3. Governing standards must be established.
4. The needs of the residents must be ascertained, and the centers tailored to meet these needs.
5. The government must adopt a leadership role in the development of the community correctional center, but the community and the ex-offender must have principal roles of participation in that development.

Evaluating the Community Correctional Center

Innovative programs in corrections, particularly in the area of community-based corrections, have begun to proliferate in every state and in every major population center in the United States. This development has been uncoordinated and of patchwork design. Programs are developing in the absence of any critical evaluation of effectiveness, and no model has been developed for universal guidance. This can be explained on the basis of the fact that the ineffectiveness of traditional penal methods is now so well conceded that alternatives are being pushed first and evaluated later.

THE COST FACTOR

The cost factor is always raised in considering the effectiveness of community-based corrections, as if success must always be less expensive than failure. If a community-based program reduced the recidivism rate significantly, but at a per person cost that exceeds jail or prison incarceration, is cost to be the overriding factor? The Correctional Economics Center, a project of the American Bar Association Commission on Correctional Facilities and Services, did a cost analysis of community correctional centers in Indiana. It was ascertained that the daily per capita operating cost for the Indiana State Prison was $6.80, whereas the comparable cost for Community Corrections Center was $17.63.[42] Does this constitute an index of failure for the Community Correction Center?

[42] American Bar Association, Correctional Economics Center, *Cost Analysis of Community Correctional Centers, A Case Study: Indiana,* January 1975, p. 24.

As the cited study so effectively points out, the financial investment in community-based corrections must be viewed in terms of savings effected *in the entire criminal justice system.* It is not the immediate cost of the innovative program that is important; it is, rather, the predicted savings that are spread among the various components of the criminal justice system. A reduction in recidivism, for instance, means a reduction in police activity, court processing, and penal maintenance, which cumulatively offset the initial per capita cost of community-based corrections. This does not mean that economic factors are of no consequence. Intelligent programming should always be subjected to cost-benefit analysis when feasible.

THE NEED FOR DATA

It is the impact on the total criminal justice system that needs evaluating. The philosophic justification for community-based corrections is well settled. What has yet to be secured is sufficient hard data to enable a pragmatic confirmation of the wisdom of the philosophic change. As this pilot study observed, "The evaluation of the Community Corrections Center, while in large part able to stand alone, would be enhanced by more specific information directly related to measurable objectives and more complete cost estimates."[43] The contemporary pioneers in community-based correction must provide this information.

Review Questions

1. Distinguish between *work release* and *work furlough.*
2. Analyze the causes of the failures in the furlough programs in Washington, D.C., and California.
3. To what do you attribute the apparent success of the New York work furlough program?
4. Is work release a sound concept? Why?
5. Critique the California prerelease experiment undertaken in that state in 1965.
6. What were the historical forerunners of the halfway house?
7. Describe the Dismas House program.

---

[43] *Ibid.*, p. 41.

8. If you were going to develop a halfway house, what essential steps would you take in planning and implementing the program?
9. What is the role of the Federal Community Treatment Centers, and how extensive is the Federal program?
10. What were the major findings of the Canadian Task Force with respect to the Community-based Residential Centres?

7

COMMUNITY DRUG PROGRAMS

Weave a circle round him thrice, and close your eyes with holy dread, for he on honey-dew hath fed, and drunk the milk of Paradise

Kublai Khan

The term "drug" automatically brings to almost everyone's mind such substances as heroin, morphine, marijuana, benzedrine, LSD, and similar classes of sedatives and stimulants. But which of these can be described as the most destructive of drugs? Heroin? Morphine? LSD? No. That distinction is reserved for alcohol.

The Most Destructive Drug

There is probably a much wider general knowledge of alcoholism in the public at large than there is of opiate addiction. Alcoholics Anonymous is almost a household word in the United States, and vast numbers of citizens are familiar with the Serenity Prayer of AA.

God grant me the serenity to accept
the things I cannot change,
the courage to change the things I can,
and the wisdom to know the difference.

THE PROFILE OF ALCOHOLISM

It is generally conceded that there are approximately 9 million alcoholics in the United States. Remedial care for alcoholism costs in excess of $25 billion annually. Three-quarters of the adult population in the United States use alcohol. Alcoholism is said to be rampant in Los Angeles County, with over $75 million being spent annually by that county to combat this plague. Nationally, it is estimated that one out of every ten drinkers is an alcoholic or a "problem drinker."

Traditionally, male alcoholics outnumbered female alcoholics by about a 4:1 ratio, but the rapid increase in the ranks of the female is an interesting and recent phenomenon. It was reported to the North American Congress on Alcohol and Drug Problems, in 1974, that for the three preceding years women accounted for 31 percent of AA's new members.

A large number of heroin and morphine addicts who have "kicked" the habit become alcoholics. In reviewing a number of pertinent studies, the Consumers Union Report stated that "The most striking finding in this study concerned the very close relationship between alcoholism and abstinence from narcotics." [1] Despite this shared relationship, it is worth noting that the American Psychological Association classifies alcoholism as a form of drug dependence separate from other forms.

There are notable parallels between alcoholism and opiate addiction, and there are striking dissimilarities. Not every one who uses alcohol is prone to alcoholism, but everyone can be "hooked" on heroin after very limited use. Alcohol is socially acceptable, and may be readily purchased without stigma; heroin is legally outlawed, and its possession constitutes a crime. Alcohol excess will directly cause organic damage, and death can occur from protracted use; heroin is not intrinsically harmful to the organs, but *one* overdose can cause death.

The harm from the intemperate use of alcohol is literally incalculable. Most fatal automobile accidents are drink-related. The misuse of alcohol is responsible for more arrests than any other type of unacceptable behavior. It burdens welfare agencies, which have to care for the countless dependents of alcoholics, and it is a major problem for industry. Alcohol abuse has sent innumerable patients into mental hospitals. Countless marriages have been ruptured by this drug. Collectively, the problems generated by the abuse of alcohol dwarf the problems generated by the misuse of all the other drugs combined.

---

[1] Edward M. Brecher and the Editors of *Consumer Reports, Licit and Illicit Drugs* (Boston: Little, Brown and Company, 1972), p. 85.

THE DYNAMICS OF ALCOHOLISM

Attempts to explain alcoholism have been quite varied. It is obviously a problem of social maladaptation. It is sometimes suggested that certain ethnic groups are more predisposed to alcoholism than others, which presumes a genetic susceptibility. It has also been observed that alcoholism has a tendency to run in families.[2] Alcoholism is said to be rare among Jews because they use wine ritually from early childhood. For those of Anglo-Saxon tradition, who usually prohibit a child from using alcoholic beverages until the teen years, there is a significantly higher incidence of alcoholism. This clearly suggests a cultural influence. Irrespective of the etiological base for abuse, the person who becomes an alcoholic develops an insatiable craving for "the grape." The imprudent use of alcohol has been repeatedly cited as a principal factor in failure on parole.

TREATING THE ALCOHOLIC

It is usually said that a multidisciplinary approach is the best approach to the problem of alcoholism. There are certainly a large number of curative efforts, but the best known and possibly most successful is far from multidisciplinary. It was devised in 1935 by Dr. Bob and Bill W. in Akron, Ohio. Bill, who was an alcoholic, recovered through a "fundamental spiritual change," and later assisted his alcoholic doctor-friend to recover. Together they founded the organization that is now world famous, Alcoholics Anonymous.[3]

Unofficially opposed to traditional therapy, and successful enough to be secure in its own philosophy, AA actually uses a variation of milieu therapy, that is, the members collectively reinforce the "treatment." Group and individual counseling characterize the interaction in AA, and the group reinforces the individual in realizing that he is neither alone nor despicable, for he has countless associates in this difficulty. This enables him to feel that his great burden is shared and, therefore, lightened. Testimonials given by the successfully abstemious are a feature of AA meetings.

---

[2] James C. Coleman, *Abnormal Psychology and Modern Life,* 4th ed. (Glenview, Ill.: Scott, Foresman and Company, 1972), p. 414.

[3] Co-founder William W. addressed the American Psychiatric Association by invitation of that body in 1949. His address provides a clear exposition of the tenets of AA. See: "The Society of Alcoholics Anonymous," *American Journal of Psychiatry,* 106, no. 5 (November 1949).

The evidence indicates that AA is most successful with those individuals who have had a degree of success in life, and is least effective with the skid-row alcoholic. An increasing number of ex-addicts have become affiliated with AA, demonstrating the common affliction possessed by both the addict and the alcoholic—an insatiable craving for a chemical crutch.

AVERSION THERAPY

Aversion therapy refers to treatment methods that chemically induce an aversive reaction in the patient. One of the better known aversive therapy approaches employs the chemical disulpherim, better known as Antabuse. When Antabuse is taken prior to the consumption of alcohol, a most distressing state of being is experienced. It is related that aversive therapy was utilized by the ancient Romans, who placed a live eel in a cup of wine that the alcoholic was forced to drink.[4] It might be said that aversive therapy is designed to induce a state of revulsion in the subject which deters him from further indulgence. The main defect in this treatment is that the patient can refrain from taking Antabuse once he is released from clinical supervision.

Emetine (emetine hydrochloride), an emetic, is sometimes used by intramuscular injection. Under the influence of emetine, the alcoholic is reduced to nausea and convulsive vomiting. In this treatment technnique, alcohol is first given to the patient, followed by emetine. The consequent results are intended to induce a conditioned response of aversion to alcohol.

Conditioning by reinforced electroshock treatments has also been experimented with in the treatment of alcoholism, but the data are insufficient to permit any meaningful conclusions.

As man is largely a social product, no exclusively psychotherapeutic, or purely medical program is going to succeed. There must be a broad approach to this problem, in which the social and life forces impinging upon the individual are also given appropriate attention. The man who is "driven to drink" by intolerable living conditions—the same forces that may precipitate crime or drug addiction—quite evidently cannot respond to pure therapy unless there is a concomitant improvement in his social circumstances. It is for this reason that a multidisciplinary approach is most frequently advocated. Treatment must also be tailored to the individual's needs.

---

[4] Coleman, *Abnormal Psychology*, p. 418.

Heroin Addiction

A heroin addict whom I once counseled professionally, described an incident in his life to me. He was "hurting," meaning that he was in a state of withdrawal, and had just "scored some smack" (purchased some heroin). He went to his room and feverishly clawed under the bathroom sink for the "outfit" (injection paraphernalia) which he kept hidden there. In his feverish haste, he inadvertently banged the hypodermic needle against the sink, bending the tip of the needle and creating a sort of fishhook.

He desperately tried to penetrate a vein, without success. He made one more futile plunge with the needle, and when he withdrew it to try again he discovered that he had hooked the vein and pulled it from his arm. Aghast, I asked him what he did then. "Man, I fixed in it!" he exultantly replied.

What kind of drug program will free a man that can experience ecstasy in a circumstance that would horrify the average citizen? What can be done for the man or woman who has purchased "death on the installment plan"?

SOME GENERAL CONSIDERATIONS ABOUT HEROIN ADDICTION

Another addict once defined the euphoric state induced by heroin as "the most of the most." The implication is that the heroin sensation is the ultimate pleasurable experience. It is this "high" that drug abuse programs have to cope with, and the challenge is monumental. There is no "cure" for heroin addiction and, indeed, this is a most inappropriate term to apply. Contemporary thinking expects the addict, like the alcoholic, to episodically "fall off the wagon." A realistic appreciation of the incredible attraction possessed by the white poppy must lead one to expect regression. The treatment objective must be to lengthen the periods of abstinence intervening between regressions. The ultimate objective, hopefully, is prolonged abstinence.

It is also important to understand the addict's life style if progress in treatment is to be achieved. The addict has his own peculiar value system, ritualistic rubrics, and an insulated mode of existence, characterized by obsessive preoccupation with drugs. As heroin is both physically and psychologically addicting, it is evident that merely abating the physical craving will not terminate the psychological addiction. I have known innumerable addicts who have spent years in custody, without drugs, who have resumed use almost immediately upon being paroled from prison.

Any valid treatment program must endeavor to treat the whole person, materially, economically, socially, psychologically, and medically. It is questionable if any program qualifies in all of these requirements, although some noble efforts are under way. We will review some of the more important efforts in this chapter.

A DRUG-ORIENTED SOCIETY

We are a drug-oriented society. From infancy children learn that parents use some mystical substance to take away pain, to reduce weight, to prolong wakefulness, to induce sleep, and to stock medicine cabinets temptingly. Pharmaceutical companies have so deluged the American public with hypnotic advertising, that the solution to all bodily discomforts and mental distress is expected to come out of a small bottle in multi-colored hues. Well over 15 billion pills are manufactured each year, and half of them wind up on the illicit market.

The illicit market is also flooded with opium derivatives, both natural and synthetic. It is generally conceded that there are somewhere in the neighborhood of 700,000 heroin addicts in the United States, and there are quite likely a great many more than that. The tragedy is that they are predominantly young people. The incredible misery that accompanies this affliction is beyond belief.

Heroin addiction also spawns an enormous amount of crime, mostly property offenses. It has been conjectured that as much as 25 percent of all crime is drug-related. A Cabinet-level report to the President in 1975 estimated that heroin addiction and other drug abuse cost the American public between $10 billion and $17 billion annually.[5] These costs were broken down on the conservative side as follows:

	(In millions)
Property loss	$6,300
Loss of earnings	1,500
Operating programs	1,100
Criminal justice costs	620
Treatment and health care	200

On top of that, drug abuse is responsible for 15,000 deaths annually.

---

[5] Cited in *Los Angeles Times*, May 31, 1975.

Proceeds of a narcotic raid.

AN OPERATIONAL DEFINITION OF ADDICTION

It is self-evident that treating an affliction is enhanced by some fundamental knowledge of the affliction. But how does one define drug addiction? It has commonly been defined as a state characterized by physical and psychological dependence, and by tolerance. Tolerance means that the body's capacity for the drug increases with increasing use of the drug. The World Health Organization, dissatisfied with that definition, attempted to introduce the concept of *drug dependency*. Any abnormal use or addiction would simply be defined as "heroin dependency" or "morphine dependency," and so forth. Although this is an admirable idea, it has not been seriously adopted.

After a most comprehensive research effort, Brecher was led to conclude that an *operational* definition was needed, one that did not need to be specific about causation, but that did need to describe *the type of behavior evoked by addicting drugs.* The advantage of an operational definition is that "it specifies precisely what young people should be concerned about, and what parents and public officials should be concerned about." [6] This is Brecher's definition:

> An *addicting drug* is one that most users continue to take even though they want to stop, decide to stop, try to stop, and actually succeed in stopping for days, weeks, months, or even years. It is a drug for which men and women will prostitute themselves. It is a drug to which most users return after treatment at Lexington, at the California Rehabilitation Center, at the New York State and City centers, and at Synanon, Daytop, Phoenix House, or Liberty Park Village. It is a drug which most users continue to use despite the threat of long-term imprisonment for its use—and to which they promptly return after experiencing long-term imprisonment.[7]

It is the abject enslavement of addicting drugs that must be avoided, and the operational definition bleakly describes the effects of this enslavement.

EXAMINING THE EXPERTISE

It is a regrettable fact that the majority of those charged with the responsibility of "rehabilitating" the addict have a profound ignorance of the drug culture and the addict personality. Countless practitioners directly engaged in correctional work in the field have neither the academic preparation nor the requisite experience to deal with the monumentally complex problem of drug addiction. This was confirmed in a recent study in Pennsylvania.[8] In fact, only recently has specific material on supervising the drug addict been contained in a textbook.[9]

Ignorance of the drug problem and the drug culture is pervasive in our society, and in our criminal justice system. Even the United States Supreme Court, in the monumental decision which held that drug addiction is not a crime, used some very peculiar logic in the narrative of its decision:

---

[6] Brecher, *Licit and Illicit Drugs,* pp. 84–85.

[7] *Ibid.,* p. 84.

[8] Arthur D. Moffett, James D. Bruce, and Diana Horvitz, "New Ways of Treating Addicts," *Social Work,* 19, no. 4 (July 1974), 389.

[9] Louis P. Carney, *Probation and Parole: Legal and Social Dimensions* (New York: McGraw-Hill Book Company, 1977).

> To be a confirmed drug addict is to be one of the walking dead. . . . The teeth have rotted out, the appetite is lost and the stomach and intestines don't function properly. The gall bladder becomes inflamed; eyes and skin turn a bilious yellow; in some cases membranes of the nose turn a flaming red; the partition separating the nostrils is eaten away; breathing is difficult. . . . Good traits of character disappear and bad ones emerge. Sex organs become affected. Veins collapse and livid purplish scars remain. . . . Nerves snap; vicious twitching develops. . . . such is the plague of being one of the walking dead.[10]

It goes without saying that those who wish to devote their professional endeavors to treating the addict should be properly educated and properly trained.

Contemporary Community Programs for Drug Addiction

If "cure" was the watchword for the 1960s, then "despair" could well be the watchword for the 1970s. A vast array of innovative programs gradually unfolded for the treatment of drug addiction in this decade, but nowhere has there been any dramatic breakthrough. Millions of dollars have been funneled into the effort to cure this species of cancer, yet the recovery rate continues to hover around the 5 percent level. This fact obviously suggests that drug *prevention* programs must have priority consideration. The young must be enabled to see drug abuse in its appalling reality, as depicted in Brecher's operational definition. The false glamour must be stripped from drug abuse and it must be viewed as the horrifying affliction that it really is. Valiant efforts must also be continued to find solace for the thousands who were seduced by the false glamour.

It is obviously impossible to deal with the innumerable drug programs proliferating in this country and elsewhere. Those which we have selected are representative of the major approaches to the program, and are also fairly well known in most instances.

SYNANON

One of the better known community drug programs, Synanon, paradoxically was founded (in 1958) by an ex-alcoholic, Charles E. "Chuck" Dederich. While it might appear that Synanon is derived from the Greek,

---

[10] *Robinson v. California,* 370 U.S. 660, 666–668 (1962).

or is at least an esoteric scientific term, it actually came from a member's inability to pronounce "seminar" and "symposium." In attempting to pronounce these words consecutively, he managed to say "synanon."[11]

Dederich was searching for a meaning for his own distressed existence, and had journeyed through various philosophies in his search. Membership in Alcoholics Anonymous had enabled him to terminate his drinking, but did little to solve his other problems, including multiple failures in marriage. Dederich's personality was such that he could not be satisfied with any existing program. He had to create and dominate his own empire. Yablonsky, indeed, spoke of his "roaring ego needs."[12]

Beginning with free-association discussion groups with his alcoholic friends in Ocean Park, California, while surviving on unemployment compensation checks, Dederich developed the ruthless encounter known as the "haircut." This is the Synanon version of what is commonly called "attack therapy" in formal psychotherapy. The recipient of the "haircut" is relentlessly attacked until, theoretically, he encounters his naked self, divested of all of its false fronts. Ostensibly, rebuilding follows. Dederich reputedly noticed remarkable changes in some of the members through this process and, consequently, the "haircut" became the pivotal nucleus of Synanon. A participating group was known as a synanon, and the participants as synanists.

Synanon began as a racially integrated organization and required absolute truth about self as a cardinal principle. Although the synanons became vociferous, physical violence was prohibited and cause for ejection. Possession of alcohol or narcotic drugs was absolutely prohibited. Synanon is usually classified as a therapeutic community, or, as sociologists would term it, a mutual aid society. A most important element is the peer therapy practiced. Dederich felt that the traditional form of doctor-patient therapy was ineffective because it interposed such a wide difference in social strata between the therapist and the patient as to render the therapy ineffectual.

On the negative side, Synanon is a closed society. Despite the impassioned praise of many scholarly supporters, and an exceptional *in-house* record of success, that record is far from duplicated in the community. Dederich himself admitted a relapse rate for graduates of over 90 percent, and conceded that "if they go out of Synanon they are dead."[13] Synanon's major shortcoming is that it prepares its residents to encounter one another in utter truth without preparing them for adjust-

---

[11] Lewis Yablonsky, *The Tunnel Back* (New York: Macmillan Publishing Co., Inc., 1965), p. ix. Yablonsky has written the definitive history of Synanon, although it is a (favorably) biased version.

[12] *Ibid.*, p. 48.

[13] Quoted in Brecher, *Licit and Illicit Drugs*, p. 78.

ment to an outside world that is characterized by duplicity and conflict. As a result, they cannot make it in that world and must flee from it.

Dederich rationalizes this in the context of his belief that the family as a social institution is changing. He sees it returning to the loose-knit federation of clans that existed in primitive times. Synanon is literally creating its own society and its own institutions. As one member commented, "We invent our traditions as we go along." Synanon has "gone along" into a multimillion dollar enterprise, with vast real estate holdings, including a 3,500-acre ranch in northern California. The closed Synanon society reputedly has over 2,000 members living in communes from California to Connecticut.

DAYTOP VILLAGE

A drug program that has received unusual commendation from critics is Daytop Village, formerly known as Daytop Lodge, which was established in Staten Island, New York, in 1963. It is really an offshoot of Synanon, for its creators were profoundly influenced by Dederich's program in Santa Monica, California. The creators of this new program were an eclectic trio: Joseph A. Shelley, chief probation officer of the Brooklyn Supreme Court, Dr. Daniel Casriel, a psychiatrist, and Herbert Bloch, a professor-criminologist.

Disenchanted with past efforts to treat drug addiction, and appalled by the astronomical cost of the drug problem, the founders of Daytop Village made an on-site survey of detection and treatment programs throughout the United States. The only positive impression that they gained was from their "astonishing experience" with Synanon.[14] Dr. Casriel was surprised to discover individuals whom he had known as "hopeless cases" in New York apparently radically transformed by the Synanon program. He then moved into Synanon as a participant observer. From these activities, Daytop Village emerged.

As initially conceived, Daytop Village was structured to accommodate addicts placed on probation by the courts. "Daytop" is actually an acronym for Drug Addicts Treated on Probation. With elements borrowed from Synanon, mixed with original concepts, a halfway house program was devised that would endeavor to provide the addict resident with a new value system, and a status organization, that would ultimately facilitate reintegration into the larger community. In addition, chemical testing was integrated into the program for both research and control

---

[14] Joseph A. Shelley and Alexander Bassin, "Daytop Lodge: Halfway House for Drug Addicts," *Federal Probation*, XXVIII, no. 4 (December 1964), 47.

purposes. Thin-layer chromatography of urine samples was adopted as the psycho-chemical deterrent.

The first year of the program was nightmarish, as a succession of house managers found themselves incapable of coping with the strain. Eventually, a charismatic director was found. When he assumed direction of the program, he declared it to be corrupt, because improper prior management had allowed the ideology of the streets to set the atmosphere at Daytop Village. Every resident was given the option of honest involvement in the program or expulsion. A public confession of wrongdoings was required of everybody, and the intransigents who were the last to relent were punished. They were given a hair-cropping with electric shears.

Intensive group therapy, patterned on Synanon, is employed daily at Daytop, and the addicts are themselves the change agents. The program consists of three phases. The first involves approximately ten months of residency in which family members are encouraged to be distinctly hostile toward the resident addict, and the other residents ridicule him when he attempts to play the addict's traditional game of rationalizing and "sniveling." In the second phase, the addict lives at Daytop but is permitted to work in the community. In the final phase, the addict, still on probation, returns to live in the community, but is obliged to visit Daytop on the weekends and testify to his success.

It is emphasized to the Daytop Village resident that he will not be permitted to project the blame for his addiction on anyone but himself —not his parents, not the police, not his childhood, nor on any pseudopsychological rationale. He is pointedly told that the reason for his addiction is simply *stupidity*. The addict is an addict because he opted to act stupidly. No one is admitted to the program who does not initiate a request for admission, and even then he is tested. He may be told to call back at a specific time, and if he does not call at that specific time he will be told he has not evidenced the prerequisite sincerity. If he is accepted, he will be made to sit in a chair for several hours, during which he will be studiously ignored by all of the residents who pass by. Gradually hostility will be replaced by filial affability, and the addict will discover the genuine concern that the residents have for one another.

There are many positive things to be said about Daytop Vilage. The most important is that, unlike Synanon, it is directed toward the reintegration of the addict into the outside community. It is not designed as a haven. The accent on substituting a new value system, whether or not that can be accomplished, is also commendable, for it is obviously a defective value system that has generated the addict's problems. Abraham Maslow and O. Hobart Mowrer, two of the most distinguished psychologists in the United States, and both former presidents of the American

Psychological Association, "have proclaimed Daytop as one of the great therapeutic community developments of our time." [15]

One more crisis came to Daytop when the forceful leader was removed by the Board of Directors. Although some feared that the program would collapse without his forceful leadership, others felt that he had developed "a cult of personality and infallibility," and was too inflexible in his expulsion policy. The fears appeared groundless when, after eight months, it was proclaimed that Daytop had the inner vitality to withstand this crisis and "was alive and doing much better then ever." [16]

Of those who enter the program, 8 percent drop out within the first thirty days and 17 percent after ninety days. It is claimed that there is a 91 percent rehabilitation rate after graduation.[17] If this is accurate, it approaches the miraculous. Daytop now appears to be taking greater cognizance of the additional influence of social factors, and not hewing to its founding principle that addiction is caused by stupidity. To say that stupidity alone is the cause of addiction would be to ignore all of the subtle brutalities in our society which prepare the climate for drug enslavement.

DELANCEY STREET

One of Synanon's "turned-off" disciples, John Maher, is the organizational genius behind the controversial community drug program known as Delancey Street. Founded in 1971, it is ensconced in the former Russian and Egyptian consulates in the exclusive Pacific Heights section of San Francisco. A product of New York's delinquent Lower East Side, Maher adopted the name of one of its streets as the name for his drug program. New York's Delancey Street was historically a haven for immigrants.

Maher is aggressively proud of the fact that Delancey Street was created and nurtured without any financial assistance from the federal government or the endowed foundations usually tapped for such a project. Nor has he relied on "the cadre of psychiatrists, psychologists, social workers, counselors, and 'creep consultants' as he calls them, who 'come out of the woodwork' to dominate most other projects." [18] A reformed

[15] Alexander Bassin, "Daytop Village," in Barbara A. Henker, ed., *Readings in Clinical Psychology Today* (Del Mar, Calif.: CRM Books, 1970), p. 132.

[16] *Ibid.*, p. 133.

[17] *Questions and Answers on Daytop Village,* Daytop Village, 184 Fifth Avenue, New York 10010.

[18] Michael S. Serrill, "From 'Bums' to Businessmen: The Delancey Street Foundation," *Corrections Magazine,* 1, no. 1 (September 1974), 14. This is recommended reading.

"Delancey Street," San Francisco. © *Corrections Magazine*. *Photo by Bill Powers.*

addict, thief, procurer, and numbers runner, Maher says he simply came over to the other side and became a social reformer in his own right.

Vocal in his disdain for the parasitic life style of the addict, Maher has nearly three hundred former addicts operating his program, which he reputedly financed with a $1,000 donation from an underworld loan shark.[19] Delancey Street is unique in that it feeds, clothes, trains, and schools its communal residents largely from income derived from its own businesses. Maher bases his program on two simple propositions: (1) the best therapist for a criminal or a drug addict is a criminal or a drug addict, and (2) the best treatment is hard work in the communal residences or in the communal family businesses. These businesses include a restaurant, a flower shop, a moving company, a garage, and a maintenance service. There is also a state-chartered credit union, the first of its kind.

The ubiquitous attack therapy, spawned at Synanon, has also been carried by its apostate to Delancey Street. Maher broke with Synanon because he opposed the Synanon belief in a closed society, feeling that reintegration in the larger society is a valued objective for the ex-addict.

Part of the philosophy of the Delancey Street program is total social support of the individual, who literally becomes a life member in good

---

[19] *Ibid.*

standing, even after he has left the organization, if he remains drug-free. Of Celtic derivation himself, Maher conceptualizes a community that is patterned on the ancient Celtic clans. Resident members are divided into clans of approximately 60 members, each with a clan leader who is known as a "barber." The influence of Synanon is seen here. The "barbers" have almost dictatorial control over their clans, and are usually old-timers, in criminal history as well as in residency.

Five fundamental rules govern Delancey Street: (1) Violence is prohibited. (2) Alcohol and drugs are barred. (3) Everyone must work or go to school. (4) The resident must make a two-year commitment to the program. (5) Promiscuity is not permitted. This does not mean that residents must be formally married, but that a "couple" must be faithful to one another.

It is difficult to evaluate Delancey Street, for no recidivism statistics are kept by Maher, although he concedes that one-third "split" within six months of entering the program.[20] The program has numerous supporters among eminent community members and correctional officials, including the sheriff of San Francisco. It also has its share of critics. There are some responsible clinicians who feel that attack therapy is a potentially dangerous therapeutic tool in the hands of amateurs. Recently, Delancey Street has been troubled with idleness and overcrowded conditions. Its future is as problematic as that of every other comparable drug program.

METHADONE PROGRAMS

Methadone is an opiate antagonist employed in a great number of programmed efforts to curb drug addiction. While it is really an auxiliary tool rather than a program per se, its use is so widespread and so controversial that it deserves to be examined in any review of community drug programs. Methadone could be called a pharmacological or drug substitute approach to drug addiction, because it involves the use of one drug to counter the effects of another drug. Approximately 100,000 addicts are on methadone maintenance programs in the United States.

Methadone hydrochloride—or methadone, as it is commonly called—is a white crystalline material that is water soluble. It purportedly has the capacity to inhibit the heroin craving. In this way, through methadone maintenance, the addict is enabled to function productively in the community. Developed in 1945 by a German, who was searching for a substitute for opium derivatives which had become scarce during

---

[20] *Ibid.*, p. 23.

World War II, methadone shares all of the properties of its equivalents, heroin and morphine, except tolerance. Its proponents claim that the methadone dosage can be stabilized, usually between 10 and 50 milligrams daily. Methadone was first used in a maintenance program in New York in the early sixties by Dr. Vincent P. Dole and his associate, Dr. Marie Nyswander. Long before this experimental treatment use, the drug was well known to street addicts.

Methadone has serious drawbacks, and there is mounting concern that its drawbacks may negate its usefulness. It has generally been established that abatement in the use of illicit drugs is positively correlated with continued participation in a given drug abuse program. The opposite, however, was discovered with respect to methadone in a recent, definitive study. This study found that "a statistical inconsistency was presented by a methadone maintenance program. From the point of view of retention in treatment and proportion of clients being arrested subsequent to entering treatment, this program did poorly." [21]

Methadone is a powerfully addicting drug, and methadone withdrawal is more agonizing than heroin withdrawal. An alarming number of deaths from methadone overdosage have occurred, rivaling those from heroin. Children whose mothers have been on methadone maintenance programs during their pregnancies have been born addicted to the drug. The most distressing aspect is probably the ethical one. Methadone maintenance puts the government in the role of officially addicting addicts. The medical director of California's Department of Health, in a 1976 news conference, said it would be preferable for the government to give addicts heroin rather than methadone because "methadone may be more permanently addictive." [22]

The confused thinking on the issue is epitomized in the Proposed Policy on Drug Abuse of the National Association of Social Workers. Beginning with a call for curbs on the production of psycho-active drugs, which is a commendable position, the policy statement then advocates that the addict be worked with "towards transfer to a more practical narcotic such as methadone. . . ." This is followed by a declaration urging chemotherapy research, "especially . . . the medical, psychological, and social consequences of methadone maintenance." [23] If research is needed, how can use be advocated?

The co-director of Phoenix House, a New York-based drug program, himself a former drug addict, said: "Methadone turns people into zombies.

---

[21] George Nash, *The Impact of Drug Abuse Treatment Upon Criminality: A Look at 19 Programs* (Upper Montclair, N.J.: The Drug Abuse Treatment Information Project, Montclair State College, December 1973), Sec. 3.14.

[22] Quoted in *Los Angeles Times*, March 19, 1976.

[23] *NASW News*, 20, no. 3 (March 1975), 13, 15.

It's a politically popular and cheap gimmick that doesn't solve the underlying causes of addiction." [24] Dr. Dole had a contrary opinion. It was his view that it wasn't relevant "whether these patients ever get off methadone." That is the heart of the methadone controversy.

THE NASSAU COUNTY DRUG ADDICT WORK RELEASE PROGRAM

Researchers are still attempting to discover a chemical agent that will more effectively neutralize the craving induced by the opiates, but with none of the drawbacks which characterize such drugs as methadone. Naloxone and cyclazocine are two experimental drugs which hold promise. The latter is being used in a most unusual work release program instituted in New York in the Nassau County Jail. This program is unusual in at least two respects. First, it reflects a collaborative effort between the jail warden, the county sheriff, the Commissioner of Corrections, and their respective facilities. Second, it is directed toward the hard-core drug addict, an individual normally precluded from traditional work release programs.

Funded by the National Institute of Mental Health, and sponsored by the Nassau County Department of Drug and Alcohol Addiction and the Nassau County Jail, this innovative program employs the narcotic antagonist, cyclazocine, to fortify the jailed addict who is to be released to work in the community during the day. The individual defrays the cost of his maintenance by diverting part of his salary to the county. If his dependents are on welfare, the diversion is to his family for its maintenance. A full range of medical, psychological, social, and vocational services support the therapy of drug antagonism.

Selected inmates must be voluntary participants over twenty-one years of age, be in good health, and must agree to participate fully in the program and in a follow-up program for two years. For ten to twenty days before being permitted to go out to work in the community, the inmate is in an "induction period" in which gradually increasing doses of cyclazocine are administered, until the maintenance level is reached.

Cyclazocine is known as an antagonist because it competes with opiates for the same neural receptor sites in the brain. It thus has the capacity to neutralize the "high" experienced by opiate addicts. In addition, cyclazocine is not addictive itself. Somewhat similar to nalorphine, it will induce withdrawal symptoms if the individual is under the influence of an opiate at the time of the injection of cyclazocine.

---

[24] Quoted in Nicholas M. Regush, *The Drug Addiction Business* (New York: The Dial Press, 1971), p. 119.

Like methadone, cyclazocine renders the patient ambulatory, but unlike methadone it does not leave him with a substitute addiction. Research and behavioral scientists anticipate that this drug "should lead to deconditioning and hopefully to an extinction of the drug-seeking behavior." [25] If this is achieved, it will be greeted with the same exuberance that a cure for cancer would occasion. After all, heroin addiction is one of the worst species of cancer. The program is still experimental, so definitive data are not yet available, but considerable promise rests in this approach.

CIVIL COMMITMENT PROGRAMS

It might not appear, at first glance, that a civil *commitment* program could be considered a community-based program. There are, however, aspects that merit our considering this approach. First, the commitment is *civil,* not *penal,* that is, penal prosecution is suspended in deference to treating the addict under a civil process. Second, the commitment phase is a prelude to community treatment under supervision, ordinarily with methadone or urinalysis testing as a concomitant.

The philosophy behind civil commitment of addicts is both coercive and remedial. It is felt that addicts must receive compulsory hospitalization for detoxification, and it is also intended that criminal behavior will thereby be reduced. New York, California, and Florida are the three states in which civil commitment of addicts has been a major undertaking. It is highly significant that Florida repealed its civil commitment statute in 1970. Irrespective of the rationale of officialdom, the civilly committed addict is not deluded into thinking that he is a patient rather than a prisoner.

There are also serious constitutional issues under the surface, and although the courts have not yet ruled that coercive civil commitment is unconstitutional, it is my contention that this action can be anticipated. There have been some relevant decisions. When California began its program, it was an integral part of the penal process of the Department of Corrections, and correctional officials *assumed* that addicts committed to the California Rehabilitation Center were to be treated as if they were convicted felons. It was also assumed that, like convicted felons, the civilly committed addicts had been deprived of their civil rights. This situation was remedied in one of the relevant decisions alluded to.[26]

---

[25] Leonard S. Brahen, Thomas Capone, Victoria Wiechert, and Philip C. DeJulio, "Nassau County Pioneers Work-Release Program for Addicted Inmates," *American Journal of Corrections,* 36, no. 3 (May–June 1974), 16.

[26] *In re De La O,* 59 Cal.2d. 128; 28 Cal. Rptr. 489.

A basic presumption undergirding all civil commitment programs—that "therapeutic incarceration" will deter addicts from resumption of use—has now been thoroughly discredited. That it was a defective presumption was demonstrated as early as 1956 in a British Columbia study. That study showed that on any given day more than half of the known British Columbia addicts were in prison, and that several of them had previously served long penitentiary sentences.[27] Equally suspect are the data published which profess to show high success. Most addicts are amateur pharmacists and know all of the sophisticated techniques for evading detection. Furthermore, it is a rare drug program that hasn't been tainted with what social scientists call self-fulfilling prophecy. This means that results are biased by the researcher's expectations of success; it also means that true scientific objectivity has not been honored.

For example, discharge from the program is often the criterion of success, but that obviously does not mean that the "successful" individual has not resumed illegal use of narcotics. Furthermore, internal policies often permit liberal interpretations of failure (self-fulfilling prophecy). I know one parole officer, for instance, who always gave his addict clients "a pass" on the first "dirty" test, and his number is probably legion. Distortions in statistical data are not uncommon. An interim list of dischargees from the California Rehabilitation Center (presumptive successes) showed that more than a third of the total had been discharged *by death,* from overdoses, obviously.

Regush raised an ominous question in relation to the therapeutic community approach to addiction: "What if the addict can never permanently and completely detoxify himself from heroin? What if the problem does not mainly reside in the mind but in the body chemistry?"[28] How then is coercive "treatment" *in durance vile* justified? The prestigious National Council on Crime and Delinquency, in a formal declaration of policy, put the civil commitment of addicts in proper perspective:

> Statutes providing for the civil commitment of addicts result in involuntary incarceration, just as criminal commitments do. These statutes should be repealed. In its conditions and lack of accomplishments, civil commitment is the same as criminal commitment, with one exception: unlike the prisons, it creates an illusion that treatment is being given.[29]

---

[27] Brecher, *Licit and Illicit Drugs,* p. 60.

[28] Regush, *Drug Addiction Business,* p. 118.

[29] National Council on Crime and Delinquency, "Drug Addiction: A Medical, Not a Law Enforcement, Problem, A Policy Statement," *Crime and Delinquency,* 20, no. 1 (January 1974), 4.

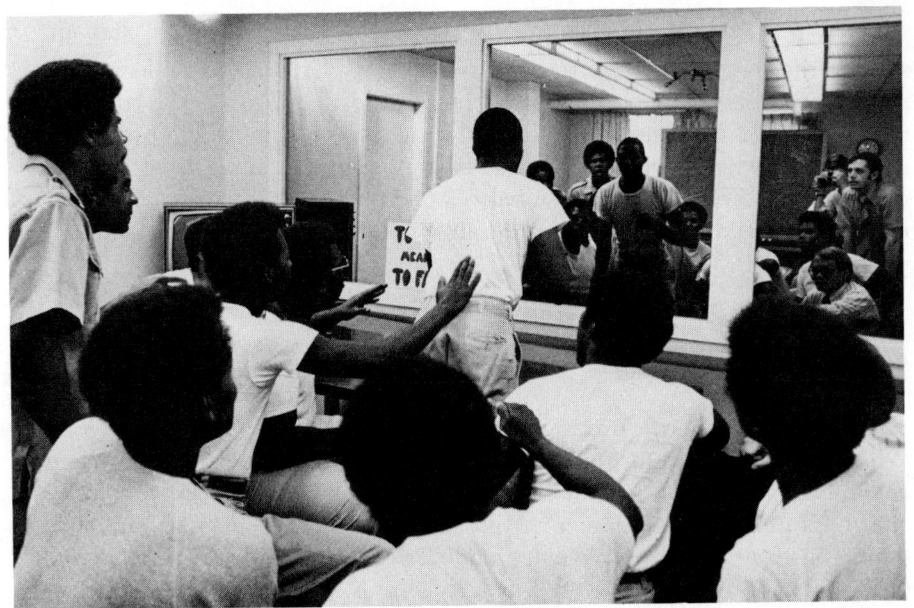

Narcotics rehabilitation unit (NARA) at federal correctional institution, Milan, Michigan, employs group encounter with videotape playback. *Courtesy U.S. Bureau of Prisons. Photo by Leo M. Dehnel.*

THE NARA PROGRAM

The Federal Bureau of Prisons, through the Narcotic Addict Rehabilitation Act of 1966, has focused its narcotic treatment endeavors in a therapeutic community species of program. NARA units have been established in several federal prisons. The program begins with an evaluative phase. This is followed by core-grouping of screened-in addicts, who are also required to participate in regular institutional activities. In the specialized addict groups, addict-inmate "linkers" select new members, and literally attempt to link (establish rapport between) the recovering addict and the prison staff. There is specialized training and vocational training, and the program includes the ubiquitous encounter group.

Prior to 1966, federal prisoners who were addicted were sent to the U.S. Public Health Service Hospitals in Lexington, Kentucky, and Fort Worth, Texas, for treatment.[30] But these facilities had a major defect.

---

30 The federal narcotic hospitals at Lexington and Fort Worth were converted to "regular" correctional institutions in 1972.

There was no aftercare. The present program, as if in expiation, heavily stresses the importance of aftercare. When NARA addicts are released on parole, counseling and anti-narcotic chemical testing (urinalysis) are part of the continuing program. The federal program is committed to providing a high quality aftercare that is based on three factors: intensity of service, continuity of service, and individuality of service.[31] The general criticisms made with regard to similar programs naturally apply to the federal program.

Perspective

The profound, perplexing, agonizing problem of drug addiction is clear. What to do about it is far from clear. There is an incredible and distressing amount of ignorance even among the professionals who should be holding aloft the torch of enlightenment. Millions of dollars have been spent maintaining institutions which have not made a dent in the problem. Antagonistic drugs have been employed which have only enriched pharmaceutical companies. The effort persists to treat addiction as if it were purely a medical problem or purely a psychological problem, despite contrary evidence in abundance.

We are a drug-ridden society, with an unholy fear of pain. Modest pain is nature's warning system, not an invitation to "trip out." So we banish headaches, blemishes, sleeplessness, avoirdupois, and conscience with an amazing variety of medicants. We also try to banish the warning pains of social injustices with flights into materialism, racism, exclusive neighborhoods and schools. That is why we will never conquer the drug problem until we make a frontal assault on the imperfections in our institutions, and in the irrationalities in our value system. Ghettoes and barrios incubate the drug culture; so do unduly affluent neighborhoods with surrogate parenting.

The addict is a product of our culture and a member of the brotherhood of man. Being an addict may be a distressing human condition, but it hardly calls for punitive, penal sanctions. Until we right the fearful wrongs in our society that impel our troubled youth to this form of escapism, we might begin by accepting the "problem" as a natural consequence of our omissions. We might also ponder the fact that compassion is a purely human attribute, and dispense it freely.

A nationally prominent psychiatrist once expressed the opinion to me

---

[31] Donald M. Petersen, Richard M. Yarvis, and Gerald M. Farkas, "The Federal Bureau of Prisons Treatment Program for Narcotic Addicts," *Federal Probation,* XXXIII, no. 2 (June 1969), 39.

that heroin addicts should have access to all of the heroin they need. I immediately thought of the traditional argument against this viewpoint, that tolerance develops with heroin usage. But I also wondered, after further contemplation, when has the limit on that tolerance ever been tested? It cannot be infinite.

The reader will have possibly noted that a thread of philosophy runs through programs such as Synanon and Delancey Street, and, for that matter, Alcoholics Anonymous. It is a distrust for traditional psychotherapy, *because traditional psychotherapy has failed the addict.* Millions and millions of dollars have been spent maintaining futile institutional programs for coercively incarcerated drug addicts. Millions more have been spent by partisans of countless unsuccessful programs and "creep consultants" who have not produced. Further millions have gone to pharmaceutical companies to purchase their ineffective antagonists.

One thing is certain. If these funds could be diverted instead to biochemical research, community-based treatment, and social reform, we would be a lot closer to a solution for the hell of heroin addiction.

Review Questions

1. What data can you produce to support the contention that alcohol is "the most destructive drug"?
2. Is antabuse, as an aversion therapy substance, effective? Why?
3. What is Brecher's "operational definition" of an addicting drug?
4. Describe the drug program at either (a) Synanon, or (b) Daytop Village.
5. In what significant ways does the Delancey Street program differ from the Synanon program?
6. What is methadone, and how would you critique its success as an opiate antagonist?
7. What are the essential characteristics of the Nassau County Drug Addict Work Release Program?
8. What is the philosophy behind the civil commitment of addicts, and what is the policy of the National Council on Crime and Delinquency in this regard?
9. Describe the federal NARA program.
10. If you were to write a "position paper" on the state of drug addiction programs in the United States, what would you say?

8

THE SPECIAL STATUS OF THE JUVENILE

A child is God's opinion that the world must go on.

Robert Frost

In seventeenth-century England, "an infant of eight yeares" who "had knowledge of good and evill" could be held guilty of homicide and hanged for it.[1] In 1875, after the passage of more than two centuries, 10-year-old children were being indiscriminately incarcerated in the county jails of Ohio with adult recidivists.[2] In the 1970s, after another century of "progress," huge numbers of juvenile offenders have been committed to institutions which, like New York City's Youth House, have been described as "hell holes."

The number of books, journals, and articles that have been produced on juvenile delinquency and the treatment of the juvenile is staggering. The task force report of the President's Crime Commission on Juvenile Delinquency and Youth Crime *was over one hundred pages longer than the main report of the Commission.* Yet in view of the "progress" noted above, it must be concluded that while these writings may be enriching

---

[1] Wiley B. Sanders, ed., *Juvenile Offenders for a Thousand Years* (Chapel Hill, N.C.: The University of North Carolina Press, 1970), p. 11.

[2] *Ibid.*, p. 433.

publishers, authors, and paper companies, they have contributed little to the resolution of the problem.

The Dimensions of the Problem

Juvenile delinquency is not exclusively a problem of modern times. Severe punishments were reserved for juvenile offenders under the oldest code of laws known, the Code of Hammurabi. For striking his father, for example, a son could have his hands cut off. Socrates expressed exasperation with delinquent behavior, and when the Clay Tablets of Nippur, dating from about 1750 BC, were translated, they were found to contain a father's admonitions to his son concerning the latter's misbehavior. Even the master psychologist of literature, William Shakespeare, deplored the delinquency of his time:

> I would there were no age between ten and three-and-twenty, or that youth would sleep out the rest; for there is nothing in the between but getting wenches with child, wronging the ancientry, stealing, fighting. . . .[3]

It is rather interesting that Shakespeare set the lower limit of his grief at ten, for in modern times the ages ten to seventeen are those which behavioral scientists refer to as the "delinquency years."

DEFINING DELINQUENCY

How do we begin to define a phenomenon, the criminal transgressions of youth, which the President's Crime Commission called "the most serious single aspect of the present crime problem"?[4] What constitutes "typical" delinquency? In the United States, legal criteria and social conceptions differ so markedly among the various jurisdictions that it is impossible to develop a standard definition of delinquency. It is easier to define what a delinquent is, for that merely involves the recognition of a legal status. *A juvenile delinquent is one whose status as such has been adjudicated in a court of competent jurisdiction.*

But textbook definitions do not include all of the salient factors about social phenomena. For instance, according to the Uniform Crime Reports, 606,548, or 9.8 percent, of all those arrested in 1974 were youngsters under

---

[3] *The Winter's Tale,* Act III, Scene III, 59.

[4] See *Task Force Report: Juvenile Delinquency and Youth Crime* (Washington, D.C.: U.S. Government Printing Office, 1967), p. xi.

fifteen years of age.[5] How is that to be translated? In terms of changing mores? More efficient police work? Greater social concern? Increased citizen apathy toward the needs of its youth?

In considering the behavior that is associated with juvenile delinquency, we must keep in mind that a critical factor is society's tolerance for that behavior. The same behavior may be tolerated or prohibited at different times. The changing mores on smoking and drinking alcoholic beverages provide classic examples. This vacillation of the public attitude prevents a qualitative definition of delinquency and introduces a relative degree of flexibility into the concept. The difficulty in definition is not with serious infractions of the law, obviously, but with lesser offenses, and we shall examine that issue more fully in subsequent sections.

THE NATURE AND CAUSATION OF DELINQUENCY

We indicated above that juvenile delinquency indicates a status. A juvenile is never arrested. He is taken into "temporary custody." This means that delinquent behavior, although it may involve breaches of the penal code, does not constitute criminality. It means that society does not wish violations of the criminal code to be considered as crimes when they are perpetrated by a certain age group. While this has political as well as social implications, it essentially involves a recognition of the minor's immaturity. Society's concern for the child is analogous to the parent's concern for the child. It is a protective solicitude which is normally withdrawn when the child reaches adulthood and inherits full responsibility for his actions.

It is a pointless undertaking to attempt to reduce delinquent behavior to a principle of causation. There is no single cause of delinquency. A vast number of young people are being thrust into the meshes of the criminal justice system for a vast number of reasons. Our principal concern should be to reduce that number without undue jeopardy to the community. The critical nature of this challenge is generally recognized. The Law Enforcement Assistance Administration, which was created by the Omnibus Crime Control and Safe Streets Act of 1968, is charged with the responsibility of improving the entire criminal justice system. In listing its priorities, it named juvenile and youth corrections as its first priority.[6]

---

[5] Federal Bureau of Investigation, *Crime in the United States 1974: Uniform Crime Reports* (Washington, D.C.: U.S. Government Printing Office, 1975), p. 186.

[6] Law Enforcement Assistance Administration, U.S. Department of Justice, "Corrections Program LEAA," Descriptive Pamphlet, 1971, p. 14.

THE STATISTICAL PROFILE OF DELINQUENCY

Several definitive comments can be made about delinquency. First, it has been increasing at least four times faster than the per capita population increase of those in "the delinquency years." Juvenile courts handled over one million cases for the first time in 1970.[7] In that same year, the male-female juvenile delinquency ratio abruptly dropped from the traditional five males to every one female, to 3:1, and it continues to drop. This is mainly due to the radically altered roles of the female, including her increasing freedom of movement. This trend is not confined to the United States. For example, in 1974, in Japan, there was a 27.2 percent increase in the arrest of female juveniles over the previous year.

Another important fact is that delinquency is overwhelmingly a group phenomenon. It is not a series of disparate actions by a large number of isolated individuals. A large amount of cumulative research indicates that 60 to 90 percent of all delinquency is group activity.[8] This has significance not only for understanding the dynamics of delinquency, but also for attacking and treating it.

Of particular gravity is the increase in violence among juveniles. Vandalism in the public schools is costing the American taxpayer $500 million a year and there are over 70,000 assaults on teachers annually. On top of that, there are more than 100 murders perpetrated in the public schools each year. Gang violence in the Los Angeles school system was described as being of near epidemic proportion. In 1975 there were 125 gang-related deaths in that city. Through the first seven months of 1974, a total of 186 students had been expelled from the Los Angeles school system for offenses ranging from possession of weapons to pulling a knife on the teacher. Over 100,000 juveniles are arrested in Los Angeles County every year, and the juvenile hall has been described as a "powder keg of rage." [9]

---

[7] U.S. Department of Health, Education, and Welfare, National Center for Social Statistics, *Juvenile Court Statistics, 1970* (January 7, 1972), p. 2. In 1972, 1,112,500 juvenile cases were handled by the court. The estimated number of children involved in these cases was actually 959,000 because, in some instances, a child was referred more than once during the year. It is of interest to note that in 1972 the number of delinquency cases actually decreased (1 percent) for the first time since 1961: U.S. Department of Health, Education, and Welfare, *Juvenile Court Statistics, 1972* (Office of Youth Development, 1974), p. 2.

[8] President's Crime Commission, *Juvenile Delinquency and Youth Crime,* p. 358.

[9] *Los Angeles Times,* May 17, 1974.

In 1974 the U.S. Congress determined that juveniles account for almost half of the arrests for serious crime in the United States.[10] The Congress also found that overcrowded and understaffed juvenile courts, probation services, and correctional facilities, as presently constituted, are incapable of providing the individualized services needed for the juvenile in trouble with the law. Worse, the failure to provide protective services for the needy nondelinquent, often causes dependent children to bcome delinquent. Add to all of the facts we have considered the further fact that there are approximately 100,000 children detained *in jails* in the United States, and you have a potent argument for a redirection of the criminal justice system as it applies to the minor.

PREVENTION

The most effective countermeasure for juvenile delinquency, like that for adult criminality, is prevention. No matter what type of *ex post facto* program we develop, it will always be a question of closing the barn door after the horse has gone. Measures must be energetically taken to forestall delinquent behavior wherever and however possible.

Most juvenile delinquents outgrow their delinquent youths. If this were not so, the adult criminal justice system would be so burdened that it would be incapable of operating. It is really for those who are seriously involved and reinvolved in delinquency that we plan treatment and rehabilitation programs. The eminent authority Marvin E. Wolfgang has even suggested that it might be better to leave first-time juvenile offenders alone, for the data show that among juvenile offenders, recidivists commit the more serious offenses.[11]

Prevention can mean many things. It can indicate the utilization of psychometric tools for detecting the predelinquent before he or she has the opportunity to act out delinquently. It can imply the use of intervention strategies. It can refer to any of a number of pragmatic programs or tactics to divert youth from the criminal justice system. We will touch upon the major concepts throughout this chapter, but some preliminary thoughts will be helpful in developing a frame of reference.

As was recently stated in the journal of the National Center for Youth Development, the concept of prevention too often smacks of the stitch in time philosophy, in which much is made of the preventive stitch but little

---

[10] *Juvenile Justice and Delinquency Prevention Act,* Public Law 93-415, 93rd Congress, S. 821, September 7, 1974.

[11] Marvin E. Wolfgang, *Youth and Violence* (Washington, D.C.: U.S. Government Printing Office, 1970).

recognition is given to remediation of the conditions that made the stitch necessary.[12] The National Center takes the position that *prevention* is synonymous with *community development,* but has also "suggested a clear-cut distinction between remedial activities in reaction to the problems of an individual and preventive activities affecting numbers of people." [13]

In short, crime and delinquency are the products of social conditions. When those conditions prevent normal fulfillment and normal need satisfactions, a prospective end product is crime or delinquency. Pathological home conditions, discriminatory educational systems, inadequate vocational opportunities, denial of life's necessities, distorted socio-political values, and the welter of other negatives are not conducive to healthy development for many children. Prevention will be most meaningful when it is applied in these broad areas. Community development must be recognized as the primary objective of prevention. How many times has a child returned from juvenile hall to the same pathological environment? The environment—the community—must be redeveloped to preclude the further incubation of crime and delinquency.

Recent legislation in California has empowered the California Youth Authority "to exercise leadership on behalf of the state to develop, establish, and operate comprehensive community-based programs for crime and delinquency prevention." [14] One of the basic sentiments adopted by the California Youth Authority is that delinquency prevention strategy must seek to "strengthen attachment of young people to society by enhancing the community's capacity to provide a participating stake in societal institutions for all youth." [15]

There could be no better place to begin than with the juvenile justice system itself, because the evidence is by now compelling that instead of countering delinquency, the juvenile justice system actually contributes to delinquency. That system, therefore, merits at least passing review.

The Juvenile Justice System

The first juvenile court is this country was established in Cook County, Illinois, in 1899. It represented the apex of a long battle to separate minors from adults in judicial proceedings. The first effort to provide separate

---

[12] William A. Lofquist, "Exploring the Meaning of Prevention: Some Common Fallacies," *Soundings,* 2, no. 2 (March–April 1975), 1.

[13] *Ibid.*

[14] Doug Knight, "A California Strategy for Preventing Crime and Delinquency," California Youth Authority, Sacramento, California, January 1975, p. 1.

[15] *Ibid.,* p. 15.

confinement of children occurred in New York with the establishment of the first House of Refuge in 1825, but the juvenile court was the repository of all of the hopes for more humane treatment of the child.

THE JUVENILE COURT

The juvenile court was founded on the doctrine of *parens patriae,* inherited from Feudal England when the Chancery Court, on behalf of the *pater patria* (the king), exercised jurisdiction over all the children in the kingdom. In the United States this doctrine evolved into the belief that the welfare of the child was paramount in importance over any criminal proceeding. The judge of the juvenile court, usually presiding informally in a setting other than the more formal courtroom, would be the solicitous father surrogate. That was the beginning of the dream. What has been the reality?

Every state now has a juvenile court, but not every state has a separate court for juveniles. In California, the juvenile court is a branch of the Superior Court. In Illinois, it is a branch of the Circuit Court. In Michigan, juvenile cases are disposed of in specially designated sessions of a constitutional court. In New York, Connecticut, the District of Columbia, and Hawaii, the juvenile courts are separate entities, and they are courts of general jurisdiction with respect to the child and the family. In most of the states, however, the juvenile court is a court of limited jurisdiction. There are no federal juvenile courts.

When a juvenile court has been established on the basis of population, and the population of a given city is not sufficient to justify the establishment of a juvenile court, then the child can be tried in a criminal court. The Supreme Court of Georgia, in an interesting decision, ruled that a child tried as a criminal in a county not having a juvenile court was not denied the equal protection, which is guaranteed by the Fourteenth Amendment to the Constitution.[16] There are more than 2,900 courts in the United States in which children's cases may be heard. In 1971 there were 1,250,000 of those . . . court hearings, exclusive of traffic violations.[17]

CRITIQUE OF THE JUVENILE COURT

One factor often alleged for the failure of the juvenile court to attain the high ideals set for it has been the lack of qualifications in the judiciary.

---

[16] *Foster v. Caldwell,* 225 Ga. 1, 165 S.E.2d 724 (1969).

[17] National Advisory Commission on Criminal Justice Standards and Goals, *Task Force Report: Corrections* (Washington, D.C.: U.S. Government Printing Office, 1973), p. 250.

Many judges simply have had no prior experience in this particular branch of the law, nor any training in juvenile behavior or child psychology. Some are simply academically unqualified. A relatively recent survey of 1,564 juvenile court judges, which was about half of the total number in the United States, revealed that 49 percent did not have an undergraduate degree. It also uncovered the fact that 24.2 percent had not even attended law school, and an astonishing 19 percent had received no higher education at all. Only 5 percent of the judges surveyed had obtained legal education above the LL.B. level.[18]

There is conflicting evidence on the merit of judicial experience, as revealed in a study of the juvenile court system of the District of Columbia after the court was reorganized in 1970. Among the findings of this study were several facts that indicated that "experience" tended to provoke harsher dispositions and less success in advocacy. Experienced judges were also more often in conflict with the probation department and defense counsel. It was revealed in the study that probation officers were more influential with the court than were the defense attorneys, and it was determined that inexperienced judges were less punitive in their dispositions.[19]

One serious criticism of the juvenile court is that insufficient time is spent on each case. In one specific instance, I assigned a student to observe detention hearings in a major juvenile court in California in 1974. He reported that fifteen detention hearings were held in a period of three hours. That is an average of twelve minutes per case, not allowing for the time between cases. The obvious question arises: How is it possible to probe the ramifications of a delinquent's case in less than twelve minutes? Is justice even approximated in such a proceeding?

THE FEMALE, THE POOR, AND THE BROKEN HOME

The treatment of the female in juvenile court proceedings also gives evidence of blatant sexual discrimination, and highlights the dual standard of morality supported in the United States. The paternalistic court seems predisposed to presume that female delinquency is primarily sexually oriented. Female delinquents are submitted to pelvic examinations and given vaginal smears, even when their offenses are nonsexual in nature, on

---

[18] Shirley D. McCune and Daniel L. Skoler, "Juvenile Court Judges in the United States," *Crime and Delinquency*, 11, no. 2 (April 1965), 125.

[19] Jackwell Susman, "Juvenile Justice: Even-handed or Many-handed?" *Crime and Delinquency*, 19, no. 4 (October 1973), 493–507.

the assumption that sex is somehow always involved in female delinquency. Comparable examinations are not given to males.[20]

Not only is there differential treatment on the basis of sex, but the juvenile system has also discriminated on a socio-economic basis. The evidence is mounting that juvenile delinquency is not the prerogative of the poorer classes; it is pervasive among all socio-economic strata. The tendency is, however, to focus on the economic circumstances of the family, and this leads to a disproportionate number of the disadvantaged being processed and institutionalized. It is a fallacy to focus on the family's socio-economic milieu and not on the needs of the delinquent. Those needs are emotional as well as economic. A child in the upper classes may have just as many unfulfilled emotional needs as a child from the poorer classes. The child from a broken home is similarly viewed with a jaundiced eye, but an "intact" home can be a pathological one, and a "broken home" can have a great deal of restorative love in the remnants.

In addition to the defects we have spoken of above, a basic deficiency in the juvenile court is that it is designed to deal with the child *abstracted from his family*. The National Advisory Commission has recommended that the juvenile courts be reorganized as family courts, and only concern themselves with delinquent behavior that would be considered criminal if committed by an adult.[21] It also intimates that there is serious concern about the system's tendency to mature the young in delinquent behavior and, therefore, recommends that sober attention be given to keeping the less seriously involved out of the system entirely.

INSTITUTIONALIZATION

In the increasing criticism of the juvenile justice system, particular emphasis must be given to the pernicious influence of institutionalization. Seventy-five percent of all adult offenders have spent time in a juvenile institution, and recidivism among juveniles who have been institutionalized runs from 50 to 80 percent nationally. According to the National Council on Crime and Delinquency, 93 percent of all counties in the United States have no special facility for detaining those accused of juvenile delinquency, and they must therefore be placed in jails.[22] There

---

[20] For an interesting article on this aspect of the juvenile justice system, consult Meda Chesney-Lind, "Juvenile Delinquency: The Sexualization of Female Crime," *Psychology Today,* 8, no. 2 (July 1974), 43–46.

[21] National Advisory Commission on Criminal Justice Standards and Goals, *Task Force Report: A National Strategy to Reduce Crime* (Washington, D.C.: U.S. Government Printing Office, 1973), p. 109.

[22] National Council on Crime and Delinquency, "Think Twice Before You Build or Enlarge a Detention Center," 1968, p. 5.

The modern Robert F. Kennedy Youth Center, a federal complex for youthful offenders, Morgantown, West Virginia. *Courtesy U.S. Bureau of Prisons. Photo by Leo M. Dehnel.*

are 2,800 counties in the United States. A 1970 National Jail Census, conducted by the Department of Justice, reported that 7,800 juveniles were housed in 4,037 jails in the United States on a given day in March of that year. But the most comprehensive study to date indicates that "it is probable that up to 500,000 juveniles are processed through local adult jails each year in the United States." [23]

As recently as 1971, a panel created by the New York Appellate Divisions of the First and Second Judicial Departments to examine juvenile detention facilities spoke of "conditions in the juvenile centers . . . so desperately in need of correction that no further delay can be tolerated." [24]

A more appalling and more contemporary example of the perniciousness of juvenile institutions was documented by the John Howard Association in 1974, at the Illinois Youth Centers at St. Charles and Geneva.[25] Practically every influence counterproductive to rehabilitation was en-

---

[23] Rosemary C. Sarri, "Under Lock and Key: Juveniles in Jails and Detention," National Assessment of Juvenile Corrections, The University of Michigan, December 1974, p. 5.

[24] Quoted in *Report of the Juvenile Detention Visitation Committee,* February 17, 1972, p. 1.

[25] John Howard Association, "Survey Report: Illinois Youth Centers at St. Charles and Geneva," October 1974.

countered at these institutions, including rampant homosexuality, extortion, vermin-infested living conditions, health and safety hazards, idleness, obsolete equipment, theft, and staff apathy and cruelty. One is compelled to admit that community-based programming would be infinitely preferable to "rehabilitation" in the type of institution which we have just described, and which, tragically, may not be an atypical juvenile institution in the United States.

LABELING

Another issue which has generated some controversy in the literature lately concerns the question of labeling, that is, the implication that calling a child a delinquent imposes a stigma, occasions a loss of self-esteem, and may actually contribute to the development of a delinquent self-image. The thinking is that to label a person is to place that person in a particular category. If an individual is labeled, he may be constrained to form an identification with those whose behavior patterns are associated with the category in which he has been officially placed. Delinquents, then, may be officially facilitated in developing responses consistent with the status of delinquency. The label reinforces the nonconforming role.[26] This is not an empirically settled proposition, but it forms a compelling argument for re-analysis of the negative aspects of the juvenile justice system.

Legal Aspects of Juvenile "Justice"

It was the fervent desire of the reformers to protect the child from the traumatic adversary proceedings which characterize the adult criminal courts. The welfare of the child was of paramount importance. And so it was that the rules of evidence, contentious attorneys, the public, and due process were swept from the chancery arena. It is rather odd that for more

[26] The following selective sources dealing with the issue of labeling may be consulted for further elaboration: Stanton Wheeler and Leonard S. Cottrell, "The Labeling Process," in Harwin L. Voss, ed., *Society, Delinquency and Delinquent Behavior* (Boston: Little, Brown and Company, 1970), pp. 208–11; William D. Payne, "Negative Labels: Passageways and Prisons," *Crime and Delinquency*, 19, no. 1 (January 1973), 33–40; Frederic L. Faust, "Delinquency Labeling: Its Consequences and Implications," *Crime and Delinquency*, 19, no. 1 (January 1973), 41–48; Erwin Schepses, "A Note on Labels," *Crime and Delinquency*, 11, no. 2 (April 1965), 162–66. In taking the contrary position, Schepses concludes his article by observing that "many well-educated, well-informed, and well-meaning persons will continue to call a thief a thief. It might be argued that this is as it should be" (p. 166).

than half a century nobody seemed unduly perturbed by the fact that constitutional guarantees, as they applied to juveniles, had been, in effect, suspended.

THE LEGAL RIGHTS OF MINORS

In medieval times the chancellor was delegated the responsibility, on behalf of the king, to watch over minors in the kingdom and to safeguard their rights. Known as "The Keeper of the King's Conscience," the chancellor was able to effect "estoppel" of proceedings against a child in the criminal courts and have them transferred to courts of equity. Proceedings in juvenile court are often referred to as chancery proceedings, a term that derives from chancellor.

The state subsequently replaced the king, but the fundamental idea that the ruling power should exercise guardianship over the miscreant child carried over to become the foundation of the philosophy of the juvenile court. Treatment was accented over prosecution, and the state arrogated to itself the role of parent surrogate. As parents tend to exercise absolute authority, so did the state. In both situations, the "good" of the child was the justifying rationale.

As with any absolute exercise of authority, abuses develop. With respect to the juvenile, these abuses developed under the guise of treatment. We learned in Chapter 2 of the many difficulties that face us when we attempt to define treatment, and we have learned that treatment cannot be arbitrarily imposed—it must be voluntarily engaged in. For all the high-flown rhetoric, the child in chancery is still a captive, albeit one benignly viewed. In some landmark cases which we shall shortly examine, we will discover the degree of power that had been exercised over the juvenile delinquent.

In the past, smoking was included in the definitions of delinquency in Arkansas and South Dakota. At least nine states included vile language in their definitions. Gradually the recognition came that all-enveloping concern for the juvenile amounted to an all-encompassing deprivation of rights. Juvenile delinquency, by definition, is not a crime. The civil disabilities that are imposed for adult criminality do not accrue to the adjudicated juvenile delinquent, yet the history of the "treatment" of delinquent children is a history of the usurpation of their rights. The ironic thing is that those rights have not been previously delineated in law. Even the Bill of Rights in the Constitution pertains only to adult rights. But beginning in 1966 with the momentous Kent decision, the courts have begun to recognize that children have rights too, and these rights have been increasingly articulated by the courts since that time.

LANDMARK CASES

In handing down its decision in the Kent case, the United States Supreme Court, in one cogent paragraph, encapsulated the deficiencies of the juvenile justice system:

> There is evidence, in fact, that there may be grounds for concern that the child receives the worst of both worlds; that he gets neither the protections accorded adults nor the solicitous care and regenerative treatment postulated for children.[27]

Morris A. Kent, Jr., sixteen years of age, had admited to District of Columbia police that he had committed housebreaking, rape, and robbery. The Juvenile Court waived its jurisdiction, and Kent was turned over to the District Court for criminal prosecution. This procedure is not exclusive to the District of Columbia, for twelve of the states have provisions for permitting the criminal courts to assume jurisdiction over a juvenile. Kent appealed on the premise that if his juvenile court file could be used to justify waiver of jurisdiction, then his attorney had a right of access to that file to challenge the validity of the waiver. The Supreme Court agreed. The issue was due process as well as the right to counsel, and precedent was set.

Perhaps the most influential decision was made in the Gault case, decided on May 15, 1967.[28] Gerald Francis Gault, at age fifteen, was committed to the Arizona State Industrial School "for the period of his minority," for allegedly making an obscene phone call. In the ensuing Supreme Court decision, Justice Fortas described the call as being "of the irritatingly offensive, adolescent sex variety." Gault was sentenced, literally, to a term of six years for an offense which, if committed by an adult, would result in a maximum of sixty days.

Gault was taken into custody without his parents being notified. His custody was secured on the basis of a complaint by a neighbor. The complainant never appeared in court. Although a petition was filed on June 9, 1964, with the juvenile court, the Gaults did not see it until they were present at subsequent habeas corpus proceedings on August 17, 1964. The actual petition gave no factual basis for the apprehension of Gault except to state that Gault was a minor and in need of the court's protection. No transcript was made of the hearing, and the Supreme Court had to rely on

---

[27] *Kent v. United States,* 383 U.S. 541 (1966).

[28] *In re Gault,* 387 U.S. 541 (1967).

records from the habeas corpus proceedings to ascertain the facts pertaining to the original hearing. There were, in addition, grounds for suspecting that Gerald was not responsible for the more serious of the obscene statements made, that dubious honor falling to a delinquent associate.

In a particularly biting denunciation of the Arizona judicial system, Justice Fortas condemned the persistent deprivation of due process that colored every step of the Gault case. The Gault decision supplemented the Kent decision, but also enlarged upon it. The juvenile court must now afford due process to all minors, which includes the safeguards heretofore restricted to the criminal courts.

THE CONTEMPORARY TREND IN JUDICIAL REFORM

In what might almost be called a wave of judicial reform in the juvenile justice system, a series of decisions have been handed down in various jurisdictions, all extending the protections of the juvenile in a constitutional context. In a District of Columbia case it was held that a juvenile had a right to treatment; the petitioner had contended that psychiatric assistance was not available at the Columbia Receiving Home for Children.[29] In a New York case the Supreme Court held that the preponderance of evidence rule that had traditionally been applied in juvenile proceedings must give way to the more rigorous reasonable doubt rule that prevails in criminal courts.[30] It was held in a Texas case that a child placed in custody has an absolute right to challenge the legality of his confinement.[31]

The prediction is that judicial reforms will continue. It is particularly important that they do so, above all to alleviate the pathetic plight of the legion of "status offenders."

Status Offenders

The term "status offender" is used in the juvenile justice system to mean a minor who has come under the jurisdiction of the juvenile court for an act that would not be considered criminal if it were committed by an adult. It is the *status* of being a juvenile that renders the child susceptible to arrest. This term covers a wide range of behavior. Some of the more common examples are running away from home, truancy, unmanage-

---

[29] *Creek v. Stone,* 379 F.2d 106 (D.C. Cir., 1967).

[30] *In re Winship,* 397 U.S. 358 (1970).

[31] *Morales v. Tuman,* 326 F. Supp. 677 (E.D. Texas, 1971).

ability, incorrigibility, disobedience, waywardness, ungovernability, and drinking alcoholic beverages. There are a great many more.

THE SCOPE OF THE PROBLEM

The number of status offenders in the system is enormous. Of the more than 1 million youngsters placed in secure detention in the system annually, about half are status offenders. The National Council on Crime and Delinquency estimates conservatively that "more than a third" of the 600,000 youngsters who are held in detention pending court action are status offenders. Of the 85,000 youngsters who are annually committed to correctional institutions, "23 percent of the boys and 70 percent of the girls were adjudicated status offenders." [32]

Some immediate inferences can be drawn from these statistical facts.

1. The juvenile justice system, specifically the juvenile court, is needlessly overworked.
2. An inordinate number of young people are being institutionalized and contaminated by a system for behavior that hardly merits this sort of reaction.
3. The family matrix is not being reintegrated, or assisted, by the wide-scale commitment of youthful offenders.
4. As a recent editorial pointed out, "The court can take authoritative action, but it cannot solve the problems." [33] The unspoken subtlety behind this statement is that *the juvenile court may actually be hindering a solution to juvenile delinquency,* which, of course, is counter to the purpose for which it was founded.
5. It is morally repugnant to treat troubled children in the same manner as it is to treat hard-core delinquents. Such an approach aggravates rather than ameliorates the problems of these children.

THE PRESENT PHILOSOPHY

Little can be found in the classical textbooks about this problem of status offenders, but lately considerable interest has been generating for remedial

---

[32] NCCD, "Jurisdiction over Status Offenses Should Be Removed from the Juvenile Court: A Policy Statement," *Crime and Delinquency,* 21, no. 2 (April 1975), 97. In April 1975 the National Council on Crime and Delinquency formally opened a drive to remove status offenses from juvenile codes in every state. See *Criminal Justice Newsletter,* 6, no. 8 (April 14, 1975), 6.

[33] Editorial Viewpoint, National Center for Youth Development, "Status Offenses, the Juvenile Court, and Community Responsibility," *Soundings,* 1, no. 2 (March–April 1974), 2.

action. The National Council on Crime and Delinquency (NCCD) has come out with a flat policy recommending the removal of status offenders from the jurisdiction of the juvenile court.[34] In November 1974, Governor Francis W. Sargent of Massachusetts signed a bill to terminate the practice of treating children as law-violators when those children "have unmet social, psychological, medical, or educational needs." These developments not only accent the need for community-based resolutions of children's problems, but they also point up the community's solemn responsibility to provide meaningful resources to meet the challenge.

CINS, FINS, JINS, MINS AND PINS

At this point the reader will feel that we have shifted into a study of Chinese linguistics, but we haven't left the generic area of our present concern. These are acronyms for concepts in juvenile justice. As knowledge grows and becomes more complex, overburdened minds turn to lettered symbols to make it easier to capture concepts.

These acronyms are related to status offenders in that they focus on the need for concerned supervision. PINS, meaning "persons in need of supervision," was first used in the New York Family Court Act of 1962 and is now generally applied to the status offender. Sometimes CINS, "children in need of supervision," MINS, "minors in need of supervision," and JINS, "juveniles in need of supervision" are substituted. The more recent term, FINS, "families in need of supervision," recognizes that the child cannot be assisted meaningfully in isolation from the family constellation. In 1975 Florida revised its juvenile code, eliminating the category of CINS and substituting a category of dependent children. Ostensibly this permits the court to place CINS in foster homes rather than just exempting them from juvenile court jurisdiction.[35]

Treatment Tactics

In the summer of 1974 a youth awaiting a detention hearing in Los Angeles County was homosexually attacked in the detention room, adjacent to the court. The presiding judge, who had just been assigned to take charge of the court facility, personally examined the detention rooms and the adjoining corridor, where as many as 60 young people wait for hours on end for their hearings. The judge described the facilities as a

---

[34] NCCD, "Jurisdiction over Status Offenders," p. 97.

[35] For a critical article, see David Gilman, "How to Retain Jurisdiction over Status Offenses: Change without Reform in Florida," *Crime and Delinquency*, 22, no. 1 (January 1976), 48–51.

disgrace, providing an atmosphere that embittered those waiting for adjudication. This is an index of the progress made in handling the juvenile delinquent, and it confirms the futility of our past efforts to cope with juvenile delinquency and points up the need to ponder alternatives.

It would take volumes to cover all of the imaginative and not so imaginative efforts that have been made to treat the disturbed and delinquent child. It sometimes appears as if the left hand doesn't know what the right hand is doing. The commodity is so precious, however, that the effort must be relentless. But it must be consistent and it must be systematized.

THE PRESENT STATE OF CONFUSION

It sometimes appears as if the in-fighting among the behavioral scientists will achieve only one thing: it will forever obscure a true understanding of the normal, disturbed child. We use the term "normal" because sociologists do not accept the contention that most juvenile delinquents are emotionally disturbed. They are children who have been blocked in their efforts to achieve satisfaction for legitimate needs, and have been diverted into channels of behavior considered unacceptable by society. There are, of course, some children who are pathologically disturbed, but the great majority do not fit this diagnosis.

In some instances, society's concept of "unacceptable" behavior is unrealistic in terms of the human growth cycle. Rebellion, for instance, is a normal part of growing up. It bears repeating over and over again that social conditions are the breeding grounds for most crime and delinquency, and those conditions must be made conducive to normal, healthy development if delinquency is ever to be curtailed.

Status offenses, particularly, reflect unwholesome conditions in the life of a child. Running away, for instance, certainly suggests a more pointed need for family counseling than for warehousing an unhappy child in a juvenile institution. Fortunately, a positive trend is developing to eliminate status offenders from the juvenile justice machinery.

There must be a palpable concern for our disadvantaged young people, whether the disadvantage comes from emotional blocking, economic deprivation, family pathology, or racial discrimination. One suggestion calls for the creation of a youth services bureau.

THE YOUTH SERVICE BUREAU

The concept of a youth service bureau was first forcefully articulated by the President's Crime Commission, when it specifically recommended that public and private efforts be intensified to establish youth service bureaus. The commission felt that:

> Agencies should be established that provide easily accessible information, guidance, and service for youth. These agencies should refer young people to remedial education or job training or recreation or other similar programs as appears appropriate in the given case.[35]

In succeeding years, the idea caught on and youth service agencies have proliferated throughout the country. But the growth has been unregulated and marred by conflict over definition and function.

THE CONFLICT OVER DEFINITION

In several successive issues of its newsletter, the National Center for Youth Development deplored the lack of a concisely delineated definition of a youth service bureau, but in October 1973 its parent organization, the National Council on Crime and Delinquency, offered one. It defined the youth service bureau as

> a noncoercive, independent public agency established to divert children and youth from the justice system by (1) mobilizing community resources to solve youth problems, (2) strengthening existing youth resources and developing new ones, and (3) promoting positive programs to remedy delinquency-breeding conditions."[36]

If the definitions of the President's Crime Commission and the NCCD are compared, the seed of the conflict may be detected. The controversy is over whether the youth service bureau should be an intervention agency, providing remedial services for individuals, or an agency committed to amelioration of the social conditions which breed delinquency, therefore a preventive agency.

The National Advisory Commission has stated that youth service bureaus "have provided some of the most successful examples of the effective deliveries of social services within the framework of a social service delivery system."[37] The California Youth Authority considers its youth service bureaus as models of "a pioneer example of a service

---

[35] President's Commission on Law Enforcement and Administration of Justice, *The Challenge of Crime in a Free Society* (Washington, D.C.: U.S. Government Printing Office, 1967), p. 68.

[36] Frederick W. Howlett, "Is the YSB All It's Cracked Up to Be?" *Crime and Delinquency,* 19, no. 4 (October 1973), 487.

[37] National Advisory Commission on Criminal Justice Standards and Goals, *Task Force Report: Community Crime Prevention* (Washington, D.C.: U.S. Government Printing Office, 1973), p. 51.

delivery component of a comprehensive youth services delivery system."[38] After one picks his way through the bureaucratic jargon of "service delivery component" and "services delivery system," the dilemma remains: Should the role of the youth services bureau be one of direct remedial assistance, or should it focus on correcting pathological social conditions and preventing delinquency on a wider scale?

It is our position that the definition of the NCCD is superior to that of the President's Crime Commission, although they are not mutually exclusive. Direct services to youth in the community, before they become enmeshed in the justice system, are highly desirable. But the crying need is for remediation of social conditions which thwart a youth's full participation as a member of his community, and which seed delinquency. *The youth service bureau must be preeminently a preventive agency that mobilizes community resources to divert the young from the juvenile justice system.*

Because the contaminating influence of the "system" reinforces delinquent identification, it is even more important that youth be involved in community-based efforts at correction. Some notable happenings have recently occurred.[39]

THE NCCD PROJECT

In July 1973 the National Council on Crime and Delinquency initiated a new program whose basic goal is "to promote the design, development, and testing of more effective methods for the prevention, control and reduction of juvenile delinquency."[40] Originally established in Tucson, Arizona, but relocated in New Jersey in 1976, the National Center for Youth Development is committed to collaboration with professionals, professional organizations, communities, and governmental entities, in pursuit of its goals. It will stress social planning and the pursuit of nontraditional methods of coping with delinquency. It is philosophically committed to community-based corrections, and it should become the leading center for progressive research in juvenile corrections.

---

[38] *Ibid.*

[39] A good source for an overview of many projects and models is: U.S. Department of Health, Education, and Welfare, Youth Development and Delinquency Prevention Administration, "Youth Involvement" (Washington, D.C.: U.S. Government Printing Office, 1970). See also *Crime and Delinquency Literature,* 6, no. 3 (September 1974) for additional material on Juvenile Offender Community Treatment Programs.

[40] National Center for Youth Development, *Soundings,* 1, no. 1 (January–February 1974), 1.

NATIONAL ASSESSMENT OF JUVENILE CORRECTIONS

In 1974 a project of gargantuan ambition was instituted by the University of Michigan, known as the National Assessment of Juvenile Corrections. The project directors have stated that the primary goal of this research plan is to establish *"objective, empirical bases for assessing the relative effectiveness of alternative correctional programs for differing types of juvenile offenders across the nation."* [41] Such a comprehensive assessment is long overdue, and it is hoped that the results of the research not only will match the majesty of the undertaking, but will also provide some concrete directions for future treatment of the juvenile offender.

PEER CULTURE AND YOUTH INVOLVEMENT

It has long been known by behavioral scientists that peer pressures are the most influential among adolescents. This means that teenagers are more responsive to the standards and feelings set by their peers than perhaps any other age grouping.

The concept of Positive Peer Culture (PPC) as a therapeutic device originated in the late 1950s in the much discussed residential treatment program for delinquent youth at Highfields, New Jersey. Highfields was one of the earliest major innovations in treatment of juveniles. The program was based on minimum security, an absence of authoritarian leadership, short-term residency, and a normal life milieu. A peer-oriented treatment model, known as Guided Group Interaction, was introduced. This model was eventually developed into Positive Peer Culture by one of the original Highfields staff, Harry H. Vorrath.

Positive Peer Culture "is designed to 'turn around' a negative youth subculture and mobilize the power of the peer group in a productive manner." [42] It recognizes the therapeutic power in the collectivity of young people, and the greater power that is generated by caring for one another. PPC has particular importance in that it directly involves youths in the redirection of their own productive energies. A major criticism of juvenile corrections is that it has dealt with youth en masse and coercively imprinted the language of treatment upon them. Youth

---

[41] Rosemary C. Sarri and David P. Street, National Assessment of Juvenile Corrections, *Summary of Research Plan,* The University of Michigan, Ann Arbor, Michigan, undated, p. 3.

[42] Harry H. Vorrath and Larry K. Brendtro, *Positive Peer Culture* (Chicago: Aldine Publishing Company, 1974), p. 3.

A peer pressure group at a PORT facility. These group sessions permit the youths to ventilate hostility, to confront negative behavior, and to reinforce constructive behavioral changes. "Growth groups" are also employed. They differ from peer pressure groups in being composed mainly of the more mature, positively oriented residents.

was not expected to have competence to participate in full measure in society, let alone in arriving at solutions to its own developmental problems.

THE YOUTH AUTHORITY COMMUNITY TREATMENT PROJECT

In 1961 the California Youth Authority commenced a Community Treatment Project (CTP), consisting of three phases, which ran through 1974 in its experimental design.[43] The objective was to discover if certain selected wards could be allowed to remain in their own communities with intensive supervision, in small caseloads, in lieu of traditional institutionalization. The wards were classified on an Interpersonal Maturity Scale devised by Sullivan, Grant, and Grant. For each subtype determined by this classification, a particular "treatment-control strategy" was devised. Thus we have the combination of individualized treatment in a community-based setting.

The CTP approach proved satisfyingly successful, both rehabilitatively

[43] California Youth Authority, *A Review of Accumulated Research in the California Youth Authority,* Sacramento, California, May 1974.

and economically. The experimental (CTP) group experienced a favorable difference of 65 percent in arrest rates, a 19 percent reduction in recidivism rates, and an average cost savings of $1,446 per ward per year.[44]

COMMUNITY-BASED TREATMENT IN MASSACHUSETTS

There is talk and there is action. In 1972 Massachusetts acted. Having had considerable failure in its past programs to rehabilitate its delinquent juveniles, and having "inherited the grim legacy of over a century of more or less ill-conceived social and moral reform aimed at rehabilitating 'wicked' children by incarcerating them,"[45] the Department of Youth Services ordered the closure of its juvenile institutions by April 1973. Group homes, foster homes, and other community resources are being substituted in this momentous shift to community-based treatment.

What is especially important is that Massachusetts made its move on the basis of realism. The majority of the delinquents are from disadvantaged backgrounds, in which economic deprivation is prevalent. Institutionalizing victims of disadvantage and deprivation is an unreasonable approach to these problems, according to the Massachusetts philosophy. The Massachusetts Department of Youth Services has, in fact, declared that its "strategy for de-institutionalization is based on some simple and realizable goals and not on some fanciful notions of reform, based on techniques which social science has not yet invented. The strategy is to ameliorate existing conditions in the most humane ways possible at the most economical level of financial cost. . . ."[46]

The reaction to the Massachusetts experiment has been mixed among professionals in corrections, and it has caused intense controversy. Some critics are asserting that the number of juveniles in the Massachusetts system has almost doubled as a result of diversion. Others contend that more needs are being rationally and humanely met. The jury is still out.[47]

These are some of the contemporary trends. There is renewed interest in the plight of the youngsters in the criminal justice system, but more than that, there is renewed creativity in diversionary approaches to the problem. In Maryland, for example, a Community Arbitration Program

---

44 *Ibid.*, pp. 55, 56.

45 The Commonwealth of Massachusetts, Department of Youth Services, "A Strategy for Youth in Trouble," February 25, 1972.

46 *Ibid.*

47 For an excellent analysis of the present state of affairs see *Corrections Magazine*, 11, no. 2 (November–December 1975).

attempts to screen lesser offenders from the juvenile justice system through the use of citations instead of arrest, and work assignments to community agencies. Since the program's inception in June 1974, only 2.9 percent of the juvenile cases handled were referred to intake or probation.

Petitions were filed in only 3.7 percent of the youths processed through a model program in Sacramento, California, which accents family counseling by specially-trained probation officers. There is a relentless need to prevent the disadvantaged and economically deprived from processing into the juvenile justice system. The disadvantaged and economically deprived and delinquent child is saying the same thing that Archimedes said, if in a different context: "Give me a place to stand, and I will move the world." Fortunately, that cry is reaching more ears than ever before.

Review Questions

1. Why do juveniles have a special status in the criminal justice system?
2. What is your definition of (a) a juvenile delinquent, (b) juvenile delinquency?
3. If you were required to construct a statistical profile of juvenile delinquency, what basic data would you include in that profile?
4. Give the history and origin of the juvenile court and critique the juvenile court as it presently operates.
5. You are a member of a debate team. The topic of the debate is Resolved: That Juveniles Should Be Diverted from the Juvenile Justice System. You are on the affirmative side. What reasons would you put forth to sustain your position?
6. What were the facts in the landmark Kent decision, and what legal principles were involved?
7. What were the facts and the points of law raised in the Gault decision?
8. What are "status offenders"?
9. Describe the Youth Service Bureau as it was envisioned by the President's Crime Commission.
10. Select one of the treatment programs described in this chapter, outline its major traits, and evaluate the program.

9

THE HISTORICAL EVOLUTION OF PROBATION

My punishment is greater than I can bear.

Genesis

It is the fate of many a poet that despite the number of his great works, he is remembered only by a line or two from one of his poems. The Cavalier poet, Sir Richard Lovelace, seems to have suffered this fate. Few are conscious of the intricate and balanced art which he wove into such poems as *The Scrutiny*, but everyone remembers the deceitful lines;

Stone walls do not a prison make,
Nor iron bars a cage.

Despite being born into wealthy circumstances, the son of a gentleman knighted by James I, Sir Richard died an impoverished tubercular at the age of forty. Before he died, he had twice served jail terms, the result of making unpopular political choices. As a romanticist, he could employ poetic license and pretend that a maiden's memory had the power to make prison palatable. But in reality, even Sir Richard Lovelace was aware of the fact that stone walls do, indeed, make a prison, and iron bars a cage.

The Changing Climate

The prison, as we have learned, developed as a counteraction to the severe corporal punishment that was prevalent, and it was intended to facilitate rehabilitation through introspective contemplation of one's misdeeds. So much for theory. We know that as the penitentiary developed, its founding philosophy evaporated, because convicts do not readily turn to remorseful introspection, and because the physical plant of the penitentiary is not conducive to human regeneration. On the contrary, it tends to degenerate both inmate and staff.

OPPOSING THRUSTS

Though the Auburn and Pennsylvania prison systems are credited with being the genesis of the penitentiary in the United States, it was a better known institution that actually became the architectural model for the fortress prison that dominated corrections in this country for more than a century. It was at Sing Sing, opened in 1828, and fabled in legend and film, that the huge, multi-tiered inside cell blocks were built. Their long, dark corridors were to be described as "the curse of prison construction for the following century." [1]

While this "curse" was still in its infancy, in 1841, the nucleus of probation was being planted in bordering Massachusetts. The following century could probably be described as the ambivalent period in American corrections. The penitentiary was destined to proliferate in this period and to become more fortresslike. It might be said that this particular phase culminated in 1926 with the opening of the world's largest prison at Jackson, Michigan, the epitome of maximum security.

THE IMPORTANT CHANGES

But at the same time, changes were gradually taking place in man's social attitudes, in legal theory, in correctional developments, and in the philosophy of rehabilitation. These changes made probation possible. Among the more important, the following could be mentioned:

---

[1] United States Bureau of Prisons, *Handbook of Correctional Institution Design and Construction*, 1949, p. 32.

1. Acceptance of the fact that a penalty other than death could be substituted for the more serious criminal acts.

2. The recognition that there are mitigants and individual factors, such as mental and chronological incompetence, that alter criminal circumstances.

3. The adoption of a reformative philosophy.

4. The adoption of diversionary tactics in sentencing.

5. The growth of the social sciences in gaining knowledge that could lead to the classification of offenders.

6. The development of the doctrine of man's universal equality, reinforced by legal developments and consequent legal protections.

In addition to these, certain concrete events are generally conceded to be the collective forerunners of probation.

The Forerunners of Probation

Probation is basically rooted in the ancient common law of England, and in attempts to mitigate the severe penalties imposed for criminal acts. The history of punishment is one of relentless brutality, interspersed with efforts to moderate the severity of penal sanctions. Probation does not represent the automatic end result of a smooth, consistent evolution toward humane treatment of the offender. We know this from the fact that the earlier part of the nineteenth century, which saw the birth of probation, was also one of the most brutal periods in terms of severe penal sanctions. Probation was more the inevitable offspring of a series of developments, the more important of which we shall now review.

BENEFIT OF CLERGY

It is rather commonly accepted by scholars in the field that the earliest "probation device" was a practice known as "benefit of clergy." Although the origin of this practice is unknown, it dates from the thirteenth century. The Church, of course, was the dominant influence in medieval Europe, but secular kings gradually attempted to usurp its powers. Upon Henry II's insistence that the clergy be subject to the civil courts rather than to the ecclesiastical courts, the compromise known as benefit of clergy developed.

Punishments imposed by the bishop on errant clergy were less severe than those of the civil officials, and several authorities feel that benefit of clergy was fundamentally a move to mitigate the extreme penalties in vogue, especially capital punishment. Benefit of clergy simply meant that clergymen who ran afoul of the law could, on appeal, have their cases transferred to ecclesiastical courts for disposition. The immediate advantage of claiming benefit of clergy was the prospect of less severe punishments. Originally, benefit of clergy applied only to capital offenses, but these were so numerous that to all intents and purposes it constituted exemption from secular jurisdiction. Until 1706 this privilege could be claimed only once. Wines records that individuals who had "taken" benefit of clergy were then "burned on the brawn of the thumb with the initial of the offence with which they were charged" to prevent their claiming the privilege twice.[2]

By the middle of the fourteenth century, benefit of clergy had been extended to lay people who could prove their literacy. As a test of literacy, the suspect was required to recite a passage from the psalm, *Miserere mei.* In time, illiterates began to memorize the required verse, and the practice ultimately fell into disuse. It endured for some time, however, and was not finally abolished in England until 1841.

One noted writer in the field feels that it is "a bit far-fetched" to consider benefit of clergy as a forerunner of probation.[3] Most writers, however, see in benefit of clergy the beginnings of mitigation of severe punishment which is epitomized in probation.

JUDICIAL REPRIEVE

A basic ingredient of probation is the suspension of the execution of a sentence. Judicial reprieve, also deriving from the Middle Ages, was the temporary suspension of a sentence to enable the culprit to appeal directly to the Crown for clemency. Pending a response to his appeal, the defendant was usually permitted to be at liberty. Because of this, judicial reprieve is considered to be the precedent for the suspended sentence, an integral part of probation. Judicial reprieve, it must be understood, was a *temporary* suspension, whereas probation involves the *indefinite* suspension of a sentence.

---

[2] Frederick Howard Wines, *Punishment and Reformation* (New York: Thomas Y. Crowell Company, 1910), p. 76.

[3] David Dressler, *Practice and Theory of Probation and Parole,* 2d ed. (New York: Columbia University Press, 1969), p. 16.

RECOGNIZANCE

Most people today are familiar with the concept of releasing a defendant, pending further adjudication, on his honor to return for those proceedings. Technically the person is released on his own recognizance. Popularly he is OR'd. Recognizance has a long tradition in English law but the origin of this practice differed from what it eventually developed into. Recognizance originally was not a device for permitting pre-adjudication liberty, but rather a method of preventive justice, that is, it imposed an obligation on a person to refrain from future misbehavior.

Recognizance was for a specified period of time, and the individual entered into a bond, sometimes with a surety, as a public assurance that he would not engage in stipulated misbehavior. While surety is not ordinarily a part of modern probation, it is interesting to note that this vestigial practice is incorporated in probation proceedings in Ireland. The reference to surety is clearly observable in the Dublin Metropolitan District Court probation order. See Fig. 9–1.

A breach of the recognizance entitled the state to forfeit the bond or impose a sentence. Eventually recognizance became less a mechanism of preventive justice and predominantly a device in criminal proceedings to assure the future appearance of a defendant.

Recognizance was employed by the courts of England for hundreds of years, and in the early nineteenth century it began to be applied in youthful offender proceedings. In the United States the first recorded use of recognizance occurred in 1830 in the case of *Commonwealth v. Chase*, when Judge Oxenbridge Thacher of the Boston Municipal Court, emphasizing the preventive justice nature of recognizance, permitted a young woman to be released with the stipulation that no further violation of law take place. In 1836 Massachusetts, by statute, "gave legislative recognition to the practice of release upon recognizance, *with sureties*, at any stage of the proceedings, insofar as it applied to petty offenders in the lower courts." [4]

Recognizance is considered to be a forerunner of probation because of the obvious characteristics they share. These include the suspension of sentence, diversion from incarceration, and the possibility of revoking that freedom for failure to comply with the conditions of recognizance.

---

[4] Charles L. Newman, *Sourcebook on Probation, Parole and Pardons*, 3d ed. (Springfield, Ill.: Charles C Thomas, Publisher, 1968), p. 12.

AN CHÚIRT DÚICHE

THE DISTRICT COURT

DUBLIN METROPOLITAN DISTRICT

BEFORE the Court of Summary Jurisdiction sitting at the Metropolitan District Court, Inns Quay, in said District on the day of 19 ,

of

age years (hereinafter called the defendant) is charged for that he on the day of 19 , at

in said District did

contrary to the Statute in that case made and provided,

the Court thinks that the charge is proved, but is of opinion that, having regard to*

*Strike out the alternatives which are not applicable.

the character, antecedents, age and health of the Defendant,

and the trivial nature of the offence,

and the extenuating circumstances under which the offence was committed

it is expedient to release the Defendant on probation :

It is therefore ordered that the Defendant be discharged conditionally on entering into a recognizance in the sum of pounds, *with one surety in the sum of pounds,* to be of good behaviour, and to appear for conviction and sentence when called on at any time during the period of months now next ensuing, and subject to the further conditions that (*a*) (i) be under the supervision of

of

(hereinafter called the probation officer), and for the purpose of securing such supervision, that the Defendant receive at own home visits from the said probation officer weekly, or at such other intervals as the probation officer may think fit ; and, if so required by the probation officer, attend at probation officer's home for the purpose of such visits at times fixed by the probation officer, and answer truly all questions put to by the probation officer with regard to conduct, employment, or residence; and

(ii) report forthwith to the probation officer any change of residence or place of employment ;

(*b*) do not associate with thieves and other undesirable persons ;

(*c*) do not frequent undesirable places ;

(*d*) do lead an honest and industrious life.

†Insert order for compensation, if any.

And it is further ordered that the Defendant†

Given under my hand at the Court aforesaid the day and year first above-mentioned.

One of the Justices of said District Court assigned to said District.

(1871).3389--1/55.2,000--L.-P.P.LTD.

Fig. 9–1. Irish District Court Probation Order.

BAIL

Bail and recognizance are closely related, yet distinctly different. We have noted that recognizance was sometimes granted with a surety. Bail is a surety, that is, something pledged, usually money, which is subject to forfeiture in the event that the defendant fails to appear for his scheduled hearing. The intent in recognizance is to temper the proceedings, whereas with bail the emphasis is on assuring the defendant's appearance.

At common law, the bailed person was placed in the custody of the bailor. The common law bailor, like the bailor of today, had a vested interest in the bailed person, for it was the former who guaranteed the fidelity of the bailed person, and it was he whose bailment was subject to forfeiture. As a consequence, the bailor often exercised a degree of supervision over his "client." Bail, therefore, comes closer to the concept of probation, for here we have suspension of action, the prospect of revocation, conditional freedom, and supervision.

FILING OF CASES

An unusual development, indigenous to nineteenth-century Massachusetts, was the practice known as "filing of cases." It took place only after a guilty verdict. This was a provisional action utilized when the court felt that mitigating or extenuating circumstances warranted suspending sentence. It was also used to place a judgment of a lower court in abeyance pending decisions by appellate courts in similar cases. Filing of a case had to be concurred in by both prosecution and defense, and the judge had the discretion to impose such conditions as he sought fit on the defendant.

Filing of a case did not constitute terminal disposition, because the judge had the authority to take further action on the case at the request of the prosecutor or defense attorney. But, in effect, it was a terminal judgment in those cases in which no further action took place and the suspension continued indefinitely. The primary objective of "filing" was to minimize the penalties ordinarily imposed. Again we have suspension, conditional freedom, prospective reimposition of original sentence, and conditions, all of which reflect the relationship to probation.

These were among the more important of the ancestors of probation as we know it today. There were also some important pioneers, as well as some significant developments in statute and case law, and these we will discuss in the following sections.

Pioneers in Probation

In one of those unusual quirks of history, two individuals, in separate continents, simultaneously introduced a concept without being personally acquainted with one another. The year was 1841. The concept was probation.

MATTHEW DAVENPORT HILL

Matthew Davenport Hill was a young English barrister (trial attorney) who had been impressed with an experiment which he had observed in Warwickshire Quarter Sessions in the 1820s. The presiding magistrates had adopted the practice of imposing token one-day jail sentences on youthful offenders, and then placing them under the care of parents or "masters." The impression remained with Hill until he arrived at a station in life that permitted him to introduce his own revolutionary version.

A "radical," Hill was involved in a number of social causes and significant legal cases of the day. One of the more memorable occurred when he acted as counsel for "The Great Emancipator," Daniel O'Connell. O'Connell, a distinguished Irish statesman, one time Lord Mayor of Dublin, and Member of Parliament, had been convicted of "seditious conspiracy" in 1844, following a mass protest against the unwelcome English invader. Hill was O'Connell's counsel of record in the successful appeal from the Court of the Queen's Bench to the House of Lords.

Hill himself had been a Member of Parliament, and in 1839 he was appointed recorder (magistrate) of the city of Birmingham. In that capacity, in 1841, he instituted the practice of *completely* suspending the sentence of youthful offenders, placing the defendants under the supervision of approved parents or guardians. Hill was an early believer in the priority of rehabilitation over punitive punishment. He requested the superintendent of police to make discreet, periodic inquiries to see if "probationed" youths were behaving themselves, but no provision existed for revocation of the privilege in the event of continued misconduct. Hill did, however, take this misconduct into consideration in the event that the defendant appeared again in his court. Probation had almost come of age.

JOHN AUGUSTUS

The man who has been called "The Father of Probation" in the United States, John Augustus, was a Boston bootmaker. At the relatively late age of fifty-seven, he became interested in court proceedings and began to attend the local magistrate's court as a volunteer. In 1841 he petitioned the court to release a defendant on bail to him. The man was charged with drunkenness. The court acquiesced, but ordered the defendant to return to court in three weeks for sentencing. When the man returned to court, he presented such a picture of reformation that the court refrained from committing him to a House of Corrections, as would normally be the case, and, instead, fined him one cent and $3.76 in costs.

This was the beginning of a long new life of dedicated service for John Augustus. Encouraged by his first "success," the Boston shoemaker devoted eighteen years to his probation work. Probation comes from the Latin root, *probatio*, and means approval or testing. John Augustus was the first person to employ the term "probation," which occurs in his writings describing his first case.

Before his death in 1859, John Augustus had helped 1,496 individuals who were "bailed on probation." He gave additional assistance to thousands of neglected and homeless females. Although his early efforts were with male misdemeanants, he eventually widened his scope and worked with youth and adults, male and female, minor and serious offenders. Some of the probationers were taken to his home to live. For others he secured residence elsewhere. He also obtained employment for a large number of his wards, and fed and clothed countless numbers. This remarkable man is said to have had only one failure among the first 1,100 on whom he kept records.[5]

Besides being a very compassionate and humane individual, Augustus was also a careful and discerning man. He scrupulously screened the individuals whom he sought to help. This is an important point, not only because it is an insight into the personality of John Augustus, but also because it completes the ingredients necessary for probation.

While contemporary probation may have added some sophistication, it has not veered from the original recipe of John Augustus: suspension of sentence, conditional liberty, supervision with conditions, revocation for breach of conditions, and careful screening of candidates for the service. In time, public officials will stand in the shadow of the private volunteer,

[5] Dressler, *Practice and Theory,* p. 27.

John Augustus, to administer the probation service, but they will have to strive diligently to surpass his compassionate concern, or to improve upon his founding concept.

Relevant Legislation and Case Law

Every state, the federal government, and the District of Columbia currently have probation statutes, but it was more than a century after the pioneering work of Augustus that the last state codified probation for adults. By 1925 every state had probation provisions for juveniles. Before the final state extended probation to adults, probation had spread to many European and South American countries. Writing as early as 1938, Tannenbaum described the rapid expansion of "an essentially American invention" as a tribute to "the usefulness and vitality of this new method of criminal treatment." [6] But that was still almost twenty years before probation had been universally legislated in the United States.

LEGISLATION IN MASSACHUSETTS

It was fitting that the state that gave birth to probation was also the first state to pass probation legislation. That took place in 1878, when a law was passed requiring the appointment of a probation officer for the city of Boston. The appointment was to be made annually by the mayor of Boston from the ranks of the citizenry or from the police force. Captain E.H. Savage, a former police chief, is generally credited with being the first statutorily appointed probation officer, although Dressler intimates that credit should go to Lieutenant Henry C. Hemmenway who preceded Savage but served for only four months.[7]

Two years later, in 1880, *permissive* legislation was passed, allowing for the appointment of probation officers in all the cities and towns of Massachusetts. It wasn't until 1891, however, that the law mandated the appointment of probation officers for the criminal courts. In 1898 this mandate was extended to the superior courts. From 1900 through 1929 there was a fivefold growth in the granting of probation in Massachusetts. In 1900 a total of 6,201 individuals were granted probation. By 1929 this figure had risen to 32,809.[8]

---

[6] Frank Tannenbaum, *Crime and the Community* (Boston: Ginn and Company, 1938), p. 460.

[7] Dressler, *Practice and Theory,* p. 28.

[8] Tannenbaum, *Crime and the Community,* p. 469.

LEGISLATION IN OTHER STATES

In 1897 the state of Missouri passed a law which made it possible to suspend the sentences of youthful and petty offenders, although the law contained no provision for actual probation supervision. In the following year, 1898, when Massachusetts was extending the assignment of probation staff to cover the superior courts, Vermont introduced a county-based probation system. Rhode Island followed with a state system in 1899. This was a key year.

The reason this was a key year was that in 1899 the first juvenile court was established, in Cook County (Chicago), and the development of the juvenile court necessarily stimulated the spread of probation legislation. Most probation laws were passed after 1900. By 1915, thirty-three states had some form of probation,[9] and by 1956 every state was so endowed.[10]

THE FORSYTH CASE

Before probation earned legitimate status in the laws of this land, it faced an early challenge on the basis of a subtle principle of jurisprudence. From our earlier review of the evolution of probation, we discovered that many subterfuges were employed to abate the severity of the law and to thwart the imposition of harsh sentences. It became an English common law tradition that the courts had the inherent power to temporarily suspend sentences. The common law of England is, of course, the foundation upon which our own law has been built.

In the United States, however, a tradition began to develop that the courts had the inherent right to *indefinitely* suspend sentences. But there were many legal minds that did not subscribe to this view. Their position was that the court had an obligation to impose whatever sentence the law called for, and to suspend that sentence was, in fact, to subvert the law and the function of the courts.

It is generally conceded that the precedent for suspending a sentence in the United States was established in the Forsyth case.[11] This was the case of a young man, with no prior record, of good character, and an

---

[9] Sol Rubin, *The Law of Criminal Correction* (St. Paul: West Publishing Co., 1973), p. 33.

[10] President's Commission on Law Enforcement and Administration of Justice, *Task Force Report: Corrections* (Washington, D.C.: U.S. Government Printing Office, 1967), p. 27.

[11] *People ex rel. Forsyth v. Court of Sessions,* 141 N.Y. 288, 36, N.E. 386 (1894).

offense containing many mitigants. The judge opted to suspend the sentence, as provided by statute. The district attorney appealed, but the appellate court upheld the verdict of the trial court. This case in itself was not necessarily a landmark decision, but it provides the backdrop against which a much more important case was decided. The issue, remember, is whether or not the court has the right to suspend sentences.

THE KILLITS DECISION

A strong supporter of the view that the court had no right to suspend sentences was U.S. Attorney General T.W. Gregory. In the Killits decision he saw an opportunity to test his premise. John M. Killits was the presiding judge in the trial of an embezzler in the Federal District Court of Ohio. The defendant had a good background and, indeed, repaid all the money that he had embezzled. His employers at the victimized bank did not wish to press charges. In light of these facts, Judge Killits imposed a suspended five-year sentence.

Gregory thereupon went into Judge Killits' court with a motion to have the judgment vacated, on the grounds that the court had exceeded its proper authority. Judge Killits overruled the motion, and the case was on its way to the United States Supreme Court. In a memorable decision, the United States Supreme Court, citing the need to safeguard the Constitution of the United States, unanimously sustained the position of the Attorney General.[12] In the decision, which was handed down on December 4, 1916, the Supreme Court held that it was not within the competence of federal courts to suspend sentences. Ironically, federal probation was authorized by law in 1925, nine years after this historic decision.

It should also be noted that this decision did not affect recognizance. The question at issue was the court's capacity "to permanently decline to enforce the law." At first blush, the negative decision of the highest court in the land would appear to have signaled the death of probation, for without the suspended sentence, probation is, to say the least, an improbability. On the contrary, as evidenced by the fact that all states now have probation laws, the decision actually hastened the passage of enabling legislation. This decision, remember, had relevance only for the federal courts. It did not directly affect the state courts, except to spur legislation that would settle in codified law the conflicting issue of the suspended sentence.

---

[12] *Ex parte United States,* 242 U.S. 27–53 (1916).

The Development of Probation as a System

While the genesis of probation can be traced to the many influences which we have discussed, systematic probation was, in the words of Newman, "America's distinctive contribution to progressive penology."[13] Taking issue with those who lay great stress on the common law origins of probation, among whom is the distinguished American legal scholar Dean Roscoe Pound, Newman contends that where it has been a matter of planned state policy, the development of probation has been a purely statutory development. Without demeaning the contribution of English common law, it can be acknowledged that modern probation was systematically developed by statutory intent.

Newman makes another point that merits consideration. He maintains that the European philosophy of criminal law was based on "reverence for precedent," that is, it leaned more on tradition because European nations such as England had centuries of stable tradition. In America, on the contrary, tradition was not held sacred, and it was more readily challenged. Policy in the United States has been basically utilitarian, even with respect to the criminal justice system. "And probation is nothing if not utilitarian."[14]

In any event, probation was refined and systematically developed in this country, and it can be truly said that it was "America's distinctive contribution." Perhaps it was a necessary expiation for our other distinctive contribution—the penitentiary.

Review Questions

1. What were some of the broader, historical changes that made probation possible?
2. Why is judicial reprieve given importance in terms of its relationship to probation?
3. Give the definition, origin, and history of the practice known as benefit of clergy.
4. Differentiate between recognizance and bail.
5. Describe the unusual practice of "filing of cases" and point out its relationship to probation.

---

[13] Newman, *Sourcebook on Probation*, p. 12.
[14] *Ibid.*, pp. 12–16.

6. Give a brief biography of Matthew Davenport Hill.
7. Give a brief biography of John Augustus.
8. What were the *legal* origins of probation in the United States?
9. The Killits decision led to a very interesting legal finding concerning the suspended sentence. Describe the series of events leading from the Killits decision to the decision handed down by the United States Supreme Court.
10. Why does Newman call systematic probation "America's distinctive contribution to progressive penology"?

10

CONTEMPORARY PROBATION

Neither heavenly nor earthly, neither mortal nor immortal have we created thee, so that thou mightest be free . . . to be thy own creator and builder.

Pico della Mirandola, *Oratio de Hominis Dignitate*

Probation is the most extensive form of community-based corrections. There are well over one million individuals under probation supervision in the United States, and over half of all offenders sentenced to "correctional treatment" are placed on probation. At this point, we will review the contemporary state of the heritage that was passed on to us by John Augustus. It is a very important heritage. The National Advisory Commission, in its survey of corrections, predicted that probation "will become the standard sentence in criminal cases." [1]

The Essence of Probation

From our review of the historical evolution of probation we have discovered the basic elements of this correctional process. The student should

[1] National Advisory Commission on Criminal Justice Standards and Goals, *Executive Summary* (Washington, D.C.: U.S. Government Printing Office, 1973), p. 50.

now be able to compose a suitable definition of probation. Let us recapitulate at this point.

PROBATION DEFINED

A definition, to serve its purpose, must contain the essential ingredients of what is being defined. The following are the essential ingredients of probation:

1. *A suspension of sentence,* resulting in
2. *Conditional liberty,* under
3. *Professional supervision,* subject to
4. *Imposed conditions,* with a provision for
5. *Revocation* for serious breach of the conditions.

From these ingredients, the following definition can be constructed: Probation is a correctional disposition in which the court suspends the imposition of sentence, and releases the defendant on conditional liberty to supervision by an agency of government which has the power to revoke that privilege in the event of a serious violation of the imposed conditions. This might be termed a *process* definition. As the *Manual of Correctional Standards* properly points out, probation "may be defined as a sentence, as an organization, or as a process." [2]

PROBATION THEORY

Probation is founded on the theory that an opportunity for reconstruction takes precedence over automatic punishment *in certain selected cases.* Individuals with minimal criminal histories are better candidates than those with extensive criminal backgrounds, but in reality, as the National Advisory Commission insisted, the great majority of defendants should be eligible for probation. The critical factor is the public attitude. For instance, on the basis of recidivism data for murderers (less than 0.2 percent recidivate), murderers would be excellent candidates for probation, but the seriousness of the offense ordinarily causes the public to demand a different disposition.

It has been determined that the earlier a youngster is involved in delinquency the more likely he will be to get into criminal difficulties as

---

[2] *Manual of Correctional Standards* (College Park, Md.: American Correctional Association, 1971), p. 98.

an adult.[3] But these *actuarial* statistics should not foreclose on *individual* redemption. The truth is that no one can predict the moment at which regeneration may commence, nor identify those specific, positive influences which will be effective in some individual case *in the future.* Selection for probation is, therefore, obviously a critical component in any soundly administered probation system.

Probation is also based on the theory that it is sound public policy to divert large numbers of offenders from the contaminating influence of the institutional side of the criminal justice system. The American Bar Association describes it as "an affirmative correctional tool, a tool which is used not because it is of maximum benefit to the defendant (though, of course, this is an important side product), but because it is of maximum benefit to the society which is sought to be served by the sentencing of criminals." [4]

Probation, like other forms of social work, is known as a "helping process." It is, therefore, a matter of enlightened concern. But it is also a matter of pragmatic expediency. It costs considerably less to maintain an individual on probation than it does to keep him incarcerated. In probation we have the typical American blend of pragmatic expediency, and compassionate concern for the welfare of those who have fallen. These are the foundations upon which probation rests in the United States.

The Probation Agency

Probation systems are normally established as units of county government, but in a few states they are organized as part of a state system, as in Delaware. A third option exercised by a minority of states is to have a combined probation and parole agency, as in Florida. Probation departments vary in size from one-man operations in smaller counties, to the world's largest department in Los Angeles County, which has responsibility for the supervision of approximately 50,000 cases. About half of the 4,000 staff members in the Los Angeles County Probation Department are case-carrying probation officers or provide professional services in the juvenile halls and forestry camps.

---

[3] Among federal prisoners, for example, the recidivism rate for those first arrested at age 14 is more than triple that for individuals first arrested at 35 and over. For additional data, see President's Commission on Law Enforcement and Administration of Justice, *Task Force Report: Juvenile Delinquency and Youth Crime* (Washington, D.C.: U.S. Government Printing Office, 1967), p. 122.

[4] American Bar Association Project on Standards for Criminal Justice, *Standards Relating to Probation* Approved Draft (New York: Institute of Judicial Administration 1970).

STATE CONTROL VERSUS LOCAL AUTONOMY

From time to time there is debate on the respective merits of having probation centrally administered as a state agency, or autonomously run by the local counties. The best that can be said is that there are substantive arguments for each point of view. Centralized state control would enable the creation of uniform standards, both as to operation of the system and as to qualifications of professional staff. Additionally, a centralized state system would result in financial economies and uniform funding. As it presently stands, the smaller counties, with limited funding, are not able to be as innovative as the bigger counties with larger budgets.

On the other hand, with the increasing emphasis on local control of the correctional process, a good argument can be made for retention of the county-based system. A state-run system would weaken local autonomy, which is so desirable in community-based corrections. Perhaps a happy compromise would be for the state to set the standards, and subsidize the poorer counties, and have the system administered locally.

THE JUDICIAL-EXECUTIVE CONTROVERSY

Another theoretical controversy concerns whether the probation function should be part of the judicial branch of government or the executive branch. Currently, in the vast majority of cases, it is a judicial function, under the courts. Again, there are things to be said for both sides. Retaining probation in the judicial branch, it is claimed, is necessary to enable the court to be in closer touch with the agency that is carrying out the judicial intent. It also permits a wider use of probation as a diversionary sentencing option, and permits closer consultative interaction between the court and the probation department.

Opponents of this view argue that all other service sub-units are in the executive branch of government, and the addition of probation would permit closer coordination between them. In addition, budgeting stability would be achieved, as well as uniform standards for policy-making and agency administration. The National Advisory Commission is on record as favoring placement of probation in the executive branch of government, for these and other reasons.[5]

---

[5] National Advisory Commission on Criminal Justice Standards and Goals, *Task Force Report: Corrections* (Washington D.C.: U.S. Government Printing Office, 1973), p. 314.

BASIC FUNCTIONS OF THE PROBATION AGENCY

The basic functions of the probation agency can be reduced to two: investigation and supervision. In the earlier era of probation, investigation was restricted to the narrow function of providing the court with information prior to sentencing. At the present time, the probation department can conduct investigations in any of the pretrial stages. In addition, there are the specialized investigations conducted in the case of dependent and neglected children, for foster home placements, and in the initial referral of juvenile delinquents. A primary investigative function of the probation officer is to prepare the pre-sentence investigation report, which we shall deal with in a later section.

Supervision of those who have been placed on probation by the court's decision is the primary, ongoing function of this agency. Supervision puts the professional with his skills in juxtaposition with the client and his needs. The long-range objective is the protection of the community.

SUBSIDY

Earlier we took a brief look at the controversy over centralized versus local administration of probation. We noted that one of the drawbacks of local control is limited funding. Most states, however, subsidize probation in one form or another, by partial funding, maintenance of juvenile institutions, or through consultative or manpower services. This is subsidization by definition. But subsidy has come to mean a particular form of underwriting by the state, based on programs developed in California, Washington, and New York. Although New York was the pioneer among the three, California's program has drawn the most comment.

California's subsidy program was instituted on July 1, 1966, and it has been called "an unprecedented success" by the Keldgord Commission.[6] That is a highly debatable appraisal; nevertheless the program is an important experiment in diversion. The subsidy program in California is voluntary and known as a performance program, that is, the state subsidizes county probation departments for results. That means that the state pays from $2,080 to $4,000 per year for every offender diverted from the prison system to probation. The amount paid is computed on the basis of a complex formula that takes into account pro-rated costs for feeding,

---

[6] California Correctional System Study, *Task Force Report: Field Services: Probation* (Board of Corrections, Sacramento, California, July 1971), p. 66.

housing, supervising, and diverting the individual. There is also a "base rate" for reductions established for each county. The counties are obliged to supervise the subsidy cases in small caseloads (less than fifty). In 1973, forty-six of California's fifty-eight counties were participating in the program.

The Keldgord Commission was closer to the truth when it proclaimed that subsidy "represents the most innovative approach to correctional field services in California history." [7] The importance of subsidy does not lie in dubious success data, but in what it represents in terms of influencing diversionary sentencing, and in the stimulus it has for innovative thinking in corrections. In California, subsidy has had a demonstrable impact on the sentencing practices of the courts. In 1965 a total of 26.3 percent of those convicted in superior courts were committed to state prisons. By 1969 that figure had dropped to a remarkable 9.8 percent. Further, approximately 51 percent of all defendants were granted probation in 1965. By 1969 that figure had increased to 66 percent.[8]

CRITIQUE OF SUBSIDY

There are valid criticisms of the California subsidy program. First, the formula of reimbursement has not been revised since the inception of the program in 1966, so it automatically tends to favor the larger counties. More importantly, if a particular county had an excellent crime prevention record, it would, paradoxically, be penalized through reduced reimbursements—less money for fewer convictions. The subsidy program is also filtering out the better risks from the institutional system, and the prisons are, thereby, becoming centers of violence. This, however, is a problem for correctional planners, because it is a natural end product of modern correctional thinking: that only the dangerous individuals should be sent to prison. Subsidy should not be submarined because of the inability of correctional administrators to contain prison violence.

When the subsidy program was launched in California, it was legislatively directed toward four basic goals: reducing the necessity for institutional commitment, developing even-handed justice, rehabilitating offenders, and increasing public protection. In a recent progress report to the California legislature, the California Youth Authority admitted that only the first two of these goals had been met. There was no conclusive

---

[7] *Ibid.*, p. 67.

[8] Robert L. Smith, *A Quiet Revolution: Probation Subsidy* (Washington, D.C.: U.S. Government Printing Office, 1971), p. 48.

evidence available that subsidy had either enhanced rehabilitation or increased public protection.[9]

It should again be mentioned that the importance of innovative correctional programs must not be determined from immediate, local successes (or failures), but from the successful impact they have on the total criminal justice system. Subsidy is undoubtedly having an impact beyond the probation component—on the judiciary, for example. This is the frame of reference in which it will have to be ultimately evaluated.

Recommendations of the National Advisory Commission

After a thorough analysis of probation as a correctional tool, the National Advisory Commission proposed the following legislative standards (here occasionally paraphrased) to regulate this process.[10]

Each state should enact legislation (by 1975) which would:

1. Provide probation as an alternative for all offenders
2. Establish criteria for:
   - A. the granting of probation
   - B. the conditions to be imposed
   - C. the length of probation
   - D. the basis for revocation of probation

The Commission then made the following specific recommendations in each of these areas:

CRITERIA FOR GRANTING PROBATION

1. Probation should be granted over confinement unless specified conditions exist which would contraindicate this option.

2. The factors favorable for the granting of probation should be specified.

3. The decision to grant probation should be made on the basis of factors pertaining to the individual offender, and not the crime committed.

---

[9] California Youth Authority, *California's Probation Subsidy Program, A Progress Report of the Legislature 1966–1973,* Sacramento, January 1974, pp. ii–iii.

[10] National Advisory Commission, *Corrections,* pp. 578–79.

CRITERIA FOR PROBATION CONDITIONS

1. A range of specified conditions should be authorized, but their imposition should not be required.

2. Conditions imposed should be reasonably related to the treatment objectives of the individual case, and not unduly restrictive nor incompatible with constitutional protections.

3. Conditions should be fashioned on the basis of the individual's needs, and not on the nature of the offense.

CRITERIA FOR LENGTH OF PROBATION

1. Probation should not be longer than the maximum sentence provided by law for a felony offense.

2. In the case of a misdemeanor, probation should not exceed one year.

3. The term of probation should be specified in statute.

4. The court should be able to discharge a person from probation at any time.

5. Appellate review of revocation decisions should be made available to probationers.

CRITERIA FOR REVOCATION

1. Probation should not be revoked unless there is substantial evidence of a breach of a probation condition.

2. Probation should not be revoked unless the probationer has been permitted to review the official records, confront his accusers, be represented by counsel, and subpoena witnesses in his behalf.

3. Probation should not be revoked unless the court has provided the probationer with a written statement of the findings of fact, the reasons for the revocation, and the evidence relied upon.

The Probation Officer

In the recent past, textbooks were filled with unprovable assertions about the probation officer's treatment role. Current thinking views the probation officer, and the parole officer, as a manager of resources for his client. The American psychiatrist Karl Menninger sees them as overworked professionals who "cannot be praised too highly." That is because unrealistic caseloads and "systems encrusted with their own inflexible rules" have prevented the probation and parole officer from bringing their skills to full fruition.[11] Most probation and parole officers today, burdened with bureaucratic chores, inundated with report-writing, and weighted down with impossibly large caseloads, despair of ever being able to make a dent in the mountainous challenge they face. Less than 4 percent of the nation's probation officers supervise caseloads of 40 or less.[12] Yet, as a group, they are among the most dedicated and compassionate professionals in the so-called "helping services."

The role of the probation officer is rapidly changing. The Federal Probation Officers Association foresees that these "judicial aides in the sentencing process" are predestined to have increasing responsibilities in the future. "They will be called upon . . . to provide a more explicit evaluation of the needs of the individual offender and to recommend the best available alternative for meeting those needs, whether this involves probation, confinement, or variations of the two." [13] What sort of qualifiying standards should be established for this profession?

QUALIFYING STANDARDS FOR PROBATION OFFICERS

Some general observations can be made before we discuss academic or technical requirements. The individual who would aspire to work in the field of probation must, above all, have a genuine love for his fellow man. Probation is not a job, it is a commitment. The probation officer must also have a genuine concern for the well-being of the wider society, and a desire to contribute to its safety and harmonious growth. He must be action-oriented, for he must constantly seek out and mobilize resources in the community to aid in the probationer's adjustment. He will also have to be equipped with an above-average reservoir of compassion. Yet he must be ruled by reason, for some of his clients will be sophisticated manipulators and psychopaths of the most distressing degree. He must be resilient, for he will face discouraging failures, and humble, for the successes may have succeeded in spite of the system.

---

[11] Karl Menninger, *The Crime of Punishment* (New York: The Viking Press, 1968), p. 87.

[12] President's Commission on Law Enforcement and Administration of Justice, *Task Force Report: Corrections* (Washington, D.C.: U.S. Government Printing Office, 1967), p. 30.

[13] Federal Probation Officers Association, "Goals of Federal Probation Service" (mimeographed), October 1972, p. v.

More than specific training, more than expertise in any particular academic discipline, the probation officer will need to be the kind of human being who is a giver rather than a taker, who is warm rather than cold, and who is committed to the highest ideals of human service. If, then, he can superimpose upon this foundation academic training and professional expertise, he will be well equipped for the job.

TRAINING AND DIAGNOSIS

For perhaps too many years the correctional services have called for training in social casework as the *sine qua non* for effective correctional service. Social casework has been classically defined as consisting of three major elements: study, diagnosis, and treatment.[14] But the history of ineffectiveness in "treating" and "diagnosing" correctional clients should have caused this position to have been questioned long before now. More important, putting the probation officer in the position of being a diagnostician and treater placed undue responsibility upon him. Worse than that, it encouraged the probation officer to try to become the alpha and the omega of reformation. What probation or parole officer can have every skill and sensitivity necessary, can be maximally insightful, can know and employ the expertise that is spread among countless social agencies? None, of course. That is why the National Advisory Commission has deplored the overemphasis on social casework.[15]

The *Manual of Correctional Standards* recommends two years of graduate study in social work as an academic standard for probation officers, with at least one year the suggested minimum.[16] But it is quite obvious that there are not enough schools of social work available, nor is every school of social work well grounded in correctional social work. More to the point, to say that social work is prerequisite for effective correctional work in probation is to deny the high-caliber contributions made by many probation officers trained in other disciplines. One of the top correctionalists in California, with an international reputation, graduated with a degree in architecture. Academic disciplines merely give factual knowledge. The human qualities needed in probation work can emerge through any discipline.

Social work and social casework are related but they are not syn-

---

[14] Consult, for example, Cora Kasius, ed., *Principles and Techniques in Social Casework* (New York: Family Association of America, 1950), particularly the article by Gordon Hamilton, "The Underlying Philosophy of Social Casework," pp. 7–22.

[15] National Advisory Commission, *Corrections,* p. 311.

[16] American Correctional Association, *Manual of Correctional Standards* (College Park, Md.: The Association, 1971), p. 103.

onymous. Casework refers to a specific philosophy of social work, which is dominated by the medical model concept. The probation officer is a correctional social worker, which means that he works with social agencies and resources in the community to further the rehabilitative aims of his agency. He acts as a catalyst between the client and his needs, and the community and its resources. If there is any one skill that it is imperative for him to have, it is the skill of decision-making. The probation officer makes countless case decisions daily, some of which are momentous in their effects upon human destinies. He should be trained well in the analysis of facts, so that he may consistently make sound judgments.

In a more formal sense, the probation officer should be familiar with his agency and its objectives; he should know himself; he should have substantive knowledge of the field of corrections; preferably, he should be schooled in the behavioral sciences; and he should be conversant with modern trends in the treatment of the criminal offender.[17]

THE INVESTIGATIVE FUNCTION OF THE PROBATION OFFICER

The probation officer not only is responsible for the supervision of men and women (and juveniles) placed on probation, he also must perform some important investigative functions. Foster homes for juveniles must be assessed, for the welfare of a child is at stake. The intake officer must scrupulously evaluate all factors before deciding if a youngster is to be admitted to detention in the juvenile hall, or permitted to return to his home. But the principal investigation that the probation officer must perform is the pre-sentence investigation.

The pre-sentence investigation might be termed a social history prepared for the edification of the sentencing judge, and intended to give the jurist sufficient insight to enable him to impose the most appropriate sentence. It should provide a succinct and precise encapsulation of the factors in the defendant's life which are relevant to the sentencing process and its options, and it should contain treatment proposals. Other agencies besides the court will be using the pre-sentence investigation report. These include prison and parole officials as well as other probation departments. Hence it can be a very useful and helpful instrument. Whether or not probation should be granted is a specific, concluding recommendation in that report. Although the pre-sentence investigation report is a useful tool, it is not required in every jurisdiction and, where it is, it has sometimes been criticized for being overly lengthy.

---

17 The California Probation, Parole, and Correctional Association has prepared an excellent pamphlet on the desirable attributes of probation and parole officers: *The Practitioner in Corrections* (Arcadia, Calif.: CPPCA, 1967).

CRITIQUE OF THE PRE-SENTENCE INVESTIGATION REPORT

A more significant criticism is that it enhances the quasi-judicial role of the probation officer, particularly where the judge is predisposed to lean heavily on the probation officer's recommendation. The probation officer administers *the will of the court.* He should not influence judicial determinations, but should merely carry them out. This is more of a problem in theory than in reality, but legal scholars are occasionally concerned at what they see as usurpation of the judicial function.

The criticism is also made that the pre-sentence report is often automatically prepared for every case despite the fact that the options of the judge are limited. Probation cannot be granted in every case, for in certain offenses it is prohibited by law. In such a situation, the compilation of a pre-sentence report may be a waste of time and energy. Conversely, an imprisoned inmate who is sentenced on another charge while imprisoned, is obviously ineligible for probation. But he could benefit by a pre-sentence report that induced the judge to impose a concurrent rather than a consecutive sentence.

There is also reason to suspect that a great deal of the information contained in the report is unnecessary. Some reports call for identifying marks on the body of the defendant. What insight, one might ask, does the judge gain from being informed that the defendant has a tattoo on his left bicep? On the other hand, complex cases will necessitate a more extensive evaluation, so it must not be presumed that good reports are necessarily synonymous with short reports. Many agencies besides the court will eventually depend upon the pre-sentence report for assistance. The report should anticipate those legitimate needs without becoming bombastic.

There is a great need for a standardization of the pre-sentence investigation report form. The Federal Probation Office created such a document in 1965, and it was intended to be a "definitive standard" to be followed in the Federal District Courts when it was adopted in 1967. This model form contained fourteen marginal headings and, unfortunately, a mandate from the Chief of the Federal System made it obligatory to complete all fourteen sections. The end result was predictable: the reports grew cumbersome. Fortunately, revisions took place. Now "Selective Pre-sentence Investigation Reports" may be submitted, unless the court requires a comprehensive version. The term "selective" was purposefully employed, instead of a word suggesting that the report had been shortened. This was because it was feared that there would be an implication that the report was less than adequate.[18] Perhaps some day substance will triumph over semantics.

A VALUABLE SIDE EFFECT

There is an unintended but valuable side effect that can derive from the use of a scrupulously prepared, standardized pre-sentence investigation report, and it has to do with equity in sentencing. Judges are notorious for the disparity in their sentencing. At the Annual Sentencing Institute for Superior Court Judges, held in Santa Barbara, California, in 1967, the participating judges were given a hypothetical case for disposition. Only 5 percent opted for prison sentences, and the remaining jurists were almost evenly divided between straight probation and jail coupled with probation.[19] If consistent criteria could be applied to the pre-sentence report, the judiciary might as a consequence become more consistent in its sentencing.

Case Management and Supervision

The heart of the probation service is case supervision. This is the arena in which all of the skills of the probation officer, and all of the management tactics of his agency, are consolidated in the effort to abate recidivism.

THE INTERSTATE PROBATION AND PAROLE COMPACT

Although probation may be locally administered, it is national in scope. In the earlier part of this century it was far from a professional operation. Not every jurisdiction lived up to the idealistic spirit of this correctional device. Furthermore, there was a definite problem when it came to regulating the interstate movement of probationers and parolees. Some states subverted the intent of parole by releasing inmates to out-of-state parole programs and forbidding them to return to the "sending state." It

---

[18] Division of Probation, Administrative Office of the United States Courts, "The Selective Presentence Investigation Report," *Federal Probation,* XXXVIII, no. 4 (December 1974), 50.

[19] *Los Angeles Times,* April 14, 1967.

wasn't openly acknowledged, but this was a device for transferring problem cases to other jurisdictions.

As a result of the obvious need, the Interstate Commission on Crime, a federal agency, developed the Interstate Probation and Parole Compact in 1935. Congress had given its prior consent to the creation of this Compact through passage of the Crime Control Consent Act of 1934. Every state is currently a member of this Compact, as are the District of Columbia, Puerto Rico, and the Virgin Islands. The Compact established standards of reciprocity in the supervision of probationers and parolees, as well as with regard to warrants, arrests, and extradition. This does not mean that absolute uniformity has been achieved, but a cooperative working agreement has been legislated. One basic principle is that supervision of probationers and parolees in the "receiving state" must be by the same standards that apply to cases that are native to the receiving state. There were over 11,000 individuals on out-of-state probation in 1970.[20]

The number of probationers supervised under the Interstate Compact, though impressive, is but a fraction of the more than one million actually on probation in the United States. They are supervised in a number of different types of agencies, with varying conditions, as determined by a diversity of penal statutes. It is practically impossible to determine the exact number of individuals actually working as probation officers, because many jurisdictions fuse the functions of probation and parole. The *Probation and Parole Directory* no longer attempts to list probation and parole officers separately. The latest edition indicates that 24,758 individuals are collectively engaged in these professions.[21]

THE AMBIVALENT ROLE OF THE PROBATION OFFICER

While it is generally assumed that the biggest challenge facing the probation officer is his clientele, a good case can be made for the role he must play. It is a role of classical ambivalence. On the one hand, the probation officer is duty-bound to protect society; this underlines the surveillance function of his job. On the other hand, he is supposed to be a non-authoritarian treatment figure. There are few people so balanced that they can ably harmonize these competing roles. That is why the prisons feature constant confrontation between the "custody" and the "treatment" echelons. It is also why probation and parole officers tend to be labeled

---

[20] Walter C. Reckless, *The Crime Problem* (New York: Appleton-Century-Crofts, 1973), p. 571.

[21] *Probation and Parole Directory* (New York: National Council on Crime and Delinquency, 1970), p. v.

among their peers as either "cops" or "social workers." Role conflict, as sociologists will tell you, can be devastating.

The truth is that each probation or parole officer brings his own personality, his own genetic inheritance, his own biases and predispositions, and his own philosophic beliefs into his profession with him. It is essential for the probation officer to know his limitations and to suppress his personal biases. As there is no single, valid approach to rehabilitation, the primary concern of the agency should be to screen out individuals with destructive biases and personality factors that are inimical to the establishment of rapport.

PROFESSIONAL TYPOLOGIES

Several decades ago a distinguished researcher and his associates classified probation officers on the basis of three broad categories. Ohlin, Piven, and Pappenfort determined that the three categories are: (1) the "punitive officer," (2) the "protective agent," and (3) the "welfare worker." [22]

These typologies are "work orientation" theories, that is, they describe the philosophic stance that the probation officer takes toward his job. The "punitive officer" is the "guardian of middle-class community morality," and employs coercion and punishment as his methods of inducing conformity. He sees his role, essentially, as protecting the community from the depredations of his clients.

The "protective agent" is ambivalent. He is protective, but of both the community and the client. He lectures, praises, provides assistance, and vacillates in his emotional reactions to a given crisis.

The "welfare worker" is client-oriented and identifies strongly with the social work profession. His focus is on individualized efforts to facilitate his client's adjustment, and he feels that society's best protection comes from an "objective and theoretically based assessment of the client's situation, needs, and capacities." [23] Every sizeable probation agency probably has representatives of all three types on its staff. Nor is this a purely domestic phenomenon. Conrad found a "vociferous" pro and con conflict among English probation officers with respect to a social casework philosophy.[24]

---

[22] Lloyd E. Ohlin, Herman Piven, and Donnell M. Pappenfort, "Major Dilemmas of the Social Worker in Probation and Parole," *NPPA Journal* 2, no. 3 (July 1956), 215.

[23] *Ibid.*

[24] John Conrad, *Crime and Its Correction* (Berkeley, Calif.: University of California Press, 1965), p. 105.

CROSS-SEX SUPERVISION IN PROBATION

Despite the legend of the little old, white-haired lady dominating social work, usually with her hair done up in a bun, neither she nor her younger sisters have been significantly involved in the fields of probation and parole until relatively recently. In a 1970 survey conducted by the Chief Probation Officer of Washington, it was revealed that ten states had no women employed as adult probation officers.[25] These states were Alabama, Arkansas, Georgia, Hawaii, Idaho, Montana, New Hampshire, North Dakota, South Dakota, and Virginia. Puerto Rico, the Virgin Islands, and forty-two states employed females as probation officers, but only nine of the eighty-nine Federal District Courts had female probation officers on the staff. This is a rather curious phenomenon, for it would be difficult to confirm that the male alone had the magic wherewithal to induce rehabilitation.

Since the survey cited above, dramatic changes have occurred. These have been a result of both passage of the 1964 Civil Rights Act and the many movements that have sprung up to guarantee the occupational equality of women. Now practically every probation agency employs women and, more significantly, assigns caseloads without considering the sex of the officer.[26] The traditional barriers to cross-sex supervision (males supervising females and vice versa) were based on legendary misconceptions of role. The female was perceived as "weak" and subordinate. It was felt that the male was particularly susceptible to paternity charges and false allegations of rape. The last two were, in fact, the responses given by California when the survey inquired as to why males did not have females on their caseloads in that state.[27] Yet the survey determined that neither of these latter two circumstances had ever occurred in any state.

The arguments in favor of cross-sex supervision are most persuasive. In the first place, this is a heterosexual world, and cross-sex supervision therefore introduces a well-established social norm. There is also evidence that individuals relate better to the opposite sex in a helping relationship. In an unpublished survey of the inmates at the California Institution for Women, for instance, 100 percent of the residents declared that they would rather have a male case supervisor.

---

[25] Ellis Stout, "Women in Probation and Parole," *Crime and Delinquency,* 19, no. 1 (January 1973), 61–71.

[26] Meyressa H. Schoonmaker and Jennifer S. Brooks, "Women in Probation and Parole, 1974," *Crime and Delinquency,* 21, no. 2 (April 1975), 109.

[27] *Ibid.,* p. 110.

There is also concern about the critical need for correctional staff in the future. The President's Crime Commission estimated that there would be a need for a 250 percent increase in probation and parole staffs in the decade following its survey.[28] With capable and qualified women in the labor pool, it would be irrational to exclude them from these correctional services on the basis of sex discrimination.

SUPERVISING THE PROBATIONER

Before an individual is placed on probation, he goes through a selection process. The judge and the probation officer screen the individual on the general basis of potential for positive response to community-based supervision. There is also a statutory screening, for the law prohibits the granting of probation to certain cases. First-degree murder, offenses committed with deadly weapons, certain sexual offenses, and aggravated prior criminal histories are examples of circumstances that bar probation in various states. But potential is no guarantee of success. It is the supervision process that endeavors to actualize the potential.

The dual function of the probation officer again comes to the fore in supervision. He has a mandate from society to protect it, and a professional obligation to mobilize the resources of the community to assist his client in his developmental growth. The controlling framework is the suspended sentence that hovers over the probationer, and the conditions of probation which must be adhered to. Most recent textbooks on probation and parole still talk of supervision as involving the application of social casework methods to the client.[29] But we have gone beyond that narrow stricture. No pat formula can be applied to every probation officer–probationer relationship. Nor is any one therapeutic approach foreordained to succeed. On top of that we have the myriad differences in each probation officer, and in each probationer, which prevent a simplified or parochial approach.

That is why the contemporary emphasis is on the probation officer's practical function as a resource broker. Within the limits set by the probation agency, the probation officer has sufficient leeway to make judgments about the probationer's behavior. It is as a decision-maker that the probation officer must be ultimately judged. Some decisions are easily made, but the complicated ones that have to do with the retention or the

---

[28] The President's Commission, *Corrections*, p. 99.

[29] Dressler, for example, has a major section on it, and the casework emphasis pervades his work: David Dressler, *Practice and Theory of Probation and Parole* (New York: Columbia University Press, 1969).

loss of freedom have to be the basis for professional standing. All decisions are made on the basis of facts, knowledge, expertise, and intuition, and the probation officer no longer needs to stand alone in the more difficult decisions. Correctionalists are learning that group decisions not only give support to the individual decision-maker, but also contribute additional insights.

CASE RECORDING

The requirements of agencies vary as to case recording. Case recording can serve several ends. It provides a tool for review of the case dynamics. It offers a mechanism for assessing progress. It is a source of evidence for legal proceedings. And it is the reservoir of social and case material which the probation officer can draw upon as he plans his rehabilitation strategy. Brevity with succinctness is a golden rule in recording, for the overworked practitioner is already overwhelmed with paperwork requirements. The federal system discovered this with the pre-sentence investigation report, as we have seen.

One major criticism of the case record is that it becomes the repository for a great deal of extraneous material, much of which is never used in a dynamic sense. The problem is compounded by the fact that periodic recording is required, and extraneous material is heaped upon extraneous material. The Burlington, Vermont, probation department is experimenting with the utilization of what is referred to as a Problem Oriented Record (POR).[30] As the title intimates, the recording is consciously oriented to the problem(s) of the individual probationer. Minimum base data are secured, such as legal and family histories, but these are conceptualized in terms of the probationer's problem areas. Problem lists are actually recorded. This serves two purposes. First it focuses on the vital area of concern and, second, the list confronts the probation officer each time he reviews his case. He is thus persistently challenged to seek a resolution. When problems are resolved, that, too, is recorded as a case dynamic.

An interesting aspect of the Vermont experiment is that a Peer Review Committee meets regularly to hear case presentations by individual probation officers. As many staff members as are able to attend are present. The individual probation officer gains the advantage of group consensus, as well as added insights and suggestions as to how to proceed with a particularly provocative problem. The outstanding feature of the Vermont

---

[30] Robert M. Smith, "The Problem Oriented Record Used in a Probation Setting," *Federal Probation,* XXXIX, no. 1 (March 1975), 47–51.

experiment is that it is a totally dynamic, problem-oriented process. Something of this nature should have been instituted years ago, so that the billions of useless words that have been interred in case records could have been aborted.

Some Treatment Strategies in Probation

Because of the criticisms we have leveled at traditional "treatment," we use the word with some misgiving. Perhaps a better phrase would be "anti-recidivism tactics." Treatment is a much misused word in the correctional vocabulary, but a reduction in recidivism is the standard for "success." Part of the problem is what the National Advisory Commission called the correctional dilemma.[31] In short, corrections so often fail today because practitioners in the field are saddled with obsolescent machinery, outmoded traditions, and a rusting ideology. When change is sought or indicated, cumbersome systems and traditions blunt the thrust of change. A good example is the philosophy on caseload size. The traditional optimum heralded among professionals and academicians—without any empirical proof—has been the magic number of fifty. The so-called "San Francisco Project," a collaborative probation experiment by the University of California and the Federal Probation System, confirmed that a probation officer could handle a selected caseload of 300 cases under minimum supervision.[32] There are other meritorious experimental programs from which a great deal can be learned.

THE CAMBRIDGE-SOMERVILLE YOUTH STUDY

This was an intended ten-year experiment, instituted in 1935 in the Massachusetts towns of Cambridge and Somerville. It was a study of 101 predelinquent boys from slum areas, and one of the principal objectives of the study was to test the universally accepted belief that the core of effective rehabilitation was counseling. Although interrupted by World War II, it was an important undertaking. The project matched experimental and control groups with and without experienced counselors, and it was discovered that there was no significant difference in the recidivism rates of the juveniles in the two groups. The conclusion was that trained counseling was no more effective than routine treatment.

---

[31] National Advisory Commission, *Corrections*, p. 352.

[32] Joseph V. Lohman, G. Albert Wahl, and Robert M. Carter, *The San Francisco Project* (Berkeley: University of California Press, 1965).

THE HIGHFIELDS PROJECT

Highfields stands as a classic experiment. This was the program in which Guided Group Interaction was introduced as a treatment tactic with juvenile offenders in 1950. The Highfields project, established in property donated by Colonel Charles Lindbergh, developed a program featuring minimum restrictions, an absence of authoritarian leadership, an accent on self-determinative decision-making by the youthful participants, and a normalizing milieu. The key in the treatment approach was a blend of group therapy in the evenings (guided group interaction), and the opportunity to work in the community in the daytime. None of the boys was obliged to work, as in a traditional reformatory or industrial school, but each was paid for his work and could be fired for poor performance.

The founders of the program felt that the delinquent boys were normal boys with poor self-images and antisocial attitudes that could be reformed through peer interaction. Comparisons made between the boys at Highfields and the residents of the nearby Annandale Reformatory indicated that the reformatory boys developed increasingly bleak outlooks on life, whereas the Highfields boys improved their outlook.[33] Subsequent statistical studies of the results of the Highfields experiment indicated that it was significantly more successful than the traditional reformatory, as exemplified in Annandale. A first-year followup showed a 33 percent recidivism rate for the Annandale releasees and an 18 percent recidivism rate for the Highfields releasees.[34] The data from Highfields have been more critically viewed as time has passed, but the general conclusion about its success remains valid. In that it dealt with only a small number of boys (twenty-four) and a highly select sample, its limitations should be recognized. But it remains a classic experiment and an invitation to success.

THE SAGINAW PROJECT

This was a three-year program, introduced on an experimental basis in Michigan in 1957. The three years preceding the experiment were used as a control base. The intent of the experiment was a simple and straightforward one: to keep individuals out of prison and to save the taxpayers

---

[33] Lloyd W. McCorkle, Albert Elias, and F. Lovell Bixby, *The Highfields Story* (New York: Holt, Rinehart & Winston, Inc., 1958), pp. 122–26.

[34] *Ibid.*, p. 143.

of Michigan up to $14 million a year. The Saginaw County courts were involved in the experiment, and this is how the project derived its name.

The basic premise of the study was that community treatment is more effective, especially when adequately trained professional staff are available, and are permitted to individualize the treatment for the clients. The probation officers in the project were, consequently, required to have graduate training in social work. The caseloads were reduced to (that old magic number of) fifty cases, and treatment was individualized for each probationer.

The Saginaw Project, as if in defiance of the Cambridge-Somerville conclusion, confirmed its hypothesis that treatment would be more effective if undertaken in the community and if administered by highly specialized and trained probation officers with reduced caseloads. It achieved its twin objectives: keeping people out of prison, and saving the taxpayers money. A 17.3 percent reduction in recidivism was achieved, and a savings in excess of $9 million was obtained for the taxpayers of Michigan.[35]

REINTEGRATIVE MODELS

The modern trend in probation treatment is reintegrative. It is designed to emphasize the offender's functional participation in relevant social institutions, such as the family, the school, and the employment market. It also endeavors to strengthen those social institutions. In Palo Alto, California, Virginia Satir has long worked with her "conjoint family therapy" model, which essentially teaches that when an individual has symptomatic pain, that pain will be experienced by all members of the family in one way or another.[36] If the "pain" is delinquency or criminality, it should be treated by involvement of the total family, and not by taking the individual offender off into some "clinical" atmosphere which isolates him from his family and ignores its crucial role in his behavior dynamics.

Next to the family, the school is unquestionably the most important institution in the lives of youths, both nondelinquent and delinquency-prone. For those who can efficiently participate in the school programming, there are such benefits as status, tools for success, peer acceptance, and training for remunerative jobs. But not all *can* participate successfully. In New Jersey, a significant effort is under way to help those who

---

[35] Michigan Crime and Delinquency Council, *The Saginaw Project* (East Lansing, Michigan: January 1963).

[36] Virginia Satir, *Conjoint Family Therapy*, rev. ed. (Palo Alto, Calif.: Science and Behavior Books, Inc., 1967), p. 1.

can't. The Collegefield Project, operated in collaboration with Newark State Teachers College, attempts not only to upgrade the academic skills of the participants, but also to teach them how to participate effectively in the school system. The youths are assigned to the project by the juvenile court. They are involved in group counseling, and in tutorial sessions with experienced teachers. Peer pressure is a built-in treatment device. When the program is completed, the offenders are advanced into the regular school program.

There are a number of other reintegrative programs developing. They are sorely needed. It is common therapeutic knowledge, as Satir points out, that "the family behaves as if it were a unit." [37] The restoration of a constructive unity in the family is the best therapeutic bulwark against delinquency.

Throughout this text, we have reviewed some of the more imaginative community-based programs, such as PORT in Minnesota, the radical redirection with juveniles in Massachusetts, the Michigan Community Treatment Project for Repeat Offenders, and the NCCJL Alternative to Prison Program. They included the newer thrusts in probation. One of the more interesting programs, but one with a somewhat different basic philosophy, remains to be mentioned.

SHOCK PROBATION

In October 1965 the state of Ohio passed a law providing for "shock probation." [38] This unique law permits a judge to release an individual from custody to probation after he has served up to 130 days on his sentence. Shock probation is based on an emerging belief that limited exposure to the prison environment has a deterrent value. The shock of incarceration, it is felt, is most effective in its earliest stages, and with the less sophisticated offender.

This is a particularly interesting proposition because modern correctionalists, for the most part, dismiss deterrence as an influential force in rehabilitation or correction. Most of the arguments against capital punishment, for example, emphasize the fact that it is not a deterrent. In truth, no one really knows who may and who may not be affected by deterrence. The only data available pertain to those who have reentered the system.

Under the Ohio law, shock probation is granted to selected offenders, primarily less serious and first time offenders. Those excluded include

---

[37] *Ibid.*

[38] Ohio Revised Code, 2947.06.1.

murderers and rapists, and similar felons, who are barred from probation by law. After the initial shock which, as we have indicated, consists of incarceration up to 130 days at the discretion of the presiding judge, the individual is released to the community on probation. In the first nine years of the statute's operation, 5,509 convicted offenders were released under shock probation. Only 10 percent of this number recidivated.[39]

In 1972 Kentucky legislated shock probation, but with a more unusual intent. Instead of applying the Ohio criterion for selected offenders, Kentucky uses shock probation for those ordinarily not considered good probation risks. The dubious candidate is given "a taste of prison life" for sixty days and, after this "shock," the judge may grant probation. Although the method of selection differs, the intent is the same in both Ohio and Kentucky—to manipulate the shock experienced in the early stage of incarceration for a reconstructive end result. In the first twenty-nine months of the law's operation in Kentucky, 512 persons had been released on shock probation. Forty-eight were returned to prison, and fifteen received convictions for new crimes.[40]

Besides being a vehicle for testing the deterrence theory, shock probation is also an excellent method of diversion. It should be quite evident that a brief exposure to incarceration is much more likely to be efficacious than a prolonged exposure.

Evaluating Probation

Probation has the endorsement of practically all of the reputable authorities in the field of corrections. It is more economical, it keeps the offender in the normalizing community milieu, and statistical data seem to support its effectiveness. The effectiveness of probation, however, is dependent upon a complexity of factors, and if probation is to continue to receive a favorable endorsement, it must continuously upgrade those factors, as well as the quality of its service.

THE ECONOMICS OF PROBATION

Probation is an economical correctional procedure. The President's Crime Commission reported in 1967 that it cost the average state $3,400 per year, exclusive of capital costs, to keep a youth in a state institution,

---

[39] Nick Gatz, "First Shock Probation: Now Shock Parole," *American Journal of Correction*, 37, no. 1 (January–February 1975), 20.

[40] *Corrections Magazine*, 1, no. 4 (March–April 1975), 26.

whereas it cost one-tenth of that amount to keep him on probation.[41] The cost of institutionalizing a youth in California in fiscal 1970–71 was $6,754, according to the Keldgord Commission.[42]

Sutherland and Cressey point to an earlier study which showed that 84,100 California probationers, in 1956, paid $2,747,000 toward the support of their families, and $902,000 for restitution and reparation.[43] Additional savings accrue from the families that are kept off welfare, from the taxes paid by probationers, and from the training and education secured by probationers at their own cost. And the cost of institutionalization is soaring. In 1974 it was estimated that it cost between $7,000 and $8,000 to maintain a child in an institution in Pennsylvania for one year.[44] These are *financial* savings. The greater importance of the *human* savings is obvious.

RECIDIVISM

The standard of success or failure in probation and parole is the recidivism rate. Many critical comments could be made about the manner in which recidivism is determined, but it is a generally accepted, broad index of the rate of reentry into the criminal justice system. It is obvious that individuals can continue in delinquency and criminality without being detected. It is also obvious that recidivism determinants are influenced by correctional policy as well as criminal justice philosophy, and these vary and change among a multitude of jurisdictions. Nevertheless, it can generally be accepted that a program which reduces the recidivism rate is a desirable program. Among the imprisoned, approximately 70 percent have been there before. That is one recidivism index.

Numerous surveys of probation outcome data in the United States and in foreign countries, surveyed by the President's Crime Commission, showed a mean success rate (probation not revoked) of 75 percent. In addition, an exhaustive survey conducted in California—in which over 11,000 adults granted probation in 1956–58 were followed up after seven years—showed a 72 percent success rate.

---

[41] The President's Commission, *Corrections*, p. 28.

[42] California Correctional System Study, *Task Force Report: Field Services: Probation* (Sacramento: Board of Corrections, July 1971), p. VI.

[43] Edwin H. Sutherland and Donald R. Cressey, *Criminology*, 9th ed. (New York: J.B. Lippincott Company, 1974), p. 479.

[44] Juvenile Probation Department, Montgomery County, Pennsylvania, Intensive Probation Unit, *Final Evaluation Report 1974* (mimeographed, undated), p. 2.

THE FUNDAMENTAL BASIS FOR EVALUATING EFFICIENCY

If probation is to be evaluated as an efficient correctional endeavor, several interdependent factors must operate efficiently and qualitatively. First, the *initial screening* must be competent. This is the responsibility of the probation department and is achieved primarily through the presentence investigation. Second, the *judicial decision-making*, through which probation is granted, must be knowledgeably made and statutorily supported. The law properly denies probation to certain types of offenses. Still, the judiciary must improve its knowledge of behavior dynamics, the law must be updated, and the public must be educated to the benefits that accrue from community-based probation services.

The quality of the probation service itself is a critical variable. This is principally experienced in the ongoing process of *probation supervision*. If it is not of sufficient quality as to be conducive to rehabilitation, then the first two elements are defeated. Finally, even if the supervision is sensitive and professional, probation will not have fulfilled itself as a correctional tool until the mighty *resources of the community* have been mobilized in support of that sensitive supervision. Deficiencies in any of these four variables, will inevitably affect the outcome of probation, and qualify any evaluation made.

It is the considered judgment of those knowledgeable in the field of criminal corrections, that only the most serious offenders should be imprisoned. Yet the federal government will spend over $6 billion constructing penal institutions within the next few years. Between 80 and 90 percent of all correctional manpower is employed in the institutional component, which also drains about 80 percent of all correctional budgets. Society deserves to have its burden lightened. Probation has proven capability.

Review Questions

1. What are the five essential ingredients of probation?
2. What are the three basic organizational systems of probation?
3. Explain the judicial-executive controversy, and defend one or the other position.
4. What are the National Advisory Commission's criteria for granting probation?

5. What are the National Advisory Commission's criteria for probation conditions?
6. What are the qualifying standards for probation work?
7. The presentence investigation is one of the most important functions performed by a probation officer. What is the presentence report? What is its function? Criticize this instrument, negatively as well as positively.
8. Ohlin, Piven, and Pappenfort determined that there are three basic categories of probation officer. What are they and what are the philosophic implications of each? Which might you be?
9. Describe the "San Francisco Project" and enumerate its basic findings.
10. Select one of the notable treatment programs covered in this chapter. Describe its operational method and evaluate the program.

11

THE HISTORICAL EVOLUTION OF PAROLE

Here is the very place the Kaf, or Caucausus,
where I must die a daily death and
make a nightly descent into hell.

John Mitchell. Aboard the convict ship, *Neptune,* as it approached the penal colony at Van Diemen's Land, April 6, 1850.

Early Influences

The origin of parole is most often traced to the emergence of the Ticket of Leave in the inhuman penal colonies of Australia, although this widespread belief has been recently disputed. Killinger and Cromwell contend that there is little factual basis for such a belief.[1] If there is controversy on this point, it is because some writers in the field tend to confuse cause with event. The Australian experience was an important event, but it was a constellation of events that were responsible for the emergence of parole as a correctional process. We shall now review the more important of those influences. In doing so, we will of necessity have to visit the infamous penal colonies.

[1] George G. Killinger and Paul F. Cromwell, Jr., *Corrections in the Community: Alternatives to Imprisonment Selected Readings* (St. Paul: West Publishing Co., 1974), p. 400.

TRANSPORTATION

In modern times, the term "transportation" has a very prosaic meaning. It refers to modes of travel. But it once had a meaning quite different, and more deplorable. In the early evolution of punishment, transportation referred to the practice of banishing criminals to distant places. Writing with authority, Barnes and Teeters considered banishment as "probably the most tragic chapter in the entire history of criminal punishment," [2] and that is a history with many tragic chapters.

Most individuals have heard of the galley ships; and *Les Miserables*, Victor Hugo's well-known novel about the released galley convict, is a classic. The galleys were warships, and the wretched convicts were chained to the fifty-foot oars. Under the lash, they provided the energy source for the ships. Cannon fire from enemy vessels was directed toward the oars, to immobilize the ship's source of power, so the unfortunate convicts were literally subjected to double jeopardy. In early times, primitive tribes exiled miscreant members, banishing them from the safety and security of their own tribe, to experience almost certain death from alien tribes. Up through the Middle Ages, and, indeed, later in many cases, numerous nations followed the practice of sending their criminals "out of sight" for punishment. Devil's Island springs to mind, for one example.

There has often been an economic motive for the punishments inflicted on offenders. The galley slaves provided a manpower source which freed the fighting men. Convicts have extracted minerals working deep in dark mines, they have built roads, and they have colonized far-flung empires.

Technological changes have also influenced the methods and motives of punishment. When the galley ships gave way to sailing ships as fighting vessels, it marked the end of galley slavery as a form of punishment. But it didn't mark the end of prisoners to be disposed of. And because of upheavals in Europe due to the breakup of feudalism, crime was increasing rather rapidly. So it was that in the seventeenth and eighteenth centuries transportation and colonization were joined in unholy wedlock.

THE PENAL COLONIES OF AUSTRALIA

Transportation was a specific policy in England's colonization plans, particularly on the continent of Australia. The first law authorizing transpor-

---

[2] Harry Elmer Barnes and Negley K. Teeters, *New Horizons in Criminology* (Englewood Cliffs, N.J.: Prentice-Hall, Inc., 1945), p. 436.

tation from England was passed in 1597. Before the Australian adventure, the mother country first turned to her American colonies as a receptacle for her unwanted prisoners, and "between fifteen thousand and a hundred thousand" prisoners were so dispatched.[3] But the competing institution of slavery, and the severance of the colonies from the British Commonwealth, eventually aborted this practice and England had to find a substitute.

When Captain Cook made his pioneering discoveries in Australia in 1770, the English Parliament came to decide that Australia was an ideal substitute for the American colonies. Not only was it a place in which to dispose of England's unwanted prisoners, but it was an empire outpost needing colonization. And so, on May 13, 1787, Captain Arthur Phillip of the Royal Navy sailed from Spithead, England, bound for Australia with a strange human cargo. Appointed Governor of New South Wales, Phillip commanded eleven ships, including two warships, to transport the first batch of English convicts banished from the motherland to the penal colonies of Australia. The nine convict ships in the fleet contained 552 male and 190 female prisoners, and the journey took a little over eight months.

The prisoners were housed together under conditions of depravity which made the journey one of despair, resentment, rebellion, brutality, and fear. In his classic factual novel on the penal colonies, Marcus Clarke spoke of conditions aboard the convict ships:

> Each new comer was one more recruit to the ranks of ruffianism, and not a man penned in that reeking den of infamy but became a sworn hater of law, order, and "free-men." What he might have been before mattered not. He was now a prisoner, and —thrust into a suffocating barracoon,[4] herded with the foulest of mankind, with all imaginable depths of blasphemy and indecency sounded hourly in his sight and hearing—he lost his self-respect, and became what the jailers took him to be—a wild beast to be locked under bolts and bars, lest he should break out and tear them.[5]

Phillip's horrible journey came to an end in Botany Bay on January 18, 1788.

Wines contends that transportation actually originated in subterfuge. The deportee was given to understand that failure to submit to transporta-

[3] *Ibid.*, p. 438.

[4] An enclosure for the temporary confinement of convicts.

[5] Marcus Clarke, *For the Term of His Natural Life* (New York: W. W. Norton & Co., Inc., 1953), p. 53.

tion could result in execution.[6] But the conditions in the penal colonies were such as to make it a questionable substitute for execution. Those conditions led to both cannibalism and a high rate of homicide among the brutalized prisoners. Wines relates that "Within twenty months of the first landing, out of eight or nine hundred souls, one hundred and fifteen were already dead." [7] Yet the seeds of rudimentary parole were fertilized in this barbaric soil, planted by a compassionate man named Maconochie.

Captain Alexander Maconochie and the Ticket of Leave

Maconochie, too, was an officer in the Royal Navy and, in 1840, he was dispatched to become Governor of Norfolk Island, a desolate piece of land, four miles by three miles, to which the worst of the transported convicts were sent. There was a tremendous amount of degrading crime on this island: one witness in a murder trial testified that he had seen so many murders committed during his stay on Norfolk Island that he was unable to precisely recall the one in the case under way.[8] Maconochie testified, in a different circumstance, that he "had witnessed the dreadful state of depravity in which the men in the public gangs were sunk," and he concluded that "it arose from the state of slavery to which they were reduced." [9] This sparked the idea of a marks system, which was central to his reformative efforts. Incentives would be offered to counter the convicts' hopeless despair.

MACONOCHIE'S REFORMS

Maconochie set about instituting a program of reform on the island. He built churches and schools, and he walked among the convicts without fear. He instituted a five-stage program of reduced incarceration, culminating in the famous ticket of leave. A marks system was introduced, which enabled convicts to reduce their sentences by acquiring a certain number of good marks. The essence of Maconochie's program was passage through these five stages: (1) Strict custody upon admission to the penal colony. (2) Work on government gangs. (3) Limited freedom on the island, within a prescribed area. (4) Ticket of leave. (5) Full restoration of liberty.

---

[6] Frederick Howard Wines, *Punishment and Reformation* (New York: Thomas F. Crowell Company, 1910), p. 85.

[7] *Ibid.*, pp. 170–71.

[8] *Ibid.*, p. 191.

[9] *Ibid.*, p. 192.

Maconochie sought to put the fate of the prisoner in his own hands, and to enable him, through diligent and useful work, to effect a reduction in his sentence. He wanted fixed and maximum sentences abolished so that the convicts could earn time reductions through their labors. His introduction of this system marked the first time that penology had encountered such an idea, and within four years after starting his labors on Norfolk Island, he had reduced that savage island to a state of relative order. In his own words, "I found Norfolk Island a hell, but left it an orderly and well-regulated community."[10] Unfortunately, Maconochie was ahead of his time, and neither his successors on Norfolk, nor his country, were able to appreciate the greatness of his contribution.

THE TICKET OF LEAVE

The ticket of leave is so closely identified with Maconochie that some have given him credit for its origination. This is not the case. What Maconochie did was to give a new correctional use to a practice that was already in existence. Conditional pardons, which were similar to the ticket of leave, were being employed in the penal colonies of Australia when Maconochie arrived there. In fact, Captain Arthur Phillip had been given the authority, by the Crown, to grant conditional pardons when he was named governor of the colony at New South Wales. This was possible under an act dating from 1790.[11] Parole and the ticket of leave have been used synonymously because parole is a form of *conditional* release, and the ticket of leave (the parole contract in modern times) contains the conditions of that qualified release. The ticket of leave was actually a dispensation, signed by the governor, absolving a convict from required government work and permitting him to work elsewhere provided he could sustain himself.

When transportation was discontinued in 1852 (it was officially ended by law in 1857), there were about 9,000 men incarcerated in England under sentence of transportation.[12] These individuals were under long sentences because transportation was reserved for the more serious offenders. It had been intended that they could earn a reduction of as much as half of their sentences through good conduct while imprisoned. But when transportation ended, the huge number of prisoners awaiting transportation posed a king-sized problem. It was decided to discharge these

---

[10] *Ibid.*, p. 194.

[11] Killinger and Cromwell, *Corrections in the Community*, p. 404.

[12] Mary Carpenter, *Reformatory Prison Discipline as Developed by the Rt. Hon. Sir Walter Crofton in the Irish Convict Prisons* (London: Longmans, Green, Reader, and Dyer, 1872). Reprinted by Patterson Smith (Montclair, N.J., 1967), p. 45.

prisoners at home on "Tickets of License," which was accomplished through an 1853 Act of Parliament.

Parole, like probation is conditional liberty. It requires conformity with certain conditions, the breach of which can result in revocation. Similar conditions were imposed with the ticket of leave. Every convict liberated in the United Kingdom on ticket of leave had the following imprinted on his "license":

> 1. The power of revoking or altering the License of a Convict will most certainly be exercised in case of his misconduct.
>
> 2. If, therefore, he wishes to retain the privilege, which by his good behaviour under Penal Discipline he has obtained, he must prove by his subsequent conduct that he is really worthy of Her Majesty's clemency.
>
> 3. To produce a forfeiture of the License *it is by no means necessary that the holder should be convicted of any new offence. If he associates with notoriously bad characters, leads an idle and dissolute life, or has no visible means of obtaining an honest livelihood, etc., it will be assumed that he is about to relapse into crime, and he will be at once apprehended, and recommitted to prison under his original sentence.*[13]

Despite the ominous wording, the power to revoke was not "certainly exercised," and supervision was nonexistent. Some convicts even tore up their licenses so that the licenses could not become "silent witnesses" against them in the event that they were apprehended for new criminal activity. Supervision and revocation did not become actualities until the advent of the so-called "Irish System," developed by Sir Walter Crofton.

Sir Walter Crofton and the Irish System

While Maconochie should be credited with imaginative compassion in eliminating hopeless despair in the penal colony at Norfolk Island, it must be remembered that his activities were restricted to that one prison island, and they did not have the wide influence that resulted from the efforts of Sir Walter Crofton.

Sir Walter Crofton became head of the Irish prison system in 1854. Like Maconochie, he believed that prisons should not be purely places of punishment but should contain reformative programs. In this philosophy Crofton was building on the sentiments of other reformers as

[13] *Ibid.*, p. 46. Note the special provision for a "technical violation" of parole in item 3, whereby return to prison is not exclusively dependent upon conviction of a new offense.

well as Maconochie. Two other men, in the two decades preceding Crofton's work, had made notable contributions.

OTHER PIONEERS

In 1830 Georg Obermaier had been made governor of the prison at Kaiserslautern. In 1842 he was transferred to the prison at Munich. Upon assuming the post, he found almost 700 prisoners bound to one another with chains, dragging heavy weights, and in a state of potential insurrection. Obermaier struck the chains, fired the punitive guards, and placed inmate superintendents in charge of the prison workshops. Wines claims that Obermaier, "a wonderful man," was so successful "that only about seven per cent. [sic] of those at Kaiserslautern, and ten per cent. [sic] of those at Munich, relapsed into crime after their discharge." [14]

In 1835 Colonel Manuel Montesinos had been made governor of the prison at Valencia, Spain. He introduced a military-type regimen among the imprisoned and, under his system, inmates were allowed to reduce their sentences by one-third for good behavior. Montesinos believed in preparing the convicts for return to society, and felt that trade training was extremely important. At one time he actually had forty different trades being taught at his institution. The climate had been developing for the culminating endeavors of Sir Walter Crofton.

THE INTERMEDIATE SYSTEM

Although correctionalists in the United States refer to Crofton's program as "The Irish System," Crofton referred to it as "The Intermediate System." It was his opinion that convicts came into the system habituated to crime; crime was their vocation. It was the responsibility of the prison system to "amend" these criminals before releasing them. This could be best accomplished if the convicts were dealt with in small numbers and given to understand that their advancement toward freedom depended on their own efforts. He also felt that reforming convicts was not practicable in the "ordinary" prisons, that the public should be involved, and that "police supervision" should be imposed after release "to render the criminal calling more hazardous. . . ." [15]

The basic ingredients found in contemporary parole were introduced into the Irish System by Sir Walter Crofton: conditional release, community involvement, supervision, and revocation for breach of the condi-

---

[14] Wines, *Punishment and Reformation,* p. 202.

[15] *Ibid.,* p. 5.

tions of the Ticket of License. The "intermediate system" was a program featuring strict imprisonment in the initial phase, intermediate imprisonment in the middle phase, and ticket of leave with supervision in the culminating stage. Police officials supervised the paroled convicts, but in the city of Dublin, the first civilian parole officer, James P. Organ, was appointed with the title of Inspector of Released Prisoners. Organ was, by all accounts, an energetic and dedicated man, industriously engaged in activities similar to those performed by contemporary parole officers. Besides providing direct supervision over his cases, he traveled regularly about his "territory" inducing employers to provide jobs for his wards and making collateral contacts in the community.

In the first phase of the "intermediate system," the convict ordinarily served about eight or nine months in strict custody in Mountjoy Prison, Dublin. He was expected to do hard, monotonous work, and was maintained on a restricted diet in solitary confinement. If his conduct was satisfactory, he was advanced to an "Associate Prison" for the second phase of the program. Here, as little as four months could be served, marks were earned, and the prisoner was put to work on public projects. The prisoner was expected to demonstrate his reformation in this stage, mainly through the marks system. To enter the final stage, the phase of conditional release, the convict had to have a certain number of marks and had to have an employment offer waiting for him.

THE IRISH SYSTEM IN THE UNITED STATES

Crofton's "Irish System" was highly thought of in many parts of the world, but nowhere did it make a bigger impression than in the United States. In 1870 the American Prison Association held its first congress in Cincinnati, and during its proceedings the possibility of introducing the Irish System into America was discussed.

A paper entitled "The Irish System of Prison Discipline," by the Right Honorable Sir Walter Crofton, was read to the prison Congress. Some of the comments made by Crofton clearly indicate how advanced his thinking was. Many jurisdictions in the United States have not yet advanced as far. Sir Walter described his method as based on a classification system governed by a scale of marks as the measure of progress. Utilizing "this system of measuring the industry and improvement of the criminal, and crediting him with an intelligible value for it, he becomes, within certain limits, the arbiter of his own fate. . . ."[16]

[16] E. C. Wines, ed., *Transactions of the National Congress on Penitentiary and Reformatory Discipline,* held at Cincinnati, Ohio, October 12–18, 1870 (Albany, N.Y.: Weed, Parsons and Company, 1871), p. 67.

One year before the Cincinnati Congress convened, the New York legislature passed an act authorizing the establishment of Elmira Reformatory. Although the act was passed in 1869, the reformatory did not open until 1876. Elmira Reformatory was important, of course, as the first reformatory, but it has particular significance for us because the Irish System was introduced into that institution's programming. Newman categorically states that "Parole originated at the Elmira Reformatory," [17] adding to the historical controversy as to the origin of parole. The first superintendent at Elmira, Zebulon R. Brockway, not only was an ideal person to launch the new program because of his progressive correctional philosophy, he also had been instrumental in having the first indeterminate sentence law passed in Michigan in 1869 (interestingly, when Elmira was legislatively authorized), as well as in having an indeterminate sentence law passed in New York in 1876 (when he was appointed superintendent of Elmira).

Statutory and Theoretical Foundations

The first law to be passed which provided for the supervision of men released from prison was legislated in Massachusetts in 1845. The first statewide law regulating a parole agency was passed in Ohio in 1884. Unlike probation, parole did not have any major legal test of its validity, and it has been universally adopted. But it is still a bit of a puzzle to legal theorists. Attempts to explain or justify parole on theoretical grounds have led to the development of three basic theories, and the imminence of a fourth.

GRACE

According to the theory of grace, which evolved in the courts, no prisoner has the right to have his sentence diminished. As the judicial proceedings which have deprived the offender of his liberty have been in accordance with due process, the state has the right to demand that the convicted individual serve the full amount of his sentence. If parole is granted, therefore, it is an act of grace; it is a privilege and not a right. Supporting this theory, the courts have upheld the absolute discretionary powers of the parole board and have traditionally refused to intervene in parole matters.

---

[17] Charles L. Newman, *Sourcebook on Probation, Parole and Pardons,* 3rd ed. (Springfield, Ill.: Charles C Thomas, Publisher, 1968), p. 35.

This theory is easily challenged. First of all, it is a gratuitous assumption that due process accompanies every judicial process that restricts one's liberty. Furthermore, parole is part of the sentencing process. It has been intimately linked with the indeterminate sentence. It is also part of the evolution of reformative corrections. As a consequence of these considerations, it cannot be purely a matter of executive or administrative discretion.

CONTRACT

Another view, which is also a judicial point of view, is the theory that parole is based on contract considerations. This is similar to the grace theory; it differs in that it sees the granting of parole not so much as a matter of grace but as a matter of contract obligation. If you enter into a valid contract, several prerequisites have to be met. One of these requirements is that you enter into the agreement voluntarily. The contract theorists assert that the inmate does not have to accept parole. When he does, it is a voluntary act and it consequently binds him to the terms of the contract. In parole, of course, the "terms" are the conditions imposed by the paroling authority.

This theory can also be challenged on constitutional grounds. How can a party to a contract subject himself to unlimited conditions of performance? The parole board has had absolute discretion and unlimited powers to impose conditions. In a case with which I am familiar, a parole board ordered a female inmate to live with a lesbian, although the inmate was a heterosexual mother. Would these abuses of power stand up in a contemporary court of law? No civil contract would be legally binding which gave to one party in the agreement the right to impose unlimited conditions upon the other.

CUSTODY

Lawyers sometimes use quaint phrases to describe conditions. They employ the term "constructive" to indicate that a condition which is not readily apparent nevertheless exists. A paroled prisoner, for example, appears to be free, but he is legally considered to be in "constructive custody" because parole means that a prisoner is allowed to serve part of his sentence in the community. The community, in effect, becomes an extension of his prison cell. This is the basis of the "constructive custody" or "continuous custody" theory.

In this theory, the fiction of constructive custody is employed to rationalize parole. The element of privilege is also present, for parole is still considered a privilege; in this case it is the privilege of finishing a sentence in the community. Custody has simply been transferred to a more benevolent location. This has probably been the most popular of the three theories. This view can also be disputed. If a parolee violates his parole, he can be returned to prison. In other words, *he can be deprived of his liberty.* It is difficult to consider a man in (constructive) custody simultaneously being at liberty.

RESTRAINT OF LIBERTY

The United States Supreme Court used a phrase in a fairly recent decision which indicates the contemporary trend. That phrase was "restraint of liberty." [18] As we shall see in the following chapter, the courts have become more attentive to the rights of the imprisoned, and it appears that a new theory of parole is emerging. That theory would see the paroled prisoner as essentially free but conditionally restrained. This is a positive rather than a negative position. It emphasizes as the central factor, freedom, which occasionally has to be restrained, rather than custody, which must relentlessly be imposed.

OTHER INFLUENCES

Although Crofton's program gave the grand thrust to the collective efforts of the pioneers named, many influences and developments were responsible for the evolution of parole. The climate must always be ripe for a new idea to bear fruit. The efforts of Obermaier, Montesinos, Maconochie, and Crofton could not have been possible had there not been a gradual shifting in the philosophy of punishment. Centuries of brutal punishments in the name of corrections had wrought little, except to dehumanize people and blunt their sensibilities. In the early years of the nineteenth century the treatment of offenders reached a savage apogee in England, with hundreds of capital offenses and thousands of executions. The acceptance of a reformative philosophy of punishment was a natural reaction to centuries of horrifying "penology."

But it was not just a "natural reaction" that tipped the scales. Other developments were showing that alternatives existed and that the mechanics for reformative programs were present. Transportation itself was influential because it led to the development of stays of execution and

[18] *Jones v. Cunningham,* 83 Sup. Ct. 373 (1963).

Royal pardons for offenders under sentence of death. Clemency could be extended providing that the offender consented to transportation. The practice of indenture was influential, although it was not ostensibly a penal practice. Indenture was a system in which individuals were placed in service to a master for a period of apprenticeship. Some of the convicts transported to the American Colonies were subsequently indentured.

The excesses of transportation led to another positive influence, the domestic Ticket of License. The citizens of Australia had never been enthralled with England's policy of shipping its convicts to that small continent. As the influx of desperate criminals multiplied, so did the hostility of the law-abiding natives. The collective resentment eventually became sufficient to bring about the end of transportation, and to permit conditional releases without the intermediate step of transportation to a penal colony. These were some of the important influences that led to the development of parole as a correctional tool. But statutory innovations and legal changes also had to occur.

The Indeterminate Sentence

The indeterminate sentence is the handmaiden of parole. It is impossible to discuss one without discussing the other. Most of the authorities writing in the field have been unqualified supporters of the indeterminate concept of sentencing. In the Declaration of Principles of the American Prison Association (now the American Correctional Association), promulgated in 1870 and reaffirmed in 1960, Principle XV includes the statement, "In a correctionally oriented system of crime control, the indeterminate sentence administered by qualified personnel offers the best solution." [19] It has also been stated that "The acceptance of the indeterminate sentence is so general today that it is difficult to comprehend why it should have become a serious controversial issue." [20]

CONTROVERSY

The indeterminate sentence was controversial when it was first introduced. A little over a century later it has again become the subject of intense controversy. In 1975 a bill was introduced in the California legislature to abolish this one-time correctional ideal. Although the bill failed to pass, it heralded a strong tide running against the indeterminate sentence.

---

19 American Correctional Association, *Manual of Correctional Standards,* 1971, p. xxi.

20 Killinger and Cromwell, *Corrections in the Community,* p. 417.

The early promoters of the indeterminate sentence were forward-thinking men who felt that prisons should be reformative and that treatment in prison should prepare a prisoner for eventual release. An indeterminate sentence, in their thinking, permitted the inmate to be released at the most propitious time, that is, when he had reached maximum benefit from the prison treatment programs. As each man is an individual, each would be ready for parole at a time related to his own unique responses. The indeterminate sentence would permit the coordination of uniqueness with the best in rehabilitation philosophy. Such was the founding philosophy, and Barnes and Teeters called parole the "logical supplement of the indeterminate sentence." [21]

Giardini traces the indeterminate sentence back to Charles V of Germany, in 1532, asserting that it was devised as a protection against habitual offenders.[22] In the United States it was first used with juveniles at the New York House of Refuge, which was opened in 1825. But it was not until the opening of Elmira Reformatory that an indeterminate sentence, with provisions for maximum and minimum sentences, became law. The federal parole system did not have an indeterminate sentence until 1958.

The advantage of the indeterminate sentence, in theory, at least, is that it puts into an individual inmate's hands the ability to influence his own release from prison, measured by his rehabilitative progress. This was a firm supposition of the early prison reformers. But criticism of this presumption has mounted in recent years. How, it is asked, are we to determine rehabilitation? How does one tell when a prisoner has been rehabilitated? For that matter, how can anyone be rehabilitated in prison? As the spotlight of penetrating scrutiny has been placed upon the indeterminate sentence, some conclusions have been drawn that were not anticipated by its pioneer supporters. It is being recognized as an instrument of psychological devastation, because inmates are left in a state of anxious uncertainty about their release. The indeterminate sentence is predicated on a nebulous concept of "optimum rehabilitation," whatever that is.

A FLEXIBLY DETERMINATE SENTENCE

What is really needed is a compromise between the old, excessively long and rigidly fixed sentence, and the idealistic but psychologically punishing indeterminate sentence. That compromise I call the flexibly de-

[21] Barnes and Teeters, *New Horizons in Criminology*, 3d ed. (Englewood Cliffs, N.J.: Prentice-Hall, Inc., 1963), p. 423.

[22] G.I. Giardini, *The Parole Process* (Springfield, Ill.: Charles C Thomas, 1959), p. 8.

terminate sentence. We should not want to return to the long, deadening fixed sentence. Nor do we really want to lose the element of sentencing flexibility that the indeterminate sentence sought. And we do want to eliminate any inadvertent psychological torment. The resolution is a specific term sentence, with an option open to the inmate to reduce it by prescription, or to serve the full term.

This type of sentence will recognize the validity of punishment, without inhibiting the humanitarian impulse; it will end blind allegiance to an ineffective treatment model, yet will permit treatment devices an opportunity to demonstrate their efficacy.

If the inmate refuses to get involved in reformative fashioning of his own destiny, then he may serve the entire amount of the sentence. If, on the contrary, he wishes to become involved, he can reduce his sentence by fulfilling program prescriptions while imprisoned. Provisions would, of course, be made for the mentally deficient, incompetent, and exculpably psychopathological.

Suppose the inmate is illiterate. He may be programmed for literacy, with a scheduled reduction in his sentence directly related to his accomplishments in becoming literate. If he has the intellectual capacity to complete high school, but has never obtained a high school diploma, his prescription could revolve around this achievement. Prescription programming would be directed toward the inmate's self-enhancement or the acquisition of social or saleable skills. But it can also include provisions for restitution to his victim. While the law would spell out the precise parameters, program prescription should involve the innovative and imaginative ideas of the correctional staff and be tailored to the individual inmate's needs and abilities.

New York, in 1817, passed what is known as the first "good time" law. This law provided for a commutation of part of the sentence of an inmate in recognition of a good work record and good institutional behavior. This contains the germ of the flexibly determinate sentence. All that is needed is modification in terms of prescriptive programming and contemporary correctional wisdom. Parole could still be granted—for the period intervening between the release date and the statutory maximum. This, too, could be reduced on a prescription basis. The individual who refused to engage in prescription programming, and who served his full sentence, would be discharged. The indications would naturally be that he would be unresponsive to parole supervision had he not served his maximum sentence.

The important thing about the flexibly determinate sentence philosophy is that it is a motivational approach; it directly involves the individual in the process of his own redemption. There are some different philosophical viewpoints about the correctional endeavor, of course. As the rehabilitation model becomes more and more discredited, a shift has been taking place towards a punishment model. Sometimes the term "justice model" is used. By whatever term, the implication is that the moral imperatives of Kantian philosophy and the basic Christian view of punishment is being resurrected in what has long been a deterministic correctional discipline. The most prominent disciple of the new mood is Dr. David Fogel.

THE JUSTICE MODEL

It is difficult to do justice to any philosophical concept in a few restricted comments. Historical events and philosophical developments constantly conspire to change the tableau of our existence. This applies to every area of endeavor. Corrections is not exempt. The persisting failure of our correctional endeavors, the widespread and violent nature of crime, the deplorable neglect of the victim, the inefficacy of past correctional treatment efforts, and complex other factors have lead to the conviction that the criminal justice system ought to be literally committed to implementing *justice*, that treatment, if it can occur, should be a by-product of the effort to establish justice. These developments have synthesized in the mind of Dr. Fogel and resulted in a fascinating treatise on the subject.[23] Of immediate interest is his view of sentencing.

Citing a wide selection of distinguished jurists and correctional authorities who are turning from indeterminancy in sentencing, Fogel repudiates the indeterminate sentence but calls "for a system based upon a finding of *clear and present danger* to be necessary for the imposition of a term of imprisonment. . . . When a finding of clear and present danger is made, it should require incarceration."[24] Under the Justice Model, the convicted felon would be advised at the outset of the penalties attached to his particular crime, and the present law would be supplanted with a schedule of fixed sentences "keyed to the felony classification system."[25] Mitigation would be accommodated by ranges in the schedule of fixed sentences.

This is a view of sentencing that is a little more severe than the one that I have suggested. Once more we face the challenge of defined dangerousness, and once more we will have endless difficulty in doing so. Fogel's Justice Model is of particular interest, however, not only because of the thoughtful and scholarly manner in which the problem of crime

---

[23] David Fogel, ". . . *We Are The Living Proof* . . ." *The Justice Model For Corrections* (Cincinnati: The W.H. Anderson Company, 1975).

[24] *Ibid.*, p. 247.

[25] *Ibid.*, p. 254.

and punishment is surveyed, but because it epitomizes a very influential trend in contemporary correctional thinking. Irrespective of the direction we take philosophically, it can be anticipated that radical changes will take place in the indeterminate sentencing structure, and that it will eventually be displaced. The 1975 bill that was rejected in California would have replaced the indeterminate sentence with fixed sentencing categories, similar to those proposed by Fogel. Although the bill was defeated, it was a harbinger of future developments with respect to the indeterminate sentence.

The Parole Model in the United States

The earliest model for parole in the United States was, of course, the program introduced into Elmira Reformatory, which was based on Sir Walter Crofton's Irish System. As far as organizational structure is concerned, there have been many subsequent variations of the model. Some parole agencies are independent entities; some are subordinate components in Departments of Correction. Some are in agencies largely divorced from corrections, such as a Health and Welfare agency (Alaska), or the Department of Health and Social Service (Wisconsin).

COORDINATION OR SEPARATION

Some critics maintain that parole should be part of an integrated service which would include all of the correctional components. The National Advisory Commission takes this position.[26] The feeling is that uniformity will be enhanced and that a nonpartisan, global view of corrections has more promise of effectiveness than a fragmented system.

Opponents of this point of view feel that parole would be devoured by the institutional component in any coordinated system, because the prisons get the lion's share of correctional attention. Further, the parole board should retain its independence because it will make for a closer relationship between the paroling authority and the field services.

In controversies of this nature, it is difficult to separate political motivation from professional motivation. The Roman historian Tacitus once acknowledged that his image shone better in innocence than in eloquence. The eloquence of the competitors in the coordination-separation con-

[26] National Advisory Commission on Criminal Justice Standards and Goals, *Task Force Report: Corrections* (Washington, D.C.: U.S. Government Printing Office, 1973), p. 396.

troversy will have to be reduced to innocence before the final vote can be cast. In the meantime, it can be said that parole has developed immensely since its early seedlings in Australia, Ireland, and the United States.

Review Questions

1. Describe the practice and significance of transportation in the evolution of punishment.
2. Evaluate Maconochie's place in the history of parole and describe his Norfolk Island penal reforms.
3. Enumerate the essential details of Sir Walter Grofton's so-called "Irish System" of prison discipline and parole.
4. What system of parole did the United States adopt and why?
5. Explain the Theory of Grace.
6. What is the Contract Theory?
7. In what way does the Custody Theory differ from the two foregoing theories?
8. Name and describe the theory that appears to be currently emerging.
9. Critique the indeterminate sentence.
10. What is meant by a "flexibly determinate sentence"? Can you give an example?

12

CONTEMPORARY PAROLE

The present safety of the community requires that thousands of dangerous and persistent criminals somehow be steered away from destructive pursuits. . . .

The Report of the President's Task Force on Prisoner Rehabilitation

The final stage in the criminal justice processing of an offender is parole. Most of the inmates eventually released from prison are released on parole. Some of them are "dangerous and persistent criminals," some are harmless, modest offenders, some are bedeviled by alcohol or drugs, but they must all "somehow be steered away from destructive pursuits." How that is attempted, by whom, and with what degree of success is the focus of this chapter.

Parole: Philosophy and Objectives

The word "parole" was first used by neither Maconochie nor Crofton, but by Dr. S.G. Howe of Boston in 1846, in a letter to the Prison Association of New York.[1] It actually derives from the French *parole d'honneur,*

[1] It was Dr. Howe's wife, Julia Ward Howe, who wrote the lyrics to *The Battle Hymn of the Republic.*

which means word of honor, and was used, historically, to mean the pledge made by captured soldiers not to take up arms against their captors. The term has experienced a metamorphosis since that time.

PAROLE DEFINED

Many authorities feel that the definition of parole given in the *Attorney General's Survey of Release Procedures* in 1939 has yet to be improved upon. That definition of parole describes the process as "release of an offender from a penal or correctional institution, after he has served a portion of his sentence, under the continued custody of the state and under conditions that permit his reincarceration in the event of misbehavior." [2] This is an acceptable definition, but it does have one deficiency. It emphasizes only the negative aspects. Parole is more than unbroken custody and the prospect of reincarceration.

There are social and reconstructive elements that should grace any definition. It would be necessary only to add the intent of the parole process—social reintegration—to complete the missing link. The essential elements of parole would then be: (1) conditional release, (2) under supervision, (3) with social reintegration the agency objective, and (4) revocation the ultimate negative penalty. Parole is the privilege of serving part of a sentence outside of the prison compound, providing that conditions imposed by the parole board are adhered to. A parole officer affords active supervision to facilitate the reintegrative process and simultaneously to protect the public.

In England parole is described as:

> a scheme for the release on license of selected prisoners before they would normally be due for discharge. It provides an opportunity for those who do not have to be detained further in the public interest to resettle as law-abiding citizens and as ordinary members of the public before completing the whole of their sentence. The success of parole depends on the willing co-operation of those released who, for the period of the license, will receive the guidance, help and supervision of probation officers.[3] Though probation officers have an obligation to report to the Home Office any failure to comply with the conditions of a license, their particular concern is to assist—especially in the early period

---

[2] *Attorney General's Survey of Release Procedures* (Washington, D.C.: U.S. Government Printing Office, 1939), IV, 4.

[3] England uses the title "probation officer" to refer to what we call the "parole officer" in the United States.

> following release—a parolee's own efforts towards successful resettlement.[4]

While this is a ranging description rather than a precise definition, it does demonstrate the modern emphasis of "personal concern" for the reconstruction of the released offender, which is particularly exemplified in the last sentence.

PAROLE PHILOSOPHY

The reader should be able to deduce the philosophy of parole by this time. It should have been gleaned from the Stygian gloom of Norfolk Island, and in Dublin's Mountjoy Prison. It should have been sensed in the work of Obermaier and Montesinos, and in the winds of penal reform that began to stir in the mid-nineteenth century. The philosophy is one that embraces both individual redemption and community-based corrections.

The philosophy of parole is also intimately linked with the development of the concept of aftercare. "Aftercare" refers to many different developmental efforts to assist the products of institutionalization, whether they be mental patients, juvenile offenders, or adult felons, upon their release to the community. Keller and Alper credit the Low Countries, Switzerland, and England with pioneering the aftercare of mental patients, who were taken into private homes, usually in rural neighborhoods.[5] Concern for children in the criminal justice system led to development of the first juvenile court in 1899, and chancery rather than penal procedures for dealing with the troubled young.

Volunteer prisoner-aid societies played an important part in the development of the aftercare concept. The first of these was fittingly established in Philadelphia, the cradle of the penitentiary. It was known as the Philadelphia Society for Assisting Distressed Prisoners, and was founded in 1776. It ceased its activities in 1777, a casualty of the War of Independence, but was reorganized in 1787 as The Philadelphia Society for Alleviating the Miseries of Public Prisons. This volunteer prisoner-aid society is still in existence, now known as The Pennsylvania Prison Society.

---

[4] *Parole: Your Questions Answered,* Instructional Booklet for Prisoners, Home Office, London, England, Autumn 1972, p. 4.

[5] Oliver J. Keller, Jr., and Benedict S. Alper, *Halfway Houses: Community-Centered Correction and Treatment* (Lexington, Mass.: D.C. Heath and Company, 1970), p. 6.

THE OBJECTIVES OF PAROLE

The actual mission of parole is not to carry on an experiment in correctional therapy, nor to take the pressure off overcrowded prisons, nor to "mollycoddle" dangerous offenders. It is, quite simply, to protect society.

As far as therapy is concerned, the National Advisory Commission has stated that "Research has cast doubt on the effectiveness of psychological treatment of offenders. . . . The preponderance of the research strongly suggests that most offenders are not converted to law-abiding ways by psychotherapy." [6]

It is a fact that parole has been used to ease the pressure in dangerously overcrowded prisons, but that is not the de facto reason for the existence of parole, and it should be assumed that those paroled in such a circumstance are eligible for release according to other objective criteria.

It is a common fallacy that parole constitutes some sort of permissive indulgence and represents "mollycoddling" of convicted criminals by shortening their sentences. In 1964, the last time that national data were available on the number paroled in the United States, it was determined that parolees actually served more time than those discharged. (See Table 12–1.) In fact, as the National Advisory Commission points out, "one major criticism of present parole laws is that their administration tends to result in more severe penalties in a criminal justice system that already imposes extensive State control." [7]

Table 12–1. Number and Types of Releases in 1964 and Median Time Served

Type of Release	*Number*	*Median Time Served*
Discharge	22,883	20.1 months
Parole	42,538	21.1 months

Source: Adapted from National Advisory Commission, *Task Force Report: Corrections.*

The broader right of society to safety and immunity from criminal harm must transcend the rights of the minority of criminals who will

[6] National Advisory Commission on Criminal Justice Standards and Goals, *Task Force Report: Corrections* (Washington, D.C.: U.S. Government Printing Office, 1973), p. 515.

[7] *Ibid.*, p. 390.

recidivate. That is beyond question. Unfortunately we cannot predict future behavior with such precision as to enable us to make a simple dichotomy of rights. The compromise is to introduce a method of correctional operation that will afford maximum protection for the community and maximum opportunity for reintegration into that community by its conditionally released offenders. Parole proposes to facilitate that objective. Its methodology is to employ trained correctionalists who are able to provide professional counsel, and are able to mobilize the community and its resources in a partnership of rehabilitation. Crime is the product of ruptured social relationships and/or the lack of social skills necessary for "normal" societal adjustment. The parole officer has a mandate from society to try to remedy these deficiencies.

The Parole Board

In response to a questionnaire from the National Council on Crime and Delinquency Research Center, forty-eight states, the federal government, the District of Columbia, and Puerto Rico reported a total of 131,121 adults on active parole, and forty-nine jurisdictions reported 51,927 active juveniles on parole, as of June 30, 1974.[8] A grand total of 214,284 individuals were reported as cumulatively on active and inactive parole status. In each instance, a parole board's decision in the past had changed the status from prisoner to parolee. In most instances there was a series of negative decisions postponing parole before the affirmative decision granting parole was reached. The parole board, the fulcrum in the terminal phase of the correctional process, has been under increasing attack of late.

STRUCTURE AND COMPOSITION OF THE PAROLE BOARD

According to the Manual of Correctional Standards, there are four basic parole board structures: [9]

1. Those administering an integrated probation and parole agency
2. Those administering the parole function only
3. Those that are a subordinate component of a department which administers the penal institutions

---

[8] National Probation and Parole Institutes, *NEWSLETTER Uniform Parole Reports* (Davis, Calif.: NCCD Research Center, January 1975).

[9] American Correctional Association, *Manual of Correctional Standards* (1971), p. 124.

4. Those that are part of an agency which administers the institutional and probation services.

In the majority of states, the parole board administers an integrated probation and parole agency.

Most states have three-member parole boards, although twenty-one states have five-member boards. New York State has the largest parole board, with twelve members. The United States Parole Board, whose members are appointed by the President, has a total of eight members.

In the overwhelming majority of states, parole board members are political appointees. In forty jurisdictions they are ordinarily appointed by the governor. In only two states are parole appointments subject to a civil service merit system.[10] It is apparent that parole board members are subject to considerable political pressures, and often reflect the political and correctional philosophy of the appointing power.

QUALIFICATIONS AND FUNCTIONS OF THE PAROLE BOARD

In twenty-four paroling jurisdictions, including the federal system, there are no specified, prerequisite qualifications for membership on the parole board. Fourteen states spell out behavioral science and/or educational requirements, and the remainder rely on broad generalities, sometimes including a requirement that there be political balance on the board. It is difficult to reconcile political balance with competent correctional expertise, but that is the gift of political intervention.

At first flush, it would seem that the parole board's function is very simply to grant paroles to imprisoned inmates. That is, of course, a very important function, but the parole board has many other duties to perform. It must make determinations as to the most propitious time for paroling individuals. It must establish conditions of parole. When those conditions are breached, the parole board is the body that permits the parolee to remain in the community or orders his return to prison as a parole violator. In many jurisdictions the parole board is the body empowered to restore certain civil rights to those who have lost those rights through conviction of a felony. The parole board must also articulate its function to the public, and press for progessive legislation in its field. In some states the parole board has an active or advisory function to perform with respect to pardons and executive clemency. Finally, it is the parole board that issues the discharge to the individual who has successfully completed parole.

---

[10] Ohio, and Wisconsin.

Parole board hearing at Lewisburg Federal Penitentiary. *Courtesy U.S. Bureau of Prisons. Photo by Leo M Dehnel.*

The central function is, quite naturally, the decision-making process through which parole is granted or revoked. In the great majority of jurisdictions, parole is intimately related to the indeterminate sentence, through which the parole board exercises its decision-making discretion. There is another type of release to parole supervision, however, called *mandatory release;* this is parole that is automatically granted after a stipulated amount of the sentence has been served. This form of release is characteristic of the federal system, New York, and Wisconsin. It is also more or less the release system in England, where parole is known as "license."

Where there is an indeterminate sentence structure, the parole board can set the sentence anywhere between the statutory minimum and the statutory maximum. Normally, the minimum cannot be reduced, but this is not always the case. In California, for instance, an inmate can be paroled after serving one-third of the statutory minimum, but in no case less than six months. In Michigan, good time can be deducted from the minimum. In England, a differentiation is made between prisoners serving sentences of three years or less, and those with longer sentences. In the former situation the prisoner is eligible for parole after serving twelve months; in the latter circumstance he is eligible for parole after serving one-third of his sentence or twelve months, whichever expires first.

The indeterminate sentence is also coming under some heavy fire of late. The basis for the criticism is that an inmate is never sure of his exact release date, and is consequently the victim of needless psychological stress when parole consideration is regularly postponed. The indeterminate sentence is based on the presumption that parole should be granted at the "right" time, when the inmate has experienced maximum institutional rehabilitation. But how is that to be ascertained? The real issue is the decision-making process which leads to selection for parole.

DECISION-MAKING AND SELECTION BY THE PAROLE BOARD

It is a well-established fact that parole boards base their decisions to grant parole on three fundamental criteria: (1) the past criminal history, (2) the institutional adjustment, and (3) the risk factor with respect to future behavior. The imprecise state of the decision-making art in parole hearings can be deduced from the following considerations:

The past neither guarantees nor predetermines the future, although it may influence it. Past behavior is a guide to the *prospective* future, to be sure, but to let the past completely govern the present is to mortgage the future to cynicism.

Institutional adjustment is another charade. "Good institutional adjustment" may mean nothing more than good institutional *adaptation.* It may indicate a broken spirit, or undue submissiveness. It can also indicate inordinate dependency and passivity, or "learning how to play the game" to impress the parole board. The adjustment that needs to be examined is the *post-institutional adjustment.*

The risk factor is a valid concern, but conservative decisions made on the basis of generalized apprehension are too often made on false premises. For example, those who have been imprisoned for crimes against the person are ordinarily seen as greater risks, yet all of the reputable research data confirms that the public is in greater danger from the property offenders, at least in terms of recidivism.

All of the academic discussions notwithstanding, the fact is that decisions concerning men's destinies should be made with the utmost sobriety, and should be based on maximal knowledge of each case. Protecting society should be the governing concern, of course, but the power over lives that parole boards have exercised has been awesome, to say the least. As Russell G. Oswald said when he was chairman of the New York State Board of Parole, "The control of human freedom is a frightening responsibility. . . ."[11] The power exercised by the California Adult Authority has been described as "of almost mythical dimensions" in a leading correctional publication.[12] This is one of the reasons why paroling authorities have been consistently assailed. Following sustained criticism of its past performance, the United States Parole Board reorganized its decision-making procedures in 1974. It added a provision for notifying an inmate of the reasons for parole denial, and provided a procedure for appealing parole denial to the full board.[13] In 1975 the California Adult Authority, following the lead of the federal system, instituted a procedure for communicating to the inmate the reasons for denial of parole.

NCCD POLICY ON PAROLE GRANTING

In a 1973 policy statement, the National Council on Crime and Delinquency declared that parole should be denied only when there is a compelling reason to believe that the safety of the public would be endangered. It further asserted that the inmate should be informed in writing of the reasons for parole denial, given an explanation of the criteria for parole selection, and advised in which respect he did not meet the criteria.[14] The Model Penal Code of the American Law Institute also takes the position that parole should be withheld only if the inmate poses a substantial risk, and that parole should be the first method of release for *all* offenders.[15]

There has been an acute need for explicit paroling policy. To leave these decisions to subjective hunch or fancy does violence to the most rudimentary concepts of justice. A quartet of noted authorities in the field have developed what they term "an explicit indicant of parole selection," to facilitate sounder, more consistent parole board decisions. At the present, there is no evidence that parole boards are using "the right determinants" in parole selection.[16] The core of the problem is to find a system of weighting the most important factors, and to devise

---

[11] Russell G. Oswald, "Decisions! Decisions! Decisions!" *Federal Probation,* 34, no. 1 (March 1970), 32.

[12] Michael S. Serrill, "Profile/California," *Corrections Magazine,* 1, no. 1 (September 1974), 8.

[13] *Criminal Justice Newsletter,* 5, no. 13 (July 1, 1974), 5.

[14] *Crime and Delinquency,* 19, no. 2 (April 1973), 137.

[15] Section 305.9(1).

[16] Don M. Gottfredson, Peter B. Hoffman, Maurice H. Sigler, and Leslie Wilkins, "Making Paroling Policy Explicit," *Crime and Delinquency,* 21, no. 1 (January 1975), 34–44.

a rating chart or formula which board members could apply at the decision-making stage. Introducing equity and uniformity into the decision-making process would be most laudable. A perfect model will never be obtained, but it would be of immeasurable benefit to at least have some stability in the criteria which are the foundation of parole decision-making. The reorganized federal system adopted a "salient factor score," which was also developed by the four authorities cited above. A weighted scale is employed which introduces a greater degree of consistency into the parole factor analysis. If it can be perfected it may save the parole board from extinction.

CRITIQUE OF THE PAROLE BOARD

Criticism of parole boards has almost reached a crescendo in recent years, and it ranges from the most exacerbating attacks to more moderate suggestions for improving the qualifications and decision-making capabilities of board members. A parole violator in a California prison condemned the parole board for allegedly spending only "4 to 7 minutes in evaluating an inmate's 365-day-calendar-year." He described the Adult Authority as a "board of ruthless tyrants." [17] In her acerbic survey of "the prison business," Jessica Mitford also singled out the California Adult Authority for some biting criticism, referring to them as "eight cops and a dentist." [18] Paradoxically, a bill was introduced into the California legislature in 1975 to make the members of the Adult Authority personally responsible for the crimes subsequently committed by the parolees they release from prison.

To make an objective evaluation of the parole board would require assessment of a number of factors and processes. Not only would the caliber and qualifications of parole board members have to be scrutinized, but it would be necessary to examine the indeterminate sentence, the decision-making process, the enabling statutes, public opinion, the sentiment of the legislature, and the philosophy of a great many subdivisions of the criminal justice system. How it would be possible to do this, and emerge with a parole board that would dispense equity and justice, is a challenge that King Solomon would find insuperable. It would seem that the parole board is destined to be phased out of the correctional process ultimately, because, in the administration of evenhanded justice, its deficiencies are obviously of more consequence than its strengths.

---

[17] Quoted in San Francisco *Sun-Reporter,* January 22, 1972.

[18] Jessica Mitford, *Kind and Usual Punishment* (New York: Alfred A. Knopf, 1973), p. 86.

The Parole Officer

A parole officer whom I once observed was counseling a black parolee who had been having marital difficulties. One day, after several counseling sessions, the parolee arrived at the parole office in a very exhilarated mood which, it turned out, resulted from the fact that he had effected a reconciliation with his wife. Obviously without thinking, the parole counselor remarked, "Worked a little of that old black magic, eh, Charlie?" The professional in parole work has a very demanding role to fulfill. Wry humor is only incidental to the many credentials which he must possess.

THE ROLE OF THE PAROLE OFFICER

Unlike the welfare worker who gets involved in only a limited area of the client's life, the parole officer has a total involvement in the destiny of his parolee. The welfare worker may withdraw financial assistance, but the parole officer can withdraw freedom. He oversees the parolee's employment activities, family interactions, recreational activities, associates, and general mode of existence. Vested with awesome authority, the parole officer has a complex role to play. Simultaneously charged with the responsibility of protecting the public and servicing his client, his professional role has personified ambivalence.

As the evidence multiplies that little of a purely therapeutic nature really occurs from the parolee–parole officer relationship, the conviction has grown that the real function of the parole officer should be to provide a catalytic function in terms of the community's resources. The National Advisory Commission has pointed out that a substantial number of parolees can do quite well without much supervision. "For those parolees requiring more intensive help, the emphasis in recent years, and one worthy of support, has been toward effecting as many needed services as possible through community resources available to the general population."[19]

This means that the old tradition, which made the parole officer the alpha and the omega of the parolee's programming, must yield. It is not as a developer of resources but as a broker of resources that the parole officer will be most effective. In 1971 Studt had pointed out that the parole officer could not "possibly develop the entire range of specialized kinds of

[19] National Advisory Commission, *Corrections*, p. 410.

competence that may be needed."[20] The emphasis should be on developing a more efficient "service technology," which will tap the parolee into the vast reservoir of community resources.

QUALIFICATIONS OF THE PAROLE OFFICER

The attributes that we pointed out as desirable in a probation officer are equally desirable in the parole officer, for the positions are generic: they are relatively interchangeable professions whose members should function effectively in either agency.

The most appropriate academic preparation for parole work is generally considered to be in behavioral sciences. Graduate study in social work has also been stressed as a desirable prerequisite for correctional social work. The National Advisory Commission, agreeing with the President's Crime Commission, maintains that the basic educational requirement for a parole officer should be a bachelor's degree. Since a great many of the parole officer's tasks do not require sophisticated skills, the Commission also strongly suggested that paraprofessionals be utilized to perform these functions.[21]

Newman sees the skills of the parole officer as being employed in three main areas, (1) case assistance, (2) control, and (3) decision-making.[22] In the area of *case assistance*, the parole officer must have a comprehensive knowledge of community resources so he can mobilize the particular assistance needed in a crisis situation, as well as routinely. Resource assistance may be practical or therapeutic, ranging from job counseling to sophisticated psychotherapy. This also implies that the parole officer will develop appropriate insights about the individual parolee through observation of his behavior.

Control involves the function of surveillance, through which the parole officer accentuates his crime-prevention role, and in which the protection of society is emphasized. Control also includes the investigation of alleged criminal activities by parolees, and the imposition of special restraints, such as parole conditions and biological or chemical testing for drug addiction.

Decision-making is, obviously, the heart of the correctional function, in every component of the criminal justice system. Judgments must be made

---

[20] Elliot Studt, *People in the Parole Action System: Their Tasks and Dilemmas* (Los Angeles: UCLA, Institute of Government and Public Affairs, 1971), p. 101.

[21] National Advisory Commission, *Corrections*, p. 415.

[22] Charles L. Newman, *Personnel Practices in Adult Parole Systems* (Springfield, Ill.: Charles C Thomas, Publisher, 1971), p. 56.

about programs and program resources, about continuing or revoking parole, about legal rights and social circumstances. Here the parole officer can be seen at his professional best, or at his incompetent worst. We have stressed that judgments involving the destinies of human beings should never be made lightly, and particularly when those individuals face loss of their personal liberties. Good decisions are made on the basis of knowledge, alternative courses of action available, a sufficient reservoir of facts, and with the risk factor minimized. In-service training should include continuous examination of the decision-making process.

THE PAROLE OFFICER'S TIME

One of the more important challenges facing the parole officer is the wise utilization of his time. His activities include dictating and recording case activity, conferencing cases, prerelease activity, collateral case activities, interaction with law enforcement and other social agencies, the development of employment and other resources, and direct case servicing. The amount of time actually available for direct case services is a great deal less than one might expect. A California study showed that less than one-third of the parole officer's time is given to this primary function.[23]

It is also necessary that the parole officer be constantly alert to newly developing resources in his community. The opening of new companies and new shopping centers means the possibility of jobs for his parolees; a new Salvation Army or St. Vincent de Paul facility means the possibility of transient accommodations as well as shelter care; the opening of a new mental health center means the availability of specialized therapeutic treatment for the emotionally disturbed. In addition, there must be ceaseless contact with established agencies in the community which have the capacity to meet the broad range of needs characteristic of individuals released from incarceration.

THE PAROLE OFFICER SYSTEM

As Irwin pointed out, the parole process brings together in a close relationship two individuals from totally different worlds.[24] This, in effect, militates against the effectiveness of the relationship. It also puts the

---

[23] The actual percentage was 30.7. California Department of Corrections, *The Parole Agent Time Study*, Sacramento, 1972, p. 7.

[24] John Irwin, *The Felon* (Englewood Cliffs, N.J.: Prentice-Hall, Inc., 1970), p. 157.

parolee in an environment that is inherently conflictual. In fact, "the parolee's career entails living until discharge with structurally imposed role-conflicts that affect all aspects of his life." [25]

Depending upon his own particular training and philosophy, the parole officer comes to this relationship exemplifying any of several role models. There is the parole officer who adopts the *guardian-ward* relationship, in which he takes a moral responsibility for his client's behavior. Another model is the *superordinate-subordinate,* in which the parole officer exercises a paternalistic role. There are those who strive for an *equalitarian* model, but the relationship is not one of equality, no matter how much the parole officer is enamored of pure democracy.

The appropriate model is the *reality-oriented integrationist* model, in which the true dimensions of the parolee–parole officer relationship are realistically defined, and the function of the relationship is to facilitate the reintegration of the client into the community. The model should be one which recognizes the many roles the parole officer must play, from custodian to counselor, and which will vary depending upon whether he is supervising youths or adults.

DIAGNOSIS, TREATMENT, AND SUPERVISION

Because of the unfortunate and lingering influences of the medical model and social casework on corrections, the diagnostic comments in the case material of most parole agencies are often not only unrealistic, but sometimes quite ludicrous. For example, this was the diagnostic comment made in the case of an inmate who had escaped from prison, and who had been at large for almost fifteen years before being retaken: "If he can overcome his restlessness and settle down to steady employment, under strict supervision, he should have a reasonable chance to succeed on parole." Such a "diagnostic" comment is, of course, utterly worthless.

Yet the case history provides the basis for parole decision-making to an extensive degree, and the data recorded in it should support the validity of this process. Glaser made the observation that no correctional administrator has advocated the replacement of the subjective case evaluation by a statistical method of prediction, because correctionalists are "making moral decisions for the state," and because some case information does not readily lend itself to statistical accounting.[26] This places a responsibility

---

25 Elliot Studt, *Surveillance and Service in Parole,* A Report of the Parole Action Study, MR-166 (Los Angeles: UCLA, Institute of Government and Public Affairs, 1972), p. 24.

26 Daniel Glaser, *The Effectiveness of a Prison and Parole System* (New York: Bobbs-Merrill Company, Inc., 1964), p. 304.

on the professional to be scrupulous in his accounting and recording of case information.

We have touched upon the treatment dilemma throughout, and particularly in the chapters on probation. It bears repeating that treatment is not a commodity that is superimposed, but, rather, a regenerative process that is initiated by the object of the treatment. As a convict in a Minnesota State Prison phrased it, "they can't cure anybody unless we allow them to." [27] In supervising the parolee, the parole officer may experiment with "treatment modalities" that appeal to him, and which will presumably benefit the client. But, as Giardini has perceptively pointed out, "the officer is not to be regarded as a person who will assume all the parolee's burdens or who will necessarily lighten them. The officer's principal task is to counsel the parolee about how he may learn to carry his own burdens in a manner that will be sanctioned by society." [28]

The parole process is fundamentally a helping process, but there is no rigid blueprint for successful helping. Social work philosophy itself vacillates when it comes to the helping methodology. A parole officer writing in 1952 condemned the "established practice of social agencies to make unplanned field visits" to parolees. He spoke appreciatively of the fact that the practice had terminated, for no "social work leader" advocated such a practice.[29] But unplanned field contacts with parolees are a standard part of *contemporary* practice. This type of philosophic conflict is a further reason to redirect parole away from vacillating theory toward a posture of positive, practical assistance. This philosophy of parole has another advantage. It will make possible the acquisition of data that can be empirically evaluated, a necessity if we are to measure the effectiveness of the parole process.

PAROLE REVOCATION

Parole revocation signals the failure of the parole process. It indicates that the conditions of parole have been breached to a degree that contraindicates continuance on parole in the community. Parole may be violated through the commission of a new felony and consequent reimprisonment by the courts, or it may come about through serious breaches of the technical conditions of parole, which do not result in court-adjudicated commitment to prison.

In the past, a great deal of arbitrary discretion was exercised by parole

[27] Quoted in Michael S. Serrill, "Profile/Minnesota," *Corrections Magazine*, 1, no. 3 (January–February 1975), 7.

[28] G.I. Giardini, *The Parole Process* (Springfield, Ill.: Charles C Thomas, Publisher, 1959), p. 203.

[29] Charles Bluestein, "Parole Perspectives," *Focus*, 31, no. 1 (January 1952), 18.

boards when it came to the process of revocation, and parole officers had practically unlimited powers to deprive a parolee of his liberty. As recently as the sixties, a California parolee could be placed in custody pending "Investigation of Violation of Conditions of Parole." This meant that a parolee could languish in a county jail for a substantial period of time, while *suspicious circumstances* were investigated. If the investigation was resolved in favor of the parolee, he would be released from the county jail and continued on parole. No one thought of challenging the right of a parole officer to *sentence* a man to a period of time in the county jail for the "crime" of suspicion. Parolees often spent months in custody under these circumstances. The courts did little to discourage this practice because the parolee was deemed, in judicial language, to be in *constructive custody* while on parole, and his home was construed to be an extension of his cell.[30]

During the sixties and particularly in the seventies, the courts began to intervene, and the ancient "hands-off" doctrine gradually eroded. Under the hands-off doctrine, the courts had held that they were incapable of interfering with the prison administration. A federal decision had actually declared that "The court has no power to interfere with the conduct of the prison or its discipline."[31] Currently the opposite is true, and the courts are predisposed to rule on all aspects of prison life and administration, and substantially in favor of the inmate petitioners. In perhaps the most significant decision so far, the United States Supreme Court has ruled that a parolee is entitled to have a pre-revocation hearing to test the validity of the parole officer's charges, *in the community before he can actually be returned to prison.*[32]

Parole revocation for technical reasons should be contemplated only after much soul-searching. If it is decided upon, it should be with the conviction that the parolee cannot continue in the community without serious jeopardy to the community or to himself. This judgment, as well as the judgment to continue an individual on parole after infractions, must be based upon certain critical factors. These are (1) the nature of the violation, (2) the individual's past criminal history, (3) the calculated risk to the community, and (4) the presence or absence of community resources necessary to maintain the individual in the community.

The Parolee

The principal actor in the drama of parole is, of course, the parolee. Concern for him should be manifested before he attains the status of

---

30 *People v. Denne,* 141 Cal.App.2d 499, 507–508 (1956).

31 *Powell v. Hunter,* 172 F.2d 330 (10th Cir., 1949).

32 *Morrissey v. Brewer,* 408 U.S. 471 (1972).

parolee. In the ideal situation, the field parole officer and the institutional counselor assigned to the inmate who is to be paroled should coordinate their planning. The parole officer should visit his prospective client before the latter is released, to break the ice and to initiate a positive relationship in advance of parole. This is not always possible, for the prison is often at a great distance from the parole office, but wherever possible, prerelease contact between the parole officer and his prospective parolee should be encouraged.

PRERELEASE PLANNING

The time to plan for release from prison is long before that release takes place. The average inmate will have enough anxiety built up at his departure from the prison; he should not have any undue anxieties about his parole program and his parole officer. Some states have intensive prerelease programming, such as South Carolina, Texas, Washington, and Michigan. Most states provide some preparatory introduction to parole. California has a major reorganization under way which will enable parole agents and inmates to work closely together for the six months preceding an inmate's release to parole. Known as the Reentry Program, it is designed to maximize the effectiveness of the professional relationship, and to minimize the inmate's prerelease anxieties. It is presumed that under this system, solid release planning can be assured and recidivism thereby further reduced.

PAROLE CONDITIONS

Parole is a form of contract. Conditional release is dependent upon satisfactory fulfillment of the terms of parole. In past years, parole conditions were much more restrictive than they are today; they could invade every aspect of a parolee's life. Parolees were forbidden to indulge in alcoholic beverages of any kind, even when alcohol posed no particular problem for the temperate drinker. Infractions could lead to reimprisonment. Driving privileges could be automaticaly suspended by the parole officer, salary stubs had to be submitted to the parole office, cohabitation was closely regulated, and association with persons who had been in trouble with the law was severely dealt with. Registering to vote in a primary election was a violation of parole in New York in 1945, and church attendance was mandatory in Tennessee. These are representative examples of an earlier restrictiveness.

But since the courts have begun to scrutinize the parole process, the tendency has been to reduce the (restrictive) conditions of parole to fewer, more meaningful regulations. These include obliging the parolee to report to his parole officer and to follow the latter's reasonable instructions, to refrain from criminal activity, to maintain stability of employment and residence, and to refrain from possessing deadly weapons or use of illicit narcotics or drugs. There are usually additional regulations on the movement of a parolee, and provisions for special conditions of parole. See Fig. 12–1 and Fig. 12–2 for representative samples of parole conditions.

Every state currently has a parole system, as does the federal government. There are, as we have learned, well over 130,000 adults and well over 50,000 juveniles currently under parole supervision. In 1939 only eight states and the federal government provided supervision for parolees, and it was estimated that over 20,000 parolees were without real supervision in the community.[33] Some states have more than a dozen conditions of parole, others have as few as five. But the trend is for a gradual shrinking of the number of restrictive conditions because the courts are showing a disposition to enlarge the rights of the convicted felon and the parolee.

THE PAROLEE'S NEEDS

Some very sophisticated treatment programs have been developed for the released offender but, except where there is evidence of a serious emotional problem, it has been consistently demonstrated that the basic needs of parolees revolve around the physical and the material. In a collaborative research study directed by the Western Behavioral Sciences Institute, an attempt was made to determine the needs of parolees *from the perspective of the parolee.* It was concluded that "The most pressing needs expressed by the parolees were physical and material, including a job, money, and a place to stay. The parolees' greatest concerns were that they were not using their ability, they lacked money and their education was inadequate." [34]

The findings of such studies should provide the operational parole officer with some programming insights. A man without a job, and with all of the consequent humiliations that are attendant on being unemployed, will not be very responsive to an esoteric discussion of the "dynamics" of being unemployed. He will be responsive to a satisfying

---

33 The National Conference on Parole, *Parole in Principle and Practice* (New York: National Probation and Parole Association, 1957), p. 10.

34 Rosemary J. Erickson, Wayman J. Crow, Louis A. Zurcher, and Archie V. Connett, *Paroled But Not Free* (New York: Behavioral Publications, 1973), p. 97.

Following is the parole agreement that you are entering into with the State of Michigan. The rules outlined are not intended to punish you or to prevent you from doing things other citizens are allowed to do. Their intent is to guide you away from situations which might lead you to commit another crime. You should always remember that parole is a privilege and not a right.

CONDITIONS OF PAROLE

1. RELEASE: Upon release you will proceed directly to your destination and contact your parole agent as indicated on this parole certificate.
2. RESIDENCE: You must obtain permission from your parole agent before changing your approved residence. You must obtain his written permission to leave the state.
3. REPORTS: You are to submit a truthful written report once a month, or as often as your parole agent may require. As soon as possible between reports you must inform your parole agent of any arrests or other matters which might endanger your standing on parole.
4. MOTOR VECHICLES: You must obtain written permission from your parole agent before driving, buying, or providing money for the purchase of any motor vehicle. You must have a valid driver's license and adequate public liability insurance.
5. WEAPONS: You cannot own, purchase, possess, use, sell or have under your control any deadly object, weapon, firearm, or imitation thereof, or be in the company of any person possessing the same.
6. WORK: You must work steadily at an approved job and obtain authorization from your parole agent to change employment.
7. ASSOCIATION: You are not to associate with persons having a police record without authorization of your parole agent. You may not visit any correctional facility without the permission of your parole agent.
8. CONDUCT: You are not to engage in any antisocial conduct which could cause you to be a hazard to yourself or the person or property of another.
9. LAWS & ORDINANCES: You are to obey all state and federal laws, local ordinances and court orders.
10. SPECIAL CONDITIONS: You will live up to such special conditions of parole that may be ordered. You will comply promptly with any written or oral request made of you by your parole agent.

AGREEMENT OF PAROLE

In consideration of the parole granted me I hereby accept and agree to abide by the above rules which I have read, or have had read to me.

By acceptance of this parole I agree to waive extradition to Michigan from any jurisdiction, and to return to the State of Michigan whenever required by the Michigan Parole authorities.

If found guilty of parole violation, I understand that the Parole Board will consider my entire history in determining the action to be taken.

I realize that by accepting this parole I am agreeing to conduct myself at all times according to the privileges and responsibilities of citizenship.

Signed ______________________ Signed ______________________
Witness Parolee

Released by ______________________ Date ______________________

CONDITIONS OF PAROLE

Some of the more common special conditions imposed by the Parole Board or agent are:

No drinking of alcoholic beverages.

Cannot associate with anyone having a criminal or police record.

Not to leave the county without written permission of PA.

Cannot change jobs without prior permission.

Not to marry without written permission of the PA.

This flexibility in special conditions permits the Board or the agent to construct controls tailored to the needs of the case. For instance, a common condition imposed on certain sex offenders is "No association or contact with female minors." Such a condition would be unnecessary for any but a small number of parolees.

Fig. 12–1. Michigan Parole Conditions.

CSR No.________________

TO:____CSP No.________________

The COLORADO STATE BOARD OF PAROLE, in session at________________________________
on____ has considered your application for parole and believing you can abide by the conditions set forth in your parole agreement, hereby grants you parole effective on____________________________.

PAROLE AGREEMENT

I agree to be supervised by the Division of Parole and to be accountable for my actions and conduct to the Division of Parole, including urinalysis or other tests for narcotics or chemical agents, and search of my person, my residence, other premises under my control, or any vehicle under my control.

I further agree to abide by all conditions of parole as set forth in this agreement, including any additional conditions consistent with the laws of the State of Colorado. I fully understand that violation of any condition can lead to suspension or revocation of my parole and return to the institution from which I am paroled. Should I be charged with an additional crime while I am on parole and be permitted to post bond, I understand I may be returned to the institution to await the decision of the Board of Parole.

CONDITIONS OF PAROLE

1. RELEASE: Upon release from the institution, I shall go directly to____________________________
______________________________________as designated by the Board of Parole and report to
____
____
____
____by mail / in person.

2. RESIDENCE: I shall establish a residence of record and shall remain at this residence in fact and on record and shall not change this residence nor leave the State or County to which I have been paroled without the knowledge and consent of my Parole Agent.

3. CONDUCT: I shall obey all state and federal laws and municipal ordinances, and shall at all times and in all respects maintain myself as a law abiding citizen. I will not associate with known criminals.

4. REPORT: I shall make written and / or in person reports as directed by the Parole Agent.

5. WEAPONS: I shall not own, possess, nor have in my custody nor under my control any firearm or other deadly weapon.

6. ADDITIONAL CONDITIONS:

I have read, or have had read to me, this entire document and I have full understanding of it, and I have received a copy of this document.

____
Signature of Parolee

____
Notary Public

____
Date

Fig. 12–2. Colorado Parole Conditions.

job, which will sever his financial dependence on others. Idealism and selflessness are most desirable attributes, but we live in a money economy, and to be deprived of purchasing power in a capitalistic economy is a devastating experience. We also ascribe status in our society in terms of a person's vocation or profession. This explains why the parolees surveyed felt their education was inadequate. Functional field planning should emphasize and give priority to productive, meaningful employment, and to academic and vocational advancement so that the individual will feel an increasing sense of worth and earn his place in the sun.

THE IMPORTANCE OF EMPLOYMENT

Every year our prisons disgorge about 100,000 men and women. Within two years, more than half of that number will be reincarcerated. There are many reasons, of course, but a primary one is that many of these individuals simply do not have adequate programs, specifically including remunerative, satisfying work. The ex-felon is rarely trained to compete vocationally, and is too often obliged to take menial jobs. The solution is not merely to have the government pour money into what is known as "supportive work" programs. These are ordinarily menial jobs, such as raking leaves, for which an inflated salary is paid. The solution is to provide adequate training, and to secure substantial employment—and to involve the community in this reconstructive effort.

An organization known as Project Second Chance began operating out of the black ghetto area of Brooklyn in 1972, as a pilot program in placing ex-offenders. Voluntary participation, both of client and of prospective employer, was a fundamental principle. The staff began working with inmates before they were released, and provided applications to the major prisons in New York State. They also visited prisons and made presentations about the program. Most of the staff were black ex-offenders. Three years after the program commenced, half of those placed on jobs were still employed. More than 400 jobs were secured for ex-offenders in the first two years of the program's operation. Only seven men (1 percent) had returned to prison. The interesting thing about this pilot project is the rationale behind it. "We started Project Second Chance not because we felt exconvicts are entitled to a decent job, but simply to help those who really want to work find jobs for which they are either qualified or willing to be trained."[35] This is a very practical philosophy, but it also demonstrates that the problem of employment for the ex-offender can be positively dealt with, and that there is a vital correctional role for both the nonprofessional citizen and the paraprofessional.

---

[35] Sol Chaneles, "Project Second Chance," *Psychology Today*, March 1975, p. 46.

The National Clearinghouse on Offender Employment Restrictions, an affiliate of the American Bar Association, has prepared a *Handbook on Remedial Legislation and Other Techniques for Alleviating Formal Employment Restrictions Confronting Ex-Offenders.* Despite its overwhelming title, it is a most useful guide to job opportunities for ex-offenders, as well as a manual of techniques for alleviating legal restrictions and empowering the licensing of qualified ex-offenders. This manual also gives evidence of the progress that is being made in enhancing the employability of the parolee.

STIGMA AND PARDON

There are other problems besides employment facing the parolee upon his reentry to the community, of course. There is a need to restore interfamily relationships, and the sensitive parole officer provides a catalytic service here. The ex-offender is also often oppressed with the stigma that his ex-felon status brings in our society. The word "stigma" derives from the Greek, and recalls the Greek practice of mutilating or marking slaves and criminals so that they would be avoided in public places. Every state has a pardon procedure, and the parole officer should familiarize himself with the appropriate procedures so that he might guide his client in securing a pardon, which will go a long way toward legal resolution of the social stigma.

Evaluating Parole

There are really so many complex variables in the parole process that evaluating its success on the basis of the number of parolees reinvolved in criminal behavior is not really a valid index. Each parolee has his own unique background, and some shared experiences in the criminal justice system. A parolee is the subject of numerous past decision-making judgments by criminal justice personnel. He is also the product of his own genetic heritage, and the subject of a unique prison experience. All of these factors influence him. There are also countless other social and psychological variables impinging upon him and influencing his behavior.

THE RECIDIVISM INDEX

An agency must render an accounting to the modern Caesar, the state, and it cannot endure if it cannot justify its existence. A parole agency resorts to recidivism data as the arbiter of its success. Recidivism implies a relapse.

Recidivism rates are negative indices. The recidivism index is an absolute, all-or-nothing index, which does not record the positive gains or growth that may have occurred even where the individual recidivates. It is not reasonable to expect the citizen at large to look for progress or growth in a parolee who has again commited a crime, but the fact is that he might have experienced some interim growth.

CALIFORNIA RECIDIVISM DATA

In the California Correctional System Study, it was ascertained that a significant reduction in recidivism occurred after the California Department of Corrections introduced the Work Unit Program.[36] The Work Unit Program embodied a progressive parole concept, in which a sophisticated effort was made to assign cases on the basis of the needs of the individual case, rather than on the traditional bases of caseload size or of geography. It is common knowledge among probation and parole officers that some cases require a lot more time to service than others. It is unreasonable to expect efficient case servicing when a caseload is unreasonably large. An alcoholic or a drug addict will demand much more of the professional's time than, say, a murderer or a first-term second-degree burglar. The Work Unit Program classified cases in three categories based on time demands. Smaller caseloads were established as part of the program, and the expectation was that the parole agent would be able to spend more creative time with his clients, thereby reducing recidivism.

Citing a "remarkable improvement," the California Correctional System Study revealed that recidivism had been reduced from a high of 47 percent returned to prison within two years for those released on parole in 1962, to 32 percent returned within two years for those released in 1967. The Work Unit Program was launched in 1965. Of those paroled in 1962, within two years new felonies had been committed by 20 percent. For those paroled in 1967, only 12 percent had committed new felonies within two years of release.

FEDERAL RECIDIVISM DATA

In what was described as "the first major recidivism study of the federal prison population in 10 years," the U.S. Attorney General reported, in 1974, that "Two of every three offenders released from the Federal Prison

[36] California Board of Corrections, California Correctional System Study, *Parole Task Force Report,* Sacramento, July 1971, pp. 54–55.

System in 1970 did not return to prison for a serious offense within a two-year period." [37] This approximates the "success rate" in California under the Work Unit Program. The federal study used any revocation, or a sentence of sixty days or more (to prison, jail, or probation for a new offense) as the criteria for recidivism. The National Advisory Commission, commenting on recidivism the year before the federal study was published, said, "The Federal system, like those of the States, does not collect statistics on recidivism that can be considered valid." [38]

NATIONAL RECIDIVISM DATA

One of the more bothersome problems faced in attempting to assess parole is the fact that the several states and the federal system have different parole statutes, philosophies, policies, and regulations. To develop standard conclusions from such a welter of complexity is well nigh impossible. Nevertheless, a Uniform Parole Reports program was started in 1964 by the National Council on Crime and Delinquency Research Center. It is the only program in existence that endeavors to secure nationwide data on parole. Data for 1972 were based upon complete returns from thirty-six parole jurisdictions, and partial returns from an additional ten other states. Partial returns are usually random samples.

Using essentially the same definition as the federal system for recidivism, that is, sentences of more than sixty days, the Uniform Parole Reports indicate that 79 percent of the males and 81 percent of the females paroled in 1972 had not recidivated within the first year. Included in the survey were 21,823 males and 1,532 females.[39] It is apparent from the data provided in the California and federal surveys that recidivism is a progressive phenomenon. The recidivism rate increases as the period of evaluation increases. What is really needed is a multi-year follow-up of outcome (which the Uniform Parole Reports will eventually produce). But the nagging question persists: For how many years should recidivism be plotted before a true success rate can be established?

The inherent difficulty of obtaining precise information on parole "failure data" is evident. The methods used to determine violation vary, and the definitions of recidivism vary. Professor Lunden commented on this when he pointed out that New York, in 1962, declared 2,280 parolees

---

[37] United States Department of Justice, Bureau of Prisons, "Success and Failure of Federal Offenders Released in 1970," *Advance Copy,* April 11, 1974.

[38] National Advisory Commission, *Corrections,* p. 603.

[39] National Probation and Parole Institutes, *NEWSLETTER Uniform Parole Reports* (Davis, Calif.: NCCD Research Center, March 1975).

(15.6 percent) delinquent. But only 1,986 or 13.6 percent were returned to prison.[40] In his own study of recidivism in Iowa from 1950 to 1963, he found a recidivism rate ranging from a low of 19.8 percent in 1958 to a high of 38.5 percent in 1954. For the fourteen years surveyed, the mean recidivism rate (percentage of those paroled actually returned to prison) was 34.8 percent.[41] The rate of failure (recidivism rate) most frequently reported among the numerous jurisdictions submitting data invariably falls somewhere betwen 30 and 40 percent. Obviously the jury is still out.

PAROLE'S VULNERABILITIES

The courts have taken an increased interest in the correctional system, including the parole phase, and are insisting that due process accompany its procedures. As the legal rights and constitutional protections of the offender and ex-offender are progressively elucidated, there has been a mounting wave of criticism regarding rehabilitation, which has been condemned as "one of the great myths of twentieth-century penology."[42] Parole, which has long been supported as a beneficent mode of correctional treatment, is being attacked, and its abolition has actually been called for.[43] It has its vulnerabilities.

In West Virginia, former Governor Barron was paroled after serving nearly four years of a twelve-year sentence. In California, 78-year-old L. Ewing Scott, convicted of murdering his wife in 1957, in a sensational case in which the body was never found, refuses parole and remains in his room beneath the San Quentin infirmary. To accept parole is to admit guilt, he avers, and he claims he is innocent. In another California prison, another murderer accepted parole after serving forty-five years in Folsom Prison. "Old Fitz" commented, "If I had a friend out there, I might have been out sooner. If you ain't got nobody you're dead."

How to be consistent and equitable in the paroling function is truly an imponderable. Whether the injustices that necessarily occur can be offset by sensitive, constructive aftercare is problematical. Parole will certainly be increasingly tested in the future. It may not survive that test, at least as it is presently constituted.

---

40 Walter A. Lunden, *The Iowa Parole System* (Ames, Iowa: The Art Press, 1964), p. 57.

41 *Ibid.*, p. 59.

42 Robert W. Kastenmeir and Howard C. Eglit, "Parole Release Decision-Making: Rehabilitation, Expertise, and the Demise of Mythology," *The Aldine Crime and Justice Annual* (Chicago: Aldine Publishing Company, 1973), p. 400.

43 See, for example, *Summary Report on New York State Parole* by the Citizens' Inquiry on Parole and Criminal Justice, Inc. (1974); and Herman Schwartz, "Let's Abolish Parole," *Readers Digest*, August 1973.

Review Questions

1. Define parole and give its objectives and philosophy.
2. Name the four basic parole board structures.
3. What are the principal duties of the parole board?
4. What are the fundamental criteria upon which parole boards traditionally base their decisions to grant parole? Are these reasonable criteria? Why?
5. What are the essential elements of the parole granting policy of the National Council on Crime and Delinquency?
6. What is the real function of the parole officer?
7. What particular skills and qualifications should a parole officer possess?
8. *Morrissey v. Brewer* was a landmark decision affecting parole. What was the issue in this case and what effect did this decision have upon parole?
9. What are some of the needs of the parolee?
10. How would you evaluate parole? Is the recidivism data given in this chapter helpful in your evaluation? Why?

13

THE VOLUNTEER AND THE PARAPROFESSIONAL

Talent develops in solitude, character in the stream of life.

Goethe

An anonymous punster once wrote that *community* cannot be spelled without U and I. This is an awful pun, but it contains a profound truth, because a community *is* the totality of its members. It is not defined as an elitist group, nor as any particular fragment of the population. A community is sociologically defined as a group of people in an identified geography, having common interests, a sense of belongingness, and the capacity to have their fundamental needs met in the communion that results. This definition necessarily includes the ex-offender. It is because of the basic sense of interdependence in a community that volunteers reach out to help. It is for the same reason that paraprofessionals must be recruited to assist in solidifying the community. Volunteers and paraprofessionals have much to offer corrections in the community.

Volunteers are nonprofessionals citizens who freely offer their services in the correctional effort. Paraprofessionals are individuals who bring particular skills or insights to the correctional arena—which they have gained from personal experiences in the criminal justice system as former offenders. In this chapter we will explore both of these phenomena.

The Volunteer in Corrections

As long as there have been troubled people, there have been those in the community predisposed toward compassionate intervention. The Biblical Good Samaritan was not a professional social worker, nor a public official charged with responsibility for the victims of robbery. He was simply a concerned citizen-volunteer, willing to invest himself in the welfare of his brother citizen. In contemporary times the volunteer is being recruited to assist in the broad reintegrative objectives of corrections. As the California Probation, Parole, and Correctional Association recently noted, "corrections cannot hope to resolve the problems of crime and delinquency by itself since they are, by their very nature, social or community problems." [1] The contribution of the volunteer is not only a noble gesture, it is an imperative necessity. But it is not an innovation.

THE PRISON VISITOR

The lay prison visitor has been a well-established volunteer in corrections, and has been active in England for more than two centuries. In the United States, the Philadelphia Society for Alleviating the Miseries of Public Prisons has been visiting prisoners since Colonial times. One of the better known prison visitors was Elizabeth Fry who, in 1813, began her voluntary career in prison work by visiting the women's section of the Newgate Prison in London. She was so appalled by the desolate condition of the imprisoned female that she literally set about to correct the abuses single-handedly. The sight of almost naked babies, born in the prison, tore at her heart. She was particularly distressed by the lack of clothing for the inmates, the insufficiency of straw for beds, and the general state of degradation and misery in the prison.

Elizabeth founded the Association for the Improvement of the Female Prisoners in Newgate in 1817. Before she died in 1845, Elizabeth Fry had visited other English prisons, as well as penal institutions on the Continent. She was a source of inspiration for many others who followed her pioneering footsteps. Her name is a familiar one in corrections. In Los Angeles a halfway house bears her name, and the Elizabeth Fry Society is active in different parts of the world, notably in Canada where it has been

---

[1] California Probation, Parole and Correctional Association, *Developing Community Resources*, Sacramento, California, July 14, 1972, p. 1.

involved in developing a model plan for the treatment of female offenders.[2]

Concern for the ex-prisoner was necessarily linked to concern for the prisoner. The problem of post-prison social reintegration was as real yesterday as it is today. Keller and Alper express the opinion that probation was a logical development of the community's concern for the welfare of the discharged prisoner.[3]

RATIONALE FOR THE VOLUNTEER

There are many reasons favoring the use of the citizen-volunteer in community corrections. Some of the more obvious include the following: (1) Volunteers provide a critically needed reservoir of manpower. (2)

Civilian volunteer conducting study group at Federal Correctional Institution, El Reno, Oklahoma. *Courtesy U.S. Bureau of Prisons. Photo by Leo M. Dehnel.*

---

[2] Louis P. Carney, *Introduction to Correctional Science* (New York: McGraw-Hill Book Company, 1974), p. 222.

[3] Oliver J. Keller, Jr., and Benedict S. Alper, *Halfway Houses: Community-Centered Correction and Treatment* (Lexington, Mass.: D.C. Heath and Company, 1970), p. 6.

They bring additional skills and talents into the battle. (3) There are economic gains from voluntarily contributed services. (4) Volunteerism is a way to gain support from the community for the correctional endeavors. (5) It provides a manifestation of community concern for the edification of the ex-offender.

The most important reason, however, is that *corrections simply cannot successfully perform its mission without the broad support and involvement of the larger community*. The National Advisory Commission commented on this fact:

> Implementation of community corrections requires citizen involvement on an unprecedented scale. In fact, the degree of citizen acceptance, involvement, and participation in community-based corrections will decide not only the swiftness of its implementation but also its ultimate success or failure.[4]

The Commission blames both community and correctional system apathy for the fact that the "correctional system is one of the few public services left today that is characterized by an almost total isolation from the public it serves."[5] This state of affairs points up the contribution that volunteers can make.

THE HISTORY OF THE MODERN VOLUNTEER MOVEMENT

The principal pioneer in the development of the volunteer movement in modern times was Municipal Court Judge Keith J. Leenhouts of Royal Oak, Michigan. In 1959 the judge and eight other concerned citizens engaged in a discussion of the needs of the court. Neither pre-sentence report nor probation services existed. The group decided to find an alternative to the only options open to the judge at the time, fine or a jail sentence. They constituted themselves as volunteers in what was to become known as Project Misdemeanant, and began to voluntarily service their "probationers." In time, the founding eight recruited other volunteers and the program began to proliferate. The expertise of professionals was obtained at a reduced cost, and volunteers and professionals joined in a collaborative rehabilitation effort.

Several recidivism studies were made in which the probationers from the Royal Oak court were compared with a similar group of probationers

---

[4] National Advisory Commission on Criminal Justice Standards and Goals, *Task Force Report: Corrections* (Washington, D.C.: U.S. Government Printing Office, 1973), p. 600.

[5] *Ibid.*

from a comparable court which had one "fine" but overworked probation officer. Each of the courts had the same budget. The study was made of those placed on probation in 1965. Through September of 1969 (a period of four years and nine months), 14.9 percent of the Royal Oak probationers were convicted of new offenses, compared to 49.8 percent in the other group. It was also shown that the Royal Oak probationers had 0.23 convictions per probationer, compared to 2.70 in the control group. As Judge Leenhouts observed of these figures: "The research simply adds proof to what must be true. Many thousands of hours of intensive services are more effective than one overwhelmed probation officer who can only administer a telephone and letter reporting system." [6] Unfortunately, that is exactly what too many probation and parole officers are actually operating, a phone and paper service, because they are inundated with cases. This is another rationale for mobilizing volunteers.

VOLUNTEERS IN PROBATION

Judge Leenhouts was instrumental in the establishment of volunteer programs in over 2,000 locations. In 1969, four years after he and his colleagues "first began to promote the volunteer program," Volunteers in Probation, Inc., was founded, initially funded by two anonymous businessmen. In 1972 this organization affiliated with the National Council on Crime and Delinquency, and its name was changed to VIP-NCCD. VIP, of course, is usually an acronym for "very important person," an intended subtlety. But VIP in this organization actually means Volunteers in Prevention, Prosecution, Probation, Prison, and Parole. The implication is clear that volunteers should be a part of the entire criminal justice system.

The first National Forum for volunteer leaders was conducted in Detroit in 1970. Others followed in Memphis, Denver, and Tampa. In 1975 the Forum was renamed The National Forum of Volunteers in Criminal Justice, and convened in San Diego, California. This meeting commemorated the decade since Judge Leenhouts, now Executive Director of the NCCD Volunteer Division, "revived the concept of lay involvement in corrections. At the end of that decade, over 300,000 concerned citizens were volunteering 20 million hours annually to criminal justice agencies and programs." [7]

---

[6] Keith J. Leenhouts, "Royal Oak's Experience With Professionals and Volunteers in Probation," *Federal Probation,* XXXIV, no. 4 (December 1970), 48.

[7] National Forum of Volunteers in Criminal Justice, San Diego Forum Planning Committee, Press Release, August 1975.

Some Volunteer Projects

The Volunteer movement that is spreading throughout the criminal justice system established its beachhead in probation and with the courts. Prior to the Royal Oak development, there had been experimental volunteer programs in Lawrence (Kansas) and Eugene (Oregon) in the mid-fifties. Judge Horace B. Holmes of the Boulder, Colorado, Juvenile Court began using volunteers in his court in 1961, and the Boulder National Information Center on Volunteers in Courts is a prominent referral center today.[8] In 1964 the Lane County Youth Project in Eugene, Oregon, successfully used volunteer citizens as "case aides."[9]

THE ABA NATIONAL SURVEY

Because of the "renewed interest" in the participation of volunteers in the criminal justice system in the preceding decade, the National Parole Aide Program, a project sponsored by the American Bar Association, undertook a national survey in 1975 "to determine the extent of correctional volunteer services presently provided to state correctional systems."[10] A questionnaire designed to determine both the attitude toward the volunteer and knowledge of volunteer programs within the department was sent to every director of state corrections. "The ultimate objective of the survey was to provide usable and concrete profiles of existing volunteer programs which could be utilized by other states and agencies wishing to develop their own volunteer systems."[11]

Thirty-one states (62 percent) responded. Of these respondents, eighteen indicated that their states actually funded the activities of volunteers, with amounts ranging from $650,000 in New York to $11,041 in New Mexico. The number of staff specifically assigned to volunteer programs was similarly skewed. New York has twenty-one full-time positions assigned. Georgia has ten. Many, such as Arkansas, Delaware, and Nevada, have no funded staff positions. California, surprisingly, leaves

---

[8] Ivan H. Scheier, "The Professional and the Volunteer in Probation: An Emerging Relationship," *Federal Probation*, XXXIV, no. 2 (June 1970), 12.

[9] Robert J. Lee, "Volunteer Case Aide Program," *Crime and Delinquency*, 14, no. 4 (October 1968), 331–35.

[10] Trisha Streff, "Volunteer Programs in Corrections," *A Survey Report*, ABA National Volunteer Parole Aide Program, A Project of the American Bar Association Commission on Correctional Facilities and Services, Washington, D.C., June 1975, p. 1.

[11] *Ibid.*, pp. 1–2.

the matter in the hands of private organizations, and has neither budget nor staff allotted on a state level.[12] In a number of states the Young Lawyers Section Volunteer Program of the ABA provides volunteer services. In Alabama, for example, the volunteer program primarily consists of young lawyers working with newly released parolees. Four of Georgia's full-time volunteers are parole officers or ex-offenders. VISTA representatives are used as volunteers in both Florida and Georgia.[13]

The activities performed by volunteers cover a wide range, but volunteerism is also limited in some jurisdictions. In Alabama, for instance, it is restricted to adult probation and parole. In North Dakota, which has no organized volunteer program, only limited assistance is available, and that is voluntarily provided by law students. Delaware takes the position that the State Division of Adult Corrections must assume the responsibility for volunteer programs, and it anticipates making such a transition. Maine has an extensive program which includes literacy volunteers, and New York has an imposing expanse of activities ranging from volunteers who provide Afro-American dialogue and Latino awareness, to pre-college orientation.

The national survey concludes that "citizens are becoming involved in almost every aspect of the correctional system," but "the volunteer's most important role. . . , is that of 'public relations' in the best sense of the term—showing both the agency and the offender that people of the community do care and will get involved." [14]

THE ABA NATIONAL VOLUNTEER PAROLE AIDE PROGRAM

In 1972 the American Bar Association launched its National Volunteer Parole Aide Program, a project designed to stimulate volunteerism in the United States. Funded by the U.S. Department of Justice, Law Enforcement Assistance Administration, and under the sponsorship of the American Bar Association's Young Lawyers Section, its Commission on Correctional Facilities and Services, and the Federal Bar Association, the project pairs ex-offenders and lawyers, with the latter serving as volunteer parole counselors.

The American Bar Association feels that there are particular advantages in using lawyers as volunteers in parole. One advantage is that it can develop an increased respect between the legal and the correctional

---

12 This reference is to the adult components of the State Department of Corrections. The California Youth Authority is extensively engaged in volunteerism.

13 VISTA is Volunteers In Service To America, the federally funded domestic version of the Peace Corps.

14 Streff, "Volunteer Programs in Corrections," p. 3.

professions, and enhance the opportunity for cooperating in correctional reform. The National Volunteer Parole Aide Program is currently active in more than one-third of the states.

As a case in point, Missouri, which had only "a handful of volunteers . . . personally involved with the problems of Missouri ex-offenders," used the VPA program as a testing ground to discover for itself how to effectively administer a volunteer program.[15] By June 1975 over 400 volunteers were working with men and women under parole and probation supervision.

In the Missouri experiment a steering committee was formed, composed of the Chief of Probation and Parole, the Chairman of the Parole Board, two young lawyers, and other individuals. A two-day seminar was conducted at which 200 attorneys were trained for the program. The steering committee was formed of the people who would be essential to effectively support and administer such a program. The large-scale involvement of the legal profession was also necessary.

A problem was encountered when the correctional administrators promised to match each volunteer with a client within two weeks. Objectively this was desirable, for "it is generally agreed that rapid matching must occur in order to not lose the interest of the volunteers. . . ."[16] The difficulty arose from negative or indifferent attitudes on the part of some field parole officers. The first lesson was learned: Line staff, as well as top administration and supervisory personnel, must be apprised of the design, intent, and impact of the project. It was also learned that there must be an adequate monitoring and record-keeping system, to offset hostility and apathy by the field workers. It was further determined that a central coordinator was essential.

In January 1973, fortified with a $100,000 grant from LEAA, Missouri initiated its own state program, having had the advantage of the pilot ABA experiment. The funds granted were to educate the public, to expand volunteer recruitment into the entire community, and to provide two full-time paid staff positions to accomplish these objectives.

SAN DIEGO VOLUNTEERS IN PROBATION

A most extensive volunteer program was initiated in 1970 in San Diego County, California, known as Volunteers in Probation. San Diego is the third largest county in California, and its probation department has responsibility for approximately 14,000 clients, 11,000 of whom are adults. Adult caseloads average 120, with juvenile caseloads being approximately

---

[15] Trisha Streff, *Volunteer Program Development and Structure: A Missouri Profile*, National Volunteer Parole Aide Program, ABA, Washington, D.C., June 1975, p. 1.

[16] *Ibid.*, p. 4.

half that size. "The central idea of Volunteers in Probation (VIP) is to use citizen volunteers to expand and enrich traditional probation services."[17] The county gets about twelve and one-half hours of volunteer time for every hour that the professional staff supervises the volunteer.

There are about 700 volunteers in San Diego, and they participate in every facet of the probation service, from institutional work to narcotic programs. "Most volunteers who provide individualized service to clients tutor, furnish cultural enrichment, and act as role model. . . ."[18] Although there is practically no formal recruitment, the San Diego Probation Department receives an average of fifty volunteer applications a month. This reveals that there is a great deal of public interest in assisting in the correctional effort.

The volunteers are "unpaid employees," but they are protected by medical and accident insurance when on the job. An ongoing orientation program of five weeks duration is presented nine times during the year for the benefit of the volunteers, and each one receives an operational handbook containing legal and agency data as well as procedural regulations. A very sophisticated program, the San Diego Volunteers in Probation project has been the recipient of numerous awards.

COMMUNITY SERVICE VOLUNTEERS IN ENGLAND

In England, following the presentation in Parliament of the Seebohm Report in 1968, "The thrust in England has been for greater community involvement and innovative kinds of programming."[19] One type of program is known as Community Service Volunteers (C.S.V.) and it endeavors to utilize young people from all types of backgrounds in some type of service to the community. It is somewhat comparable to our VISTA program except that it utilizes younger people.

Florida's Model Program

On January 19, 1968, legislation was passed in Florida enabling the Probation and Parole Commission to establish a Department of Community Services to recruit and train volunteer citizens, to maintain liaison with state and federal reintegration agencies, and to stimulate com-

---

[17] E.S. Miller and Beverly DiGregorio, "Volunteers in Probation: A Program of the San Diego County Probation Department," *Crime Prevention Review,* 2, no. 1 (October 1974), 29.

[18] *Ibid.,* p. 30.

[19] The formal title of the report was the *Report of the Committee on Local Authority and Allied Personal Social Services.* See Clementine L. Kaufman, "Community Service Volunteers: A British Approach to Delinquency Prevention," *Federal Probation,* XXXVII, no. 4 (December 1973), 36.

munity programs for probationers and parolees.[20] The volunteer program was begun in 1969, and it was the first statewide program servicing probationers and parolees in the United States. At present, there are more than 3,200 volunteers in Florida contributing an average of 12,000 man-hours per month to the reconstruction of the convicted offender.

THE ROLE OF THE VOLUNTEER

The Florida program stresses the fact that the volunteer is not an authority figure, and that this role is reserved for the professional. The volunteer is seen as a friend who can often get closer to the client than the authoritative professional. It is pertinent to quote another pioneer in the volunteer movement in this regard, Judge Horace B. Holmes of Boulder, Colorado: "volunteers are not a free gift. They are an investment . . . an investment in time, effort and intelligence." [21]

The qualifications that must be possessed by the volunteer are enumerated in the Florida Volunteer Handbook as including "warmth, concern and the sincere desire to help by projecting your influences as a successful law-abiding citizen in a fashion that will assist the offenders in successfully reintegrating into a free society." [22] It is stipulated that the volunteer is not "an authoritarian figure," and "when reprieve, reprimand, or another authoritative measure is in order, recommend a course of action to the Parole and Probation Officer but DO NOT take such an action yourself." [23] The role of the volunteer is one that precludes the exercise of disciplinary authority.

Volunteers are engaged in two ways in the Florida program: on a one-to-one daily association and counseling basis, or on a group specialist basis providing legal services, marriage counseling, and comparable resources. Volunteers are also engaged in Structured Treatment Programming (STP). Here the volunteer works as a "motivating catalyst," helping the probationer or parolee complete the "package of treatment programs" designed for his restoration.

THE VOLUNTEER RECRUITMENT POOL

A good volunteer program obtains its volunteers from a broad base in the community, and selects people of diversity in age, race, sex, and levels of academic and vocational achievement. The Florida volunteers

---

[20] Charles E. Unkovic and Jean Reiman Davis, "Volunteers in Probation and Parole," *Federal Probation,* XXXIII, no. 4 (December 1969), 41.

[21] *Ibid.,* citing *Juvenile Court Judges Journal,* Winter 1968, vol. 18, no. 4.

[22] Florida Parole and Probation Commission, *The Volunteer Handbook* (October 1974), p. 6.

[23] *Ibid.,* p. 7.

come from the ranks of the police, the business community, the clergy, housewives, tradesmen, retirees, construction workers, attorneys, and other professionals such as psychologists.

There is also a wise and conscious effort made to recruit volunteers who share the particular life style of the client and who live in the same community, for this makes the volunteer not only more capable of understanding the ex-offender, but also more accessible. Recruitment is actively engaged in through churches and civic organizations.

THE VOLUNTEER'S RESPONSIBILITIES

Any program, to be effective, must have a degree of structured direction. The responsibilities of the volunteer must be clearly defined for him, and he must evidence an appreciation for the agency's goals and operational procedures. In Florida the volunteer is oriented to some basic counseling concepts and given a suggested list of DOs and DON'Ts (see Fig. 13–1). Beyond this, the following responsibilities, here paraphrased, are imposed upon the volunteer: [24]

1. A minimum of one hour per week must be contributed to the case assigned.
2. If the offender fails to keep an appointment, the Parole and Probation Officer must be notified.
3. A minimum of one contact per week must be made with the offender, "and sufficient collateral contacts" with the family and other sources.
4. A monthly summary of contacts must be submitted to the Parole and Probation Officer.
5. Personal contact must be made monthly with the Parole and Probation Officer.
6. The volunteer must be alert to innovative approaches to problems, and communicate the ways and means to the professional staff.
7. All information of a classified nature acquired during activity with the agency must be held in confidence.
8. The volunteer must be empathic but objective.

While the human factors must always be primary, the economic factors in corrections also demand attention. The volunteer program is an auxiliary in reducing the cost of corrections. Not only are the services voluntarily donated, but those services share some credit for the savings

[24] *Ibid.*, pp. 6–7.

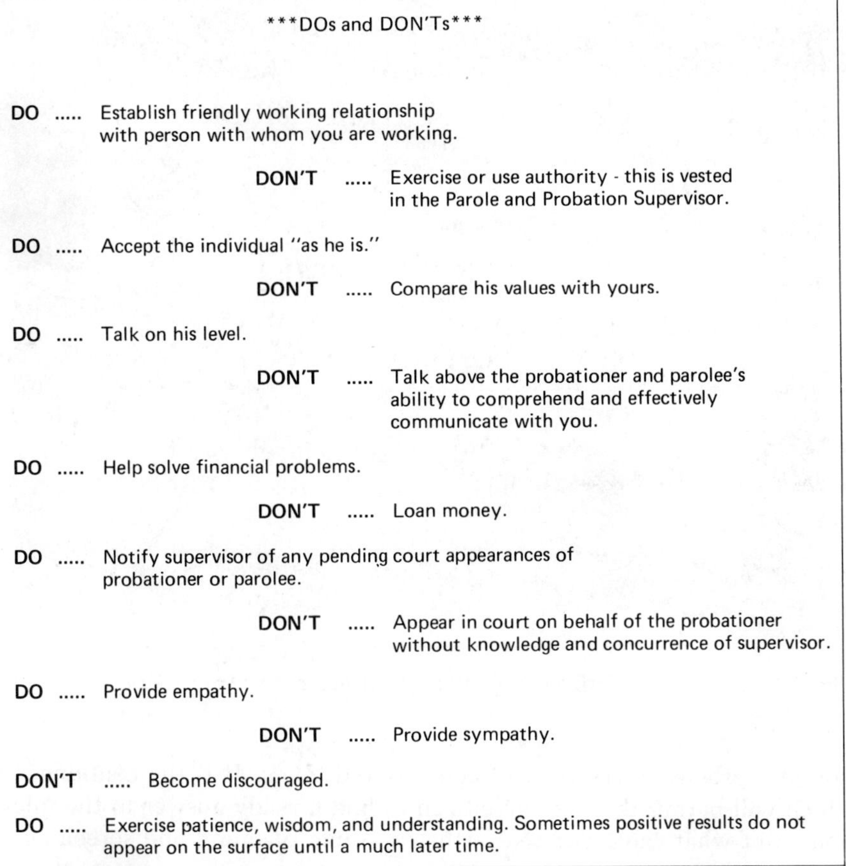

DOs and DON'Ts

DO ..... Establish friendly working relationship with person with whom you are working.

DON'T ..... Exercise or use authority - this is vested in the Parole and Probation Supervisor.

DO ..... Accept the individual "as he is."

DON'T ..... Compare his values with yours.

DO ..... Talk on his level.

DON'T ..... Talk above the probationer and parolee's ability to comprehend and effectively communicate with you.

DO ..... Help solve financial problems.

DON'T ..... Loan money.

DO ..... Notify supervisor of any pending court appearances of probationer or parolee.

DON'T ..... Appear in court on behalf of the probationer without knowledge and concurrence of supervisor.

DO ..... Provide empathy.

DON'T ..... Provide sympathy.

DON'T ..... Become discouraged.

DO ..... Exercise patience, wisdom, and understanding. Sometimes positive results do not appear on the surface until a much later time.

Fig. 13–1. DOs and DON'Ts in the Florida Volunteer Program.

made by the ex-offenders' being kept in the community. In Florida it costs the taxpayers \$7.37 a day to maintain an individual in prison, but only 80 cents per day to supervise an individual on parole or probation. For their contributions, the volunteers of Florida are highly esteemed and are provided with appropriate certificates of appreciation. (Fig. 13–2.)

Guidelines for the Use of Volunteers

Corrections, like many other areas of human endeavor, is subjected to faddism from time to time. The Bandwagon Effect operates, and there is occasionally a tendency to adopt a program because it is the "in" thing of the moment. Volunteerism is not a fad. It is a rational, logical exploita-

Certificate of Appreciation

PRESENTED
TO

IN RECOGNITION OF YOUR SERVICE
AS A

CITIZEN VOLUNTEER

ASSISTING THE

FLORIDA PAROLE and PROBATION
COMMISSION

IN ITS EFFORT OF COMMUNITY INVOLVEMENT IN CRIME PREVENTION
THROUGH RECLAMATION

Date — Place

Paul Murchek
Director

Fig. 13–2. Florida Citizen Volunteer Certificate of Appreciation.

tion of a promising reservoir of concern and talent. It is the enabling act which will permit the average citizen to find a ready answer to the question, "But what can I do?" Nevertheless, some planning and screening is necessary.

SELECTION

At the very minimum, the individuals recruited as volunteers must have an interest in corrections and be motivated to assist in the rehabilitation effort. They must have something to offer. Too often overburdened correctionalists are subjected to additional burdens in playing nursemaid to student "volunteers" or citizen "volunteers" who have not been prepared for a contributing role. As was wisely pointed out in an important national survey, "sheer massiveness of citizen involvement is not necessarily a benefit. Poorly managed programs can lead only to mistakes on a massive scale, rather than the positive impact originally intended."[25]

---

[25] Ivan H. Scheier and others, *Guidelines and Standards for the Use of Volunteers in Correctional Programs,* U.S. Department of Justice, LEAA, Technical Assistance Division, Washington, D.C., August 1972.

That same survey emphasized that screening, recruiting, and training should not be separated. "They are part and parcel of the same process: putting the right volunteer, properly prepared, in the right job." [26] One point should be made here: it must not be forgotten that *the professionals* will often need to be trained—to accept the volunteer. Despite the fact that approximately 70 percent of the criminal justice agencies have some type of volunteer programs, many professionals feel threatened because they do not fully understand the role of the volunteer. In the Hennepin County (Minnesota) Department of Court Services it was discovered that many of the volunteers were quite capable of performing the same functions as the professionals. This did not indicate that the professionals were expendable but, on the contrary, that they "will be called upon to perform roles that are likely to make better use of their talents." [27]

Because the products of the criminal justice system are the poor and the disadvantaged for the most part, volunteer programs should consciously strive to increase the number of volunteers from the disadvantaged and minority groups. This is not only a tribute to justice, but it recognizes the fact that cultural peers are much more likely to reach offenders than those from an alien life style.

TRAINING

Many, if not most, volunteers will be entering a strange, new world when they become involved with a correctional agency. They may be bringing enthusiasm and compassion, but they will also be bringing a natural measure of ignorance. It has been suggested that there are six fundamental components of volunteer orientation. Training of the volunteer should be related to these fundamental components: [28]

1. *Translate the job that the volunteer will do,* in terms of what the job is and what it is not, and in terms of "clearly specified goals of the volunteer program."
2. *Orient the volunteer to the "system,"* that is, the laws, rules, and regulations under which he will operate in the correctional agency.
3. *Educate the volunteer about the offender* and his culture. "Your job is to puncture fantasies and replace them with reality."
4. *Provide the volunteer with community resource information,* and

---

[26] *Ibid.*, p. 62.

[27] Ira M. Schwartz, "Volunteers and Professionals: A Team in the Correctional Process," *Federal Probation*, XXXV, no. 3 (September 1971), 49–50.

[28] *Ibid.*, pp. 78–80. Adapted and paraphrased from this source. For a supplementary view, see also Charles R. Horejsi, "Training for the Direct-Service Volunteer in Probation," *Federal Probation*, XXXVII, no. 3 (September 1973), 38–41.

keep it updated. More than that, show the volunteer how to utilize the community's resources.

5. *Ground the volunteer in the basics of counseling and other treatment tactics.* This does not mean to create an overnight professional. It means that the volunteer can be easily schooled in such techniques as the art of listening, and can be acquainted with the fundamentals of human need and appropriate responses to those needs.

6. *Don't forget the "ceremonial components."* The seriousness of his commitment will be impressed upon the volunteer through formal welcomes, graduations after training sessions, and the receipt of certificates or diplomas of appreciation.

RIGHTS AND LIABILITIES

For the agency contemplating a volunteer program, it is important not to overlook the legal and quasi-legal aspects of the volunteer function. Dealing with these issues early will head off a lot of subsequent embarrassment. For example, what about confidentiality and privileged communication? Should the volunteer have access to confidential case material, and will his communications be protected by the same degree of privilege as accorded his professional colleague? Should the volunteer be required to sign waivers granting immunity to the agency from his negligent actions? The problem of visiting penal institutions will also arise. What happens if the volunteer is an ex-offender? What about situations requiring the arrest of a client? There are some nonhazardous things to consider also, such as insurance coverage for the citizen volunteer, and the use of governmental property, such as automobiles.

Some of these issues cannot be resolved simply; the answers will depend upon the various statutes governing the correctional agency. It is wise to have the volunteer execute a waiver, which will exempt the state agency from the negligent acts of volunteers, but the form should be constructed with competent legal counsel. There are *specific* waivers and *general* waivers, but a waiver is a contract at law. "General waivers have the disadvantage of possibly being too broad and at times may be found by courts not to be applicable to specific situations and therefore not binding. On the other hand, specific waivers may be too narrowly drawn and so many exclude the specific situation which causes the injury." [29]

---

[29] Peter J. Gurfein and Trisha Streff, *Liability in Correctional Volunteer Programs Planning for Potential Problems,* The National Volunteer Parole Aide Program, A Project of the American Bar Association Commission on Correctional Facilities and Services, Washington, D.C.: June 1975, p. 7. This is an excellent source reference on the rights and liabilities of the volunteer, as is the ABA's 1974 publication, *Volunteers in the Criminal Justice System: Rights and Legal Liability.*

Immunity itself is a complex concept at law, and sovereign immunity may or may not be possessed by the governmental agency in a given circumstance. This is but one more reason for having these issues scrutinized by legal counsel. The other issues which we raised will depend for their resolution upon the degree of permissibility in controlling statutes in the various jurisdictions. They should be resolved before any volunteer program is launched.

The Volunteer Looks at Corrections

Both the President's Commission on Law Enforcement and Administration of Justice, and the National Advisory Commission on Criminal Justice Standards and Goals, in their task force reports on corrections, strongly emphasize the importance of volunteers as a manpower source, and advocate their recruitment in corrections.

A MEASURE OF PROGRESS

As recently as 1969 it was stated that "correctional administrators remain divided on the value of the volunteer for the correctional agency as well as on the question of the most appropriate role and function of the volunteer in the correctional program." [30] In the intervening years, however, considerable progress has been made. Nineteen states now actually have an office on volunteerism in the governor's office, and all of the governors have committed themselves to stimulating the growth of volunteerism in their respective states.[31]

Volunteerism is a correctional partnership. How does the volunteer see himself and his role? What type of person is the man or woman who is motivated to engage in the correctional partnership? The Joint Commission on Correctional Manpower and Training commissioned Louis Harris and Associates to conduct a national survey to determine who the volunteers were, why they were volunteers, what they did, and what the attitude of the correctional agency was toward the volunteer. The following facts and conclusions have been taken from that survey.[32]

---

[30] Report of a Survey made by Louis Harris and Associates for the Joint Commission on Correctional Manpower and Training, *Volunteers Look at Corrections,* Washington, D.C., February 1969, p. i.

[31] National Volunteer Parole Aide Program, *The Parole Release,* Summer 1974, p. 1. The nineteen states are Arkansas, Connecticut, Georgia, Illinois, Indiana, Massachusetts, Michigan, Nevada, North Carolina, North Dakota, Oklahoma, Oregon, Rhode Island, South Carolina, Texas, Utah, Vermont, Virginia, and Washington.

[32] Report of Survey by Harris, *Volunteers Look at Corrections.*

PROFILE OF THE VOLUNTEER

The Louis Harris survey revealed that the volunteer is an unusual individual, unique in many respects. This group reflects the nation's religious distribution almost precisely. Approximately half are women, and they tend to be younger as a group than those professionally engaged in correctional work. The sexual breakdown is interesting because corrections at the present time is approximately 90 percent staffed with males. There is also a tendency for the younger volunteers, and for the females, to gravitate toward working with juveniles. Blacks are underrepresented in the volunteer group.

In terms of the labor force, the volunteer group contains an inordinately high number of professionals, such as doctors and lawyers, and is underrepresented in blue-collar workers. As a group, the volunteers are much better educated than the public at large, although not as many have college degrees as do the professionals in correctional work. The volunteers are "joiners." Twenty percent belong to two or more community organizations. Speaking of the differences in background and training between the volunteers and the incumbent professionals, the survey pointed out that they "may make it more difficult for volunteers to be accepted into . . . the system. However, the differences also permit them to bring a fresh perspective to corrections. . . ."[33]

WHY VOLUNTEER?

Just over half of those surveyed were having their first experience in a correctional agency as a volunteer, and about the same percentage were simultaneously engaged in volunteer work in noncorrectional agencies. Less than 20 percent had prior experience in corrections. When queried as to their reasons for working as volunteers in a correctional setting, the almost universal reply was that the work was interesting. In addition, three "groups of reasons" were encountered: (1) a desire to help others, (2) a recognition of the need for volunteers and a sense of obligation to serve, and (3) anticipated personal benefits.[34]

The volunteers do not see themselves as needed merely because there are not enough professionals to do the job; they are convinced that they have something unique to contribute, such as an ability to operate

[33] *Ibid.*, p. 3.
[34] *Ibid.*

without the negative cloud of authority hovering over the relationship. The volunteers are much more predisposed to lay the blame for crime and delinquency at the doorstep of social conditions than are the professionals, who tend to talk in terms of personality disorders. The opinion was expressed that this made the volunteer "in some ways . . . better suited to serve as the offender's advocate in the community."[35]

There are grounds for believing that the volunteer is the more enthusiastic participant in the correctional partnership. Less than one-third said that the agency had initiated the original contact, and only 41 percent had been interviewed by an agency representative for screening purposes. Only 15 percent indicated that they had to meet any educational or experience requirements. These facts led the Harris Survey to comment that "corrections, at least in the initial phases of contact, appears to be the passive partner in its relation with the volunteers."[36]

The volunteers generally have a favorable opinion of their experience in correctional activities, with 40 percent evaluating the program as "excellent." But more than half indicated a belief that there was a need for organization improvement by the agency in terms of the volunteer program. The major shortcoming in the volunteer is that he or she tends to be overconfident, and not capable of recognizing the behavioral subtleties in the correctional client.

The Paraprofessional in Corrections

It is a simple matter to differentiate the paraprofessional from the volunteer: the paraprofessional gets paid. The paraprofessional is a nonprofessional who exercises a supportive function for the paid professional. In a parole agency, he might transport parolees to job opportunities. Working in a mental health agency, the paraprofessional might assist the patient in getting to the outpatient clinic. The scope of his activities will be determined by the agency and its needs.

THE "INDIGENOUS PARAPROFESSIONAL"

The individual who comes from the same cultural milieu or class structure as the client is known as an "indigenous paraprofessional." He shares the same life style. He has the advantage of being able to establish rapport more readily and to open lines of communication with greater

---

[35] *Ibid.*, p. 4.
[36] *Ibid.*

facility, because he talks the "language" of the client. He performs another important function: He can gain entrée for the professional into a world or a culture that the professional too often does not understand. The ex-offender is one type of indigenous paraprofessional.

All of the major commissions have urged the use of paraprofessionals as well as the use of volunteers. The California Correctional System Study put it succinctly: "It is abundantly clear that a vast source of additional correctional manpower is to be found among volunteers and para-professionals." [37] There are areas in which the paraprofessional can be uniquely effective and can employ his unique skills to advantage. The modern professional in corrections must learn to respect the contribution that the paraprofessional can make, and must realize that effective corrections is a teamwork proposition, not a competitive sport. Who knows the world of the ex-convict better than the ex-convict? That reservoir of knowledge should be tapped.

It is an interesting fact that the overwhelming majority of paraprofessionals working with alcoholics are themselves alcoholics.[38] But this is in contrast with the situation in corrections, where many paraprofessionals are noncriminals. Many are students. This is by no means a disparagement of these groups, but the correctional profession is going to have to make wider use of that great reservoir of manpower talent that is in the community in the guise of the reconstructed ex-offender.

HIRING THE EX-OFFENDER

Employment is of paramount importance to the ex-offender. There was a time when the ex-offender was someone to be exploited, a source of cheap labor for unscrupulous employers. This has changed, fortunately, with the passage of time:

In 1975 Hawaii became the first state in the nation to pass a law prohibiting discrimination against ex-convicts in private employment.[39]

In a 1974 clarification of policy, the Department of Defense categorically stated that companies under contract with the Department were "clearly entitled to employ persons with a past criminal record." [40]

---

[37] Board of Corrections, *California Correctional System Study, Task Force Report: Probation,* Sacramento, 1971, p. 55.

[38] George E. Staub, ed., *The Para-Professional in the Treatment of Alcoholism* (Springfield, Ill.: Charles C Thomas, 1973), p. 3.

[39] American Bar Association, National Clearinghouse on Offender Employment Restrictions, *Offender Employment Review,* no. 9, July 1974, p. 1.

[40] American Bar Association, National Clearinghouse on Offender Employment Restrictions, *Offender Employment Review,* no. 10, October 1974, p. 5.

Since 1973, the office of the Illinois Secretary of State has been employing selected ex-offenders. Named after the Secretary of State, Michael J. Howlett, "The Howlett Program of Rehabilitation Through Employment is a low-budget, direct action prototype program." [41] It gives the opportunity to selected offenders to be competitively judged for positions for which they have qualified. "Once in a position, they receive no more job assistance or supervision than any other employee. They are judged upon their job performance without relation to their pasts." [42]

Despite the wide range of treatment theories, the practitioner in the field is becoming increasingly convinced that the foundation for rehabilitation is satisfying, dignifying employment. Correctional agencies, specifically charged by law with responsibility for rehabilitating the ex-offender, should be setting the standard in hiring ex-offenders. Paraprofessionalism is one way of developing that standard.

THE PARAPROFESSIONAL AS A MANPOWER SOURCE

In 1965 a total of 121,163 persons were employed in corrections programs. The President's Crime Commission predicted that this figure would experience almost a threefold growth, to 304,000, in 1975.[43] As the criminal justice system is increasingly burdened, and as corrections moves increasingly toward a community base, it is expected that the need for staff in correctional programs will experience a constant growth.

A fertile source of supplementary manpower is the large population of ex-offenders. The major barrier against conscription of the ex-offender into the correctional labor pool in the past has been statutory or legal impediment. But the National Advisory Commission noted that, "While some States still have these legal barriers to the employment of offenders and ex-offenders, the greatest obstacles come through agency policy. In 1969, fully half of all correctional personnel interviewed in a survey for the Joint Commission on Correctional Manpower and Training objected to hiring ex-offenders as full time correctional workers." [44]

This results from a combination of factors, including fear, distrust, insecurity, an inflexible philosophy of punishment, and an ignorance of the role that the paraprofessional will play. It must be clearly demonstrated by administration that the ex-offender has something to offer

---

41 *The Candle*, III, no. 6 (December 1974), 1.

42 *Ibid.*

43 President's Commission on Law Enforcement and Administration of Justice, *Task Force Report: Corrections* (Washington, D.C.: U.S. Government Printing Office, 1967), p. 99.

44 National Advisory Commission, *Corrections*, p. 478.

corrections, most notably his insights, his ability to understand the thought processes of the criminal mind, and his capacity to establish rapport with the ex-offender because he has shared a life style. Administration must also demonstrate that the professional is enhanced, not threatened, when indigenous paraprofessionals join the correctional work force.

The chasm that has traditionally existed between the "free man" and the convict or ex-convict is largely the product of a mental set and it has disappeared when an opportunity to interact on an intensive basis has presented itself. During a unique educational venture conducted at the Massachusetts Correctional Institution at Norfolk during 1967–69, a regular Boston University Seminar in Criminology was conducted at the prison with five career offenders, between the ages of thirty-four and fifty, who had a cumulative 109 years served in juvenile and adult institutions. Professor Albert Morris of Boston University, and five to eight university students, met with the inmates in the weekly seminar. It was discovered that "very shortly the class became a primary 'in-group' in which the dichotomy between the B.U. and Norfolk members largely vanished, the instructor became primarily a moderator, and each person became an individual whose knowledge, experience, and attitudes were his own to be shared with others." [45]

We are suggesting that the correctionalist and the paraprofessional in concert should be permitted to develop a correctional primary group, in which each contributes, but in which the professional remains the moderator. In this way, the contributions of all are recognized and valued, and the pride of none is vanquished. It has been successfully accomplished in other professions, such as education, social work, the medical arts, and mental health.[46]

NEW CAREERS

Closely related to the concept of paraprofessionalism is the concept of "new careers." The difference between the two is that the paraprofessional supplements and supports the endeavors of the correctional professional, whereas the new careerist is an ex-offender who has been programmed into a professional level position. In one sense, the concept of

[45] Massachusetts Correctional Association, "The Involvement of Offenders in the Prevention and Correction of Criminal Behavior," *Correctional Research,* Bulletin No. 20, October 1970, p. 6.

[46] Donald W. Beless, William S. Pilcher, and Ellen Jo Ryan, "Use of Indigenous Nonprofessionals in Probation and Parole," *Federal Probation,* XXXVI, no. 1 (March 1972), 11.

new careers is taking the concept of paraprofessionalism to its logical conclusion.[47]

In 1963 the National Institute of Mental Health (NIMH) sponsored a conference to start a systematic study of people who had experienced significant social problems, in particular to examine their potential to professionally deal with those problems on the basis of their personal experience—in other words, to provide "new careers" for those who had been products of social problems. A specific problem was selected for the conference focus—crime and delinquency. As a result of the conference, a demonstration project was sponsored, called the New Careers Development Project. Its goal "was to build a participation model which would merge the resources of the professional with those of offenders in the field of social change and development." [48] The first recruits were eighteen inmates from the California prison system, who were placed in nonprofessional public service jobs. Only one of the original recruits committed a new crime and was returned to prison. The rest went on to positions earning up to $15,000 per year. New careerists have been a vital part of the Los Angeles County Probation Department's programming since 1965.

In 1968 the Vocational Rehabilitation Act was amended to include a Special Projects section that empowers the Secretary of Health, Education, and Welfare to make grants to state vocational rehabilitation agencies for the purpose of developing new career programs.[49] In 1967 the California Department of Corrections initiated a parole aide program, in which 33 individuals from the ghetto sections of the larger cities were hired to work in the new career concept with the Parole and Community Services Division. Although 33 is a modest number, it was an important beginning, because three years later, in 1970, the California State Personnel Board developed a career ladder of three new classes of entry-level positions through which a new careerist can progress to the position of parole agent. Those with felony convictions are not eligible unless they have been pardoned, but they can still progress up a number of rungs on the career ladder.

The Federal Probation Office in Chicago also has an extensive parole aide program under way, funded by the National Institute of Mental Health. Paraprofessionals are engaged both full-time and part-time. Congress was so impressed with the Chicago results that it appropriated funds

---

[47] It should be noted that the new career concept, in its broadest implication, has application to the unskilled, undereducated, disadvantaged resident of the poverty community. We narrow the reference here to mean the disadvantaged ex-offender.

[48] Joint Commission on Correctional Manpower and Training, *Offenders as a Correctional Manpower Resource,* Washington, D.C., June 1968, p. 2.

[49] *New Careers,* II, no. 4 (Fall 1968), 1.

for additional paraprofessionals in 1973. Several other states employ the ex-offender in correctional classifications. Included are Florida, Hawaii, Iowa, Michigan, Oregon, and Rhode Island. The National Advisory Commission placed the responsibility across the correctional spectrum: "Correctional agencies should take immediate and affirmative action to recruit and employ capable and qualified ex-offenders in correctional roles." [50] There are four types of tasks identified in a Joint Commission study, that could be carried out by paraprofessionals: (1) direct service, (2) data gathering, (3) escort, (4) agency and personnel development.[51]

If rehabilitation is to be meaingful, it must be attainable in the ultimate; if it is to be tested, it must be tested in the ultimate.

Review Questions

1. Give five reasons to justify the use of the citizen-volunteer in corrections.
2. What is the modern history of the volunteer movement?
3. Describe the ABA National Volunteer Parole Aide Program. What was the particular significance in its Missouri program?
4. The volunteer program in Florida is described as a model program. How is that program organized, and what are some of the conditions imposed upon the volunteer in the Florida program?
5. It has been suggested that there are six fundamental components of volunteer orientation in any good training program. What are they?
6. What did the Louis Harris profile of the volunteer reveal?
7. What is an "indigenous paraprofessional"?
8. What basic reasons would you give for the utilization of paraprofessionals in corrections?
9. Why is employment so important to the ex-offender?
10. How would you describe the concept of "new careers"?

---

[50] National Advisory Commission, *Corrections,* p. 478.

[51] Joint Commission on Correctional Manpower and Training, *A Time to Act* (Washington, D.C., 1969), p. 30.

14

BLUEPRINT FOR THE FUTURE

If rehabilitation is your goal, it ought to be done in the community.

Norman Carlson, Director
U.S. Bureau of Prisons

There is, of course, no likelihood that we will ever see the Utopian society in which perfect harmony characterizes the human community. There will always be some members of society who are marauders and predators against their fellow citizens. The rational objective of each component of the criminal justice system should be, therefore, not an unattainable Utopia but an attainable improvement in the degree of social harmony. Correctional harmony will more likely be enhanced through community-based programming, but it is even more important to reassess some of our basic values and rearrange our priorities.

Value Surgery

Although there are practical changes that need to be made in the criminal justice system, there are also changes that need to be made in our system of values, particularly those which are conducive to law-breaking. In a society that creates haves and have-nots, the emphasis on

Contemporary jail. *Courtesy South Carolina Department of Corrections. Photo by Ken Sturgeon.*

material possessions is a constant source of pressure on the have-nots to acquire status through material symbols, which cannot always be licitly secured. A more suitable distribution of wealth must be achieved if this country is going to reduce crime and make corrections meaningful. If we are not concerned about the fact that one-fifth of our population exists on a poverty level, how can we become disturbed about the impact that poverty has upon crime?

Empty pet food containers have been found in the garbage cans of elderly poor who own no pets but who have been surviving on a bare subsistence level. Meanwhile, the pet food retail market grosses approximately $2 billion annually, and there is more pet food than baby food sold in our food markets. What kind of value system can support a balanced diet for animals while leaving a large human population malnourished throughout the world? How do we learn to deplore the loss of human dignity if we can show more concern for animals than we can for human beings?

A decent reverence for life will have to be instilled in our youth in their formative years, and this value will have to be reemphasized in our basic institutions, the church, the family, and the school. We read daily of crimes that evidence the most callous disregard for human life. An elderly lady, sitting among a group of children in front of her apartment house in Chicago, attempted to console a little boy who had been mistreated by an older boy. The latter then turned to the elderly lady and demanded her purse. When she refused to yield it, he shot her to death.

In a New York subway a brilliant young graduate student was stabbed to death for the $82 he carried in his wallet, while 40 passengers looked on and did nothing. They should have been in attendance at the 1975 graduation at Fairfield University. Judge John J. Sirica, of Watergate fame, told that graduating class: "Democracy is not a spectator sport. It requires a high degree of participation." If the inequities in the criminal justice system actually promote disregard for the law, then the criminal justice system *is* a spectator sport. We must remedy the inequities.

It is wrong for the great weight of the law to come down on the heads of the poor, if the rich are exempt; on the heads of the untutored, if the sophisticated are absolved; on the unimportant, if the important are immune. And it is wrong for the law-abiding victim to be left with a sense of injustice. But where are the role models of rectitude? In recent years the following people, among a great many of similar stature, have had their criminal involvements publicized across the country: a Michigan Supreme Court Justice, the former Educational Commissioner of Florida, a famous bandleader, a New Mexico senator, a top Los Angeles official in the U.S. Department of Housing and Urban Development, a congressman from Idaho, the former governor of Oklahoma, the stenographer to the Speaker of the House, a member of the Los Angeles County Crime Commission, a federal judge, and a Vice-President of the United States.

In Galveston, Texas, the district attorney recommended a $25 fine for a coach who had been convicted of altering the transcripts of two recruits for the University of Oklahoma football team. The district attorney stated, "I can't think of a more laudable reason to do wrong than to try to help a kid." [1] If that type of reprehensible logic and appalling ethic is displayed by the chief law enforcement prosecutor of a county criminal justice structure, then how are we to expect the impressionable young to develop honorable behavior patterns and respect for the law? These examples will indicate rather clearly some of the areas in which value surgery is radically needed.

THE CRIMINAL JUSTICE SYSTEM IN RETROSPECT

The criminal justice system has so many defects that the inclusion of "justice" in its title is practically indefensible. For one thing, consistency and equality are simply not present in the system. Criminologists and correctionalists tell us that crime could be radically reduced if we could introduce certitude of apprehension into the criminal justice system. But, as we have learned, only a fraction of those who have committed crimes are apprehended, and only a fraction of that fraction are subjected to penal servitude.

Justice requires that every man be given his due. The system should not discriminate on any basis in the dispensation of justice. But the residents of our prisons and jails and other correctional facilities are predominantly the disadvantaged. Deficiencies are so entrenched in the criminal justice system that a goodly number of people accept them as ineradicable parts of the justice apparatus. This viewpoint is epitomized in the popular phrase, "What are you going to do, fight city hall?" The answer must be a resounding "Yes!" if the fight is against the perversion of justice.

The concept of community-based corrections is a promising correctional strategy. It has the potential for advancing equity and harmony. Harmony in the community is, indeed, the objective of the criminal justice system. As a sensitive former chief prosecuting attorney aptly phrased it, "The fair settlement of private disputes, the evenheaded enforcement of the law, and the sensible and sensitive handling of antisocial conduct are all essential to people's living together in peace." [2]

---

[1] Quoted in *Los Angeles Times,* January 11, 1975.

[2] Whitney North Seymour, Jr., *Why Justice Fails* (New York: William Morrow & Company, Inc., 1973), p. xiii. Seymour says that his book is about "the injustice actually *created* within our established legal system."

We are not being challenged to *begin* a reappraisal of our system. Many efforts have already been made to bring justice to the justice system. The American Bar Association, in a monumental project (1964–73), created a series of standards covering every important facet of the criminal justice system. Formally known as the American Bar Association Standards for Criminal Justice, they were formulated and developed "when the criminal justice system was increasingly seen as neither fair nor effective." [3] There are seventeen of these standards covering everything from the police function and norms for sentencing, to imprisonment and diversion. They should be consulted by the serious student of criminal justice reform.

In concluding our case for community-based corrections, we will briefly overview the criminal justice system and make some consummatory statements about changes that could occur and must occur if we are to make any headway in the battle against crime and delinquency. Our basic premise retains its validity: The majority of offenders should be dealt with in the community. There is overwhelming evidence that traditional institutional methods have failed to effect any significant rehabilitation of the offender.

The Police

The police component is the doorway to the criminal justice system. Because the primary function of the police is to apprehend the lawbreaker, there is a tendency to overlook the great potential that the police have for diverting individuals from the justice system. This is especially important with respect to juveniles. The police officer has a great deal of discretion in determining whether or not to place a juvenile in custody. In view of the negative impact of criminal justice processing, the police officer should be trained well in his diversionary functions and in the significant dynamics of juvenile behavior.

POLICE RECORDS

If we are to inspire rehabilitation in its best sense, then we should do something about the relentless police records that doggedly pursue the completely rehabilitated ex-offender. Rehabilitation must at least mean restoration to an honorable state. If criminal records constantly bob up during job interviews and other activities, then the rehabilitated offender

---

[3] Chamber of Commerce of the United States, "Modernizing Criminal Justice Through Citizen Power," Booklet Distributed by the American Bar Association Section of Criminal Justice, Chicago, 1973, p. 5.

is constantly being reminded of his second-class status. Most agencies could operate quite efficiently without a great number of the criminal records which they presently maintain, especially those for minor offenses. In 1974 California's attorney general, Evelle Younger, authorized the destruction of 2.1 million outdated criminal records, "to protect the privacy and reputation of persons who are no longer even remotely involved in criminal activity." [4]

It will not be easy to convince most police agencies that they can dispense with criminal records, however. In 1975 the Associated Press broke a story which led Senate Intelligence Committee investigators to probe the Law Enforcement Intelligence Unit (LEIU). This is a consortium of 230 police agencies who exchange information between law enforcement officers in the United States and Canada, ostensibly on organized crime. But according to the evidence uncovered by the Associated Press, member agencies of LEIU have been gathering data on citizens, such as attorneys for the American Civil Liberties Union.[5]

THE COMMUNICATION GAP

The job of the police agency is an enormous one, complicated by too few resources, at times, and a limitless burden of problems. There is also a grave communication gap between this agency and the public it serves. The executive director of the Police Task Force of the National Advisory Commission on Criminal Justice Standards and Goals said that the communication gap is so wide today that "it threatens to become an unbridgeable gulf of total misunderstanding." [6]

The police must develop a more harmonious relationship with the community. A scholarly article in the prestigious *Annals* has made this significant observation: "Virtually every major disturbance in the last three years has been triggered, in the immediate sense, by an incident involving the police and a Negro or Puerto Rican." [7] While the police haven't always been wrong in these confrontations, they have often acted unwisely. The police do not have an enviable record when it comes to race relations. It must be improved. The minority American is entitled to the full protection as well as the full respect of the law and the lawman.

---

[4] Quoted in *Los Angeles Times,* October 22, 1974.

[5] Cited in *Criminal Justice Newsletter,* 6, no. 11 (May 26, 1975), 2.

[6] U.S. Department of Justice, LEAA, *Progress Report of the National Advisory Commission on Criminal Justice Standards and Goals,* Washington, D.C., May 1972, p. 14.

[7] Bruce J. Terris, "The Role of the Police," *Annals of the American Academy of Political and Social Science,* vol. 374 (November 1967), 61.

There is no need for the chasm between the police and other agencies involved in the correctional process. This has been exemplified in a pioneering police–social work project initiated in the city of Wheaton, Illinois. Cooperatively sponsored by the Illinois Law Enforcement Commission, the city of Wheaton, and the University of Illinois, the police–social work team model is an effort to develop an effective method of alleviating the overloading in the criminal justice system. The project recognizes that the police and the courts are frequently overloaded with cases that actually require social rather than criminal justice services. Psychological and family counseling, and crisis intervention services, are provided to selected cases for an average period of two and a half months for each case. The project has proved its worth in many ways: in the reduction of recidivism among misdemeanants, in a marked reduction in referrals to the Wheaton juvenile court, and in enabling the professionals to identify gaps in community services.[8] This project could serve as a model for many police–social agency interaction projects.

THE POLICE AND DIVERSION

Finally, the police agency must become more sensitively aware of its diversionary function. The National Advisory Commission's Police Task Force, which was almost totally composed of police practitioners, gave diversion this emphasis:

> Every police agency, where permitted by law, immediately should divert from the criminal and juvenile justice systems any individual who comes to the attention of the police, and for whom the purpose of the criminal or juvenile process would be inappropriate, or in whose case other resources would be more effective. All diversion dispositions should be made pursuant to written agency policy that insures fairness and uniformity of treatment.[9]

The Courts

The American system of justice is centered in its courts and in the constitutional and legal principles upon which they operate. But the courts,

---

[8] This project is more fully described in: Harvey Treger, Doug Thomson, and Gordon Sloan Jaeck, "A Police-Social Work Team Model," *Crime and Delinquency,* 20, no. 3 (July 1974), 281–90.

[9] National Advisory Commission on Criminal Justice Standards and Goals, *Task Force Report: Police* (Washington, D.C.: U.S. Government Printing Office, 1973), p. 80.

like every other component in the criminal justice system, have become encrusted with archaic traditions and are in desperate need of reform. Such issues as disparity of sentencing and plea bargaining have drawn down upon the courts a veritable torrent of criticism. Reform in any branch of the criminal justice system, however, is hampered not only by archaic tradition, but also by public apathy, and sometimes public hostility. Apathy permits outmoded traditions to continue, and anger at the volume of crime and criminal behavior is an effective barrier against diversion and modulated sentencing practices. Nevertheless, reason and experience clearly indicate that certain improvements in the judicial process are overdue.

SENTENCING

One of the chief complaints leveled against the judiciary is that it exercises wide disparity in sentencing. The reader is reminded that *unjust* sentences, not *different* sentences are the source of our criticism. This results both from differing penal code provisions in the various jurisdictions, and from variations in the philosophies of sentencing judges. Examples are only too numerous. In a case in New York a judge's sentence was so severe that *the prosecutor* called it "unconscionable." The judge had given a young man a 30-year prison sentence for selling less than one gram of heroin to an undercover police officer. In California an 82-year-old man was released from Folsom Prison after serving thirty-five years; he had held up a train and stolen $300 from the passengers. In Brazil a murderer was sentenced to six years in prison for having his son-in-law killed by hired gunmen; the defendant was 107 years old. In Texas a marijuana seller on his first offense before the court was sentenced to 88 years. The litany is endless.

But while there is vociferous criticism of disparate sentencing, there is an interesting aspect of sentencing that is too often overlooked by the critics. Professor Herbert S. Miller, of Georgetown University's Law Center, points out that the disparity does not really lie with the sentencing judge, but with "the fact that sentencing decisions are frequently made before that sentencing hearing occurs." [10] In other words, "the roles the different actors play" in the whole criminal justice process leading to judgment in court must be analyzed, because it is these actors who create the sentences and have the vicarious impact upon the sentencing judge. This can be illustrated by looking at the data for sentenced prisoners.

Miller cites one study of 1,500 Crime Index Offenses [11] handled by the U.S. attorney in the District of Columbia. Of this grand total, only 300 appeared before the judge for sentencing. The 1,500 crimes represented one-fifth of the total number of offenses reported. Therefore, the court was actually sentencing only 4 percent of the criminals (300 out of 7,500) and, obviously, this indicates that the judge even in disparate sentencing has a very limited impact on sentencing.[12]

The antidote for disparate sentencing is not, therefore, a matter of educating judges, but of educating "the actors" throughout the system, including legislators. More important, the public must be educated, because when it is afraid it clamors for severity in sentencing, even where scientific evidence contraindicates severity of punishment. In Michigan, for instance, a 1974 survey revealed that 67 percent of those surveyed felt that "the courts have gone too far in making rulings which protect people who get in trouble with the law. . . ." [13] In 1973 that sentiment had been expressed by 58 percent of the respondents.

In the 1974 survey, 48 percent of those surveyed felt that the courts had

---

[10] Herbert S. Miller, "Judges, Prosecutors and Lawyers in the Criminal Justice System—Research Potentials for the Future," Paper prepared for the Annual Meeting of Directors of Criminal Justice Research Centers, Harvard Law School, May 5–6, 1974, p. 8. Quoted with permission.

[11] The Crime Index Offenses are murder, robbery, forcible rape, burglary, aggravated assault, motor vehicle theft, and larceny-theft.

[12] Miller, "Judges, Prosecutors and Lawyers," p. 8.

[13] Office of Criminal Justice Programs/The Michigan Commission on Criminal Justice, *The Michigan Public Speaks Out on Crime (Second Annual Survey, January 1974)*, March 1974, p. 3.

become too lenient, compared to only 2 percent who felt that the courts had become too strict.[14] These respondents indicate a hardening of the public attitude toward the offender, and affirm the need to educate the public concerning criminal justice reformation and the ineffectiveness of excessive sentencing. A contrasting practice, plea bargaining, is constantly mentioned when court reform is under discussion.

PLEA BARGAINING

Plea bargaining, the cooperative process between the prosecuting attorney and the defense attorney in which sentencing concessions are made in exchange for a guilty plea, has been the subject of bitter debate. Sociological critics tend to condemn this practice, which is also referred to as the "negotiated plea." The Task Force on Courts of the National Advisory Commission has roundly condemned plea bargaining and asserted that it should be abolished no later than 1978. But the practice is defended by the American Bar Association in its *Standards Relating to Guilty Pleas.* It does not appear that plea bargaining can be dispensed with unless and until there are sufficient courts to fully try every issue.

More to the point, plea bargaining can be interpreted as part of a diversionary policy. The American Bar Association's support of plea bargaining is predicated, in part, on the fact that it can have positive benefits for the criminal justice system as well as for the individual. One of those benefits could be the tempering of justice with mercy, which is an unspoken proposition in the philosophy of community-based corrections. There are abuses, to be sure, in plea bargaining, but the advantages may be enhanced if the abuses are eliminated. In a study aimed at examining the causes of pretrial delay, it was concluded that it is not possible to eliminate plea bargaining, because we simply do not have enough courts, judges, attorneys, courtrooms, and jurors to permit full trials for every case.[15] This affirms our contention that we would be better directed to see plea bargaining as a prospective part of a diversionary process, and work to eliminate the abuses that exist.

DIVERSION

The courts should be decentralized, so that the dispensation of justice literally takes place in the community and not in a distant and impervious

---

[14] *Ibid.*

[15] Lewis Katz, *Analysis of Pretrial Delay in Felony Cases: A Summary Report,* Law Enforcement Assistance Administration, U.S. Department of Justice, Washington, D.C., May 1972, p. 7.

bureaucracy. Justice must be a vibrant, vital thing, not a packaged commodity. An emphasis on community-based corrections, however really means that the courts should basically be an agency *to be avoided* wherever possible, particularly in dealing with youthful offenders. A survey of the Juvenile Court operation in Cook County (Illinois), published in 1975, resulted in the same conclusion: "No matter how many quasi-judicial components . . . may be created in the process of decentralization of the juvenile justice system, unless efforts are made to avoid use of the court in the first place, the system will not be altered to any appreciable degree." [16]

The Cook County Juvenile Court, the first juvenile court to be established in the United States, currently handles over 26,000 juvenile cases annually. The need for diversion in the juvenile court is graphically portrayed in a statistic such as this one. But diversion is also necessary because the court has actually been able to do little for juveniles. Interviews conducted with Cook County Juvenile Court staff almost universally confirmed the impersonality and ineffectiveness of the juvenile court operation. A representative comment was the following ". . . the way I look at it, when I refer a kid down there [Juvenile Court] I want something to happen. Nothing ever does. *Nothing.*" [17]

The concept of pretrial diversion has caught on fairly well and is actually rather widespread today. There are literally hundreds of these programs in different parts of the country. What is now needed is standardization and unification of diversionary programs. One development that would immeasurably help the whole sentencing process would be a national penal code, standardized with respect to definitions and penalties, but independently administered by each state. This would enable consensus with respect to the types of offenders that would be eligible for diversion. Diversion has to be selectively administered and would ordinarily be reserved for the less serious offender. It has a twofold objective: to abort criminalization, and to forestall what one writer called "the disastrous social and economic results" of arrest, fingerprinting, and detention.[18] Model programs do exist. The Court Employment Project in New York City is a good example.

---

[16] Ramon J. Rivera and Richard M. King, "Juvenile Court Decentralization: Implications for Communities in Effecting Juvenile Justice in Cook County," *Final Report*, Youth-in-Crisis Project, Berwyn, Ill., February 1975, p. 46.

[17] *Ibid.*, p. 28.

[18] John W. Palmer, "Pre-Arrest Diversion: Victim Confrontation," *Federal Probation*, XXXVIII, no. 3 (September 1974), 12.

THE NEW YORK COURT EMPLOYMENT PROJECT

The adult courts as well as the juvenile courts have been overburdened, and diversion is as much an effort to reduce this burden as to develop intelligent dispositions in the criminal justice process. In New York, for example, the number of felony and misdemeanor arraignments went from 46,694 in 1968 to 77,066 in 1971.[19] It is at this intake stage that cases are screened for New York's Court Employment Project. The New York program started out as a funded project, and it is currently a New York corporation. Established in 1968, the Project is a diversionary program that serviced approximately 2,500 nontraffic criminal cases in 1974. Cases are selected by an examination of court records of individuals awaiting arraignment in the boroughs of Manhattan, Brooklyn, and the Bronx. Selected individuals are counseled, assisted in finding social service programs in the city, and aided in securing employment.

Those who do not get re-arrested, or who return to school (in the case of the younger defendants), have their criminal charges dismissed. It has been confirmed that "The Project does not constitute a risk to community safety. Only one participant in fourteen is re-arrested during treatment, and fewer than one out of four participants is re-arrested during the year after being terminated from the Project." [20] Professor Zimring points to an important aspect of the Court Employment Project. The Project was able to provide more supervision than would have been provided in the criminal justice system, as most of the individuals would have served jail time if they had not been diverted. Some in-depth evaluations of this project are under way, but it can be concluded that it is a meritorious endeavor.

Incarceration

Incarceration—jail and prison—has been a major instrument of intended correction since the infancy of our nation. But the jail has been condemned as the nadir of the criminal justice system, and the prison has become a center of controversy. The prison has been soundly denounced for its failure to rehabilitate, but it has also been strenuously advocated by a frightened citizenry alarmed by the growth in violent and senseless

[19] Franklin E. Zimring, "The Court Employment Project," unpublished evaluative study prepared for the New York City Human Resources Administration, November 1973, p. 1.

[20] *Ibid.*, p. 2.

crime. It should be plain that the advocates of community-based corrections are not endorsing unconscionable risks to the general public. They are endorsing more rational methods of corrections. The criminal justice system is actually a process consisting of a series of calculated risks. Community-based correctional efforts, and measures to abate the perfidious influence of incarceration, cannot be justified if they pose excessive risks to the public. The premise is, as was demonstrated in the New York Court Employment Project, that *soundly devised* diversionary programs are not intrinsically dangerous.

THE JAIL AND THE PRISON

The monstrous conditions of many of America's jails, if not most of them, has been well documented. The deplorable conditions are, in themselves, an eloquent plea for diversion. The really appalling fact is that over half of the inmates in our jails have not even been convicted of an offense, but are merely awaiting adjudication. Dr. Menninger, in recounting a visit he made to the Cook County (Chicago) jail in 1967, described himself as "shocked and frightened" by what he saw. The jail superintendent admitted to Dr. Menninger that "deviate sex practices, beating of inmates by other inmates, smuggling of contraband and other vicious practices were routine in the jail." [21] Our jails are populated with tens of thousands of addicts and alcoholics who should be diverted into treatment facilities, and with juveniles, who should be diverted away from adult reprobation.

We know that the prison will not fade away—at least not for some time. But thoughtful people will insist that only the dangerous offenders be sent to prison, and that the prisons themselves be radically altered to contribute to the positive redirection of its inmates. It is worth recalling to mind the indictment of the National Council on Crime and Delinquency: "Prisons are destructive to prisoners and those charged with holding them." [22] The American Bar Association also recommends that only dangerous offenders be imprisoned and states that "the least amount of custody which is compatible with the public safety, the severity of the offense and the rehabilitation of the offender should be imposed." [23]

---

[21] Karl Menninger, *The Crime of Punishment* (New York: The Viking Press, 1968), p. 40.

[22] National Council on Crime and Delinquency, *The Nondangerous Offender Should Not Be Imprisoned,* A Policy Statement, *Crime and Delinquency,* 19, no. 4 (October 1973), 449.

[23] ABA Project on Minimum Standards for Criminal Justice, *Standards Relating to Sentencing Alternatives and Procedures,* #2.4(d), September 1968.

THE "PUNISHMENT MODEL"

The inability of the prisons to rehabilitate has been amply demonstrated. But in the wake of this discovery, an ironic shift in emphasis has led some correctional theorists back to a punishment philosophy. Notable among the adherents of the new "punishment model" are the Director of the Federal Bureau of Prisons, Norman A. Carlson, and the former Director of California's Department of Corrections, Raymond Procunier. The punishment model is sometimes equated with the justice model, such as has been espoused by David Fogel, which we touched upon earlier.

In its extreme sense, the punishment model maintains that prisons are instruments of punishment and not rehabilitation, and that this is their proper function. The indeterminate sentence is usually condemned, and parole is often attacked. The punishment model, at least as interpreted in the federal system, means, among other things, that inmates will not be compelled to pursue an educational or vocational program while imprisoned.

In view of the fact that the majority of the prisoners are undereducated and unskilled, this amounts to a failure to meet their most basic needs with respect to the competitive markets of the outside world. The shift in the federal philosophy led one psychiatrist-warden to resign from the Federal Bureau of Prisons after indignantly condemning the "warehousing" approach to the prisoners. The fact that rehabilitation has not been demonstrated, and the fact that the medical model has been debunked, do not mean that the only alternative is a return to programless warehousing. Inmates should be programmed and trained for reintegration into society when they are inevitably released. This is quite different from being plied with unpalatable and ineffective therapeutics.

It is unfortunate that the emergence of a punishment model has to occur after the Atticas and the Soledads have pointed to options other than a pure punishment perspective. The distress of the public is understandable in the face of rising crime. The surrender of correctionalists is more difficult to understand. They should have the academic grounding to understand that a great deal of crime is not the product of willful criminality but rather the end result of ethnic and cultural dispossession.

A popular magazine of current events makes this assessment: "As experts see the future, sentences will become more punitive, surer, more swiftly imposed, more definite in length. . . . And certain types of criminals, particularly the career and violent offenders, will be dealt with more harshly." [24]

---

[24] *U.S. News & World Report,* August 25, 1975, p. 21.

Sentences will more likely become dichotomized, that is, sure and severe for the dangerous offender and serious recidividist, and more diversionary for the lesser offenders. It would be nice to believe that sentences will be surer and more swiftly imposed, but that is an unlikely proposition given the congested criminal justice system that we have. It is to be hoped that sentences will become definite in length, but flexibly determined rather than rigidly punitive. The proponent of community-based corrections holds no brief for the premature release of dangerous offenders into the community.

THE ERA OF CONTRADICTION

There is a great deal of irony in this shifting philosophy. In California a subcommittee was established in the Department of Corrections to plan programs for new institutions. A list of goals and objectives was developed and these were grouped under three headings: "Anti-Deterioration," "Constructive Adjustment to Provided Opportunities," and "Preparation for Return to Society." The subcommittee then solicited the viewpoint of the inmates at San Quentin. The inmates suggested that the first category be renamed "Retain and Reinforce Human Values"!

Perhaps we are not so much changing philosophy as wrestling with philosophy. While it is reported that the punishment model is deposing the rehabilitation model, prominent religious groups have been vocal and active in support of such bodies as the National Advisory Commission in recommending something quite other than a punishment model. The National Council of Churches sponsored a conference in 1975 to examine alternatives to prison programs on the federal, state, and local levels. In 1974 the United States Catholic Conference issued a formal statement in which it was asserted that, "There is increasing and strongly convincing evidence that a large center of incarceration should not be the major instrument for dealing with convicted offenders. . . . Smaller, community-based facilities are beginning to prove that they are more appropriate and effective." [25]

REFORM OF THE PRISON

Rather than a pure punishment model, what is really needed is a pure justice model, patterned on the type of philosophy that is emblematic of the Minnesota Mission Statement, to which we have made previous refer-

[25] *A Formal Statement of the United States Catholic Conference, The Reform of Correctional Institutions in the 1970s,* Washington, D.C., November 1973, pp. 6–7.

Modernistic federal correctional institution, opened in 1976 in Butner, North Carolina. It was originally designed as a hospital and research center for incorrigible inmates, but mounting opposition to behavioral modification programs caused it to be converted to a "regular" institution. *Photo courtesy U.S. Bureau of Prisons.*

ence. To speak of punishment without speaking of justice is to speak of discrimination. As the Statement of the United States Catholic Conference also pointed out, "It behooves us to be aware that, despite well-publicized exceptions, prisons are largely filled with the poor, the disadvantaged minorities, and the 'losers' of our society. *We need to examine whether we may not have a 'poor man's' system of criminal justice.*" [26] (Italics added.)

If the prison is not ready to fade away, it can certainly be reformed, and it must be. The author of one of the acknowledged classic studies of imprisonment called the prison a "despotic regime in a democratic society." [27] The fate of hundreds of thousands of individuals, and the responsibilities of rational men, cannot be simply disposed of in a debate

---

26 *Ibid.*, pp. 4–5.

27 Gresham A. Sykes, *The Society of Captives: A Study of a Maximum Security Prison* (Princeton, N.J.: Princeton University Press, 1972), p. 130.

over the merits and demerits of punishment and rehabilitation models. Some hard facts confront us. The prison suicide rate is 59 percent above the national average. The abnormal prison atmosphere is conducive to sexual aberration and exploitation (or sexploitation, as the movie industry would phrase it) of the ingenuous prisoner, because it is a total, entrapping environment.[28] The prison epitomizes the abnormal, and any concern for normalizing offenders must include concern for prison reformation. There are some improvements that can be introduced.

A PRISON OMBUDSMAN

The concept of a correctional ombudsman is gaining in popularity. It is one readily available solution for a great measure of the frustration that inmates feel in being buried in an unresponsive bureaucracy. Gellhorn

Minnesota's ombudsman visits prison inmate. © *Corrections Magazine. Photo by Bill Powers.*

[28] For an excellent analysis of the problem of homosexuality in prisons, see Peter C. Buffum, *Homosexuality in Prisons* (Washington, D.C.: U.S. Government Printing Office, 1972).

defined an ombudsman as "that high level, independent, legally constituted, greatly respected officer to look into citizens' dissatisfactions with government." [29] It is a relatively recent concept in corrections, although it has a long historical tradition in civil affairs. One scholar traces the origin of the ombudsman to thirteenth-century Norway,[30] although it is generally conceded to have begun in Sweden in 1809.[31] The concept has received a great deal of discussion in the United States in recent years, but the general climate has not been one of universal and ready acceptance. Gellhorn attributes this mainly to the self-interest attitudes of legislators, and the fact that they fear that the creation of an ombudsman would open them to criticism which they have previously been insulated against.[32]

The same may be said of correctional administrators who oppose the idea. The doctrine of administrative discretion—which, in the past, made wardens supreme rulers of the prisons, with whom the courts would not interfere—is now being eroded by judicial fiat. But the tradition dies hard. California's former director of corrections, Raymond Procunier, for example, placed himself in opposition to an ombudsman for the California correctional system with the comment, "I'm supposed to be the ombudsman in this state." [33]

Wherever the concept has been implemented, however, it has been favorably evaluated. It is, of course, quite refined in Scandinavia, particularly in Denmark where it has been significantly developed. It is enthusiastically supported in New Zealand, which has had an independent ombudsman–Member of Parliament since 1962, and in Great Britain, three provinces of Canada, Guayana, and several other countries.

Minnesota appointed the first independent correctional ombudsman in 1972. Michigan's correctional ombudsman is a convicted murderer who served 36 years in prison before being appointed to the position. In all, a total of fourteen states have "conflict mediators" in their correctional systems. New York is the only jurisdiction with a statewide program exclusively servicing youth.[34] Difficulties have arisen, and will have to be ironed out, but the fundamental concept of someone impartially listening to legitimate grievances, and having the power to do something construc-

---

[29] Walter Gellhorn, "The Ombudsman Concept in the United States," in Edgar A. Schuler, Thomas F. Hoult, Duane L. Gibson, and Wilbur B. Brookcover, eds., *Readings in Sociology* (New York: Thomas Y. Crowell Company, 1971), p. 409.

[30] *Ibid.*, p. 408.

[31] Hing Yong Cheng, "The Emergence and Spread of the Ombudsman Institution," *The Annals of the American Academy of Political and Social Science*, vol. 377 (May 1968), 21.

[32] Gellhorn, "The Ombudsman Concept," pp. 408, 411.

[33] Quoted in *Corrections Magazine*, 1, no. 1 (September 1974), 32.

[34] Edgar May, "Prison Ombudsman in America," *Corrections Magazine*, 1, no. 3 (January–February 1975), 46.

The Federal Youth Center at Pleasanton, California. *Courtesy U.S. Bureau of Prisons. Photo by Leo M. Dehnel.*

tive about them, must have a place in the correctional apparatus. It is subsumed in the concept of the Minnesota Justice Model.[35]

THE OPEN PRISON

A phrase that has come to mean both a particular type of prison, and increased interaction between the prison community and the outside world, is "the open prison." The open prison concept is an inevitable corollary of community-based corrections, because the emphasis is on maximizing interaction with the community. At England's Spring Hill Prison, for example, some of the inmates work for civilian employers in the community and on surrounding farms. They wear civilian clothing. In addition, a variety of activities such as sporting and musical events and church activities bring the inmates into intimate interaction with the surrounding community. There are also annual Christmas parties put on by the inmates in the village hall for the local children.[36]

Some of the newer institutions being built by the Federal Bureau of

---

[35] For a capable presentation of the need for a correctional ombudsman, see Timothy L. Fitzharris, *The Desirability of a Correctional Ombudsman* (Berkeley, Calif.: Institute of Governmental Studies, University of California, 1973).

[36] For a more extensive description of this institution, see *Prison Service Journal*, no. 11 (London: H.M.S.O., July 1973), pp. 6–7.

Man and wife, both inmates, visit at the co-educational Federal Correctional Institution, Fort Worth, Texas. *Courtesy U.S. Bureau of Prisons. Photo by Leo M. Dehnel.*

Prisons are open and revolutionary in their design. The Federal Youth Center at Pleasanton, California, a coeducational institution, is, as claimed, a veritable break with the past. A convicted cocaine dealer provided the best advertisement for this new facility when he said: "You've got something here to stimulate your mind. Not clanging doors, fights and all that stuff. . . . This place fills you with something other than hate and desperation."[37] At Pleasanton, the architecture of the prison was designed to influence the attitude and behavior of the inmates. Pleasanton has a wide open, village-type design. Long corridors have been eliminated in favor of living areas that simulate residential homes in the larger society. "The correctional process is based on the development of a supportive atmosphere relatively free of the corrosive effects of the traditional prison environment."[38] Coeducational institutions are expanding, and they currently exist in Fort Worth, Texas; Lexington, Kentucky; Morgantown, West Virginia; and Framingham, Massachusetts, in addition to Pleasanton.

---

[37] Federal Bureau of Prisons, *Breaking with the Past: The Changing View of Correctional Facilities,* undated informational brochure.

[38] *Ibid.*

For those who cannot be diverted from the institutional system, this type of incarceration is infinitely preferable to the "despotic regime" of the past.

Epilogue

In a very cynical projection of crime and criminal justice, one distinguished scholar anticipates the possibility of a complete breakdown of the criminal justice system before the end of the twentieth century. He says, "I find little upon which to base hopes of the survival of law as a viable social control mechanism." [39] One of the reasons for his apprehension is the pressure that increasing control places upon those in the system. Without sharing his cynicism, we can note the National Advisory Commission also took cognizance of pressure in the system, but it emphasized the pressure for change, and recommended "increased diversion out of the criminal justice system for certain types of offenders."[40]

Pressure for change became insistent in the sixties and seventies. It suggests that another model be added to the ones that we have discussed—the conflict model. In the recent past, certain social "movements," particularly among ethnic self-help groups, civil rights advocates, and prisoner organizations, have abandoned the traditional "orderly process" and have sought their objectives through conflict or direct intervention. And they have been largely successful. Many changes in the penal system have been brought about by conflict and its resolution. The conflict that is bred in the prison and the conflict that festers in society are also tributes to society's failure. Redirecting corrections to the community will bring no panacea, perhaps, but it may build a few more escape valves to reduce the anger and the hostility that breed abrasive conflict in the penal world.

Community-based corrections is not one big integrated system, but a conglomerate of diversionary efforts. It is philosophy and it is practice. In some areas it is embryonic; in other areas it has achieved a measure of maturity. It is the long-established practices of probation and parole, and the relatively new programs such as PORT in Minnesota and the Community Treatment Project for Repeat Offenders in Michigan. It is the infant Orange County Halfway House in California, and it is the

---

[39] Leslie T. Wilkins, "Crime and Criminal Justice at the Turn of the Century," *Annals of the American Academy of Political and Social Science,* vol. 408 (July 1973), 15.

[40] National Advisory Commission on Criminal Justice Standards and Goals, *Task Force Report: A National Strategy to Reduce Crime* (Washington, D.C.: U.S. Government Printing Office, 1973), p. 114.

patriarchal Dismas House in St. Louis. It is the 1974 Connecticut Plan for Action, and a host of other diversionary tactics.

It is concern and it is action. It is a battle against overcriminalization. It is the voice of Voltaire warning that "A multitude of laws in a country is like a great number of physicians, a sign of weakness and malady," and it is the compassionate spirit of St. Francis. It is the renowned judge, Learned Hand, "making muffled noises at people who may be no worse than I," and it is corrections moving toward adulthood.

It is also Dr. Samuel Johnson's wisdom reminding us that the future is purchased by the present, and it is the President's Task Force on Prisoner Rehabilitation declaring, without equivocation, that:

> "Community-based corrections" is no visionary slogan but a hard contemporary fact. We support wholeheartedly the proposition that the community is the appropriate place in which to prepare offenders for useful participation in community life.[41]

The criminal justice system has found no solutions for criminal deviancy. We really cannot anticipate success until we solve our socioeconomic and political problems. What we are really trying to do is to develop solutions. Community-based corrections should be viewed in that context.

It can be viewed in another context, as a response to the echo of Attica, as an effort to avoid what the McKay Commission called "The tip of the fury of hell."

Review Questions

1. The term "value surgery" has been used in this chapter. What exactly does that mean? Can you give some examples of value surgery?
2. In retrospect, what are the major deficiencies in the criminal justice system?
3. What particular changes could the police component accomplish to facilitate justice in the criminal justice system?
4. In what fashion could the police agency employ diversion in its routine operations?
5. What major reforms could be introduced into the judiciary?
6. What reforms in sentencing would you suggest?

---

[41] "The Criminal Offender—What Should Be Done?" in *The Report of the President's Task Force on Prisoner Rehabilitation* (Washington, D.C.: U.S. Government Printing Office, April 1970), p. 7.

7. Would you attack or defend plea bargaining? On what grounds?
8. What is meant by the "punishment model"?
9. The prison will not simply fade away, of course. What reforms should be introduced into the prison?
10. If you could see into the future, what would you see as the main features of the criminal justice system in the year 2000?

APPENDICES

NATIONAL ADVISORY COMMISSION ON CRIMINAL JUSTICE STANDARDS AND GOALS

A

STANDARD FOR DIVERSION

Standard 3.1

Use of Diversion

Each local jurisdiction, in cooperation with related State agencies, should develop and implement by 1975 formally organized programs of diversion that can be applied in the criminal justice process from the time an illegal act occurs to adjudication.

1. The planning process and the identification of diversion services to be provided should follow generally and be associated with "total system planning" as outlined in Standard 9.1.

a. With planning data available, the responsible authorities at each step in the criminal justice process where diversion may occur should develop priorities, lines of responsibility, courses of procedure, and other policies to serve as guidelines to its use.

b. Mechanisms for review and evaluation of policies and practices should be established.

c. Criminal justice agencies should seek the cooperation and resources of other community agencies to which persons can be diverted for services relating to their problems and needs.

2. Each diversion program should operate under a set of written guidelines that insure periodic review of policies and decisions. The guidelines should specify:

a. The objectives of the program and the types of cases to which it is to apply.

b. The means to be used to evaluate the outcome of diversion decisions.

c. A requirement that the official making the diversion decision state in writing the basis for his determination denying or approving diversion in the case of each offender.

d. A requirement that the agency operating diversion programs maintain a current and complete listing of various resource dispositions available to diversion decisionmakers.

3. The factors to be used in determining whether an offender, following arrest but prior to adjudication, should be selected for diversion to a noncriminal program, should include the following:

a. Prosecution toward conviction may cause undue harm to the defendant or exacerbate the social problems that led to his criminal acts.

b. Services to meet the offender's needs and problems are unavailable within the criminal justice system or may be provided more effectively outside the system.

c. The arrest has already served as a desired deterrent.

d. The needs and interests of the victim and society are served better by diversion than by official processing.

e. The offender does not present a substantial danger to others.

f. The offender voluntarily accepts the offered alternative to further justice system processing.

g. The facts of the case sufficiently establish that the defendant committed the alleged act.

B

STANDARDS FOR COMMUNITY-BASED CORRECTIONS

Standard 7.1

Development Plan for Community-Based Alternatives to Confinement

Each State correctional system or correctional system of other units of government should begin immediately to analyze its needs, resources, and gaps in service and to develop by 1978 a systematic plan with timetable and scheme for implementing a range of alternatives to institutionalization. The plan should specify the services to be provided directly by the correctional authority and those to be offered through other community resources. Community advisory assistance is essential. The plan should be developed within the framework of total system planning discussed in Chapter 9, Local Adult Institutions, and State planning discussed in Chapter 13, Organization and Administration.

Minimum alternatives to be included in the plan should be the following:

1. Diversion mechanisms and programs prior to trial and sentence.
2. Nonresidential supervision programs in addition to probation and parole.
3. Residential alternatives to incarceration.

4. Community resources open to confined populations and institutional resources available to the entire community.

5. Prerelease programs.

6. Community facilities for released offenders in the critical reentry phase, with provision for short-term return as needed.

Standard 7.2

Marshaling and Coordinating Community Resources

Each State correctional system or the systems of other units of government should take appropriate action immediately to establish effective working relationships with the major social institutions, organizations, and agencies of the community, including the following:

1. Employment resources—private industry, labor unions, employment services, civil service systems.

2. Educational resources—vocational and technical, secondary college and university, adult basic education, private and commercial training, government and private job development and skills training.

3. Social welfare services—public assistance, housing, rehabilitation services, mental health services, counseling assistance, neighborhood centers, unemployment compensation, private social service agencies of all kinds.

4. The law enforcement system—Federal, State, and local law enforcement personnel, particularly specialized units providing public information, diversion, and services to juveniles.

5. Other relevant community organizations and groups—ethnic and cultural groups, recreational and social organizations, religious and self-help groups, and others devoted to political or social action.

At the management level, correctional agencies should seek to involve representatives of these community resources in policy development and inter-agency procedures for consultation, coordinated planning, joint action, and shared programs and facilities. Correctional authorities also should enlist the aid of such bodies in formation of a broad-based and aggressive lobby that will speak for correctional and inmate needs and support community correctional programs.

Standard 7.3

Corrections' Responsibility for Citizen Involvement

Each State correctional system should create immediately: (a) a multipurpose public information and education unit, to inform the general public on correctional issues and to organize support for and overcome resistance to general reform efforts and specific community-based projects; and (b) an administrative unit responsible for securing citizen involvement in a variety of ways within corrections, including advisory and policymaking roles, direct service roles, and cooperative endeavors with correctional clients.

1. The unit responsible for securing citizen involvement should develop and make public a written policy on selection process, term of service, tasks, responsibilities, and authority for any advisory or policymaking body.

2. The citizen involvement unit should be specifically assigned the management of volunteer personnel serving in direct service capacities with correctional clientele, to include:

a. Design and coordination of volunteer tasks.

b. Screening and selection of appropriate persons.

c. Orientation to the system and training as required for particular tasks.

d. Professional supervision of volunteer staff.

e. Development of appropriate personnel practices for volunteers, including personnel records, advancement opportunities, and other rewards.

3. The unit should be responsible for providing for supervision of offenders who are serving in volunteer roles.

4. The unit should seek to diversify institutional programs by obtaining needed resources from the community that can be used in the institution and by examining and causing the periodic reevaluation of any procedures inhibiting the participation of inmates in any community program.

5. The unit should lead in establishing and operating community-based programs emanating from the institution or from a satellite facility and, on an ongoing basis, seek to develop new opportunities for community contacts enabling inmate participants and custodial staff to

regularize and maximize normal interaction with community residents and institutions.

Standard 7.4

Inmate Involvement in Community Programs

Correctional agencies should begin immediately to develop arrangements and procedures for offenders sentenced to correctional institutions to assume increasing individual responsibility and community contact. A variety of levels of individual choice, supervision, and community contact should be specified in these arrangements, with explicit statements as to how the transitions between levels are to be accomplished. Progress from one level to another should be based on specified behavioral criteria rather than on sentence, time served, or subjective judgments regarding attitudes.

The arrangements and procedures should be incorporated in the classification system to be used at an institution and reflect the following:

1. When an offender is received at a correctional institution, he should meet with the classification unit (committe, team, or the like) to develop a plan for increasing personal responsibility and community contact.
2. At the initial meeting, behavioral objectives should be established, to be accomplished within a specified period. After that time another meeting should be held to make adjustments in the individual's plan which, assuming that the objectives have been met, will provide for transition to a lower level of custody and increasing personal responsibility and community involvement.
3. Similarly, at regular time intervals, each inmate's status should be reviewed, and if no strong reasons exist to the contrary, further favorable adjustments should be made.
4. Allowing for individual differences in time and progress or lack of progress, the inmate should move through a series of levels broadly encompassing movement from (a) initial security involving few outside privileges and minimal contact with community participants in institutional programs, to (b) lesser degrees of custody with participation in institutional and community programs involving both citizens and offenders, to (c) partial-release programs under which he would sleep in the institution but have maximum participation in institutional and outside activities involving community residents, to (d) residence in a halfway house or similar noninstitutional residence, to (e) residence in the com-

munity at the place of his choice with moderate supervision, and finally to release from correctional supervision.

5. The presumption should be in favor of decreasing levels of supervision and increasing levels of individual responsibility.

6. When an inmate fails to meet behavioral objectives, the team may decide to keep him in the same status for another period or move him back. On the other hand, his behavioral achievements may indicate that he can be moved forward rapidly without having to go through all the successive stages.

7. Throughout the process, the primary emphasis should be on individualization—on behavioral changes based on the individual's interests, abilities, and priorities. Offenders also should be afforded opportunities to give of their talents, time, and efforts to others, including other inmates and community residents.

8. A guiding principle should be the use of positive reinforcement in bringing about behavioral improvements rather than negative reinforcement in the form of punishment.

C

STANDARDS FOR VOLUNTEERS

Standard 12.8

Manpower for Parole

By 1975, each State should develop a comprehensive manpower and training program which would make it possible to recruit persons with a wide variety of skills, including significant numbers of minority group members and volunteers, and use them effectively in parole programs.

Among the elements of State manpower and training programs for corrections that are prescribed in Chapter 14, the following apply with special force to parole.

1. A functional workload system linking specific tasks to different categories of parolees should be instituted by each State and should form the basis of allocating the manpower resources.
2. The bachelor's degree should constitute the requisite educational level for the beginning parole officer.
3. Provisions should be made for the employment of parole personnel having less than a college degree to work with parole officers on a team basis, carrying out the tasks appropriate to their individual skills.
4. Career ladders that offer opportunities for advancement of persons with less than college degrees should be provided.

5. Recruitment efforts should be designed to produce a staff roughly proportional in ethnic background to the offender population being served.

6. Ex-offenders should receive high priority consideration for employment in parole agencies.

7. Use of volunteers should be extended substantially.

8. Training programs designed to deal with the organizational issues and the kinds of personnel required by the program should be established in each parole agency.

Standard 14.5

Employment of Volunteers

Correctional agencies immediately should begin to recruit and use volunteers from all ranks of life as a valuable additional resource in correctional programs and operations, as follows:

1. Volunteers should be recruited from the ranks of minority groups, the poor, inner-city residents, ex-offenders who can serve as success models, and professionals who can bring special expertise to the field.

2. Training should be provided volunteers to give them an understanding of the needs and lifestyles common among offenders and to acquaint them with the objectives and problems of corrections.

3. A paid volunteer coordinator should be provided for efficient program operation.

4. Administrators should plan for and bring about full participation of volunteers in their programs; volunteers should be included in organizational development efforts.

5. Insurance plans should be available to protect the volunteer from any mishaps experienced during participation in the program.

6. Monetary rewards and honorary recognition should be given to volunteers making exceptional contribution to an agency.

INDEX

DATE DUE

MAY 15 '78	MAY 10 '78		
DEC 10 '81	DEC 3 '81		
MR 4 '82	APR 13 '82		
[illegible] 29 '89	DEC 6 '89		
DEC. 05 1991	DEC 5 '91		
DEC. 05 1992	DEC 9 '92		
FEB 22 '97			
GAYLORD			PRINTED IN U.S.A.